No other way to tell it

MANCHESTER
1824

Manchester University Press

Derek Paget

No other way to tell it

DOCUDRAMA ON FILM AND TELEVISION

Second edition

Manchester University Press

Manchester and New York

Distributed in the United States exclusively by Palgrave Macmillan

First edition published 1998 by Manchester University Press

This edition published 2011 by Manchester University Press
Oxford Road, Manchester M13 9NR, UK
and Room 400, 175 Fifth Avenue, New York, NY 10010, USA

Distributed in the United States exclusively by
Palgrave Macmillan, 175 Fifth Avenue, New York,
NY 10010, USA

Distributed exclusively in Canada by
UBC Press, University of British Columbia, 2029 West Mall,
Vancouver, BC, Canada V6T 1Z2

British Library Cataloguing-in-Publication Data
A catalogue record for this book is available from the British Library

Library of Congress Cataloging-in-Publication Data applied for

ISBN   978 0 7190 8446 1 hardback
ISBN   978 0 7190 8447 8 paperback

This edition first published 2011

Typeset by
Special Edition Pre-press Services, www.special-edition.co.uk

Printed in Great Britain by
the MPG Books Group

Contents

Acknowledgements

Researching and writing this second edition I have benefited from new interviews with people who work in the theatre, film and television industries. Sarah Andrew, Simon Armitage, Simon Boswell, David Edgar, Brian Hill, Peter Kosminsky, Ian McBride, Bella Merlin (who manages – somehow – to be both actor and academic) and Patrick Swaffer have added greatly to my understanding and have helped me to try, as I did in the first edition, to bridge the gap between the academy and the arts. I am particularly grateful to David Edgar in this regard; he has found time between writing his plays to discuss docudrama with me for over twenty years. I remain grateful to Ray Fitzwalter, Tony Garnett, Oliver R. Goodenough, Martin McKeand, Alasdair Palmer, the late Jeremy Sandford, Irene Shubik, Sita Williams and Leslie Woodhead for interviews given for the first edition.

I am grateful to academic friends and colleagues in all sorts of ways. I owe most to a group I think of as 'The Documentarians': Stella Bruzzi, John Corner, Jonathan Dovey, Tobias Ebbrecht, Craig Hight, Annette Hill, Peter Hughes, John Izod, Richard Kilborn, Steven N. Lipkin, Chris Megson, Gareth Palmer, Janelle Reinelt, Jane Roscoe, Alan Rosenthal and Brian Winston. I first met many of them through the excellent 'Visible Evidence' international conference series. My world would be the poorer without their publications, their conversation and their friendship. Peter Hughes, Steve Lipkin, and Jane Roscoe are in many ways more like family to me now. All of them have shaped and reshaped my ideas about the challenges docudrama presents to makers, actors and audiences (and, of course, academics).

Some of the material in this edition has appeared in different forms in journal articles for *Jump Cut*, *Studies in Documentary Film* and *Studies in Theatre and Performance*. I thank all the editors concerned – Chuck Kleinhans and Julia Lesage, Deane Williams, and

Kate Dorney and Peter Thomson – for opportunities in their journals to try out ideas that are developed further in Chapter 8. Serving on the Editorial Boards of the latter two journals I count as a particularly rewarding experience. While rewriting the book I was especially fortunate to become part of the Department of Film, Theatre and Television at the University of Reading in 2003. My thanks to students and colleagues past and present for their stimulating company in and outside the lecture room. But particular thanks must go to Jonathan Bignell and Lib Taylor for their support and friendship. Between 2007 and 2010 the three of us, along with our indefatigable postdoctoral researcher Heather Sutherland, have been part of the Arts and Humanities Research Council (AHRC)-funded research project 'Acting with Facts: Actors Performing the Real in British Theatre and Television since 1990'. 'Acting with Facts', for which I was Principal Investigator, has been a thoroughly enjoyable collaboration for me. I thank 'my' team, the many actors who have given their time to talk to us about their work for stage and screen docudrama, and the AHRC for the opportunity and the support.

I would like to thank Corinne Orde, my copy editor, for all she has done to improve this edition; it has been a real pleasure to work with her. Thanks also to my editor and friend Matthew Frost and the staff at Manchester University Press. The caveat to these particular thanks, of course, is that any errors in the book are my responsibility.

Finally, my love and grateful thanks go to my family. Throughout our life together my wife Jessica has shown exemplary patience in trying to help me understand that there is more to life than an obsessive interest in docudrama. Since our son Joseph and daughter Emily have been part of our lives, they have greatly enhanced this understanding. I hope the three of them will feel their efforts have not been entirely in vain.

Introduction to the second edition

New documentary, new docudrama

Although docudramatic formats have burgeoned in recent years, it is hard to shift the pervasive notion that docudrama is either poor drama or poor documentary – *plus ça change* in this regard. I believe that this is to miss the point: the best new docudramas challenge the very basis of common understandings of both documentary and drama. They ask audiences to adjust their views of both these fundamental ways of making sense of the world. A belief in the docudrama led me to write *No Other Way To Tell It* in the first place; a renewed belief leads me now to this revision.

Since I wrote the first edition in 1998 docudrama has become centrally important not only in television production but also in film. Added to this, there has been an increased profile for documentary forms in theatre production too. In the UK, David Hare's 'verbatim' plays about the British rail transport system (*The Permanent Way*, 2003) and the Iraq War (*Stuff Happens*, 2004), and a series of 'tribunal' plays at London's Tricycle Theatre (*Guantanamo*, 2004; *Bloody Sunday*, 2005), have all demonstrated documentary theatre's new cultural importance. In America, too, a similar appetite for the kind of testimony now used in docudrama has long been evident in the work of Anna Deveare Smith (*Fires in the Mirror*, 1992; *Twilight: Los Angeles*, 1994). More recently Jessica Blank and Erik Jensen's 2002 play *The Exonerated* (about prisoners on death row) mirrored *Stuff Happens* by making a successful trans-Atlantic switch in 2006. Factual dramas in all media are enjoying a heyday, and the synergy that now exists between entertainment industries is evident in, for example, Peter Morgan's work. For television he has written *The Deal* (2003 – about the alleged agreement between Tony Blair and Gordon Brown to take turns as British Prime Minister) and *Longford* (2006 – about the peer Lord Longford and his attempts to get the child killer Myra Hindley released from prison); for the cinema, *The Queen* (2006 – about the monarchy's struggle to absorb the meaning of Princess Diana's death) and *The Last King of Scotland* (2006 – about Idi Amin's reign of terror in Uganda); and for the theatre, *Frost/Nixon* (2006 – about the celebrated 'confession' of the disgraced former President live on air).[1]

I believe this burgeoning of interest in docudrama to be in part due to a *zeitgeist* crisis in representation. Documentary 'proper' began to go through this in the 1990s. In my 1998 Introduction I cited the (then-current) case of Michael Born, a German filmmaker jailed for four years. His 'crime' was to fake a series of documentaries made for German television. I wrote: 'It is hard to avoid the thought that the somewhat draconian punishment meted out to him is a reflection of documentary's cultural status as a kind of faith.' On his release, Born was anything but a martyred figure. He was cheerfully insouciant about his apostasy and more than happy to parlay it as a claim to fame. He was, perhaps, among the first of a media-literate generation more interested in exploiting the possibilities of a cultural stance in which anything goes than in preserving his status and dignity as a *bone fide* maker of factual films.

In 1998 the British independent television company Carlton was fined in a similarly draconian way by the UK's television industry regulator. This body's attention had been drawn to the company's bad practice by a series of articles in the *Guardian*, which concluded that the makers of a primetime independent television documentary, *The Connection*, originally screened in 1996, had faked scenes. A swingeing fine was imposed on the network responsible.[2] Late in 2003, print journalism in its turn was rocked by an ethical scandal. It was revealed that one of the world's foremost newspapers, the *New York Times*, had published a series of articles plagiarised by one of its journalists, Jayston Blair. When he resigned in May 2003 the newspaper suffered the indignity of having to print a correction/retraction that ran to *four* pages. By 2004 the artist David Hockney was arguing that the digital revolution in photography had made an insupportable nonsense of the notion of photograph-as-truth. As an instrument of documentary record, he opined, the photograph was finished. Could anything be trusted as a carrier of fact and information in this millennial dispensation?[3]

My feeling now is that end-of-century lack of faith in documentary-as-record can be compared to the end of the nineteenth century's Nietzschean questioning of religious faith. In the explosion in 'Reality TV', an apparently shameless exploitation of both documentary presence and dramatic licence, the Last Days seem to many observers to have arrived. These mixtures of social engineering, game-show, soap and documentary formats have proved as popular to watch as they are cheap to make but have caused much hand-wringing amongst cultural commentators and politicians alike. Whether this phenomenon is a 'dumbing down' of television culture or a movement of populist democratisation, Reality TV clearly marked the coming of what John Corner has termed the 'post-documentary' period in which the very values of the historical documentary movement have been thrown into doubt. The drive to analyse this cultural moment has been the subject of a large number of recent academic books in many different countries.[4]

Docudrama has necessarily had to adjust to this and in some of its manifestations has moved towards a seriousness of purpose more usually associated historically with the documentary 'proper'. Much docudrama production, it is true, is not greatly different from what was going on in 1998, but the variety of hybrids now available has benefited the docudrama in ways I did not foresee previously and which I want to explore in this revision. The current spectrum of 'intergeneric hybridisation'[5] in film and television can be represented graphically. It is a continuum stretching from the mode of non-fiction (or documentary) at one end and the mode of fiction (drama)

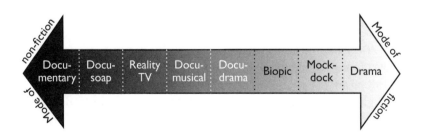

at the other. Even at the extremities of this continuum the forms are losing their purity, importing as they do conventions and structures from elsewhere.[6] Modern film and television drama, of course, has for some time been framed and organised to capture the 'buzz' and immediacy available in other forms – of 'direct cinema', for example, whose techniques so revolutionised documentary representation from the 1960s onwards. And it has been far from unusual for 'documentary proper' to structure itself according to dramatic rules (of plot and character) and even to incorporate elements of dramatic re-enactment, whether the subject is historical or contemporary. It is worth remembering, too, that the 'biopic' has always had a research dimension (of however dubious a kind) and often uses newsreel or documentary inserts (even if they only consisted of spinning newspaper headlines). George Custen's indispensable 1992 book on the biopic situates the genre in a not dissimilar relation to the fields of documentary and drama as I have the docudrama.[7]

In forms old and new an appetite for the factual has become a defining feature of the twenty-first century. Its place in current film production is an important factor in its rise to prominence. Cinema occupies a particularly privileged position in many practitioners' – and indeed commentators' – hierarchies of screen arts. Peter Kosminsky told me:

> For a director [of film drama] it is a much bigger canvas on which to work, a much tougher technical challenge ... Let me put it this way: if you talk to directors who work in television, you will find they have this slightly chippy attitude towards those who work exclusively in the movies. I say chippy because it's seated in jealousy. Most directors who work in drama in television would love to be working in movies.[8]

By 2003 docudramas made up around ten per cent of the top 100 films screened in the UK – an awful lot for what I described in 1998 as an 'occasional' genre.[9] Biopics alone in the period 2005–6 included films about Ray Charles, Alfred Kinsey and Howard Hughes (*Ray*, *Kinsey*, *The Aviator*), Truman Capote (*Capote* and *Infamous*) and Johnny Cash (*Walk the Line*). Docudramas have continued to revisit events from recent history – often employing the rubric of an historical anniversary. In 2005, ten years after the Rwandan genocide, there was Terry George's *Hotel Rwanda*; Raoul Peck's *Sometimes in April*; Michael Caton-Jones's *Shooting Dogs*; and Nick Hughes's *100 Days*. In 2006 the historical sore of 9/11 was picked at in Paul Greengrass's *Flight 93* and Oliver Stone's *World Trade Centre*. The more distant past, too, has been mined for its suggestive parallels with current history. *Good Night and Good Luck* (2005) explored current American right-wing mendacity through the historical prism of Ed Murrow's principled 1950s stand against the extreme Right of his day. *The Wind That Shakes the Barley*, Ken Loach's *Palme d'Or* winning film at Cannes in 2006, similarly coded an attack on current British foreign policy through a docudramatic reflection on the galvanic formation of modern Eire.

I took a somewhat gloomy view of the future for the docudrama in 1998. I concluded it was 'drifting towards Hollywood', losing that hard edge delivered by investigative research methods and realist filming practices. These were being softened, I felt, in favour of the kind of melodramatic sentimentality that is Hollywood's speciality. As Annette Insdorf remarks in her book on Holocaust films: 'there is a danger that the aesthetic can become an anesthetic [*sic*]' (1989: 126), and this is never more true than when something profoundly serious is smoothed into a three- or four-act structure. If I could see only decline towards a low common denominator, and away from the sober, high-concept docudrama I valued so highly, I was not alone: Julian Petley's observation that 'the dramatic look is displacing the documentary one' found wide assent, as did his feeling that the form was 'decreasingly marked out *stylistically*, from other forms of television drama' (1996: 18–19 – my emphasis). Practitioner Leslie Woodhead (who gave me my book's title) reluctantly noted that in the new television ecology it was 'necessary to go on talking to your audience in a language which they're willing to receive'.[10]

But the extent of creative hybridisation post-1998 has taken me somewhat by surprise. If US production of docudrama has been concentrated into movies, the television docudrama in the UK has pretty much reinvented itself, albeit in a form difficult to take for the generation brought up with a vision of television as a public service and documentary as a frowningly serious form. Developments in forms and modes of access have meant that all the codes and conventions of traditional documentary have been made available for mixture with other kinds of representation. The new success of documentary, too, has been phenomenal and marked by a willingness to be subjective rather than objective. At the time of the first edition, for example, the idea that a documentary film could fill a multiplex would have seemed absurd. Michael Moore was at that point an engaging but hardly culturally central maker of 'agit-TV' shows such as *Video Nation*. By the early years of the twenty-first century he had become a multi-award winning filmmaker who, almost single-handedly, had put documentary back on the cultural map through his 2003 film *Bowling for Columbine*, a film that used a personal angle of approach that made a character of Moore himself.[11]

Documentary film has since seized the political agenda in a major way, with Moore seeming to set himself the task of winning an American Presidential election through his films. In 2004 his anti-Bush, anti-Iraq War film *Fahrenheit 911* was seen in some quarters as nothing more than propaganda for the Democratic Party. In spite of Moore's efforts George W. Bush did get re-elected, but who in 1998 could have predicted that a documentary filmmaker would ever be in such a central political as well as cultural position? To many observers outside the USA Moore began to look and sound like the real opposition to the neo-conservative techno-industrial complex currently holding power. Formally, Moore imports many non-documentary devices into his films: innovative mixes of theatre-style agitprop stunts, MTV-style newsreel compilation, cartoon direct address, and not least his own pieces-to-camera. These, arguably, centre all his work, his performances constituting the central *characterisation* in all his films. Michael Moore is always the star of his own show.

Unique television

The argument of this book is still that docudrama is first and foremost a television form, even though industrial convergences during the past twenty years have raised docudrama's cinematic, and there-

Table 1. **Rethinking the docudrama: comparative table of 'documentary' and 'drama' features**

Documentary	Drama
THEORETICAL CATEGORIES	
Realm of 'non-fiction'	Realm of 'fiction'
Heavy emphasis on 'fact'	Light emphasis on 'fact'
Cool medium	Warm medium
Sobriety	Entertainment
Reason/the rational	Imagination/the intuitive
Authenticity	Credibility
The prior referent	Imitation of an action
Objectivity	Subjectivity
Particular truth	Essential truth
CONTENT	
Data/information	Feelings/emotions
Current affairs issues	'Human condition' issues
Public over private	Private over public
Institutions	Individuals
PRACTICE	
Research/accuracy	Invention/creativity
The journalist/researcher	The writer/creator
Unrehearsed pro-filmic events	Rehearsal prior to filming
Commentary/statement	Dialogue
Real-world individual	Character
Behaviour	Acting
Exegesis (e.g. captions)	Diegesis
Montage	*Mise-en-scène*
Location/non-design	Setting/design
Natural light	Key light
Location (messy) sound	'Balanced' (clean) sound
AUDIENCE	
Belief	Suspension of disbelief
Convergent thinking	Divergent thinking
Consideration of issues	Identification/empathy with characters
Comprehension (understanding through the mind)	Apprehension (understanding through the senses)
Distance	Closeness

fore its public, profile. Sub-textually, docudramas have asked audiences questions about the ways any 'drama' can be 'documentary', or any 'documentary' 'drama', partly because on television they join the flow of other programming. They offer a form, as it were, 'not-documentary/not-drama' that offers an experience through which audiences are challenged to reconstruct their mental model of the real through codes *both* documentary *and* dramatic. The two areas can be contrasted through the matrix in Table 1. This highlights the essential intertextuality of docudrama. It not only negotiates a path between documentary and drama but also provokes questions about where, if at all, any balance might be struck between the opposing claims of each category. In practice, particular examples will oscillate between one side and the other.

Intertextuality in examples of docudrama can be actively traced against this matrix. The connecting of texts with each other in this way signals more than just a simple relationship of similarity or dissimilarity. A way of viewing the world through texts or as text can be articulated, in which the more texts you know, the more likely they will 'show through' the one you are dealing with. For the practitioner, too, there is a use in intertextuality, even if they might regard the term suspiciously. Today they can certainly count on an audience not being phased by either overt or covert reference to other texts. Leslie Woodhead is, perhaps, representative of practitioners in the sense that he is 'confident of the audience's abilities to decode':

> It seems to me that an audience that can read *Hill Street Blues*, or a rock video, or can respond at a speed that popular drama now hits them, is well able to deal with notions of dramatic re-creation.

At a functional level, for a viewing audience, the docudrama, the drama and the documentary *share* territory rather than dispute it.

The docudrama is inherently more indexical than the drama, less indexical than the documentary. It inevitably points more insistently towards its origins in the real world than other kinds of drama. In another context, Richard Maxwell observes that the very act of pointing first 'draws attention to the pointer', and then diverts it towards that which is pointed at (1992: 183). So, in docudrama, we are always aware of both dramatic pointing and a place-(or person)-pointed-to. This can often give the form a campaigning edge. From its 'moment of presentation' in fictional, dramatic, form, docudrama points beyond the realm of fiction to a realm of non-fiction that is already-lived. In one sense, all drama, all fiction, aspires to this condition, but docudrama quite literally 'indexes' an explicit reality in ways difficult to ignore.

Thus, so far from pointing out from itself towards a universalised, generalised 'reality', the docudrama seeks to overlay the Stanislavskian emotional equivalence of 'As If' with a documentary-indexical 'See This!'. The relation to reality claimed in the solely dramatic 'as if' through equivalence and parallel, is present in docudrama through reconstruction/re-enactment (these words/actions, in this place). At the same time viewers will usually be aware that the events dramatised really happened; they exist, as it were, in parallel to acted ones. The docudrama is, in effect, part of the repertoire of a late twentieth-century culture that is highly dependent upon the television medium. Although variants exist in speech and music theatre, on radio, in the novel, or even in poetry, only television docudrama reaches mass audiences, with all that that implies. Experimentation in television has never been as radical as it has, say, in the theatre and the novel, or even the film. But the special 'take' on mixtures of fact and faction in television is what has made the docudrama a known quantity in modern culture. For over fifty years the form has been a kind of 'public service' in itself.[12]

Consider the range of docudrama subjects over this period: the form has dealt with social problems (housing and poverty in *Cathy Come Home*, 1966), contemporary history and international affairs (Soviet foreign policy and the Cold War in *Invasion*, 1980). In the USA, in its 'made-for-TV movie' form, it has similarly approached aspects of American history in series such as *Roots* (1977) and difficult 'human' issues such as cancer (*Brian's Song*, 1971), and AIDS (*And The Band Played On*, 1993). Television programmes and films that mix fact and fiction are now so commonplace throughout the world that to attempt to list even those made in the UK and the USA since the genre acquired its status in the 1960s would be a mammoth task indeed.[13] Suffice it to say that audiences continue to be drawn to the docudrama in numbers significant enough for it to remain a major cultural phenomenon. Although audience numbers may be small in relation to the big battalion television genres (soaps, sit-coms, cop and hospital series), the form has great 'TV talk' power, especially when it is controversial. Major audience studies have confirmed this. The Independent Television Commission's 'Research Monograph' *Television and the Public's View* (1992)[14] used the category 'drama-documentary' in two of its chapters (on 'Viewing Habits and Preferences' and 'Impartiality') even though the programmes with which it is being compared are much more frequently transmitted. In the chapter on 'Impartiality', for example, the other four categories are news, current affairs, drama, and entertainment. As Ian McBride observed, drama-documentary 'makes large numbers of people talk … about something they wouldn't otherwise have talked about.'[15]

In 2003, just before the British Standards Commission was merged with the new Office of Communication (or 'Ofcom'), the organisation published a study titled *Dramatic Licence*. This far-reaching piece of research examined the whole area of fact-based drama and came up with some counter-intuitive conclusions. Not least among these was the indication that the popular audience was more than ready to cut the industry some slack on *contemporary* docudrama but was less forgiving when inaccuracy became evident in historical films. The reasoning seemed to be that, while basic facts might be difficult to establish in respect of current events, they really should be known in the case of past history. As I shall try to show in Chapter 8, audiences and producers seem to have become more comfortable with, and increasingly interested in, the ironising play-off between fact and fiction. New forms have explicitly worked with the tension between the two. It is not only a case of documentary borrowing, or appropriating, dramatic codes and conventions, drama has also been enlivened by its equal and opposite appropriation of documentary and factual codes, especially in regard to actors' performances. And the evidence suggests that audiences have kept up with this. The 'Executive Summary' of the BSC's report notes:

> Although entertainment is the most important factor for viewers, they still expect the story or situation to be based on fact. They expect a realistic portrayal with an element of factual accuracy, but viewers also accept

that, for drama's sake, exaggeration of a situation or concentration on one possible outcome is needed to entertain. (Gatfield and Hargrave, 2003: 1)

Audience research done for the industry by academic Annette Hill (2005) similarly shows an audience that may be unschooled in academic theories of deconstruction but which remains innately sceptical. Through controversy docudramas can easily become media events, but this is far more common in television. Martin McKeand, producer of the 1980 ATV documentary drama *Death of a Princess*, recalled it being 'one of those programmes everyone had an opinion about, even if they hadn't actually seen it'.[16] Such is the ambition to make a difference many docudramas begin by hoping for direct effects in the external world. Of course Paul Kerr was right to point out that controversial docudrama has always been the exception rather than the rule: 'such programmes are not always so explosive – and that fact is far too easily forgotten in the wake of whatever is the latest "controversy"' (1990: 74). George Custen draws attention to the fact that television fame tends to focus on ordinary people: '[n]otoriety has ... replaced noteworthyness as the proper frame for biography; short-lived, soft news has replaced the harder stuff, history' (1992: 216). In spite of such just caveats, it is still the case that television docudrama, even more than film docudrama, can impact directly on the public sphere.

The new documentary

Docudrama draws its power to be important publicly from its association with documentary, its power to explore human reactions from its association with drama. As Alan Rosenthal says, many makers of docudrama enjoy 'the ability to break free of the limitations of documentary, and yet still aim to change the world' (1995: 229). Documentary's privileged status in Western cultures in the twentieth century was gained principally through an inherent seriousness of tone and purpose that has more recently been thrown into doubt. Bill Nichols, whose scholarship is central to documentary studies, coined the phrase the 'discourses of sobriety' in 1991 in order to express documentary's fundamental seriousness of content and purpose. Documentary was linked, he remarked, to some heavy-duty public discourses – politics, economics, and the law, for example. Brian Winston (2000: 40) observes that documentary constitutes one of television's 'duty genres', foisted upon the institution by the regulatory frameworks he provocatively labels 'quango-laws' (Winston, 2000: 12, and see also Chapter 2 of this volume). Docudrama lives in the shadow of such seriousness; it too, is something of a 'duty genre' – in the history of the British institution anyway. But new forms that emerged in the final decade of the twentieth century have radically reconfigured this seriousness. They depend upon a popular audience attuned as never before to what cultural theorists would call post-modern reflexivity, but which I want to call innate media intelligence. Those that are most closely related to I consider in Chapter 8, but I want to say something in this Introduction about the wider spread of hybrids – about docusoaps, Reality TV and cognate modes.

It seems to me that these hybrids narrativise in a very dramatic way, while also utilising set-ups that recall direct cinema. They have grown in response to, and because of, technological development and innovation, and late capitalist industrial convergence. Computer-generated imagery (CGI) and other modern technologies complicate matters, often making fictions easier to believe for audiences but also making it easier to fake material. Especially in the popular press, this has led to a narrow focus on issues of evidentiality and authenticity in recent debates. While cultural critics stress the relativities inevitable in any argument about 'fact' and 'truth' (for example, citing angle of vision, context, history, race, class, gender as positioners of such concepts), tabloid newspapers trumpet demands for the kind of monumental 'Whole Truth and Nothing But the Truth' that is hard to deliver. 'Truth' is always simple in one sense – when compared, for example, to provable outright lies. But at each complex and multi-levelled moment of history the most interesting 'facts' seem to be the ones most open to dispute, and in practice truth seems to become elusive. The contesting of the various 'truths' of the Iraq War is an indication of this.[17]

Technology is a double-edged sword in the search for truth-in-representation in another way: cheap digital cameras may have democratised filmmaking, but at the same time they have provided nation states and their institutions with new tools for keeping law and order. The Orwellian 'Big Brother' nightmare is played as farce on primetime television courtesy of Endemol and its competitor companies, but it is played differently in tropes of surveillance and control through closed-circuit television (CCTV) systems in parking lots, public buildings and gathering places (see Palmer, 2003). Emerging programme formats that are cheap for producers, appealing for participants, and entertaining for consumers have reinforced the growing split between defenders of 'public service' documentary and those aligned with neo-liberal notions of a public sphere.

There is considerable industrial and commercial pressure now bearing down on any broadcaster or programme maker with a background in, or continuing concern for, the concept of 'public service'. The threat is not just to developed 'Reithian' models of public service (with a full-blown commitment to giving the public what it needs as well as what it wants). Even the thoroughly commercial remit of the American terrestrial system has not been without an honourable history of public service, and this is also under threat. The technical and distributive developments of cable, satellite and digital channels ensure that any film- and programme-maker not working within the intrinsically popular will potentially have a problem placing their product. This has undoubtedly fuelled the drive towards hybridisation.

Documentary films for theatrical and televisual distribution increasingly import essentially dramatic structures. Fiction films routinely raid documentary practices in their search for an immediacy that signals authenticity. Macdonald and Cousins remarked in the late 1990s upon the dual developments of a 'desire to make films which although educational and informative are also entertaining' (which led, in their view, to a resurgence of the form in multiplexes) and 'a willingness to challenge the boundaries between "documentary" and "fiction"' (1996: 311).[18] Annette Hill (2005) rightly describes television in particular as 'cannibalising itself' in its quest for new forms. The largest question of all is do these forms open up or close down the 'public spaces' of television and film? No one can doubt that documentary output in the twenty-first century is being more widely viewed and more widely discussed than at any time since the 1930s. *Survivor, Castaway, Temptation Island, Big Brother* and their 'celebrity' clones are multi-national phenomena as much as they are products of individual national cultures. The fact that such programmes began to appear around the cusp of the millennium gives them a Janus-face in terms of documentary history. Like Walter Benjamin's Angel of History, they gaze back at documentary practices of the past as they are precipitated into a future apparently mortgaged to the ratings, sustained by the new digital revolution's proliferation of channels. But there are democratic possibilities in the new documentary, as I hope to show in Chapter 8. They can articulate questions of ethics, values and morality, and can allow a popular audience to access serious questions through factual entertainments that establish knowing, playful and sometimes teasing relationships with audiences. These relationships continue in the manifest afterlives of many documentary hybrids further to challenge audience expectations.

The internet especially carries evidence of the 'excess' that allows both player/producer and consumer/audience to set new agendas. In the concluding chapter to the first edition of this book, I suggested that programme makers might allow the research base that underpins the responsible docudrama to be made more widely available via the internet. This has happened, and in this edition I examine the results. Some of these are remarkable, and certainly go beyond what I expected as I looked into the future in 1998. As digitalization further re-forms the economy of broadcasting worldwide, questions about the ethics and values that obtain will continue to drive both popular and academic debate. Reflecting such change as I have outlined above is always difficult for an academic book. In the first edition, I used the 1992 Granada television film *Hostages*, plus two or three other illustrative examples from the period 1992–96, to try to be as up-to-date as possible. As I write now, my aim is to reflect more broadly on trends in docudrama across time. I have retained aspects of the *Hostages* case study only because the subject of the clash between Western and Middle Eastern cultures is as relevant now as it was then. Until this fundamental geopolitical problem is resolved, this will surely continue to be the case in dramatic representation as well as in news and current affairs. Otherwise, I have drawn my illustrations more widely from film and television docudramas past and present – hence the change in the book's sub-title.[19]

The new subtitle: 'docudrama on film and television'

Having noted a 'growing synergy between American and British television' in 1998, I proposed a neologism – 'dramadoc/docudrama'. Its purpose was to show 'typographically the meeting of the distinctively different British and American traditions of "docudrama" and "dramadoc"'. The first word indicated an American tradition of entertainment-led, 'based on a true story' films; the second marked a British tradition of investigative documentaries made as fictions predominantly within current affairs departments of television companies. The neologism's clumsiness was, in a sense, its recommendation: there was – still is – confusion between the concepts of 'drama documentary' and 'documentary drama' (see Chapter 4) highlighted in the typography. Ultimately, I regard all attempts to standardise definitions, including my own, as worthy but doomed. The two terms are routinely used (often shortened to 'dramadoc' or 'docudrama') in journalistic commentary about widely different examples, as if they were the same thing. In general, awareness of what I have described as the British tradition leads to the use of 'drama-documentary' and 'dramadoc'.

But I believe now that 'docudrama' is effectively the term of choice for discussion of this subject – academic or otherwise – in anglophone cultures. Its breadth brings some advantages, some disadvantages. After I had gone through my 1998 definitions with a class at Reading in 2004, a student asked: 'Is *NYPD Blue* a docudrama, then?' This celebrated example of cop-show longevity does have a research base – like the first of the cop shows, the 1950s *Dragnet*, its plots and characters come from a police department and its representatives. It does exhibit many of docudrama's stylistic markers, and it does play into the public sphere in a way that I habitually claim for the docudrama. Its exemplary figures and circumstances are not unlike those of *Cathy Come Home* – composites intended to convey broad truths about something of social importance. The full range of 'border genres' mentioned diagrammatically above would certainly include *NYPD Blue* and other series developed by 'show-runners' like Steven Bochco. For Bochco in the USA, read *Cathy Come Home* producer Tony Garnett in the UK: his 'World Productions' company similarly animates drama series like the 1990s *Cops* with a visceral documentary style. The live episode of *ER* in which the doc(tor)-show incorporated a doc(umentary) crew making a real-time film about County General would similarly have furnished a fascinatingly intertextual example of inventive hybridity in a television drama series. The hybrids I discuss above, even soaps, all utilise research, and many pride themselves on being issue-driven and therefore potentially socially useful in a documentary and docudrama way.

But, ultimately, none of these are docudrama. To be a docudrama is to be altogether closer to *documents* – to factual templates. Docudramas' indexical links to real-world occurrences can always be established in more thorough-going ways – as I hope to show more clearly in the chapters that follow, especially those concerned with the form's history and development. As single dramas or miniseries, docudramas capitalise on an 'out-of-story' awareness – of issues, events, people in the news and in history. Docudrama plots are to some extent predetermined through news, current affairs, and the histories of nations, peoples and social groups in ways that fiction cannot be. Docudramas may have changed since 1998, as – again – I hope to show, but they retain this quality even when they are speculative.[20]

As Steven N. Lipkin observes, the trends in docudrama continue to reflect the differential targeting strategies of film and television industries and the demographics of their audiences. Docudramatic subject matter, he points out, tends to be gendered differently for film and television. Male subjects and their issues *tend* to be made into film docudrama, female into what Lipkin shortens as 'MOW ('movie-of-the-week') docudrama'. I pointed out in the first edition's final chapter that there was a superabundance of the feminised 'ethic of care' in MOW television docudrama. And writers such as Jonathan Dovey (2000) and Annette Hill (2005) have observed that the public sphere itself has become feminised and individualised as never before as 'grand narrative' certainties give way to post-modern anxieties and relativities. It is in this new broadcasting ecology – multi-channel digital technology, an increasingly privatised industry of publishers rather than producers, a 'privatised' audience – that the docudrama has 'come of age'.

Academic studies

If a second edition has afforded me the opportunity to consider important alterations in the landscape, it also enables me to pay tribute to new interventions in the field to which the first edition contributed. As the discipline of Media Studies has grown in confidence (and in its capacity to distinguish what it does from the activities of Film Studies and Communication Studies) it has begun to generate both key texts (such as dictionaries, encyclopaedias and collections that define terms and forms) and new scholarship. This has been the case with docudrama, the study of which has been immeasurably enhanced by the appearance of several important texts since 1998. The first, Alan Rosenthal's collection *Why Docudrama?: Fact-Fiction on Film and TV*, gathered together twenty-eight of the most important published interventions on docudrama up to the point of its own publication (1999) – the essays therein demonstrate how the academic community has carved out understandings of the form, and how docudrama can be bracketed off from other forms. The second, Jane Roscoe and Craig Hight's 2001 *Faking It: Mock-documentary and the Subversion of Factuality*, marks off the docudrama from the mock-documentary, and in doing so indicates how the power of the documentary idea has returned as farce in an increasingly sophisticated media environment. The mock-documentary, as they point out, now looks far more like a classic documentary than the fiction film-influenced docudrama; the essential joke of the mock-documentary depends fundamentally on audience recognition. Finally, Steven N. Lipkin's 2002 *Real Emotional Logic: Film and Television Docudrama as Persuasive Practice* has taken the debate on the form into new and important territory. He explores in particular the moral and ethical landscape of the docudrama's address to its audience, and gives due prominence to the use of docudrama by the film industry. This has always been the prime mover of change in the USA. As the subtitles of both Lipkin's book and Rosenthal's collection indicate, film and its industrial muscle account in large measure for the current ubiquity of the docudrama. But of equal importance is the convergence between film and television industries that is such a feature of the current entertainment industry landscape. These are the kinds of considerations that have generated some of my 'second thoughts' about docudrama.[21]

Why docudrama? A personal reflection

The title of Alan Rosenthal's 1999 collection is important, and for this new introduction I want to explain more fully my own fascination with docudrama. It is of all things vital that the critic remains a keen spectator – an enthusiast – while also trying to retain some distance on the subject. Spectating at the theatre and in front of television and cinema screens links me to my readers (for without this common interest, I would not write nor would you have picked up this book). But I believe it is also necessary to know from *the inside* what it is like to make a documentary play, to have practical experience of wrestling with the problems of form and medium. I have not only taken an interest in plays with a factual background, I have also made and researched them. Making has been exclusively in a theatrical context, as professional theatre worker and teacher at a variety of educational establishments. My academic research straddles theatre and screen media.

Lipkin's *apperçu* that 'this mode of presentation offers *attractive* instruction' (2002: xiii – my italics) perhaps explains why I have occupied myself so exclusively with docudrama. I believe I am not alone in having an interest in – indeed deriving an enjoyment from – being instructed by those who know more than I do. This applies both to facts and expertise and to life experiences. I am, of course, attracted to drama in general as an *expressive* mode whether documentary or otherwise. My attraction to the didactic has been acquired and I recognise it as an unfashionable taste. It may be on the increase as a consequence of people more and more 'looking for answers' in a sometimes bewildering modern world. It is to Steven Lipkin also that I owe the important perception that the docudrama can primarily be seen as a means of persuasion – a *rhetorical* mode. The value of docudrama as 'second order experience' is something I want to dwell on second time around, and which I develop in Chapter 8.

In some ways my research into fact-based plays has been founded on two ground-breaking examples: Theatre Workshop's *Oh What a Lovely War* (1963) and Jeremy Sandford's *Cathy Come Home* (1966). In some ways these two works typify the limitations, possibilities and excitements of the fact-based drama in different media. These theatrical and televisual pieces condense between them many of the qualities of the socially oppositional and formally inventive docudrama. They are both works of the 1960s, and they both bear the marks of that decade (both positively and negatively). They quintessentialise the capacity of drama to work *with* facts and *through* entertainment to provoke a questioning stance towards historical events (the First World War, in the case of the theatre piece) and social policy (housing, in the case of the television play) and the political consequences of both. The two media have vastly different reaches and grasps in terms of operational technique and audience. When asked what the fascination of the fact-based drama consists in, I am always tempted to say, 'See these two works, then tell me if you still don't get the idea.' 'See' rather than 'read' – reading the published texts of both plays is fine, but as John McGrath memorably said, the text is what is left when the play has gone.[22]

My interest in – indeed my continued enjoyment of – these dramas derives in a major way from the fact that they once marked out important moments of cultural turbulence. Their continued visibility states very openly that drama *is* important. Both plays made quite straightforward claims in exciting ways. In doing so they opened up debates that rapidly turned into complex arguments about historical circumstance, human agency and representation itself. They still do that in a residual form whenever they are performed, shown, read and discussed. The former drama says, among other things, that the 1914–18 War was visited upon, and suffered heroically by, the unempowered masses at the behest of arrogant and incompetent ruling elites. The latter says, amongst other things, that society is needlessly cruel to its poorer members and could easily do a great deal better. These messages were, of course, open to dispute at the time of first production and are so still.[23] But I continue to believe they contain useful information both in form and content.

In common with many people of my generation and profession I have spent a good deal of my life defending the arts, and particularly the dramatic arts, against the rationalist accusation that they are fundamentally useless. I have always believed that the arts can be of *use* as well as *decoration*. Where better to take this stand than with a mode that offers both instruction and entertainment, and that in certain examples can claim equal measure for these things? A determination to continue to focus on docudrama left me with some hard decisions as to how far to pursue discussion of the other provocative hybrids. In the end I have concentrated in the new final Chapter on two of the most extravagant ones: documusical and docuopera. The overt theatricalisation of these forms delights the Brechtian in me and their profound emphasis on *drama* is my excuse for including them. Finally, I have radically re-arranged the chapters of the original book, and introduced new material, in order to account for newly flourishing mixtures of documentary and drama. They have renewed my faith in the ingenuity and imagination of the film- and programme makers of the new century.

Notes

1 Documentary Theatre's resurgence led to the *Tulane Drama Review* running a special edition on Documentary Theatre in 2006 – see *TDR* (Fall 2006, 50: 3 – T191).

2 See Chapter 2 for more details on this case.

3 Hockney was interviewed in the *Guardian* on 4 March 2004. His idea was not new, of course; Brian Winston was pointing it out in 1995 (see his *Claiming the Real* for more on the effects of new technologies on documentary's historic truth claims).

4 John Corner first trailed this idea in *Media, Culture and Society* in 2000 (see Bibliography – this lists a number of books that deal with Reality TV).

5 The phrase 'intergeneric hybridisation' is, again, John Corner's. He has used it in a number of places, but put it forward first in 1997 in an essay in *Media, Culture and Society* (see Bibliography).

6 To take just one new form on the continuum – the mock-documentary – this, arguably the most *fictional* mode, often looks more like old-fashioned documentary than documentary itself (see Roscoe and Hight, 2001).

7 See especially Custen's Chapter 6, where he cites movie-of-the-week docudrama as the film biopic's direct heir.

8 I interviewed Peter Kosminsky at his home in Wiltshire on 28 June 2005.

9 This is according to the Film Distributors' Association *Yearbook* for 2003.

10 'No other way to tell it' is Woodhead's telling phrase from his 1981 BFI/ *Guardian* lecture. I also interviewed him in London on 26 October 1994.

11 The distinctive style was, of course, set up in Moore's early film *Roger and Me* (1989 – see Corner (1996, Chapter 9) for an excellent analysis of this documentary).

12 In March 2007, Channel 4's *Fifty Greatest Television Dramas* programme included eleven docudramas in its list (with the iconic 1966 *Cathy Come Home* highest placed at no. 5). Six more were heavily based on fact – however suspicious one is about lists of this kind, the inclusion of so many docudramas and near-docudramas is an indication of the maturity and importance of the form.

13 Andrew Goodwin and Paul Kerr (1983: 39–53), Alan Rosenthal (1995: 231–6) and Steven Lipkin (2002: 57, 63–4) provide some interesting information, as does Alvin Marill's 1987 reference book, *Movies Made For Television*. Also see *Reel Life Real Life* (Horenstein *et al.*, 1994).

14 The archive section of Ofcom's website (www.ofcom.org.uk) has the more recent of these yearly-surveys.

15 Interestingly, a 1990 study of the effects on an audience of Granada's 1990 *Who Bombed Birmingham?* found that 76% of those questioned believed they had acquired fresh information through the dramadoc, but only 59% believed that most of the information offered was true (see Kilborn and Izod, 1997: 236).

16 I spoke to Martin McKeand at the '*Médias: entre Fiction et Réalité*' conference in Dijon, 27–8 November 1992.

17 For example, the presence or absence of weapons of mass destruction in pre-War Iraq has been much contested. A ray of hope amongst the plethora of facts appearing during this period was that considerable social extension was evident in the debate – even if the level of the debate at times descended to playground name-calling.

18 They quote as examples of the first development *Unzipped* and *Crumb* (both 1995 – the former about fashion designer Isaac Mizrahi, the latter about cartoonist Robert Crumb, and the work of Chantal Akerman, Errol Morris and Chris Marker as (high-status) examples of the second. In this section of their book (Section 11 'Diversity' – 311–63) they include pieces on *Thin Blue Line* (1989) and *Shoah* (1985) and on the work of 'participatory' documentarists like Nick Broomfield.

19 In hindsight, the Granada film *Hostages* (1992) was in many ways the

first of a series of representations of the hostages' experiences. Channel 4 in Britain ran a documentary – *Hostage* – examining the experiences of British and American hostages in Beirut across three weeks in January 1999. Brian Keenan and John McCarthy, two of the released Beirut hostages who so resented the film that, ironically, had been made to help make them free, did eventually make their own film *Blind Flight* (2004). Frank McGuiness's play *Someone Who'll Watch Over Me*, endorsed so eloquently by Brian Keenan at the time of its first production in 1992, played London's West End again in 2005.

20 I refer here to the new wave of 'conditional tense'/'what if'/'speculative' docudramas dealing with anxieties surrounding a global future consistently reported and perceived as uncertain and threatening (see Chapter 8).

21 Docudrama has also, of course, featured in several important studies of documentary, such as Winston (1995 and 2000), Corner (1996), Kilborn and Izod (1997), Bruzzi (2000). *No Other Way To Tell It* has had recognition in reference books and edited collections. Sections of the book have been anthologised in collections such as Allen and Hill (2004), and in Rosenthal and Corner (2005). It has often been cited too; see, for example, Casey *et al.* (2002), and Creeber (2001, 2004).

22 See McGrath's seminal 1981 book (5–7). For an evocative illustrated book on Theatre Workshop that will give some idea of the group's theatrical inventiveness, see Melvin 2006. *Oh What a Lovely War* is, of course, also available idn a third medium, film, through Richard Attenborough's 1969 version.

23 Many historians now dispute the central thesis of *Oh What a Lovely War* – just one example is Gordon Corrigan's *Mud, Blood and Poppycock: Britain and the First World War* (London: Cassell, 2003). For the furore created by *Cathy Come Home* – in 1966 and subsequently – see Paget (1999).

1

Working on docudrama

Research and writing

Docudramas require pre-production research and this is a key marker of difference between docudrama and other kinds of drama. Sita Williams, researcher as well as producer, tellingly described to me the kind of knowledge acquired through docudrama research as 'real short-term memory stuff, like revising for an exam!' Kathy Chater, writing on the work of the researcher in television, notes that there are 'two forms of factual research'. The first comprises the collecting of generally accepted facts. This research is unlikely to be controversial. Chater calls the second form 'the exposé method'. Here the aim is to find 'facts that have either not been considered or which have been rejected by the general consensus' (1992: 16–17).[1] The stakes here become higher. The information-gathering methods used to provide material for the classic British investigative 'drama-documentaries' of the late twentieth century were identical to those used for documentary proper; the films were prepared like any other piece of television journalism. As a matter of course some docudramas ran identical risks to any documentary that attempted to shine a light into dark places.

The docudramas produced for many years by Granada were underpinned by a flagship current affairs programme *World in Action* (1963–98). In former times, an employees-only library, an archive of film and video tapes, journalists' own newspaper cuttings collections and personal contacts, plus the usual public information services, underwrote the research background to a docudrama as it did to a documentary. Looking back, producer David Boulton has said, 'We really did turn the world of TV current affairs on its head, even if the world itself remained stubbornly the right way up.'[2] Today, with a television ecology comprising more independent production companies, independent agencies deliver this kind of service, and anyway computers are there to back up 'hard copy' archives.

'Field work', which might include interviews with real-world individuals, is also a factor in any research process. In the case of Granada's 1992 *Hostages*, returned hostages such as Frank Reed, and families and friends such as Jill Morrell, working for the release of their loved ones in Beirut, were interviewed by Alasdair Palmer the Associate Producer. For *The Government Inspector*, a 2005 Channel 4 film about the British weapons inspector Dr David Kelly, producer Simon Chinn and his researchers worked for eighteen months and conducted 120 interviews.[3] The facts portrayed in television docudrama are subject to pre-production checks, with the script drafts constantly referred to lawyers to ensure that films will be legally defensible at the level of fact (see Chapter 2). In the case of the 'co-pro' (co-production with other countries' television companies), other lawyers too will check material against their own national law. There is a widespread anxiety in television especially about getting right the facts of any television film. Professional and ethical motives are behind this anxiety, but legal – and ultimately financial – concerns are ever present. It is rare (though not unknown) for the facts of a television docudrama to be disputed in a law court. Even in times where competition and cost-cutting are the order of the day the research effort still has to be made. Anything already in the public domain is beyond legal dispute, of course, and a good deal of the material used in docudrama is likely to be in Chater's first, uncontentious, category.

Because the lead-time in film production is different from television, and because film is not subject to such stringent regulation as television, there tends to be less anxiety within the film industry. It is hard to imagine, for example, a television docudrama on the Guildford Four being able to get away with the sometimes extravagant liberties taken with facts in the 1993 film *In the Name of the Father*. This film has been accused of

debasing its own authenticity with its final, hollow court-room scene which is not only completely invented and inaccurate in its portrayal of British procedure, but is played like the climax from a Perry Mason movie. (Halliwell and Walker, 2002: 406)

In the scene in question, Emma Thompson plays defence lawyer Gareth Peirce and passionately harangues the jury. Peirce was actually a behind-the-scenes legal figure at appeal, and so she never had to speak to a jury at all. There were other invented scenes. For example, Giuseppe and Gerry Conlon (Pete Postlethwaite and Daniel Day-Lewis) were depicted inhabiting the same jail cell. They were never even held in the same prison. These aspects of his film have been vigorously defended by writer/director Jim Sheridan:

> Films always and necessarily distort the truth: Daniel is not really Gerry Conlon, and the bomb did not really go off in slow-motion. (Domaille 2001: 70)

Sheridan made no secret of his intention to wring heart-strings rather than produce a factual report in his film. His insouciance regarding factual accuracy can be seen as provocation, an articulation of a political point about Irish oppression by Britain. But, to repeat, it is hard to imagine such a version of the facts being prepared for a television audience.

For television docudrama makers the situation is more complicated and they more generally adduce research as evidence of their probity in the event of post-transmission attack. Docudrama makers habitually describe their research in adjectives signifying conscientiousness. Research is never other than 'detailed', 'extensive', 'painstaking', or 'voluminous'. Yet as any researcher knows, no matter what the field, it is always possible to do more research (and who in any case would ever deliberately describe their research as 'sketchy', 'superficial' or 'incomplete'?). There is also an ongoing stand-off between print and television journalism, the former exulting whenever it can show slipshod work in the latter. A classic argumentational move for the television filmmaker is the one Peter Kosminsky used when discussing *No Child of Mine*, his ITV film about child-abuse, at a 1997 BAFTA debate. He angrily contrasted his own (faithfully-kept) promise not to reveal the identity of 'Kerry' – the main protagonist, a prostituted child – to the door-stepping depredations of the tabloid hacks who had made the real girl's life a misery in the weeks following transmission.

In addition to researchers working with individuals and information agencies, docudramas also employ writers who occasionally do their own research. Writing docudrama is a specialist task, one not relished by all writers. Factual material must be turned into believable dialogue for actors to exchange in scenes organised into a narrative text. Just like works of the imagination, docudrama text is composed with aesthetic as well as factual considerations. Research material is passed to the dramatist, who tends either to benefit from this work and acquire ownership of it as they shape it further, or to feel like a kind of 'hired hand' as they begin to resent the straitjacketing that working with facts can impose. Dramatists are expected at the very least to familiarise themselves with often highly detailed research material very quickly. Michael Eaton's case on Yorkshire Television's 1990 *Shoot to Kill* (also directed by Kosminsky) is instructive here. At the moment in which Eaton entered the project, the journalists on the team had already done three years research into the Stalker affair.[4] His job was to synthesise what was there. 'We are', Eaton has said, 'structuralists rather than dramatists – producers want us to supply form and structure.'[5] Some writers enjoy the constraints this inevitably provides, but others find them irksome. As far as the industry is concerned, it is the job of drama to supply form and structure and ultimately a 'shooting script'. This more or less final print version will have had many drafts, all of which have to be run past lawyers in what amounts to a negotiation. This tricky process has two protagonists: a writer keen to represent the facts but focused on creating meaningful dialogue, scenes and narrative; and a lawyer focused on combating prospective libel suits.[6]

The method by which a production team works on a docudrama text is then broadly that of any fiction film. In the first stage there is concept, writing and setting up finance. In the next stage there is casting, negotiating with actor's agents, finding a director and a crew, drawing up contracts, organising schedules to ensure the smoothest possible running of read-throughs, rehearsals, location work, and studio sessions. Writers draft, and actors work with scripts, rehearse and perform for the camera. Realisation in performance before the camera depends upon skills from outside the world of factual journalism – skills of credible performance in environments both simulated and actual, recorded on film by complex technical means. Dubbed, shaped and edited by further exercise of technical skill, the docudrama then reaches its audience. The process for a feature film docudrama is similar in many respects to television but crucially different in its focus: less hedged around by regulation, it has a freer attitude towards the letter of the fact and more focus on narrative dynamics. But film and television docudrama have converged gradually over a quarter of a century, and many films that start as features end up as 'movies-of-the-week', or are even aimed at both film and television markets.

Take the example of two 2002 docudramas about the Bloody Sunday incident. *Bloody Sunday* was first to be screened on ITV. In the week of first transmission this film also had a limited cinema release, neatly illustrating the current synergy of the film and television industries. In the same week another film on the subject, *Sunday*, was broadcast on Channel 4. The research background for both *Sunday* and *Bloody Sunday* included input from historical participants and the films were made in a new context of interest in the historical incident. In 2002 an official inquiry into the actions of 30 January 1972 (when the British Army's Parachute Regiment entered Londonderry, shooting 13 civilians) was in process. *Bloody Sunday* was directed by Paul Greengrass; *Sunday* was written by Jimmy McGovern. Both these individuals have catalogues that heavily feature docudrama.[7] Neither film could be called a 'documentary' in the usual sense of that word, even though they were prepared in a similar way, and had some similar intentions to those of documentaries on this subject (to expose original tragic injustices in a context in which the case of Bloody Sunday was being re-examined by the British judiciary).[8]

The very fact that actors had rehearsed specially written scripts is enough to deny these films any documentary categorisation. But nor were the films strictly 'dramas' in the sense of freely-imagined works of fiction, made 'originally' in the mind of writers. In the case

of Granada's 1992 *Hostages*, writer Bernard MacLaverty was not the
only 'creative' policed by facts. Producers Alasdair Palmer and Sita
Williams intervened so often on the set – to correct or to insist upon
particular matters of fact – that they were only semi-jokingly dubbed
by disgruntled members of cast and crew, the 'fact fascists'. For the
'artists' involved – the director and the actors – any hint of improvisation, any deviation from the legally-vetted script, was quite simply
out of the question. Like it or not, the 'fact fascists' had an on-set role
– as mouthpieces for off-set lawyers.[9]

Treating facts

Docudramas begin – as do films and television programmes of all
kinds – with someone's bright idea developed into a formal 'pitch'
or 'proposal' made to someone with the power to produce and/
or finance a film. If a pitch is given the green light, it is developed
into a 'treatment', or an outline that includes the subject matter of
a proposed film or television programme, a description of the kind
of approach the film might take, and details about characters and
incidents to be portrayed. According to Sita Williams, 'the treatment
isn't a straitjacket, it's only to give whoever needs to know a kind of
feeling for the story' (the people who 'need to know' being principally executives likely to have commissioning powers). A treatment
defines genre or genre-mix, too, the citing of film or programme
categories helping in its turn to mark out the kind of audience to
whom the finished product might appeal, and (for television) the
scheduling slot for which it will be most suitable. If researched facts
are evident in the treatment this in itself marks the intended territory and trajectory of the film for planners in both film and television
industries. A successful treatment also becomes the basis for budgetary and logistical planning. It will eventually shape a writer's work
in fundamental ways. This has been described by Todd Gitlin as a 'fil-
tration' process through which the industries control ideas (1994:
21). In the open competition that characterises American film and
television the process reduces thousands of ideas pitched each year
'by a factor,' says Gitlin, 'of five, ten, or thirty' at each stage. Only
a handful of ideas can survive this Darwinian process. Even highly

successful writers and directors can point to numbers of unrealised projects at various stages of aborted preparation.

The dramatic element in docudrama makes for many of the form's complications. Just as the concept of the 'unrehearsed' is fundamental to documentary, so the 'rehearsed' is integral to drama. In the classic narrative film the spectator is sucked into the frame through the cathartic power of identification with a fictional 'other'. By contrast, the spectator in classic documentary is positioned as 'person-to-be-addressed' and held at the distance appropriate to a dispassionate observer. Latterly these spectatorial positions have become far more complicated, but the clash between these competing 'ways of seeing' is still a factor. In the USA many of docudrama's difficulties are resolved financially, by bringing actual participants in historical events 'on board' with projects. Alan Rosenthal notes that 'most of the [US] networks and major producers of docudramas not only employ scouts to search for the hot stories, but also spend vast amounts of money in purchasing the story rights' (1995: 26). This has led occasionally to bizarre consequences at the tabloid end of docudrama production (see Chapter 8). Home Box Office (HBO) wittily satirised the sensational excesses of tabloid docudrama in their 1992 *The Positively True Adventures of the Alleged Texas Cheerleader-Murdering Mom*. The jokey quality of this reflexive docudrama is evident in an early scene that depicts the eponymous 'Mom' objecting vociferously to the idea of actress Holly Hunter playing her in the film. It is of course Hunter speaking this objection.[10]

Historically the British drama-documentary tradition has been far closer to the project of the journalist and the documentarist than its American cousin. As Jeremy Tunstall notes: 'British documentary film-makers see themselves as heirs to two great traditions – one in public service broadcasting, the other in 1930s documentary film-making' (1993: 33). The BBC and Granada in particular have highlighted journalistic values in the past, working invariably with stories already in the public domain. In refusing to enter into story-auctions British producers in general have invoked a system of rights and ethics shared with the investigative journalist. But the cultural crisis over ownership of real-life stories, social anxieties around the

concept of privacy, and the increasing convergence of broadcasting
institutions now complicate this apparently straightforward moral
stance. A fierce turn-of-the-century public debate about celebrity
and privacy has raised the stakes even higher.

In the UK, the stages of proposal, optioning, production and
transmission were re-shaped in the 1990s owing to the 1990
Broadcasting Act, and re-shaped again by the 2003 legislation
that spawned Ofcom. The independent production sector and
the phenomenon of co-production have increased, with the way
smoothed by 'lighter touch' regulation. Many former employees
of large broadcasting organisations shifted into independent production during the 1990s.[11] The digital revolution has caused further 'niche-marketing' changes in the ecology of broadcasting and
further emphasis on audience interaction with broadcasters (via, for
example, mobile phones and interactive video handsets). Public service broadcasting is still energetically debated, and strong enough in
terms of tradition for there to be some hope of continuity. But global
media change has shifted the overall emphasis – in the television
industry at any rate – to a greater concern with commerce and consumers than the founding fathers of the BBC would have wanted.
Large organisations like the BBC and the ITV franchise holders have
increasingly worked with co-producers worldwide – with American
companies like HBO and European partners like France's Canal +
(see also Chapter 8).

With single dramas harder than ever to pitch in television, and
fraught with difficulties in film, drama that plugs into major issues
has a built-in advantage. Allied to the publicity boost of a campaign,
an anniversary or a *cause célèbre*, factual drama is more likely to
be made than fictional drama in the new dispensation. Television
docudrama can win out when schedule space is difficult to come
by. The main result of the changes is that British dramadoc (which
had been drifting towards Hollywood from the late 1980s onwards)
has become more and more like American docudrama. The synergy
between American and British television has increased through co-
production, but it was a factor well before Granada, the BBC and
others began to work with HBO. Some would see it as an inevitable
consequence of the American cultural imperialism that has been

invading national television cultures consistently since the end of the Second World War. Some mourn the apparent death of the British dramadoc. But whatever the changes, the form still retains crucial differences from conventional television drama and from the general run of feature film fiction. There are two aspects to this difference: the research dimension, and the vulnerability to regulation (in the case of television) and to the law (in the cases of both television and film). In the research and project-development stage and in post-transmission/post-screening there is often more sensitivity to possible real-world repercussions, more direct fit with the real world, than with any other drama genre.

The process of production

This can be summarised as follows:

- *Pre-production* 'Pitch' or concept → research → treatment → further research → draft scripts + ongoing research + legal vetting → final script (continuous legal vetting) → cast and crew assembled.

- *Production* Read-through → rehearsal → shooting in studio and on location → ongoing research + re-drafting/script editing + legal checks.

- *Post-production* Editing → dubbing → research updating for website + continued legal checks → television: scheduling + press preview/film: focus-grouping + re-editing.

- *Television transmission/Film release* Docudrama reaches audience.

- *Reception post-transmission/post-release* Public discussion (for example: radio and television studio debate, newspaper articles, internet activity, follow-up television/radio).

The final category above is a reminder that where television docudrama is concerned the process does not terminate at transmission: the moment of reception is equally important, as are any repercussions arising from this moment. Only when film and audience meet is any docudrama (indeed, any drama) finally complete. Here the docudrama sometimes collides in unexpected ways with the world from which it has emerged (see Chapter 7 for more discussion on this point).

Both Media Studies and the broadcasting institutions have long taken an interest in the audience for television.[12] Research is no longer simply a matter of quantifying ratings or even 'audience share', though these remain important indicators. Increasingly, research into the way we watch television has asked questions about qualities as well as quantities. In 2005 Annette Hill noted an increasing 'triangulation' in the UK between the audience research of regulatory bodies like Ofcom and its predecessor the Broadcasting Standards Commission, the television industry's own agencies, and analyses originating in the academy. This is especially important in a fragmenting television culture. When docudrama is controversial, it becomes possible to observe an historical process feeding back on itself. The history to which docudrama points can work in and through the programme, creating further turbulence in the real world. This was clearly the case on 21 September 1992, when released Beirut hostages wrote a letter to the *Guardian* objecting to Granada's film version of their experience.

Four of the hostages depicted in the film – John McCarthy, Brian Keenan, Terry Waite and Terry Anderson – wrote to protest:

> We are greatly concerned that Granada Television is promoting the film *Hostages* (to be shown this week) as the 'true story' of those depicted in it. From the information released from Granada's publicity department it is clear that the film contains scenes involving us that are pure fiction. Granada is grossly misleading the public by giving them the impression that they will see what actually happened.

The letter was the culmination of a campaign to have the film withdrawn altogether. It ensured a level of controversy for the actual transmission that raged on for some time. With the real hostages claiming that the film was 'pure fiction', an 'untrue' story, Granada's 'documentary' claim was thrown into doubt and the issue was energetically taken up by the press.[13] The acute awareness of the boundaries between fact and fiction during the pre-production and production periods was mirrored closely at the point of reception. There was the kind of active questioning not seen in any other kind of genre in any other medium, whether print or audio-visual.

The costs of preparing and making these programmes are generally less than those of drama but more than those of documentary. *Hostages*, for example, cost over £1 million to make in 1991–92. By 2001, producer Peter Bazalgette was quoting costs of over £0.5 million per hour for ordinary television drama.[14] Cheap by feature film standards, this kind of costing still represents a considerable commitment of resources for a television company, even with co-production. British and American network executives continue to see the docudrama as a cheap means of marketing single television dramas, while the subjects of docudrama can still attract big stars for reduced fees. This was the case with *Hostages*.[15] As Lipkin points out, the qualities of the already-known are, and remain, a valuable asset:

> TV movies based on actual subjects are potent weapons in the ratings battle for three reasons. First, docudramas can exploit story subjects that are highly recognizable for their audience. Second, docudramas offer easy and efficient promotion possibilities. Third, docudramas have come to target directly the very audience the networks are attempting to win back. (In Rosenthal, 2005: 454–5)

Hence what he describes as the 'Mantra' of American television executives: docudrama works because it is 'rootable', 'promotable', and 'relatable'.[16]

Performing docudrama

For the remainder of this chapter the focus will be on the dramatic performance itself – in terms of the realisation of the docudrama in front of the camera-eye and microphone-ear, and in terms of what actors do when they act. It is common practice for those who write on docudrama to use a deficiency model, as I argued in the Introduction. Generally speaking, objectors concentrate first on documentary deficiencies before turning to dramatic ones. I propose to take as read documentary deficiency (though this is not necessarily to be seen as a weakness, as I hope to show). Documentary is a logocentric form, whatever the performative aspects of its current fashion, and docudrama has incontrovertibly become more and more fiction-filmic over the years (and thus less and less reliant on words to carry narrative detail). In effect, then, the argumentation that constitutes a documentary claim (made up of the words and the images that accompany them) is more pre-production – however much newsreel, CCTV or home-movie footage might be incorporated. Documentary for the modern docudrama exists mostly *behind* rather than *within* the drama. It exists 'off-set', so to speak, in pre-production research activity, in publicity and in 'legalling' (see Chapter 2). So it seems to me that it is worth looking first at the pro-filmic moment of docudrama (in other words, the real-time rehearsed dramatic action that takes place in front of the camera).

From time to time the language and vocabulary of Film and Media Studies theory have a precision that is useful in making subtle intellectual points about dramatic action before cameras (although my own suspicion is that heavily theoretical language has become something of an instrument of control in the academy). The notion of the 'pro-filmic' is especially useful because the events that happen in front of the camera are in a real sense original in documentary (or purport to be so) and are (normally) rehearsed in drama. Dai Vaughan puts it succinctly when he asks: '[w]hat exactly is the pro-filmic? Fiction does not need to ask, since its only interest in the pro-filmic is to eradicate it.'[17] The documentary, on the other hand, relies on a 'total assimilation of the pro-filmic' in order to make its meanings (1986: 174–5).[18] I consider further the documentary aspect of the mixed form elsewhere, but an initial focus on dramatic practice will illustrate that, fundamentally, there is no real difference at the point of performance between the generality of film and television drama and the docudrama. This is because the disciplines of performance are pretty much the same for both.[19]

For the pro-filmic event in the television or film studio or on location, there is no audience other than a 'surrogate' one constituted by camera and microphone. These 'stand in for' the eventual watchers and listeners. Their business is to record for the eyes and ears of a deferred 'real audience'. The pro-filmic event of the docudrama is inevitably more inflected by performance than that of the documentary because it is constituted as *drama*. Drama is the most problematic element of the mixed form because its basic qualities are so different from the more evidential qualities of the documentary. This is often at the root of real-world individuals' objections to their portrayal in docudrama. It was the basis of the Beirut hostages' objections, for example.

I shall therefore make comparisons between the television studio and the theatre space, between the activities taking place within each, and between the relative juxtapositions in the two spaces of performers, crews, and audience. My purpose is to illuminate the performance values that are now firmly part of contemporary film and television practice. This view of practice will, I hope, be helpful when more abstract concepts of 'documentary' and 'drama', and when institutional factors, are discussed later.

In the studio

In 1995 I spent time with Granada in Manchester observing studio and location filming. Some of what I saw was filming for a docudrama about euthanasia eventually broadcast just after New Year 1996 (a poor spot in the annual schedule). Its working-title, *Final Act*, was deemed rather pessimistic, and furthermore was uncomfortably close to the title of the source book written by Derek Humphry the film's main protagonist.[20] It was re-titled as the more ambiguous *Act of Love*, but Granada then discovered that a 1981 NBC made-for-TV movie had already used this title. The NBC film was sufficiently well-known for this to be a problem. It had Ron Howard (Richie Cunningham in the hit television series *Happy Days* and now a noted film director), starring and had achieved a 21.7% rating and a 35% audience share when first transmitted. It was also frequently repeated on US television (see Gitlin 1994: 172). Although NBC's film was adapted from a novel rather than from actual events, it was also about euthanasia. Granada executives considered that their hopes of selling their own film to PBS (Public Broadcasting System) in America would be better served by finding another title. The film became *Goodbye My Love* – still somewhat ambiguous as a title, perhaps.

Work began with eight days of location shooting in the USA (13–21 October 1995), followed by a read-through and rehearsal of Peter Berry's script in Manchester (24–5 October 1995). Intensive filming took place in the Granada studios and on location in the Manchester area (26 October to 13 November). Then followed post-production editing and dubbing during early 1996. At the time I attended shooting the producer Sita Williams' hope was that the film would be transmitted in a two-hour slot on the ITV network in spring 1996 – the difference between this hope and the endless delays that resulted in transmission in a less than prestigious late evening slot on Saturday 4 January 1996 speaks volumes about the tricky process of making and placing television drama. After transmission Desmond Christy's review in the *Guardian* opined that the film 'was worth any number of discussion programmes about mercy killing' (6 January 1996). Although the film fell some way short of the producers' expectations and has pretty much disappeared, I am concerned not with judgement but with description.

Technical considerations

Goodbye My Love was partly filmed in Granada's Quay Street complex in Manchester. Studio 12 most resembles a giant Cottesloe Theatre (the 'experimental' space at the National Theatre's South Bank site in London). It has affinities both with film sound stages and 'black box' theatre studios. Generically, such spaces are large, high-ceilinged, light-tight boxes, with flexible units of seating available for audiences. For this film Studio 12 contained ten sets of rooms built according to the production designer's research in the actual historical locations where some of the events depicted had originally taken place. Details of the interiors of two houses in particular had been noted and photographed during an eight-day trip to the USA. For one of the 'houses', the whole of the downstairs floor-plan had been reconstructed down to the last detail. Location shooting in the USA provided exterior shots of these houses, as well as contextual 'neighbourhood' shots.

Heavy with naturalistic detail, and for all the world like a West End or Broadway theatre set, the structures were erected on Sunday

29 October during a break in filming – a process not dissimilar to a theatre 'get in'. The rooms included ceilings, but were open on one side just like 'fourth wall' stage sets. Each change of scene during the day involved the crew re-locating camera, light and sound equipment in new set-ups, all organised with a view to economy. The schedule was not in story-order but in filming-order (the usual case). This tends to reduce unnecessary hiatuses in a process that is characterised by a hyper-awareness of costs. Within each scene, camera set-ups required re-arrangement of the equipment to cope with the exigencies of new camera angles, and the technical crew were busily occupied for anything up to a quarter of an hour between takes. During this time the actors returned to their dressing rooms. The scene on location was not dissimilar, except that dressing rooms were now coaches and caravans, camera set-ups could be miles apart, and the whole process was to some extent dependent on weather conditions. Location work is something of a travelling *caravanserai*, with a financially disadvantageous ratio of film footage shot to time spent moving around.

Filming in Studio 12 on 31 October 1995 – my representative day – began at 8.00 a.m. and was scheduled to finish at 7.00 p.m. but continued into more than an hour of overtime. During this long day, the team filmed half-a-dozen A4 pages of 'dialogue' (some scenes were in fact wordless). Ten scenes were shot from a number of angles, the main establishing shots sometimes needing three or four takes. Reaction shots were sometimes accepted as satisfactory after a single take. Rehearsal was minimal and was related to camera position, movement and focus, not to actors and their motivation. Location work again was broadly similar, but the time between set-ups much longer. The camera on this particular day was mounted throughout on track and hydraulic trolley to facilitate movement backwards and forwards, up and down. On the previous day there had been a good deal of hand-held operation – more often a feature of location filming. For some shots two microphones were used, but more usually a boom microphone picked up the speakers' lines. Actors, after being given or finding a position on set, had to move to their marks in multiple takes. Lighting, rigged and re-rigged for each set-up, made much use of diffused, 'bounced' light from large, gold and silver reflectors. 'Key lighting' was the dominant convention, with a suitable naturalistic acknowledgement of 'real' light sources within the room set-ups.[21]

The technical work contrasted interestingly with the no less precise but broader requirements of stage lighting and sound. Since the sets were such realistic room-simulations, lighting followed two main priorities: to light actors for the camera and to maintain the naturalistic illusion of real-room light as required by the script. It is only necessary to compare a studio play of the 1960s with one from the present day to become aware of how much more sophisticated the capturing of this illusion is now. Some of the sound and lighting equipment being used had originally been developed for news programmes that relied mainly on on-scene lighting boosted by lightweight equipment (digital sound recording, radio mikes, clip-fixing mini-spots). This equipment is now standard for television drama too; thus the major priorities of a network television service – news and entertainment – are enacted at the level of technology.[22]

Technology was, of course, ever-present in a way it is not for most theatrical rehearsal. The majority of those present were camera or lighting crew concerned with the image; they were tending the camera and its field of focus. The sound crew was smaller, but was equally intent on creating through the medium of its technology a sense of the reality of that room – the 'soundscape'. The only other person (besides me) from 'outside' the film crew was a photographer present throughout the day taking publicity shots (for use pre-transmission and in press reviews). We all moved around the studio for the different scenes, rather as one does for a promenade theatre performance. And yet no promenade performance could sustain the level of detachment evident in this audience. This was an 'audience' involved almost solely in its own work. The actors may at any one time have had anything up to twenty people 'watching' them. But more exactly their watchers were 'servicing the image', as it were. Many of them (including the producer) gathered *during* takes around a small black-and-white monitor. They watched a tiny image, even though the real actors were six feet away. It cannot be stressed enough that what the camera was seeing was far more important than any quasi-theatrical view of the action available by watching the set. The requirements of the camera were paramount and could only be assessed by this kind of watching.

For anyone whose training is in the theatre, accommodations to the camera are the most striking feature of the rehearsal and filming process. The actors were constantly making these accommodations. The effort to look 'right-in-the-situation' was left to the actors; the consensus about the greater importance of getting things 'right-for-the-camera' unspoken. The necessities of framing and focus marked the parameters of action, as the concepts of sightlines and lit space mark the parameters of stage action. These seemed non-negotiable givens rather than adjuncts to the process of performance. On takes that were likely to be supplementing the main action (for example reaction shots and reverse-action shots) minor changes in actors' positioning and orientation (the film set equivalent of 'cheating' a stage position) were speedily accepted and often volunteered by the actors. The focus upon eyes and faces in these dialogue scenes was most apparent, perhaps, in the camera crew's frequent measuring of distances between lens and actors' eyes, to ensure precision of focus. Screen drama is pre-eminently a drama of faces and eyes, and television drama still concentrates on small (room) spaces, the smaller screen allowing proportionately less to the drama of space than cinema. The fixed audience perspective of theatre, meanwhile, is less flexible in terms of focus.

The routine before a take illustrated the more technology-driven concerns of the screen drama. Where theatrical rehearsal would tend to settle after a break with perhaps a call for quiet from stage management and instructions from the director ('Let's pick it up from ... '), in the film studio, preparation for re-entering the drama had a distinctive and different rhythm of words and action. The assistant director (AD) called 'Turn over' to the camera operator once there was quiet. The sound recordist then announced 'Sound on.' The clapper board operator marked the take (or unit of action) for the crew and the editor, and only then did performance occur. At the end of the take, the AD called 'Cut!' on the director's instruction. The lens of the camera was checked for dust specks before the take could be included in material to be seen later in 'rushes'. The director had the last word on whether another take was needed, often consulting with the producer on this. Throughout, there was the ritualistic quality of a finely honed work routine concentrated upon technological 'eyes' and 'ears', busy about their task of recording faithfully for the human eyes and ears of a deferred audience.

As a theatrical deputy stage manager (DSM) runs the rehearsal or show logistically, the First AD ran the studio, with the Second AD assisting 'back stage' in the studio like a theatrical assistant stage manager. The Third AD was mostly responsible for moving the cast between studio and dressing room. The parallel is not total, for in theatre the DSM will normally record stage movement on the prompt copy in rehearsal and call cues in performance, and an assistant stage manager will normally look after props in both situations and operate sound or other effects in performance. In the film studio the marking up of the script is undertaken by continuity personnel, the latter tasks by 'action props' and 'set dressers'. The heavily-annotated continuity script for *Goodbye My Love* closely resembled the theatrical prompt copy. Continuity, props and make-up also made much use of Polaroid cameras; prop desks scattered around the studio bore evidence of the importance of this activity.

The practical exigencies of delivering a television product exacerbated the habitual working-against-time that characterises all drama preparation. In an ideal world, Sita Williams told me, *Goodbye My Love* would have had three more days of filming. Forced as the film was through budgetary considerations into a race against the schedule, occasional urgent conferences between Williams and the director Richard Signy were often to do with the cuts and elisions in the script needed if the production team was to stay the right side of its tight timetable.

To sum up: the agencies of organisation and technical presentation have a far greater prominence in television at the fragmented moment of performance than they do in theatre. For the live stage these matters would come under the aegis of two theatrical sub-groups – stage management and lighting/sound personnel. The former group facilitates the rehearsal and 'runs the show' in performance. The latter group will be involved in design and logistics pre-performance, with occasional rehearsal input, and will be involved in technical operation in performance (though this is sometimes the province of stage management, especially in small-scale touring). The only time that a show is given over to the stage managers, lighting and sound designers and technicians is during technical rehearsal. In 'mainstream' productions actors are excused this task, as junior stage managers 'walk' their parts in order to mark technical cues and actors are kept fresh for other technical and dress rehearsal(s). Once cues have been fixed and tested, the expectation at subsequent technical rehearsal, whether 'cue to cue' or 'continuous action', is that actors will hold back from performance levels, reserving their full commitment for the presence of an audience. On the set of *Goodbye My Love* the pace and rate of the action were decided almost entirely by the wants and needs of sight and sound, camera and tape recorder. All this caused a different rhythm to the event of shooting – and a different kind of focusing for performers – from the rhythm at a theatrical rehearsal. It was like working on individual pieces of a large jigsaw where the printed script is the picture on the box. The business-like atmosphere was similar but was noticeably more low-key.

In contrast to the theatre director's somewhat mythical power of textual interpretation and the film director's equally mythical power of inspired seeing, Richard Signy's efforts were focused on the attempt to realise the script as written for the camera and the microphone within the time constraints. For example, at 4.15 p.m. a rapid conference between Signy and his two assistant directors concluded that the day's filming would need to run into overtime in order to stay on course with the remaining part of the schedule. The priority was to get as much of the script as possible given the time, in as acceptable an amount as possible, so that sufficient 'raw material' existed for the editor(s), director and producer to work on in post-production. Whereas the technical matters are more in the nature of 'actor-support' in the theatre, the balance was noticeably different in the film/television studio. The concept of author or authority is in any case a problematic one, but it is easy to see why producers have a higher profile in the logistically demanding world of television drama. Individually crafted pieces of a narrative jigsaw of recorded performance are assembled in the post-production phase. Here, actors may be present for the dubbing of sound, but the significant shapers of the audience experience are editors, directors and producers. These people have the privileged overview – both metaphorically and literally – of pre-transmission or cinema release; these people prepare the docudrama for the audience.[23]

All this, of course, happened some time ago now, but the fundamentals remain the same. The biggest change has been an even greater squeeze on time available, given costs involved. As a direct result, more hybrid forms of docudrama have utilised face-to-face interview and archive footage that reduces the costs of actors/ rehearsal (see Chapter 8 for more on these changes).

Acting a part

The theatrical process depends upon a specific occasion when audience and actors meet in the same time and space. The event-of-theatre is something actors speak of in exalted tones; it is an event actors known more for their film work sometimes seek out, as a kind of 'touching base' for their craft. The liveness of the theatre event is denied the screen actor. The filming process contrasts vividly with theatre work. Its effect is to *miniaturise* acting technique. Dramatic moments, rather than sequences, drive actors inwards. They take what are in themselves tiny sections of dialogue or action and expose these moments (and, of course, themselves-in-role) to the camera over and over again.

Docudrama performance-before-camera is, as has been noted, very different from the pro-filmic event of the documentary film. This latter occurs in real time and records the behaviours of people caught up totally (or supposedly totally) in an unfolding actuality. Rehearsal for performance in the theatre, especially early on in the process of realisation, may concentrate heavily upon discrete moments in just this way, but directors will generally have more opportunity to help actors establish themselves-in-role in continuous temporal action, thereby developing the 'through line', which in character terms is the *sine qua non* of the Stanislavski-based Western acting tradition. This, however effective, can only ever be an approximation to the real, fuelled by technique, experience and confidence in the actor.

Theatrical rehearsal may 'chop up' the chronology of a naturalistic drama for specific developmental purposes, then, but rarely does it do so to the extent of a film's fractured shooting order. An actor works with a split-consciousness, managing both the self and the self-in-role. In naturalistic theatre performance, part of an actor's task is to manage character in a chronology – a chain of events constituting the plot of the play. On their return to a temporal 'off-stage' ('wings', 'dressing-room' or whatever space exists outside the action) actors may even, according to levels of conscientiousness or the nature of their preferred acting theory, seek to retain their character through exercises of various kinds. The relative lack of continuity for film actors reinforces the tendency to miniaturise by always magnifying and privileging the moment against the sequence. The brief read-through period constitutes one of the few formal occasions in film and television drama when actors can engage in the kind of free-ranging, intuitive and associative activity that constitutes 'building a character'. Time before the camera, as we have seen, is extremely limited, and any 'inner work' of this kind must be done in private. Docudrama, of course, does not have characters in any conventional dramatic sense. It attempts to portray real-world individuals who are accessible in a way fictional characters are not (a factor that often raises the temperature of debate about this genre – and to which we must return).

In the theatre success with an audience habitually depends upon controls developed in acting training and mobilised through rehearsal to ensure the actor's dominance over, and channelling of, the energy inherent in the theatrical moment. This moment is as much vocal as physical, the striking of balance between voice and body being different in a theatre from that in a screen setting. In poor performance, an audience's attention tends to drift, to become atomised; they cease to be an 'audience'. In effective performance, enough spectators can be relied upon to be 'in' the moment with the actor to weld what can always disaggregate into a disparate collection of individuals into a (temporarily) self-reflexive, compact collective unit. Actors and audience become, jointly, absorbed and carried along by the mutually-satisfying energy inherent in successful performance.

Being re-made for transmission or theatrical release in post-production through editing and dubbing, all film drama is 'audience-less' at the moment of its performance for the recording agents. In the deferred moment of reception, with an audience both closer to and further from the performance, it is re-made yet again. The moment of reception for television drama is different in certain regards from that of film. This has, I believe, important consequences – and not just for performers. I believe it necessary to understand the dynamics of such moments, the better to deal with them as audiences. In theatre, the dramatic moment is *outwardly* displayed – in semiotic terms it is 'ostended', or held up for view.[24] Before the camera, something more interior, more private, is required. All this is generically true for film and television drama. The docudrama, once again, makes special demands in terms of 'being-before-the camera'. Because of this the docudrama tends to attract particular kinds of writer, actor – and, indeed, audience.

In drama of any kind communication between actor and audience is fundamental to the communication circuit. While actors (and those who study them) rely on essentially similar working methodologies that theorise the transformative process undertaken by the performer,[25] there are vastly different approaches to 'knowing' the audience. Media Studies has been concerned about the audience almost since their inception (as have the media industries themselves), while Theatre Studies has on the whole had very little to say.[26] The theatre industry is conscious of numbers, with Broadway and West End runs ever vulnerable to the exigencies of raw data. But in its day-to-day discourse, the industry is primarily anecdotal, mystifying not quantifying. 'A quiet house' denotes disappointment with a group taken to be too reserved about what is being offered, 'a good house' likes the show in some obvious way, 'a papered house' (an audience largely composed of those with free tickets from the producer) tends to react over-eagerly. Actors solemnly dilate on 'evidence' that would be laughed out of a Media Studies seminar. In theatre, if actors are to be believed, experience alone helps you to 'know' an audience through its every rustle and whisper.[27]

In television and film, the audience is courted, counted and its reactions analysed more systematically. Focus-grouped by the industry, worried over by regulators, eagerly sought by advertisers, badgered by academics, their views are actively canvassed, mulled over, then fed into planning.

In film and television drama it tends only to be the actors in television sit-coms that are in contact with an actual audience, but on stage this contact is fundamental. The actor's place in the production hierarchy, too, is pretty much unchallenged; they are the focus in rehearsal and performance. Once technical rehearsals have been done, once the director has seen the show launched, actor and audience can settle down to some pretty direct interaction. The actor is thus inevitably the point around which Theatre Studies converges, with a heavy proportion of theory devoted to tricky philosophical negotiation around the 'mind/body split' that dominates acting theory and is so much a feature of the mainly Stanislavskian discourse that dominates the industry and to a lesser extent the academy. Actors have to be professionally schizophrenic. While they act, they monitor what is happening with a split-consciousness alert for anything in the way of audience response. This could take many forms: a laugh where there's never been one before, a technical problem (a door on set suddenly sticking, for example, or a prop not being where it should), a fellow actor's aberration (a 'dry', or a line from Act 2 offered suddenly during Act 1).[28] This state of adrenalin-fuelled arousal, of maximal alert, must not reach overload because this tends to inhibit. The ideal state is to be oxymoronically, alertly relaxed. This is still important to the screen actor, but if the set door sticks or if a fellow actor dries there can always be a re-take. To compensate, some method actors will go to extraordinary lengths. Marlon Brando was a celebrated example of an actor fabled for efforts to stay 'in role' over long periods of filming. Oliver Stone persuaded Tom Cruise that it would be a good idea to inject a drug 'that would have totally paralyzed him for two days' when the actor was playing paraplegic Vietnam Vet Ron Kovic in the 1989 *Born on the Fourth of July*. The film's insurance company refused to cover this, '[b]ut the point was he was, he was willing to do it'.[29]

In Media and Film Studies, by contrast, the literature on screen performance is certainly not negligible, but it is scarcely overwhelming.[30] Nor is study of screen acting a major focus for many drama schools. The screen actor is something of a hired hand reliant on skills prepared for the stage and at the mercy of technical expertise. As I remark above, it is the activity going on around the actor that is fascinating in film and television studios and on location. A theatre stage manager would never openly treat an actor like an object, but on film set and location alike this occurs routinely. Technical personnel have to behave in this way at every new camera set-up. In television, the only difference for the performer is when the *number* of cameras to be addressed changes. Single and multi-camera dramas, whether recorded on video or film, need slightly adjusted skills, slightly different camera-awareness and body-positioning.[31]

Watching the actors

At the screen docudrama's centre, and rarely remarked in any but the most obvious ways, is the actor. In the presence of the actor, docudrama audiences confront the most visible sign of a docudrama's essential inauthenticity as documentary. Busily acting a part, the human agent on screen is always both more and less than the real individual being impersonated. They are more in the sense that their body signifies an excess that is always fictional (as any acting is); they are less in the sense that this body emphasises the structuring absence of the Real Person Subject. However (and acting apart), even the most trite movie-of-the-week docudrama still contains and confirms one vital feature of documentary heritage: straight information is placed higher in its hierarchy of discourses than it is in pure fiction. Several elements constitute the information: an assumed pre-knowledge of real-world events; intertextuality with other representations of these events in other media; and, possibly, new information to add to the mix.[32] Prior knowledge and new information cut both ways; they influence both actors and audiences. Both parties are similarly implicated in the future of the knowledge field in which the film seeks to resonate, and which it sometimes disturbs.

For example, *Conspiracy* (2001) was an international co-production docudrama about the 1942 Wannsee conference at which historians allege that a branch of the Nazi leadership determined upon extermination as a means of solving the 'Jewish

Question'.[33] Both actors and audience almost inevitably bring a baggage of information, quasi-information and disinformation to such a subject, across a potential spectrum that might even include Holocaust-deniers at one extreme. The literate modes of print and talk (newspaper reports, books, articles) are likely to be at least as involved here as the visual record (still photographs, newsreel footage, previous documentary and fiction films on the subject). In performance, the actor marks with voice and body the space of an active and/or latent knowledge that has been, is being, and will be articulated more fully elsewhere. In docudrama in general, this knowledge often manifests itself more obviously in the public sphere than with other drama. Such works trail debate in their wake – in talk shows, articles, water-cooler and classroom talk. The actor bridges the spaces of these various knowledges in performance, negotiating backwards and forwards across the space between non-fiction and fiction. Audiences undertake a similar negotiation, which is relative to their empathetic and intellectual involvement with the film. Whenever the Holocaust is the historical event being represented the stakes seem higher. This is inevitable given the ongoing debate about this event within Western cultures. Leaving aside other kinds of representation, docudramas on the Holocaust in the theatre, on film and on television have been frequent and regular across the years since the scale of the event was made available to the public in 1944.

The actor's means to affect (or fail to affect) an audience are the specific skills born and bred through training, experience and 'talent' – the latter especially context and fashion dependent. Audiences can be assumed to be seeking second-hand experience through acted performance. To be convinced by an actor – Kenneth Branagh playing Heydrich in *Conspiracy* for example – an audience will look for confirmation that the actor can represent an experience that is also, necessarily, second-hand. In a realist drama, fundamentally these are matters of belief on both sides: does Branagh look like Heydrich? Yes, he does; one look at photographs of the Nazi policy maker will confirm this. Do we believe that Heydrich might have behaved in this way? A 'yes' response will again be inflected by the knowledge that *Conspiracy* was based on actual minutes taken at the Wannsee Conference but will also be affected in its turn by any pre-knowledge (or denial, if it comes to that). The 'factual basis of the story', in David Edgar's classic formulation, 'gives the action of the play its credibility' (1988: 52). The task of the docudrama is to persuade an audience to take a view on the issues (defined through research), and it does this in a fundamental way by seeking belief in the actors' performance.

A docudrama like *Conspiracy* gets as close as it can to first-handedness, and in the famous Stanislavski phrase, the actor works 'as if' from the first-hand. The audience, if convinced, reacts in similar terms – 'suspending disbelief' (in the equally famous, Coleridgian, phrase) and operating imaginatively 'as if' it were present at originary actions that shaped an historical event. Since the advent of portable cameras and sound equipment the most useful tool for the working screen actor has been the kind of unfussy, understated performance that audiences readily take as a token of first-handedness. This is a style that, at least superficially, rejects excess in performance, eschews the overtly theatrical, plays the 'ordinary'.

In its British cultural manifestation, it is a style grounded in the theatrical traditions of two London theatres, the Royal Court, Sloane Square, and the Theatre Royal, Stratford East.[34] These theatres produced very different plays, but grounded their acting techniques in believable performance. Sometimes this could look 'stagey' in its most voice-producing manifestations; more often it tapped an awareness of what Brecht described as 'gestus' – a behaviour recognisable within concepts of social being, an acted behaviour founded on social observation. In the USA, a cognate realist style was grounded in a brand of theatrical psychologism. If this derived historically from Stanislavski and his American interpreters (Strasberg, Adler), it was linked culturally to Freud and the twentieth-century turn towards psychology. This major paradigm shift took root easily in the distinctively American quasi-religion of individualism. At one end of the performance spectrum, this can lurch uncomfortably into a kind of therapy, at the other it produces authoritative performance because it secures an identity for the duration of a performance. To put it another way, it introduced into screen drama an authenticity founded on badges of the idiosyncratic.

Understatement in acting has equalled the Real over nearly forty years of film and television dramas. It works especially well with anything additionally claiming the Serious and the Social. Actors play structured psychological tricks on themselves in order to create a coded and conventionalised reality in which an audience will, in its turn, play its own unstructured psychological tricks. Both parties do this to access a mental space outside reality (the theatre, or cinema, or living room in which they sit) where ideas and beliefs can be tested. They are, as it were, mentally transported to a parallel reality. Directors and writers connive to create situations in which this psychological trickery is facilitated. For example, director Ken Loach reveals the plot to his actors gradually, in order to help them play the moment and not the result; Mike Leigh has perfected a way of writing based on improvisation (always thought somehow to be 'fresher' than acting – by actors, anyway).[35]

The actor training methodology that seeks to facilitate these psychological leaps of faith is still predicated heavily on theatre performance. In the UK, an October 2001 report by the National Council of Drama Training found that newly-trained actors consistently found themselves at a methodological loss on their first day in the film or television studio. What was worse, this was often their first engagement in their chosen profession, so much has screen work now superseded theatre.[36] Training still follows quite a simple input–output model based on, and suitable for, real-time theatrical performance in which establishment of a role's 'through-line' (the kind of moment-to-moment continuity that secures a recognisable, stable and readable identity) is pre-eminent. Actors are also taught to seek information for a role both from within and without a text. They must assess a role's 'given circumstances' as written; these comprise the keys to a character's actions in the articulated dramatic situation. Given circumstances are understood from information within a text (revealed intellectually), and from information supplied through an actor's imaginative engagement with that text (understood emotionally and even physically).

Take as an example the playing of Juliet in *Romeo and Juliet*. Reading the text offers a broad range of information on this character and her situation within the play. She is young, rich, upper-class, naïve, strong-willed, physically attractive – implicated through all these factors in a social and political mode of marriage in which the patriarchy holds the upper hand (at least conventionally). Through research, her interpreter can access further information: academic editors' explication of culture and context, their gloss on words, phrases and textual cruxes no longer current in contemporary society and thus difficult to decipher; similarities and differences in terms of current social and political mores; and so on. These reading and thinking activities are vital to the work, fuelling discussion and possibly improvisation with other actors – for theatre preparation is essentially collective and collaborative.

But intellectual activity alone will never be enough to support a performance of Juliet. Thinking like this would help with an old-fashioned English Literature 'character appreciation/analysis'. The kind of intellectual centring offered by an essay question ('What aspects, if any, of post-feminist theory would you use to work on and animate the character and situation of Juliet in a modern-dress production of *Romeo and Juliet?*') might even achieve an interesting set of production ideas. But to act Juliet, to 'embody' the character at least for the two hours' traffic of the stage, a very different set of abilities is needed. The projection of a personality (your own and not-your-own) into a recognisable if artificial social sphere is only part of it. Actors on stage, in a studio, on location must repeat this activity over time, each time as if for the *first* time. It is in this latter discipline that the amateur actor most often falls short, the professional perennially struggles, acting manuals labour to promote, and directors attempt to facilitate.

The actor's state of split consciousness might be sanity-threatening were it not for discipline and training, for intellectual understanding of 'given circumstances' is supplemented with material from direct experience. Juliet's age-specific readiness to fall in love, for example – easy to remark, but how to communicate it? Must it be lived, or must it 'have been' lived, in order to achieve projection? Again, second-order experience (novels, poems, paintings, music) about being in love may help to *imagine* the mental state of 'falling and being in love'. Better still, however, is direct experience of this mental state, direct experience you can input via yet another classic concept 'emotion memory'. This is the core of Stanislavskian realist acting, since the remembered emotion can, it is believed, trigger physical (and hence communicable) *action*, rather than thought-about-action. Ideally, an audience will see 'Juliet' fall in love; if the performer 'plays the result' of falling in love, however, an audience merely notes 'Juliet is in love'. This is much debated in acting theory, especially because influences from Eastern cultures have impacted discussion of the body/mind split. The process of understanding a role by living it is somewhat undercut by actors' legendary propensity to literalness. For example, falling in love with your Romeo (at least for the duration of a West End run) might seem a promising approach, but is likely to make the complex process behind your creation of Juliet seem shallow. Made thus vulnerable to tabloid newspapers, gossip-culture magazines and *schadenfreude* outlooks alike, your genuinely artistic act of transformation can so easily be confounded.

Real acting

Acting the role of a real individual in a filmed docudrama ratchets up the complications in two very obvious ways. Firstly, there is the distance between a real person and the projection; secondly, there is the distance between film and stage acting. The effort to adjust to playing real individuals is marked by actors' more public affirmations about finding authentic emotion memory to carry into performance. Just as writers and producers are forced into expansive claims for their 'painstaking' and 'voluminous' research (an article of faith in their pursuit of the authentic), so actors characteristically cite any primary experience with zeal. In proportion to the 'already-known-ness' of the person being portrayed, more needs to be claimed when portraying the famous or notorious. There are not so many problems in disease-of-the-week docudrama, where the protagonists are the lesser-known individuals of celebrity rather than fame. But in the case of the well-known historical figure, declarations of seriousness of purpose in acquiring emotion memory are almost *de rigeur*.

Colin Firth, playing John McCarthy in Granada's 1992 *Hostages*, made a big point in pre-screening interviews, about *actually* being wound with packing tape like a mummy and coffined under a lorry.

Just like the real McCarthy being moved around Beirut by his captors, Firth experienced being driven from one place to another in this stupefyingly claustrophobic way. In January 2002, newspaper and television interviews with the cast of Channel 4's *Shackleton* revealed them eagerly making their first-hand contemporary Greenland into a second-hand Antarctica. It is easy to be sceptical about all this (unlike McCarthy, Firth always knew he'd be unwrapped; Kenneth Branagh *et al* may well have been cold, but Shackleton and his men didn't have a warm trailer to retreat to and didn't know how long they would have to suffer).[37]

But it is more productive to look beyond scepticism and consider the seriousness with which the problem of portraying something so manifestly real is so earnestly addressed. Not so much wishing to 'claim the real' as 'assert connection with the real', actors make such hardship the kind of 'Rite-of-Given-Circumstances-Passage' that seems to generate a quasi-religious belief. Just as medieval monks believed self-flagellation brought them nearer to God, actors hope to get closer to public-domain subjects through replicating something of that real-world protagonist's suffering, thinking, being. In this important sense, I believe they can be seen as 'bearing witness' on behalf of a real-world subject. I also believe it is why some actors (as well as some writers and, indeed, some audiences) are drawn emotionally to the form.

It is instructive to read how a thoughtful actor approaches the task of playing a real-world villain. A given for realistic acting is that, since no real-world individual categorises themselves as 'evil' (the exercise of self-justification being as familiar to the 'bad' as to the 'good' personality) you cannot just 'play evil' in a realist drama. But particular difficulties remain from cultural training. The theatre scholar Eric Bentley once remarked that, although Hitler was known to like dogs and to be kind to small children: 'a portrait of that man conceived in hatred might be more valid than one written' [or, I would add, acted] 'according to the dogma that all men are a blend of good and evil'.[38] Playing one of Hitler's Nazi hierarchy is always likely to be difficult, because the personalities involved have become historical limit-cases in Western culture. But in realist drama the challenge to an actor is to understand and excuse these bad guys.

Charlton Heston (playing Josef Mengele in Egidio Eronico's 2001 film *Rua Alguem 5555*) took the latter option, telling an interviewer: 'It's only a movie, you have to remember ... The bad guy comes out the bad guy ... and he dies in the end.'

Brian Cox, a thoughtful actor who has brought therapeutic Shakespeare to Broadmoor, approached his portrayal of Hermann Goering in the mini-series *Nuremberg* (Channel 4, 20–21 May 2001) more systematically.[39] He argued that within a widespread denial of evil in Germany (following revelations of the full horror of the Holocaust) there was a psychological kernel playable for the realist actor:

> At this point the individual's psyche suffers what can only be described as a form of spiritual stroke resulting in an emotional blackout. Over the years, I have portrayed numerous characters of a dubious and diabolical nature. But you cannot act evil; the element of evil is dormant. Evil manifests itself in action. Power and control are the active ingredients that bring evil awake. As an actor I go one step further and try to combine power and control with a lack of awareness or concern about self-motivation. A paradox which I believe to be the human condition.

Like any good actor, Cox avoids demonising a real-world historical individual ('emotional blackout' is something we could all suffer, thousands of perfectly ordinary Germans did) in order better to do his job:

> My job is to examine the detail of lives. That detail takes into account motivation, excuse, mindlessness, emotions such as envy, malice and resentment. But when these motives are examined, they actually become quite fine and nobody is exempt. In consequence, evil does dwell within us all.

This assertion, an admission of personal culpability, underwrites the claim of authenticity and constitutes a philosophical justification. He finds, or makes, useable emotion memory through the *condition humaine* of self-justification. Emotion memory enabled, he can then use research details to feed his portrait of Goering: the war hero (a kind of German Biggles); the despairing patriot adrift in post-First World War Germany ('eventually he had a massive nervous breakdown'); the dedicated public servant ('he returned to Germany to try and repair the wreckage exacted by the war'). He can even admit and partially excuse the Jew-hater ('the source of his anti-semitism [was] not so much racial as political and economic'), accommodate the fascist ('Goering believed that Hitler would unite Germany. He believed passionately that this was where the salvation of his country lay'). Finding explanations and excuses for ethical and political transgression, 'He/Goering' and 'I/Goering' gradually merge and a stable acting identity is forged. By this kind of process a doubtlessly good man can bear witness even for an undoubtedly bad one. Goering is a figure so thoroughly demonised within Western culture that Cox is constrained to go through the process described in order to 'be' his character. He can do no other than try to find a way to humanise someone so widely considered inhuman.[40]

Docudrama is so grounded in negotiation with the intertextual that it is an element for audience as well as actor. For the audience, the founding principle in psychological terms is the 'testing of reality' or 'realities'. Audiences are drawn to dramas by the question 'what if', rather than the actor's 'as if'. In the 'what if' situation of drama, audiences' imaginations are stimulated to consider what it might be like to be another person ('like me but not me') in another situation, in another place, at another time. The basis of these hypotheticals is a 'universal': the fear of aloneness, or rather the desire to be connected with others.[41] Connection occurs through realization of an 'equivalent centre of self' (a resonant phrase that appears at the end of Chapter 12 of George Eliot's 1871–72 novel *Middlemarch*). In all but the most malign, stunted and anti-social pathologies, this desire exists as a basis for the humanity we count on to be (and stay) alive. Link this imaginative projection existing within performance to the ratification of a factual base, and you have a potentially powerful rational and emotional cocktail.

Acting, even moderately good acting, uses experiential intensifiers drawn from emotion memory and seeks to supply them to an audience who will absorb and endorse these features. The documentary element, however weak, supplies a heavily indexical assurance: that this did happen. What we see and hear marks the space of prior happening – enacting absence and presence simultaneously. A drama like *Conspiracy* and a mini-series like *Nuremberg* are made up of clusters of metonyms, performed actions standing for real ones. These docudramas work in much the same way as religious ceremonies do to mark moments of significance for believers. Often docudramas from both ends of the quality spectrum deal with worst-case scenarios that are ordinarily dreaded. Audiences going to docudramas for confirmation as to the feelings engendered around these scenarios may well use and get information, but consolation may well be the ultimate reward.

Emotional intensification is necessary for actor and audience for different reasons, but sometimes it has strikingly similar effects. Playing his historical villain, Brian Cox had constantly to make clear, if only for himself, the boundary between Self and Acted Other:

> During the making of the Nuremberg mini-series there came the moment when the actual documentary film of the Holocaust victims was presented to the make-believe court. We, the cast and crew, had to watch the film take after take. It was a fairly harrowing experience, and several members had to be excused from the room. The documentary film is filled with the shocking images that have come to represent that horrific event; layer upon layer of cadaverous skull-like creatures, the barely-alive survivors dressed in the uniforms of Buchenwald, Dachau and Auschwitz. These images, while shocking, nevertheless numb the senses. Disbelief that human beings can be treated in such a horrific fashion. The eye and heart are out of sync. But then about one minute into the documentary the body of a young woman is lifted out of a mass grave and, as she is raised, her long hair cascades down her back. Every time we came to this point in the replay, an audible gasp could be heard throughout the ensemble and the tears began to flow.

George Stevens' documentary film images, Cox argues, caused 'the dam of grief' to break; the cast's tears are offered both as marker of authenticity in performance and as justification in human terms. In Cox's own performance, even his Goering is shaken, his blustering personality momentarily undermined. When talking about 'this horrid film' Goering tries of all things to allege media manipulation to his American guard: 'Propaganda! Anyone can do it. You show a little bit of this, a little bit of that. And before you know it ... ' After a pause, he adds reflectively, 'Still ... ' as he moves out of shot.

In a contribution to Michael Renov's influential 1993 collection

Theorising Documentary, Bill Nichols discusses performance in film. He seeks to make distinctions between what happens when real historical individuals 'perform' for the cameras on newsreel footage and documentary, and what occurs when imitators of real individuals 'reconstruct' on location and in the studio for the docudrama. He talks of 'a body too many' and 'a body too few' to explicate the differences (Renov, 1992: 177). In fictional representation of historical events, he claims, we find 'a body too many'; in documentary representation, there is always 'a body too few'. Thus, fiction enacts a kind of *excess*, non-fiction a kind of *dearth*. This matters not only to makers of films (directors, crew, performers) but also to viewers.

So, for example, in contemporary newsreel or in documentary films about the Second World War, the figures of Winston Churchill and Hermann Goering will often appear, marking the presence of historical individuals significant to the narrative of that conflict however one interprets history. The appearances alert us to the presence before real historical cameras, at or around the time specified by the authors of the films (this a matter primarily of belief for an audience) of real historical individuals. However, the fact of the real historical individuals' deaths in 1946 and 1964 means that any celluloid representation in the real time of the film's showing marks absence not presence. The historical space of bodies now absent is represented by continuously exposed film frames – the film Churchill or Goering is a 'body too few'. Irrespective of the final absence of any body through death, all documentary representation, all photographic representation, shares this time-based disjunction – the you and me of the family photograph is no longer the you and me looking at it in the family album. The pro-filmic moment, the 'moment on film', and the spectatorial moment of viewing are compelled to exist within their own time specificities.

The British actor Albert Finney represented Winston Churchill in *The Gathering Storm*, a 'high-concept' 2002 HBO docudrama aimed at the Anglo-American television market.[42] This was a very different case from Cox representing Goering. Finney marked with his own 'real' (actor's) body the absence of the historical Churchill by presenting a very conventional 'Performance-Churchill'. 'Absence' was here covered by the presence of direct imitation – an instantly recognisable version of Churchillian weight and mannerism, of both physique and voice. Thus was the corpse animated, as it were, and brought to a kind of life for an audience. The imitation was widely taken to be a rather good one – apt and accurate, serious, non-parodic. At the very least, it encouraged audiences to suspend disbelief in 'Finney-Churchill' and accept the performance as 'Churchill'. The 'body too many' of the actor is an ever-present in the docudrama, and will tend to flit in and out of a viewer's consciousness. It is not necessary to be what Ben Jonson would have called an 'Over-curious Critick' to be aware of the 'body too many'. Every time you think, 'What a good actor!', you are negotiating between the historical and the acted.

In its emphasis on personality, modern docudrama adheres to a US 'made-for-TV movie' mode that Todd Gitlin has described as 'little personal stories that executives think a mass audience will take as revelations of the contemporary' (1994: 163–4). A Holocaust drama like *Nuremberg* is composed of anything but 'little' stories, but its style does accentuate the personal, and some have objected to its use of documentary images. Granada executive Ian McBride takes the view that audiences have to be 'attracted to the subject' in the first instance but that, thereafter, a subject's potential in the abstract must be sustained by the particular of the drama.[43] In common with other writers, I have argued elsewhere against this inexorable individualising of issues which is an almost inevitable concomitant of naturalism's descendant, television realism.[44] The industry itself, however, has little or no sympathy with this view. Williams, for example, defined dramatic coherence itself as 'a story told through character', saying: 'if you're doing drama-documentary you're inevitably locked into naturalism. I don't see how else you can do it. I don't see what you would gain by stylising it in any way, really.'

From the legal angle, however, a different view began to emerge as docudramas became more and more filmic in the 1990s. The more like a fictional film a docudrama becomes (the more 'light' on dialogue, for example), the more difficult it becomes to 'legal'. In the legal process, the documentary part of the docudrama must be accessible if a lawyer is to be able to defend it. An increased emphasis on the drama of the unsaid has re-inflected the distinctive contribution of lawyers to the making of the modern docudrama, and it is to this aspect of the preparation of these programmes that I now turn.

Notes

1 Kathy Chater has written a number of books on research for the media, and is an active researcher herself (see also note 4 in Chapter 4). I quote here from the 1992 second edition of a book updated again in 1995. Useful on research and other matters relating to documentary production is Chapman (2007). While not directly relevant for docudrama, this book does consider the logistics and expenses involved if reconstruction scenes are contemplated (see especially pp. 47–50).
2 See Finch (2003: 189).
3 Although, as director Peter Kosminsky pointed out in his article about the film, no one in the British government was prepared to talk ('"The answer is no"', *Guardian* G2, 8 March 2005, pp. 1–4). On research in general, see also Holland (1997: 162–5).
4 This docudrama dramatised the way the Stalker Inquiry, a 1990 investigation into the practices of police in Northern Ireland, was effectively hobbled for political reasons.
5 Eaton was speaking in a Keynote Lecture for the 'Reality Time' conference, University of Birmingham, 12–14 April 1996.
6 Again, see Chapter 2 for more on docudrama and the law.
7 Greengrass was the director of the 9/11 feature film *Flight 93*. On television he also directed ITV's *The Murder of Stephen Lawrence* (1999). McGovern organised the writing of the 1999 Channel 4 docudrama *Dockers* and wrote the 1996 docudrama *Hillsborough*.
8 This judicial process finally reached its conclusion in 2010, twelve years after it began and thirty-eight years after the actual historical incident. The Bloody Sunday Inquiry was the longest and most costly in British legal history. It drew a public apology from the newly-elected Prime Minister, David Cameron, to the people of Northern Ireland.
9 The story was recounted to me by *Hostages* producer Sita Williams, whom I interviewed several times in Manchester (15 March, 15 April, 27 June and 10 November 1994, and 31 October 1995). I also quote from her working scripts (*Hostages*, *Fighting for Gemma*, and *Goodbye My Love*). For more on the 'fact fascists', see Chapter 2.
10 Hunter won an Emmy for this performance. In Chapter 8, I use Rod Carveth's term 'headline docudrama' to describe such films. The actual 1991 news story which inspired this film also led to another network – ABC – making *Willing to Kill: the Texas Cheerleader Story*. Rosenthal (1995: 237–44) offers an interesting comparison of these two docudramas.
11 Leslie Woodhead and Ray Fitzwalter, for example, both former Granada

employees, followed this path.

12 For a useful summary of theories of the audience from a Media Studies perspective, see Tim O'Sullivan *et al.* (1994).

13 See Chapter 7 for more detail on this case, and for the *Hostages* producers' letter of refutation published the following day.

14 Bazalgette, producer of *Big Brother* in the UK, gave the 2001 Royal Television Society 'Huw Wheldon Lecture' – transmitted on BBC2 on 29 November 2001.

15 Kathy Bates and Harry Dean Stanton in *Hostages*, Rutger Hauer and Martin Sheen in *Hostile Waters*. Sita Williams certainly took this view on costing when I spoke to her, but Kilborn and Izod (1997: 150) quote Ian McBride's opposite view: 'They cost as much as full-blooded drama, and more because you have all the journalistic work in advance.'

16 Steven Lipkin gives further details about the 'Mantra' in Chapter 5 of his 2002 book *Real Emotional Logic*. Interestingly, in *BioPics*, George F. Custen draws attention to movie producer Darryl F. Zanuck's belief in the importance of what he called the 'rooting interest' for audiences (Custen, 1992: 18).

17 He might have added the crucial term 'realist' before 'fiction' in the second sentence here – for only realist dramatic technique seeks to 'eradicate' the idea that what we watch is not *really* happening. There are many styles of dramatic performance, and I shall be considering some alternatives to realism in Chapter 8.

18 See also Corner (1996: 20–1).

19 One of the clearest things to emerge from the 'Acting with Facts' research 2007–10 is that actors themselves make little or no distinction between film and television acting. This led the Project Team to shift their analytical vocabulary, and to talk always of 'screen' rather than just 'television' docudrama. Hence also the changed subtitle of this revised edition.

20 Humphry's book is titled *Final Exit: The Practicalities of Self-deliverance and Assisted Suicide for the Dying*. It was used by the members of the religious cult 'Heaven's Gate' in preparation for their 1996 mass suicide. Humphry's greatest success, celebrated at the conclusion of *Goodbye My Love*, was to persuade the authorities in the state of Oregon to pass the 'Death with Dignity' act in 1997. This act permitted doctors in certain specified situations to 'assist' in a death. In 2006, this was still the only such act in the USA. Its upholding in that year by the US Supreme Court (against a 2001 directive by the then Attorney General John Ashcroft) will, according to some commentators, lead to other states considering whether they might introduce their own version of 'Death with Dignity' (see *The Week*, 21 January 2006, p. 8).

21 The 'key light' convention takes note of the principal light source in any situation, but builds around it to optimise definition of actors' faces. As in the theatre, the face of an actor is even more important as a vehicle of com-

munication than in film (where *mise-en-scène* really comes into its own. Key light is a naturalistic convention. For an audience, the expectation is that they will be able to accept the light as 'real-in-the-drama'.

22 Phil Smith, an experienced Granada sound recordist who worked on this film, gave me a telling explication of the essential unreality of the long-shot convention which uses radio-mikes to allow an audience to 'overhear' dramatic protagonists' conversations while we see them within a landscape. The technology, he explained, was first used in news broadcasting, then adapted to the conventions of television drama – the audience's desire to hear always overcoming any doubt about the actual impossibility of hearing over such huge physical distances. See also Chapter 8.

23 See Tunstall (1993) and Gitlin (1994) on the television producer as the real power in the industry. It should be noted, however, that a director can acquire prestige and power in television and parlay it into a career in film – as both Paul Greengrass and to a lesser extent Peter Kosminsky have done.

24 For an introduction to theatre semiotics, see Aston and Savona (1991). For a similarly excellent introduction to media semiotics, see Bignell (2002).

25 Here, of course, the theories of Constantin Stanislavski are fundamental. In an extensive literature, a useful short guide to the terminology I shall be using in this article is Benedetti (2000).

26 To list book-length studies of audience in Film and Media Studies research would need an extensive bibliography. In Theatre Studies, Susan Bennett's 1990 *Theatre Audiences: a Theory of Production and Reception* (2nd edn, 2001) stands virtually alone, and her bibliography leans heavily on literary reader-response theory.

27 There is some truth in this, of course, as every teacher and lecturer also knows.

28 An actor who forgets a line and fails to recover from this is said to have 'dried'. Lines from the wrong Act are frequently delivered in productions of plays like Samuel Beckett's *Waiting for Godot*, where the repetitive, absurdist, dialogue denies the actor 'through-line' logic.

29 Stone told interviewer Richard Corliss this anecdote – see 'Tom Terrific', *Time*, 25 December 1989. The insurance company was conscious that there was a chance that Cruise might become permanently disabled.

30 A useful collection is A. Lovell and P. Krämer (1999). Like most of the available material, it has to be said that this collection concentrates on film rather than television acting, and acting in docudrama is considered not at all.

31 I owe this insight to a 2002 Birmingham University M. Phil. thesis, 'Ready to Record?: Acting Technique within the Television Production Process'. Significantly, the writer Kim Durham is himself an actor (a regular on the long-running radio series *The Archers*).

32 This was the case, for example, with Granada's 1996 docudrama *Hillsborough*. During the filming, a CCTV engineer came forward to the

writer Jimmy McGovern with new information about the 1989 football stadium tragedy.

33 *Conspiracy* was a BBC/HBO co-production, directed by Frank Pierson. It was based on notes taken by one of the Wannsee conference participants.

34 Again, there is a vast literature on British acting styles, but a useful collection that combines material on theory and practice is Hodge (2000). See also Luckhurst and Veltman (2001).

35 See Fuller (1998) on Loach, and Clements (1983) on Leigh. Loach's penchant for non-actors has a bearing on the notion of 'real acting' – film directors who like working with non-actors generally appreciate the 'technique-less-ness' of such individuals.

36 See the Draft Report of the NCDT 'Recorded Media Working Party', a group that included the late actor Sir Nigel Hawthorne amongst its membership. A 1998 Arts Council report by Edward Birch, Charles Jackson and Ruth Towse, 'Fitness for Purpose: Dance, Drama and Stage Management Training – an examination of industry needs and the relationship with the current provision of training', came to broadly similar conclusions.

37 *Shackleton*, another 'high concept' docudrama/biopic, was a two-parter filmed for Channel 4 in May–June 2001 and broadcast in the UK on 2 and 3 January 2002.

38 See Bentley (1968: 215).

39 Charlton Heston was interviewed in the *Guardian* on 21 May 2001 (Section 2: 8); Brian Cox's article 'The Face of Evil' was in the same newspaper on the same date (Section 2: 16–17). Broadmoor is a high-security psychiatric hospital in England.

40 Even though the Nazi period of German history closed half a century and more ago, docudramatisations about it continue to attract filmmakers. Robert Carlyle played Hitler in another Anglo-American mini-series *Hitler: The Rise of Evil* (2003). In 2004, Bruno Ganz played Hitler in *Downfall*, and in 2006 Hannes Hellmann played Goering in *Nuremberg: Goering's Last Stand*.

41 'Universal' has been almost a proscribed word in the academy for over twenty years. I believe it to be deserving of re-consideration. It is difficult to speak of some 'invisible realities' without this word, and the academy has signally failed to unhitch it from day-to-day discourse (part of the original project) in any meaningful way. See Chapter 8 for more on this subject.

42 For more on the notion of 'high' and 'low' concept docudrama, see Edgerton 1991.

43 I first interviewed Ian McBride in Manchester (15 March 1994) then again in London (5 June 2003). His April 1996 paper at Birmingham University's 'Reality Time' Conference was published in A. Rosenthal (1999: 111–18).

44 See Paget (1990: 86–111).

2

The law and regulation – docudrama in the new millennium

Legalling – fact fascists and accuracy police

This chapter aims to outline the main legal and regulatory issues that concern docudrama. 'Legalling' is the term used for the vetting of a docudrama by production company lawyers. The process must take account of two separate systems: regulation (especially of television services but to a lesser extent of film too); and the law itself (as it applies to screen representations). Lawyers' advice is designed to provide 'a broad penumbra of restraint, confining the investigative journalist not merely to the letter of the law but to an outer rim bounded by the *mere possibility* of legal action,' as Geoffrey Robertson and Andrew Nicol remark in their standard work on media law (1992: xvi–xvii – my emphasis). Television is 'policed' through regulatory structures more closely than any other medium, and the press tends to have an especially vigilant eye for television, so lawyers have to be careful. They do their work both before and during filmmaking, and are on hand afterwards for any fallout from transmission or cinema release, for legalling is indispensable whether a film is destined for multiplex or for television screen. It is more high profile in the case of docudrama than for ordinary drama simply because real people are likely to be involved. By the late twentieth century media law in the UK generally was being described by Robertson and Nicol as 'lucrative ... high in profile ... and in a state of exponential growth' (1992: xvi). The rise of co-production has meant that legalling must be carried out by lawyers from the co-producing nation or nations, too, with a resultant rise in costs.[1]

As the twentieth century drew to a close, lawyers were encountering more and more problems with the inherent ambiguity of dramatic realism, the dominant performance style in television and film drama. Realist dramatic conventions have always meant that as much is *concealed* in dialogue as is revealed. With each reconfiguration of screen dramatic realism, dialogue has attenuated and modern screen acting puts a premium on the subtleties of sub-text (see again Chapter 1). This inevitably poses problems for legal teams because lawyers like to deal with what can be demonstrated directly. The indirect is always tricky. These non-professionals (in terms of drama) have become increasingly important to television docudrama production over the years. In the cinema, a film must negotiate whatever system of classification and certification is in place in any particular country, but this level of regulation is no different for any fiction film. Television docudrama, on the other hand, is sometimes singled out as a 'special case'. Although ultimate responsibility rests with studio chiefs, network owners, boards of governors, and directors of producing companies, filmmakers themselves always have to face the fact that they may be asked, in court, to justify their decisions and to demonstrate that the factual basis for their docudrama is sound in terms of the law. Legalling is a kind of anticipatory defence ultimately designed to avoid the inconvenience and the costs of defending a libel suit in court.

A major question is whether legalling acts as a brake on creativity, amounting to censorship. Commentators sometimes feel that the presence of the lawyer hovering in the background acts as an inhibiter of creative teams, leading to a kind of 'writing by committee' at odds with the ideal of free expression. The kind of creative constraints projected by those who dislike the form is symbolised by the nickname I mentioned in Chapter 1 given by actors and crew to *Hostages* producers Sita Williams and Alasdair Palmer – the 'Fact Fascists'. In a strikingly similar way, the crew working on *Apollo 13* (Ron Howard's 1995 film about the 1970 Moon mission that went wrong) saw their director as the Chief of what they called 'the Accuracy Police'.[2] An obsession with detail can be a good thing in filmmaking, but it marks a primary condition for makers of docudrama. Obsession with detail may be good for the making of a period drama, for example, but only in docudrama are the *legal* stakes so high. These nicknames powerfully articulate a resentment that lurks behind every docudrama production amongst some at least of the creative personnel.

This can be reinforced by lawyers' behaviour on and around the set. Their training and institutional practices encourage caution; Robertson and Nicol make the point that lawyers are 'inevitably more repressive' than the law itself 'because they will generally prefer to err on the safe side, where they cannot be proved wrong' (1992: xvi–xvii). With courts finding straightforward meaning more difficult to attribute to film scripts than any student of literary theory, it is no wonder experienced media lawyer Patrick Swaffer remarks that 'lawyers are cautious about meaning'.[3]

The lawyer's work

During the process of production there tend to be regular (amounting to daily) consultations between producers and lawyers. For example, the London firm of Goodman Derrick (Granada's legal representatives at the time) were sent complete scripts of 1990s docudramas to review with any proposed alterations during production faxed and/or phoned to them for immediate advice. Documentary material authenticating the developing script is gathered, with lawyers cross-checking the factual basis down to individual lines. Docudrama, with its potential for controversy, is a form that needs careful vetting, because of the sensitive nature of material that dramatises the lives of living people and active contemporary institutions. When Granada faced legal action on the 1990 docudrama *Why Lockerbie?* (US title: *The Tragedy of Flight 103: The Inside Story*) an airline company was directly involved. Researcher/producer Alasdair Palmer had on this occasion to go beyond even the normal procedures and provide lawyers with 'a script in which each line had a number which referred to a document attached to it'.[4]

The producer's marginal comments in working scripts of *Fighting for Gemma* (1993) demonstrate the close interface between the creative and legal teams.[5] The bulk of the marginal comments refer to legal matters. In this case the producers were fearful of running foul of a large institution (BNFL – British Nuclear Fuels Limited).

This can be clearly seen in Sita Williams' 'Principal Working Script'. The most frequent marginal comments are 'Q RP', 'Send to RP' and 'RP' ('RP' was Robin Perrot, a lawyer at Goodman Derrick). Next in frequency is the imperative 'Check' (i.e. with existing research and/ or undertake new research). The files compiled and held by producers constitute evidence in the worst-case scenario of a libel case coming to court. With the costs of making television docudrama tending to preclude the option of the writer-researcher, the responsibility for the impregnability of the factual base devolves primarily upon the researcher/producer and the lawyer. The writer has then to *work with* the research files and transform them into plot, character and dialogue. This creative task, like the actor's, is thus markedly different from that involved in 'freely imagined' dramatic work.

In the script of *Fighting for Gemma* legal intervention can be seen very directly. Speeches and sections of dialogue get re-phrased, cut or amended. This sometimes produces a circumlocution that is the very antithesis of dramatic plain speaking. A good example occurs on page 48 of Williams' script. The character Susan D'Arcy, talking about her daughter Gemma, originally says: 'Sellafield caused her to have leukaemia.' Lawyer Robin Perrot's view was that the line could be taken as defamatory by the lawyers of Sellafield's owners BNFL. The line is therefore changed to the more circumspect, but inevitably less passionate: 'Are you saying Sellafield didn't cause her leukaemia?' The negative grammatical form of this interrogative phrase would be altogether easier than the original line for a lawyer to defend in court. Even more direct is the alteration on page 75, Susan's: 'That place caused Gemma to have leukaemia!' becomes the anodyne but demonstrably factual: 'Gemma's got leukaemia.' This alteration removes even the faintest accusation of Sellafield's complicity in the child's illness.

One can sympathise with the actress trying to play character here – the linguistic shift diminishes the potential for emotion. The contrast with the language the real Susan D'Arcy used during her 'fight' for her daughter is revealing. For example, interviewed by *Today* reporter Penny Wark (10 November 1993) she described how she refused to allow her husband, a Sellafield contract-worker, to blame himself for their daughter's illness: 'I said, "That's not true. It's

Sellafield done it to you without you knowing."' The article's headline was even stronger, paraphrasing Susan D'Arcy in a way that
would not get past any docudrama's lawyer: 'I want them to admit
they [i.e. BNFL] killed my girl.' In law, 'Susan D'Arcy' (a character
in a filmed drama) does not, and can never, have the rights of free
speech possessed by Susan D'Arcy (the real-world individual). This is
a fundamental lesson for writers of television docudrama.

Producers tend to defend their lawyers. Media lawyers know
the media, they say, and their specialist understanding is tempered
by sensitivity to the values and aspirations of the filmmakers. The
process is often presented as one of *collaboration* not opposition.
As Alasdair Palmer saw it, a lawyer 'has this very difficult job –
not wanting to destroy the film, but wanting to protect us legally'.
Patrick Swaffer and Oliver R. Goodenough, the two experienced
media lawyers I consulted for this book, both convinced me that they
were genuinely keen to interfere as little as possible with creative
processes. Both agreed, however, that their work had become
more difficult as a result of the increasingly laconic nature of film
dialogue. Their concern was not so much with what is acted in the
finished film as with what has been *written* and *said* since the law of
libel and defamation inevitably proceeds from these things. The success of lawyers' collaboration with the 'creatives' can perhaps be best
measured by the infrequency of court action against docudramas.

Any drama 'based on fact' remains a legal minefield precisely
because it relies so much on information both in – and at the edges of
– the public domain. If the work is to have any investigative thrust at
all it will almost inevitably lead a docudrama into controversy if not
legal difficulty. Even when events are a matter of record, understandings of those events and the records of them can be contested by
those who claim to know more, or other, facts; or by those who can
assert that some facts have been misunderstood or misinterpreted.
In one sense, after all, only the most *un*interesting facts are uncon-
tested, and part of the attraction of the 'issue-based' docudrama is
its potential to disrupt and disturb. In the 2005 Channel 4 docudrama *The Government Inspector*, directed by Peter Kosminsky, different experts adduced different conclusions from available evidence at
best ambiguous. BBC reporter Andrew Gilligan's palmtop notes on

his meeting with weapons inspector Dr David Kelly were always a key item of evidence in the Inquiry that followed Kelly's death, but its status was never clear. Had Gilligan or had he not altered these notes? Kelly, who died shortly after the two men met in 2004, was not around to provide confirmation one way or the other. Gilligan himself steadfastly denied misconduct. The official Hutton Inquiry upheld the reporter's assertion, though it cast doubt on his general integrity. Peter Kosminsky, researcher/writer as well as director of the film, put his trust in new analysis from a computer forensics expert and provocatively contradicted Hutton. *The Government Inspector* featured a scene showing Daniel Ryan as Gilligan blatantly altering the notes. Gilligan complained a lot to the press about this but stopped short of court action.[6]

Research for fact-based programmes has many pitfalls. In 1996, for example, Granada was accused of plagiarism in an episode of *In Suspicious Circumstances*, a popular factual drama series of crime costume dramas.[7] The series had the obvious advantage of telling stories so far in the past that the actual protagonists were beyond suing. But in an episode titled 'Crime Passionnel', Andrew Rose claimed his book *Scandal at the Savoy* had been plagiarised. In court, the television company acknowledged that the book was known to their researchers. Their defence was that both drama and book were based upon the same material, freely available in the public domain. Ian McBride said: 'I don't think some writers appreciate how much research we do from a wide variety of sources, such as the Public Record Office, Crown Prosecution Service and newspapers.'[8] Generally, however, the volume and quality of the research conducted are not only what set docudrama apart from other television drama, they are also what enable lawyers to mount successful defences against charges of plagiarism, defamation and libel.

Being challenged on legal matters is, perhaps, rather like being in a traffic accident – you do not admit liability but have to be aware that blame could eventually be apportioned after due process. The territory of the docudrama is that of living individuals and the organisations for which they work, and these entities have the legal right to test whether they have been 'defamed' by docudrama. Since they are often turned into unwilling dramatic protagonists, this is only right. If they think they can show that the docudrama's view is inaccurate or unfair according to the facts they will seek damages, becoming the 'plaintiff' in a court case. Rich and powerful individuals and institutions (and their representatives) can command large resources and are often very jealous of their public image.

Defamation

'Defamation' in legal terms is the publication or broadcast of false information likely to cause damage to a plaintiff's reputation in the eyes of the world – as laid out in the most recent legislation, the 1996 Defamation Act. It is understood as either 'libel' (the written form of defamation – hence 'publication') or 'slander' (the spoken form – or 'broadcast' in its most general sense). A television programme could thus be regarded as both publication and broadcast, but:

> The 1990 Broadcasting Act re-asserts that for the purposes of defamation, publication by broadcast is to be treated as libel rather than slander. (Welsh and Greenwood, 2003: 498)[9]

A potential plaintiff can demand through a court order that a recording of the offending broadcast be made available to their lawyers ('television publication' being as retrievable as print publication). Although docudrama would seem especially vulnerable to charges of defamation, actual court cases are relatively rare. This is partly because of the expense and uncertainty associated with litigation, partly because, with sufficient attention from 'the accuracy police', the research element can always be mobilised to justify what has been published or broadcast to the satisfaction of the law. This is why good research is so fundamental to docudrama. The law in many countries, and certainly on both sides of the Atlantic, is also amenable to the democratic notion that 'fair comment' on a public subject, made in an informed manner, is justified in the wider public interest.

British law is enshrined in the 1996 Defamation Act. In *McNae's Essential Law for Journalists* the defences available are listed as follows:

(a) justification;

(b) fair comment;
(c) privilege;
(d) accord and satisfaction;
(e) offer of amends.

The final two defences, 'accord and satisfaction' and 'offer of amends', need not detain us since in both cases the perpetrator of the defamation will already have admitted fault and obviated the necessity of going to court either by offering the plaintiff 'accord and satisfaction', or by being about to make direct 'amends'. In both cases satisfactory apologies or retractions will have been offered, perhaps a damages figure agreed, and the plaintiff will withdraw from action. For defamation that was unintentional this is the best course; it stops the case from proceeding and, for the price of loss of face and some financial cost, avoids much greater potential harm to the defendant. The other defences deserve more attention because they imply rejection and contestation of the accusation.

In a case of 'justification' the defence hinges on proving that 'the words complained of are substantially true' (Welsh and Greenwood, 2003: 244). 'Substantially' is important here since *absolute* truth is notoriously hard to establish. The defence of 'fair comment' is part of a democratic society's more general guarantee of free speech. This road is the one more frequently travelled by embattled researchers, journalists and makers of docudrama. The cornerstone of the defence will be the claim that the disputed words were used 'honestly on a matter of public interest' (p. 255). In 2001 there were two cases that increased the likelihood of this defence being used by the Press and broadcast media. Previously, if 'malice' could be shown to be an element in the disputed words, the plaintiff's case would be accepted by courts. But the 2001 judgements established a freer scope to comment on public figures and public matters (briefly, it was accepted that adverse comment might *by its very nature* be perceivable as malicious by a plaintiff and therefore should not stand in the way of comment 'in the public interest').

The defence of 'privilege' is accorded absolutely, for example, in certain instances of common law such as the reporting of court proceedings – a valuable thing for investigative journalists since 'what is said in court ... is often highly defamatory' (p. 260). Working from court transcripts can be, then, a failsafe for the docudramatist.[10] Finally, investigative journalism has frequent need of the defence of 'qualified privilege', about which *McNae* notes: 'There is privilege at common law for the publication of defamatory statements in certain circumstances' (263). This is usually a defence in which the concept of the 'public interest' can again be seen to be paramount. Within this kind of legal phraseology can be discerned the workings of a democratic 'free speech' ideology.

The other significant development in the law that has taken place since this book was first published is the 'Reynolds Defence'. Patrick Swaffer sees this as having developed the law *potentially*, insofar as it was likely that a defence against libel might be able to argue fair comment more readily than before. The editors of *McNae* note that, following Reynolds, 'English law in effect recognises a public interest defence' (p. 243). Much discussed by lawyers since it was first promulgated, the Reynolds case was originally brought by a former Irish Prime Minister, Albert Reynolds, against *Times* newspapers. The article in the *Sunday Times* that caused the trouble followed Reynolds' resignation from his leadership of both Ireland and his party in 1994. In 1998 in the Court of Appeal, Lord Bingham (Lord Chief Justice at the time) applied what he called 'the duty test' to investigative journalism, and in the House of Lords in 1999 Lord Nicholls spelt out a list of ten circumstances under which such a defence might be mounted. The original trial against which Reynolds appealed had resulted in a judgement that famously awarded Reynolds one penny of damages – a ruling indicating, perhaps, the extent to which the law was prepared to protect adverse and critical comment against the powerful. The nugatory damages awarded spoke volumes in this regard, as did the upholding of the judgement on appeal.

Lawyers remain divided on the actual usefulness for libel cases of the Reynolds defence, which has not been used as much as anticipated.[11] Ian McBride's view as a television executive, however, is more positive. He told me in 2003:

> Changes in the libel law such as qualified privilege defence and the Reynolds test have theoretically made the documentarian's and drama-documentarian's life ... not easier, but if they go about their work particu-

larly diligently and professionally they can be less worried by the law of libel than they were, say, 10 years ago. It's harder for people without just cause to mount a libel claim against you than it was.

This is a good thing since an unfortunate dimension to the libel laws, very evident in the UK, has been that the lawsuit became for a while the privilege of the rich and litigious. Robertson and Nicol remark: 'Libel actions launched by wealthy and determined individuals can be enormously expensive to combat' (1992: 43).

Any shifts in emphasis in vetting docudrama pre-transmission, McBride told me, have actually been more concerned with new regulatory arrangements (see next section) and anxieties about privacy and media intrusion. Some kinds of legalling have receded in the new dispensation; for example, solicitors (especially those retained by wealthy individuals and organisations) were once fond of the 'letter before action' as a ploy to try to prevent publication or transmission. The letter characteristically warned an organisation or individual that action may be taken against them. The request for withdrawal and/or emendation of the offending material was then made either overtly or tacitly. The print media were willing enough on such occasions to follow up on this, smelling the blood of inaccuracy. Solicitors' letters before action are now, according to McBride, 'about privacy – and start quoting Human Rights provision at us'. 'Lighter touch' regulation, he explained, tends to mean that action is deferred until it is clear that regulation, rather than law, has been infringed. Thus it occurs more after transmission than it did heretofore. Gathering cultural concerns about the issue of privacy – especially concerning celebrity privacy – and ownership of 'story rights' have also had an effect in recent years on the legal activity around docudramas. BBC lawyer Sarah Andrew observed that there has been a pronounced 'shift in balance between libel and privacy' in media law:

> day to day in my job I find the considerations of threats of invasion of privacy now far outweigh libel in terms of the chill factor of the likelihood of action.[12]

The 'chill factor' for makers of documentary and docudrama may have changed, but for media lawyers the task is still basically to assess risk by applying 'a working test of "potential action-ability"' to the material contained in films they legal (Robertson and Nicol, 1992: xvii). They must be satisfied that the possibilities are low to non-existent before they perform their most significant pre-transmission task – the signing of the insurance certificate which protects the television company and its employees from legal action by third parties. As Sita Williams told me, 'We cannot start shoot-ing until Goodman Derrick underwrites the script.' Having sought reassurance that the programme defames neither persons nor organisation, the lawyers' opinion allows insurers to issue the all-important 'E & O' (errors and omissions) cover. In the event of action this insurance pays for a defence (and any costs incurred should the case go against the defendants). This situation obtains in most legal systems worldwide.

But the kind of public argument that takes place about docu-drama often occurs at the margins of the law, in the contentious area of free speech. The right of free speech can be used to venti-late issues, and this is certainly what many docudramas seek to do. Mostly this occurs without there ever being occasion or justification for legal action. The cultural studies notion of a 'media event' is use-ful here. Debate about controversial issues is often focused through media presentation, and docudramas have often provided just such a focal point. Also useful is the sociological concept of the 'moral panic'. This refers to the flurry of discussion that occurs and then grows around some contentious social or political problem or event. The agenda for wider public debate is at least partly set by the media, and in particular cases politicians and even governments join the fray and raise the temperature of discussion.

Such a media event, such a moral panic, occurred around Associated Television's 1980 docudrama *Death of a Princess*, and similar circumstances attended *The Government Inspector* in 2005. In the former case, the furore occasioned a Middle Eastern nation, Saudia Arabia, to break off diplomatic relations with Britain (see Chapter 7 for further details). In the latter, a storm of publicity sought to charge a British Government with mendacities that might have brought it down. It is not unusual for the opening exchanges in such public arguments to be evident in pre-publicity and at press previews – this was certainly the case with these two films. When controversy is generated by the contesting of the programme's view of the facts, the news media tend to become very active.[13]

Regulation

If the controversies around such examples as *Death of a Princess*, *Hostages*, and *The Government Inspector* demonstrate anything, they show that docudrama has the power to disturb – and make the air thick with accusation, counter-accusation, and the threat of legal action. If this threat has somewhat receded since this book first appeared it can never entirely disappear. With most docudrama, as Ian McBride remarked to me in 1993, 'there's always somebody who doesn't want it made'. Once a distinguished programme maker, McBride is now an executive responsible for 'compliance'. This is a relatively new field and a sign of new regulatory times. As Granada's 'Director of Compliance', McBride's job, as he describes it, is 'to spend more time, and take a great deal more care [than previously], on the regulatory position post-transmission'. Calling this 'one of the liberalisings of regulation', he told me:

> the new situation is a huge bonus to us, it avoids what lawyers used to call prior restraint – at the same time you do have to second guess as you go along what the regulator's position might be two months down the track.

But, although the print media have tended to call the new system 'self-regulation', McBride demurs from this view, alleging that some of the problems with docudrama have simply been moved elsewhere:

> There is an independent regulator who can visit substantial sanctions on you. So some of the lawyers' pre-transmission correspondence is actually aimed at the regulator *after the event*. The well-heeled or aggressive combatant can more easily and cheaply – and swiftly – get a better *partial* result against you than they would from suing you.

Cases such as the heavy fining of Carlton in 1999 bear out McBride's view that the regulator is far from toothless.

Company 'codes' and statements of 'best practice' have accommodated to the new dispensation. The Granada team who produced

Hostages when interviewed for this book in the early 1990s was bound by: the *ITC Programme Code* and the ITV Network Centre's *Statement of Best Practice*. They had also to be aware of offending the Broadcasting Standards Council (BSC) and the Broadcasting Complaints Commission (BCC). Present-day makers of docudrama work in a changed environment. In 1996, the latter two organisations became one – the Broadcasting Standards Commission – and then in 2004 the Office of Communications (Ofcom came into being in the wake of the 2003 Broadcasting Act. On its website, Ofcom demonstrates the extent of ideological symbiosis with former regulators in its Broadcasting Code, a document that became operational on 25 July 2005 but which incorporates many similarities with previous regulatory publications (many of which can be found in its archive 'Legacy' section).[14] This indicates both institutional continuity and broad satisfaction (some would say complacency) amongst British media professionals and their regulators. In many ways the strongest injunction about docudrama in the new code is to be found under Section 2.2 (p. 18). This states:

> Factual programmes or items or portrayals of factual matters must not materially mislead the audience.

The key sections of the Code in regard to docudrama are Sections 5, 7 and 8.

Section 5 deals with 'due impartiality and due accuracy and undue dominance of views and opinions' (pp. 24–9). Amongst other things it defines the important concept of 'due impartiality' (p. 24). It emphasises (Section 5.5) the importance of a 'series of programmes taken as a whole'. Thus a view in one programme may be compensated for by another with a different editorial line. It offers as an example 'drama and a debate about the drama'. Sections 7 and 8 deal with 'fairness' and 'privacy'. The former emphasises the importance of 'informed consent' to factual programming, the latter emphasises the importance of 'reduc[ing] potential distress' in reconstructions and factual drama. In all these sections the references to docudrama are mostly via phrases like 'dramatic reconstructions and factually-based dramas' (p. 39) rather than 'drama-documentary', the old ITC's preferred term.

Although 'drama-documentaries' gets an entry under 'drama' in the Index (p. 81) the phrase is never used in the Code itself. This is an indication of both the changes in production practices since the 1990s and the 'lighter touch' of modern regulation.

The BBC, governed through a Charter that comes up for renewal on a cyclical basis and financed partly through the public purse, produced its 'BBC Producer's Guidelines' at around the same period as ITV wrote its *Code*. This mirrors closely the language and concerns of the *ITV Programme Code*. It now mimics closely Ofcom documentation – indeed, attaches the Ofcom Code under Section 18 of its own code.[15] The governing principles of 'accuracy' and 'due impartiality' are similarly central. In the Introduction to the *Guidelines*, the BBC articulates its 'editorial values', emphasising: 'The BBC's commitment to accuracy is a core editorial value and fundamental to our reputation.' The relevant sections in terms of docudrama are Sections 3–6 (dealing respectively with 'accuracy', 'impartiality and diversity of opinion', 'fairness, contributors and consent', and 'privacy'). The phrase 'drama documentaries' survives still in the BBC Code, in Section 3.

Pretty well all the documents produced post-1990 Broadcasting Act sing, as it were, from the same hymn sheet. They could almost have been written by the same corporate mind. They fit into a late twentieth-century culture that became increasingly focused on business practices and audit procedures. No institution would be taken seriously without its 'Statements of Best Practice' and 'Core Values', its 'Mission Statements' and all the rest. Patrick Swaffer observed to me that broadcasters in general tend to find the panoply of regulation 'onerous and burdensome', especially in comparison to makers of films. But for television documentary and documentary derivatives it is especially so, particularly when they look in the direction of theatre, film, and even print journalism. Creative personnel in these industries appear, relatively, freer from restriction. While there is no doubt that the television industry is subject to a heavy surveillance, because of its grip on the public imagination, these industries too are now watch-dogged, mission-statemented and scrutinised-through-audit in a way that inevitably causes frustration.

Nevertheless the assumptions, language and declared intentions of the regulatory instruments are clear enough. Major broadcasters have over the years taken particular note of legislators' strictures on the preservation of 'due impartiality', especially in cases where the controversy is political, industrial, or to do with matters of public policy. The important word is actually 'due', which has been defined as 'adequate or appropriate to the nature of the subject and the type of programme' (p. 26 in the Ofcom Code). There is clearly what politicians describe as 'wiggle room' here. With docudrama as with documentary and current affairs, 'due impartiality', 'accuracy' and 'fairness' are seen as obligatory. Because of its contentious hybridity, cultural anxiety about the docudrama is ratcheted up in regulatory documentation. There is widespread acceptance that boundaries between fact and fiction may indeed become 'blurred', but the 'custom and practice' answer to this is that anything which attempts docudramatic reconstruction should be 'labelled'. For many television people the notion of 'labelling' has become tantamount to an article of faith.

Another such article of faith is the self-reflexive scheduling that seeks to ensure 'due impartiality' by providing supporting information and after-transmission discussion in potentially contentious circumstances. An example of the docudrama-followed-by-discussion format was the BBC2's *The Late Show* of 21 September 1992, which included a follow-up panel reviewing the transmission of *Hostages*. Supporting information is usually provided by an end-credit sequence featuring help-line numbers or website references (see Chapters 3 and 7 for further discussion).

Freedoms of speech

Insofar as docudrama shares documentary's seriousness of purpose, it too is a 'duty-genre'.[16] And though American docudrama has had the reputation of being a 'disease/problem of the week' form, it can still claim a degree of public service. Todd Gitlin quotes an NBC lawyer, Barbara Hering: 'If justified by the facts, [docudrama] performs a public service, but if the facts are not as portrayed, the possible undermining of the public's faith in their institutions would be not only unfair but a real disservice to our audience' (1994: 173).

With public faith in the main source of its day-to-day information – the television – at issue, the law and regulation have a significant part to play in American practice too.

A standard work on the law and US television (and similar to Robertson and Nicol and McNae) is Oliver R. Goodenough and Howard J. Blumenthal's *This Business of Television*, which has sections devoted to 'docudramas' (pp. 186–7) and 'regulation of programming' (pp. 160–200).[17] The USA has a central regulatory agency, the Federal Communications Commission (FCC), developed in 1934 from the earlier Federal Radio Commission. This body, like Ofcom, has extended its control of the media to include the new technologies of satellite and cable television and the internet. Historically, it has been concerned primarily with allocation of frequency bands and the limitation of monopoly. It has had some input into content but is often seen by media commentators as a somewhat craven servant of the commercial interests that have always dominated American broadcasting.

In terms of American law, First Amendment guarantees of free speech have ensured a somewhat looser monitoring of US docudrama (see below, and also Chapter 6). At times monitoring can come down to State level rather than Federal level, and differences in State and Federal legislation can make for confusion. With 'privacy and publicity', for example, each state has its own laws. The real difference in the two systems, however, remains in the positioning of the burden of proof: in the British system, it is necessary to prove that everything claimed is true; in the American, the plaintiff must demonstrate malice and negligence. As Goodenough summarised in 1996: 'In the UK, the question is, is it the truth? In the USA, the question is, did they do their homework?'

Before a docudrama can be transmitted by an American network, the script must pass through three layers of scrutiny. These are the network's own legal, 'errors and omissions', and 'broadcast standards and practices' departments. All networks have guidelines similar to the BBC/Ofcom codes. NBC guidelines do not use the term docudrama, they refer instead to 'fact-based movies and mini-series' (see Rosenthal 1995: 248–50). This much broader swathe of fact–fiction drama is now in line with Ofcom's phrase about 'reconstructions and fact-based drama'. If the reasons for a looser definition are historical and cultural, the demands made are similar to those in British guidelines. NBC requires the producer to provide 'substantial backup, including multiple sources', and to 'send one copy of the annotated script to the NBC Program Standards Department and a second copy to the NBC Law Department.' The *NBC Annotation Guide* offers detailed instructions on this aspect of script preparation. Finally, NBC draw producers' attention to independent research agencies (formed expressly to deal with the fact-based movie and mini-series) whose assistance they recommend.[18]

'Release forms', as used in documentary proper, are recommended for docudramas too. A release form, signed by the actual protagonists in a true story, ensures that they will find it difficult if not impossible to take action after they have been portrayed in a drama. As Robertson and Nicol put it: 'Consent to publication is a complete defence' (1992: 94). 'Informed consent' is the key phrase legally, and goes right to the heart of the ethical issues that surround docudrama (indeed, documentary itself). The phrase, as I have shown, now appears more systematically in British regulation. Ethically, it points to filmmakers' responsibility to real-world individuals directly affected by their films. As Bill Nichols says:

> A common litmus test for many ... ethical issues is the principle of 'informed consent'. This principle relied on heavily in anthropology, sociology, medical experimentation, and elsewhere, states that participants in a study should be told of the possible consequences of their participation. (Nichols, 2001: 10)

To this end many recent publications on television offer advice on waivers and dummy release forms.[19] Baker's book reproduces a dummy release to copy (1995: 258–9) as does Rosenthal's (1995: 212).

The American legal system, like the British, is based on adversarial court procedures and stands in contrast to European (particularly French) systems of advocacy. The Anglo-American system in general puts its faith in juries (directed by judges), whereas judges are the focus for European courts. In the USA certain constitutional factors have determined the legal progression of the docudrama, and state as well as federal legal precedents have to be taken into account. The general situation (according to Goodenough) is:

> the [US] courts have worked out a First Amendment analysis that permits [docudrama] to be made with relative safety from legal challenge.

He stresses, however, that: 'Staying in this area of safety ... depends on the producer acting responsibly.' In this remark alone one can see similarities to the British mantra of 'due impartiality', 'accuracy', 'fairness'.

The test of potential actionability is slightly different in the USA. In Alasdair Palmer's words, 'the burden of proof is not on you as the film maker,' as it is in the UK, 'it's on the plaintiff to prove that you're wrong'. American precedent has been established that for those in public life 'recovery is only possible if it can be shown that the publisher of the false libel acted with actual malice', while for private individuals, 'a showing of negligence in the publication of the defamatory falsehood' is required.[20] The case that helped establish the US law's position in regard to docudrama was 'Davis *versus* Costa-Gavras' (1987). The latter film director's depiction of historical events in his 1982 film *Missing* was challenged by a very powerful court opponent: the US State Department. Politicians were, to say the least, unhappy with the way American involvement in Chile in 1973 was portrayed in *Missing*.

The historical background to *Missing* was that the Chilean Army had staged a coup against the democratically elected President Allende, bringing to power the right-wing General Pinochet. Costa-Gavras's film depicts an American father (played by Jack Lemmon) discovering the extent of his country's complicity with the coup. Its indirect responsibility for the death of his son is the emotional 'hook' for Costa-Gavras's critical view of US foreign policy of the time. Goodenough quotes Judge Milton Pollack's summing-up:

> Self-evidently a docudrama partakes of author's license – it is a creative interpretation of reality – and if alterations of fact in scenes portrayed are not made with serious doubts of truth of essence of the telescoped composites, such scenes do not ground a charge of actual malice. (Goodenough, 1989: 29)[21]

So it was that *Missing* and its director's principled stand was protected by the US legal system against the US government. [22]

US broadcasters have undoubtedly benefited from First Amendment-protected precedents such as the *Missing* case and the *New York Times* v. Sullivan case of 1964. Here the US Supreme Court ruled that a newspaper had a right to make allegations against a public figure, provided these could be proved to be 'honestly and diligently made'.[23] As Robertson and Nicol remark, this latter judgement paved the way for such historic exposes as Watergate and Irangate (1992: 103). It is no wonder, then, that British producers like Alasdair Palmer look at the US system with something approaching envy. 'I have to think the American system is best,' Palmer told me, 'because they actually do believe in the freedom of the press – it's constitutionally protected.' The UK's *sub-judice* procedures, of course, do tend to prevent the pre-judging of trials. Media-event trials in the USA, such as O. J. Simpson's (1995) and Michael Jackson's (2005), show an in-built disadvantage to the First Amendment. It virtually guarantees the very 'trial-by-television' that the UK Contempt of Court Act of 1981 works to prevent. Robertson and Nicol define journalism as 'not just a profession [but] the exercise by occupation of the right to free expression available to any citizen', but they acknowledge that this right has been hedged round historically in Britain by 'special rules' developed by Parliament and the courts rather than constitutional guarantees (1992: xv–xvi).[24]

The USA is not alone in its relatively greater liberality regarding freedom of speech. Robertson and Nicol further note that 'the British media enjoy relative freedom from censorship by comparison with most Third World countries' but that the situation in Canada, France, Scandinavia and Australia as well as America is actually preferable from the point of view of freedom of expression. They use as their yardstick Article 19 of the Universal Declaration of Human Rights of 1975 which reads, in part:

> Everyone has the right to freedom of opinion and expression; this right includes the freedom to hold opinions without interference and to seek, receive and impart information and ideas through any media and regardless of frontiers. (1992: 35)

Brian Winston's suggestion that 'for non-commercial, state-funded broadcasting not inevitably to mean state control requires, as a first essential, that freedom of expression be constitutionally guaranteed' remains apposite.[25]

The legal mantra: 'due impartiality', 'accuracy', 'fairness'

It would be a mistake to expect the law to have anything other than a pragmatic view because 'the law is a working-through at a societal level of ethics and morality', as Oliver Goodenough told the 'Reality Time' conference of 1996. The status of documentary as a mode of communication is routinely collapsed into its status as a mode of social exploration (a tendency I shall examine further in Chapter 4). But this chapter has argued that problems multiply when drama joins the mix – and are increased exponentially when it is so 'forward in the mix', as it were, as it currently is. Producers on both sides of the Atlantic are channelled towards related notions by *both* legal and regulatory frameworks because these frameworks share societal and cultural norms. The legal mantra – 'due impartiality', 'accuracy', 'fairness', 'informed consent' – comprises working concepts that try to give protection to both sides of a docudramatic operation. The balance in vetting systems is on the whole in favour of the 'responsible producer'. Responsible production ensures that films continue to be made for television, while the filmmaker aiming at the multiplex can count on a little more slack from the cultural police.

What happens when production is deemed irresponsible can be illustrated historically in a number of cases. In the 1989 BBC television play *Here Is the News*, for example, a character called 'David Dunhill' was so closely modelled on a real journalist – Duncan Campbell – that when Campbell sued the BBC in 1990 he won. Deploying his own investigative skills to devastating effect, he demonstrated just how much detail of his own life had gone into writer G. F. Newman's character Dunhill. A simple change of name is not a sufficient tactic *in itself* to avoid charges of defamation. As Goodenough points out: 'Merely changing names, events, locations or physical features will not in itself prevent recovery by someone who claims to be recognizably portrayed.' He cites a 1983 case in

America that was similar to the Dunhill/Campbell one, but more salacious. A 'Miss Wyoming' from an actual beauty contest 'was able to win the issue of identity against *Penthouse* magazine when it ran a story about a fictional Miss Wyoming of a different name, who twirled batons and levitated men through oral sex' (Goodenough, 1989: 5).

Nor is reference to regulatory bodies an unheard of event. For example, Ofcom's predecessor the ITC censured Carlton TV for its docudrama *Beyond Reason*. This 1996 film was based on a sensational 1991 murder case in which an Army officer's wife had been murdered by his lover. The censure followed complaints by the murdered woman's parents. By contrast, in 1997 ITC upheld as valid against a series of complaints the treatment of the subject of child abuse in Peter Kosminsky's Meridian TV docudrama, *No Child of Mine*. Doubts about the facts on the latter were dispelled by evidence involving the programme's use of unassailable confidential files made available to the filmmakers by a real-life victim. But, as I mentioned in the Introduction, regulatory teeth were shown most clearly in 1998 when a scandal followed the transmission on ITV of the documentary *The Connection*. This 1996 film about the drug trade and Columbian gangs was again a Carlton production. Filmmaker Marc de Beaufort was found by ITC (the regulator at the time) to have faked a significant proportion of the film. Carlton was fined £2 million, and British newspapers had a field day. As Winston (2000) outlines, they almost fell over themselves to condemn television journalism as irresponsible. Given the state of the British Press, especially in its tabloid manifestation, this seemed to many people a case, if ever there was one, of the pot calling the kettle black.[26]

The BBC, too, has had its problems with fact–fiction mixes. In addition to *Here Is the News*, the Charles Wood teleplay *Tumbledown* and Alan Bleasdale's *The Monocled Mutineer* caused executives problems. *Tumbledown* told the story of Robert Lawrence, a Guards officer badly wounded in the 1982 Falklands War. Necessarily, it depicted in a way that might be seen as controversial not only a number of Lawrence's actual colleagues but also the institution of the British Army itself, and it was due for transmission on the eve of a general election. Alterations were made to the film and its transmission delayed until 1987. Ian Curteis's *The Falklands Play*, meanwhile, caused almost as much of a problem even though it was not transmitted at all during this period. It had, in fact, to wait until the new BBC digital channels came on stream and were looking for material. It was finally shown, in a shortened form, on BBC3 in 2002. I have argued elsewhere that the controversy over representations of the Falklands War betrayed a society deeply troubled by, and unable to resolve, antithetical views of this conflict. Unable any longer to smooth fundamental disagreements into the kind of consensus evident in, say, 1950s films representing the Second World War, this furore presaged in some ways the fierce debates surrounding the Gulf War of 1992, the Iraq War of 2003 and the invasion of Afghanistan.[27]

A similar case occurred in 1988 when the BBC broadcast *The Monocled Mutineer*, a four-part docudrama based on a book by William Allison and John Fairley. The story of book and series was of a First World War deserter from the British Army, Percy Topliss. The *Daily Mail* was prominent in claiming errors, and several newspapers thought it important enough to run editorials on the subject. In retrospect, the right-wing press was almost bound to take exception to a story that denied the myth of the Heroic Great War Tommy in this way. In the context of a decade in which the government in power was prone to regarding the BBC as a left-inclining institution hostile to traditional values, it was perhaps not altogether surprising that the BBC lost its appetite for factually based drama for a while after these problems. The double-bind of Charter renewal (the BBC needs to be seen as a 'free' institution, but it is beholden to government for its continuation) left the BBC vulnerable at this point in its history. This situation occurred again in 2003 with the outcry that followed the Hutton Report into the death of weapons expert Dr David Kelly.

If the end-result of the combination of regulation, legal considerations, and general cultural suspicion of the form has ever been to induce defensive strategies, it seems to me that the quest for viewers and ratings has had something of a balancing effect. The fact is that hybrid modes are always likely to be under simultaneous attack from several quarters. These comprise persons or institutions depicted in a docudrama (and unhappy with their depiction); the legal representatives of such persons or institutions; regulatory bodies; filmmakers' own employers; a hostile press; a wary public. In any event British lawyers dealing with docudrama still need to tick points off a checklist before allowing producers to proceed:

1. Defamation. Is there anybody identified in the programme whose reputation is likely to be reduced because of the programme?
2. Confidentiality. Is there any material used in the programme which is confidential or was obtained in confidence?
3. Regulatory Framework.[28]

An American lawyer's list is not dissimilar, comprising 'four principal rights that real people have in relation to media depictions of them':

- Libel and slander
- Privacy
- Publicity
- Trade name (Goodenough, 1989: 5)

The shift from defendant to complainant, and the more commercial awareness inherent in 'trade name', clearly marks out a difference in the American legal view (as does an apparent absence of real worry about regulation). But the absence of a strict liability, which in the UK puts the burden of proof on the defendant, is the most notably different feature.

Regulating, legislating or censoring?

If the basic structures of criminal law, civil law and legally mandated regulatory frameworks is broadly shared by both British and American broadcasting, media agencies in the UK have been hedged round historically by the kind of informal, gentlemanly (and I use the word deliberately) lobbying and state-sponsored benign repression which has resulted from a self-protecting culture of caution in public matters. The USA is not necessarily better as a result of having had less time to practise this 'grace-and-favour' culture. The pre-eminence of the commercial interest has made things simultaneously freer in terms of the legal framework but more restricted in terms of the kinds of programme it is possible to make. Because advertisers want above all programmes which will draw popular audiences, US television has a tendency to take fewer risks with the formats of programmes – and its docudrama tradition is not as 'fact-rich', to use Goodenough's phrase, as the comparable British tradition. In recent years, however, the two cultures and their media institutions have been moving closer together under global market pressures. Robertson and Nicol's 1992 comment:

> The recent history of moral and political censorship in Britain has been characterised by a move from criminal law to statutory regulation. (1992: 594)

was certainly borne out in the ten years that followed, as we have seen.

British television's historical concept of a 'public service' BBC has been a cultural factor since the BBC was formally constituted as an organisation in the 1920s. The first US broadcasting networks were formed around the same time, but whereas they have always been commercial in orientation (the USA only acquiring a public service network in the 1960s), the BBC has presided over nearly a century of continuity in the public service tradition. Following the British General Strike of 1926 the government of the day ensured that the constitution of the fledgling broadcasting organisation guaranteed the right of military take-over. A Home Secretary still has this power and an additional right of veto on any programme or programme item (see Robertson and Nicol, 1992: 26). This threat of action has sometimes caused the BBC to dither and procrastinate on matters of public policy. The USA, as part result of its sheer size, has always given local stations greater autonomy, and the FCC regulatory function is more akin to the new, post-Broadcasting Act 'lighter touch' Ofcom than to previous models of broadcasting regulation.

An example of the British way is the so-called 'D-notice', through which British governments can take the opportunity to restrain broadcasting of subject matter deemed to be against the national interest, but without immediate recourse to the law.[29] The tendency of such convenient secrecy seems at odds with that concept of civil education for responsible citizenship which is so much the defining tradition both of British broadcasting and British education. Fundamentally ideological arguments can still be played out at the level of individual articles, films or programmes whenever a controversy occurs. The break-up of the post-war consensus in Britain has led to challenges to the network that once guaranteed acquiescence in a gentlemanly square dance between legislators and broadcasters. The tension between government pressure and broadcaster/ journalist independence has been shown vividly on a number of occasions in recent years (again, the Kelly case of 2005, especially as dramatised in Peter Kosminsky's *The Government Inspector*, offers a relevant example).

In many ways this began during the 1980s when a deteriorating situation in Northern Ireland caused the Conservative government of Margaret Thatcher progressively to remove the various public voices of the Irish Republican Army (IRA) from the broadcast media. In the case of *At the Edge of the Union*, a 1985 BBC television documentary in the *Real Lives* series, the BBC bowed to pressure and removed the programme from their schedules. In 1988 the Thames Television documentary series *This Week* investigated the killing in Gibraltar by the Special Air Services (SAS) of three IRA members earlier that year. The programme, *Death on the Rock*, went out after the Independent Broadcasting Authority (IBA) and the television company resisted government's attempt to have it removed from the schedule. The consequence of this resistance was that the Conservative Government legislated, in 1988, in order to deny what they called 'the oxygen of publicity' to the IRA. Thames lost its franchise in 1993 in a follow-up to the Thatcher government's legislative war against leftie broadcasters. Many commentators saw Thames's loss of franchise as a direct result of its resistance to covert censorship on *Death on the Rock*.[30]

Robertson and Nicol's words about the move from criminal law to statutory regulation take on a different dimension in this example: if regulation fails, there is still legislation. Broadcasting Acts in 1990 and 2003 shifted the ground further, and altered not only the outlines of regulatory frameworks but also the whole ecology of British broadcasting. The combative attitude of the Thatcher government, with its belief verging on paranoia that the British media was a hot-bed of left-wing agitation, focused the debate in the UK increasingly on the regulation of the media, with the 1990s debate on Human Rights offering a counter-balance. All this affected docudrama inasmuch as it fulfils its claim as documentary; the rigour expected of a purely factual programme is the base from which any programme must be made. The main laws that must be acknowledged by the makers of docudrama are, therefore, the criminal laws of contempt of court, official secrecy, sedition and obscenity, and the civil laws of libel and breaches of copyright and confidence. These are reinforced by the various legal and regulatory bodies on both sides of the Atlantic, behind whose rhetoric lurks the mantra of 'due impartiality' and 'accuracy' and 'fairness'. These rough rules of thumb can seem as if they are intended mainly to dissuade programme makers and broadcasters from taking risks, but they can also be seen as a permitted freedom-within-boundaries rather than a free-for-all.

Film, of course, is similarly subject to the law and to censorship, but TV executives like Ian McBride have always believed that there is effectively no comparison between the two media:

> The requirement of due impartiality is actually a duty; no feature film-maker has that responsibility. Cinema is not regulated like that because it's not seen as carrying a public information role. It's not current affairs, it's essentially seen in an entertainment role, in which the audience elects to go along and watch.

His view as a former television journalist and filmmaker and a current policy maker is that 'the reasons for the television regulations are actually sound given the more random way television is watched'.

Legal advice

Leslie Woodhead was one veteran producer I interviewed who could recall no legal problems with docudrama until the last years of the twentieth century.[31] His Eastern European docudramas *Invasion* (1980) and *Strike* (1981) had no legal difficulties, but as soon as domestic subject matter was involved things changed. The first legal problem he could recall was, significantly, on *Collision Course* (a 1979 reconstruction of a 1976 mid-air collision over Zagreb). 'We'd used the flight recorder for the last few minutes of the British Airways flight,' Woodhead recalled:

> An injunction was served by the Pilots' Association, whose representative was Norman Tebbit [later to become a Conservative cabinet minister]. They took us to the High Court to ask whether we should use this tape, which was the copyright of BA. They lost.

The Pilots' Association lost, of course, because a public interest defence was relatively easy to mount. A decreasing consensus about the degree of openness in public information has generated an increasing public distrust of information agencies. As a result, the running check that is legalling has acquired more and more importance since docudrama first became controversial in the 1960s. The legal contribution to the process is now so direct that it can easily be read as a kind of censorship, and many creatives now fight shy of working in an area overdetermined by legal and regulatory constraints. As Michael Eaton (writer on *Shoot to Kill*) noted dryly, the writer can argue points with the journalist/researcher and even win occasionally, but in any argument with the lawyer, 'the lawyer always wins'. At a public debate in 1997 the Channel 4 executive David Aukin called the control exerted by lawyers 'a terrible compromise'. This phrase drew wide acclaim from an audience principally composed of filmmakers and writers. At the same event Charles McDougall, director of Granada's 1996 *Hillsborough*, offered the stoical view that lawyers 'are there right through to post-production and you have to put up with them'.[32]

Rob Ritchie (writer of *Who Bombed Birmingham?*) has commented: 'It is a hard and exacting task to write dramadoc.'[33] The sober advice offered by the two media lawyers interviewed for this book bears this out. Goodenough lists these 'Suggested Procedures':

- Select a topic and characters of legitimate public interest.
- Get releases.
- Do voluminous research.
- Have a factual basis for every aspect of the script.
- Stay as close to literal truth as possible.

- Respect chronology.
- Do not use composites for major characters.
- Depict dead people ['death wipes out rights of libel, slander and privacy'].
- Take particular care with certain topics [gloss: especially 'sex and nudity'].
- Have a legal review of the script and film.
- Use disclaimers. (1989: 29)

Swaffer, meanwhile, lists four 'Golden Rules' which are briefer, but not dissimilar:

1. Firstly, fairness and accuracy.
2. Detailed and good quality research must underpin your description of any events.
3. Work with the evidence you have got, rather than that you wished you had; don't listen to rumour and gossip.
4. Best of all make a programme about historic events where the participants are dead and therefore can't sue.[34]

Swaffer's cautionary words regarding the docudrama must also be borne in mind. 'There is', he says:

> always the risk that, in the most extreme cases, the dramatisation of the story will overwhelm or remove the documentary element of the programme ... this problem has become more acute with the development of drama/documentaries [*sic*] dealing with personal life stories.

Specifically he was referring to the problems he had legalling *Goodbye My Love*. The emphasis on personal detail, buttressed by naturalistic acting techniques, has shifted the ground on which the docudrama stands. Even with a subject of proven public interest, such as euthanasia, the fact that the documentary element was implicit rather than explicit was a cause for concern. He remarked in general that 'more acute problems come with drama/documentaries of personal stories where events have often taken place both in public and in private and there may be entirely conflicting viewpoints on individuals' motives and, indeed, the actual events.'

'Again and again,' according to Swaffer, 'you review with the [creative] team the meaning of the film.' The lawyer must therefore be 'part of a team to assist you with identifying and reducing, or removing, risks'. As a result, lawyers have, 'a good deal of input into the meaning of the programme'. This is seen as a mixed blessing. Programme makers, as we have seen with Palmer and Williams, will often praise the sensitivity of their lawyers on this issue, but the creative shoe undoubtedly pinches at times. It may be tempting for programme makers to see lawyers as people who pick away at lines of dialogue, while artists work beyond words, trying to capture a visual and aural *zeitgeist*. It is perhaps better to see modern media lawyers having a cultural as well as a legal role. In these times of uncertainty about, and increasing challenge to, facts and information, the lawyer has become a kind of arbiter of meaning-in-the-text for the industry and – by extension – within the culture. As well as trying to fix meaning, they have come to represent a figure past whom it is necessary to smuggle other meanings. The job of 'meaning-making', theorised almost out of existence in the modern academy, has devolved upon the lawyer. Swaffer observed to me caustically in conversation that the theoretical finessing so beloved in the academy would not get far in a court of law. As a gesture towards clarification, I want now to examine the terms most commonly used to define and describe the docudrama and to move the discussion on to a review of its codes and conventions. These devices most usefully mark the docudrama out both from other kinds of film and television drama, and separate it from the 'flow' of the television schedule.[35]

Notes

1 Legal systems in anglophone countries have many common points of reference, of course, but there are enough differences to make this necessary.
2 This detail is revealed in a documentary addition to the 2005 DVD of the film, released to mark the thirty-fifth anniversary of the space mission.
3 Both Patrick Swaffer and the American media lawyer Oliver Goodenough (whom I quote extensively below) spoke at the 'Reality Time' conference Birmingham in 1996. Goodenough has worked for HBO, and legalled *Hostages* in 1992. Both lawyers gave me access to their conference papers and gave me valuable interviews during the conference. Subsequently I corresponded with them, and also interviewed Swaffer at his legal chambers in London on 5 June 2003. Goodenough is currently Professor of Law at Vermont Law School (see also note 17).

4 In 1994, with the case having been settled out of court, Alasdair Palmer felt that the problem with *Why Lockerbie?* had been that the film was 'critical of a large American company which hadn't yet gone bankrupt'. The company he was referring to was the airline Pan Am, whose jumbo jet had gone down over Lockerbie. Patrick Swaffer was the lawyer involved with the case. He pointed out to me (in letters of 14 March 1997 and 11 September 1997) that Air Malta was the company actually suing Granada, and that Pan Am was 'not involved in any legal challenge to the programme'. Palmer's remark, however, indicates the presence of Pan Am (then connected with Air Malta) in the background. I interviewed Alasdair Palmer in London on 7 October 1994.

5 Granada gave me access to such scripts, including Sita Williams' own heavily annotated copy of *Fighting for Gemma*.

6 He was still said to be considering legal action in a front page article in the *Guardian* on 8 March 2005.

7 In many ways the series was the direct descendant of the sensational 'true crime' periodical of the twentieth century.

8 As reported in the *Observer* on 27 October 1996. When the case came to court, out of twenty-one claims made for infringement of copyright, only four were upheld. The others were dismissed, representing a kind of victory for Granada. This kind of 'source duplication' occurs in academic life too. Some of Anthony Hayward's remarks about *Cathy Come Home* in *Which Side Are You On?*, his 2004 book about Ken Loach, are very similar to mine in a 1999 *New Theatre Quarterly* article on the celebrated film. Both pieces were using the same primary sources.

9 Like Robinson and Nicol *McNae's Essential Law for Journalists* (Welsh and Greenwood, 2003) is a standard work. Another indication of the importance of the law in establishing a framework for 'based on fact' material is the number of editions such works have – *NcNae's* seventeenth edition appeared in 2003. New books are also coming onto the market – for example, Barendt and Hitchens (2000) and Smartt (2006), the latter's Chapters 2 ('Privacy') and 6 ('Defamation'), being very useful. Section 34 in Winston (1995) ('What Constraints?', pp. 219–29) is particularly good on what the law can sometimes sideline – the ethics of documentary. Winston remarks that the law 'look[s] for property to protect' (p. 226) and that this complicates the ethics of documentary filmmaking considerably.

10 London's Tricycle Theatre and its director Nicholas Kent have in recent years made a speciality of 'tribunal' plays – as I remarked in the Introduction. The following are all dramatisations of court and official enquiry transcripts: *Half the Picture*, 1994; *The Colour of Justice*, 1999; *Justifying War*, 2003; *Guantanamo: Honour Bound to Defend Freedom*, 2004; *Bloody Sunday: Scenes from the Saville Inquiry*, 2005.

11 The legal profession is still working out the precise implications of legislation such as the 1998 Human Rights Act and the 2000 Freedom of Information Act (2002 for Scotland). There is also, post 9/11, a heated

debate in Western culture about the rights of religious groups. In the UK this culminated in legislation against 'incitement to religious hatred' and in cultural crises such as those around the televising of the satirical musical *The Jerry Springer: The Opera* (transmitted on the BBC in 2005) and the stage play *Beshti* (which angry protesters prevented Birmingham Repertory Theatre from staging in 2004).

12 After a decade of high-profile cases, British case law on issues of privacy has begun to clarify. The case of Michael Douglas and Catherine Zeta-Jones versus *HELLO!* magazine in particular has facilitated this. A 2005 appeal left no clear winner in the case, but clarified the situation in respect of definitions of 'invasive' photography, the difference between privacy and commercial rights, and the limited financial ceilings likely to accrue from compensation claims. But as is often the case with the Law, the possession of private means is still no hindrance to getting what you want. Sarah Andrew – who received some of her training from Patrick Swaffer at Goodman Derrick – gave me the quoted view in an email of 13 September 2006.

13 Objections to *Hostages* began to be voiced in the press at the beginning of 1992, as much as eight months before transmission.

14 See www.ofcom.org.uk – where all Ofcom's regulatory and research material, including its 90-page 'Broadcasting Code', can be found.

15 Go to www.bbc.co.uk/guidelines/editorialguidelines/edguide for full details.

16 This is Brian Winston's term – see Winston (2000: 40).

17 *This Business of Television* was first published in 1991 (second edition 1998, third edition 2006). The book's subtitle tells its own story: 'A Practical Guide to the U.S. and International Television Industries for Producers, Executives, Marketers, Performers, Writers and Entrepreneurs'. The relevant section on docudrama in the latest edition is on pages 334–5.

18 See www.nbc.com, the NBC's corporate website.

19 See for example Baker (1995: 258–9), Rosenthal (1995: 212) and Bignell and Orlebar (2005: 183–4).

20 See Goodenough (1989: 5).

21 See also Horenstein *et al.* (1994: 380–1). Like many docudrama controversies, this one has rumbled on over the years. It may not disappear even with the demise of the compromised protagonist General Pinochet.

22 What is especially interesting here is the judge's apparent invocation (indeed, his misquotation) of the celebrated definition of documentary given by John Grierson in the 1930s (the 'creative treatment of actuality' – see also Chapter 4). As is often the case, Grierson's 'treatment' is rendered as 'interpretation', and his 'actuality' becomes 'reality'. Such semantic shifts bear out a widely held critical view that documentary's aesthetic power of 'creative interpretation' has been at least as important as its claim to represent the actual/real. This slippage between 'real' and 'true' has a long history. See also Winston (1995: 51ff) for an acerbic deconstruction of the phrase (though without reference to its first use in 1933 – see Chapter

4, note 6, of this book for a full reference).

23 Again, see Goodenough (1989) and Goodenough and Blumenthal (2006).

24 Organisations dedicated to bringing constitutional change into the public sphere (like Liberty, for example) were bitterly disappointed with the Freedom of Information Act, regarding it as essentially toothless.

25 This point, which his later books all defend in one way or another, is made in Hood (1994: 39).

26 Chapter 1 of Winston (2000) gives a full account of this scandal. It also offers a critique of the language of regulators. Winston is right to be concerned about the role of the press in all this. In Britain in June 1997, there was a renewal of serious debate about press intrusion into private life following *Guardian* editor Alan Rusbridger's 'James Cameron Memorial Lecture'. Rusbridger asked whether industry self-regulation was sufficient to curb tabloid interest in the sexual peccadilloes of the rich and famous, or whether legislation was required to facilitate more serious investigations of financial malpractice. The death of Diana, Princess of Wales, on 31 August 1997, fanned the flames and new guidelines from the Press Complaints Commission were issued in September 1997. British privacy laws have moved considerably in the past few years – see Dan Tench, 'Photo finish', *Guardian* (*Media* section), 23 May 2005, p. 14.

27 See Paget (1992: 154–79).

28 Swaffer's keynote contribution to the University of Birmingham 'Reality Time' Conference of 1 May 1996.

29 The 'D-Notice Committee', formed in 1912, comprises representatives of the military, civil service, and journalism (print and radio/television) amongst others. In the *Guardian* (*Media* section, 1 October 2001: 10), Jessica Hodgson notes: 'when … the government really wants to block information, it resorts to the Official Secrets Act'. The point of the committee, as she also remarks, is that it 'create[s] a point of liaison between the media and the government on delicate issues of national security'.

30 Thames has continued to operate as an independent television production company despite losing its franchise.

31 Tony Garnett, producer of *Cathy Come Home*, was another.

32 Rob Ritchie was speaking at the 'Reality Time' conference in Birmingham in April 1996. Aukin and McDougall were speaking at a BAFTA debate, 'True to the facts', held in London in March 1997.

33 This, again, was in a presentation at the 1996 'Reality Time' conference.

34 The earlier example of *In Suspicious Circumstances*, of course, demonstrates that dead protagonists only protect programme makers from the most directly obvious litigants.

35 'Flow' is a concept that has itself been much discussed in media studies; see Williams (1992) for the original idea and Corner (1999) (especially pp. 60–9) for a useful discussion of the debate that has followed Williams' intervention.

3

Codes, conventions and change

Docudramatic functions

More than a decade on from the first edition, the 'Siamese twin' term that I favoured then – dramadoc/docudrama – is no longer one I find useful for discussing current developments. Although many British filmmakers and critics will doubtless continue to use 'dramadoc' the domination of American culture worldwide virtually guarantees that 'docudrama' is the most widely understood term. 'Dramadoc' is rarely used by American writers (academic or otherwise).[1] The two terms are so interchangeable that the distinction is lost in all but the most detailed (and context-aware) discussions. This tendency was exacerbated in the last decade of the twentieth century with cinema's increased use of the docudrama and preference for that label. Overall it is just simpler to refer to the whole genre as 'docudrama'.

However this chapter on the form's principal codes and conventions is, perhaps, even more necessary than it was at the time of the book's first edition. It is codes and conventions to which people in a media-literate environment respond, and that they recognise prior to categorising what they watch. Categorisation has, if anything, become more contentious as a result of the increased experimentation that filmmakers have demonstrated. Everyone concerned with the film and television industries relies on the public's facility with codes and conventions. The tendency increasingly to create entertaining hybrids means that codes and conventions of docudrama have expanded either side of the millennium. But the following can still be safely asserted about the docudrama's aims and intentions:

(a) docudramas *re-tell events* from national or international histories, reviewing and/or celebrating these events (often at a suitable 'anniversary' point in history);

(b)   docudramas frequently *re-present* the careers of significant national or international figures, for broadly similar purposes as (a) above;

(c)   docudramas portray *issues of concern* to national or international – even local – communities, in order to provoke discussion about them. Occasionally, they may even enter the public sphere sufficiently to alter, or at least make contributions to, social and political issues.

(d)   docudramas focus upon *ordinary citizens and their stories*. Such individuals, thrust into the news through special (and often traumatic) experiences, can thus be seen as in some way representative – and may, again, contribute to change.

Finally:

(e)   docudramas consistently provoke questions about form. Specifically, they may generate debate about the *permissibility*, *usefulness*, even the *danger* of mixing documentary and drama. More generally, they may raise issues about representation itself.

Questions about form demonstrate a 'coming of age' for docudrama in particular, and for television in general. From the mid-1960s onwards levels of sophistication in production and consumption ensured a keener awareness of form than had previously been the case (see Chapter 5 for more on this). Questions about 'referentiality' and 'representation' cluster around docudrama, probing the extent of documentary and the efficacy of dramatic codings (Corner, 1996: 42–3). As well as the question of the legal legitimacy of having actors depict real-life persons discussed in the last chapter, the ethical dimension of this creative decision is often debated, especially when a docudrama is controversial. Even when it is not, I have found it to be the single issue that most student groups want to engage with immediately after viewing a docudrama. 'Was X *really* like that?' and 'Did Y *really* do that?' are often the immediate 'FAQs' of docudrama discussion. Although it is rarely possible to answer such fundamental questions authoritatively, it is certainly necessary to take account of them before taking discussion to the next level. Discussing docudrama is not dissimilar in some ways to discussing violence in the media. Even when the particular film that has generated the debate has not been seen by discussants, they will have a view of its probity and efficacy. Some commentators will always hold that the inherent representational dangers (of misleading a public assumed always to be gullible) far outweigh any informational advantages. The predominance of drama coding in modern docudrama has had the effect of ratcheting up these debates about what John Corner calls the 'manipulation' issue.

The docudrama comes to its audience with material that is usually already familiar (or if not exactly 'familiar', then often widely known). Trails before programmes, print media advertising, and captions or voiceovers in transmission highlight this familiarity for promotional and rhetorical purposes. Closeness in time to contemporary historical events helps, because the audience's knowledge of the events depicted will not need much refreshing prior to their representation. *Hostages*, although made a long time ago now, is still a good example. HBO/Granada's co-production followed up a major news story with which people throughout the Western world would have been (relatively) familiar in 1992–93. A ready-made audience in Britain and America was available, as producers were only too aware. The structure of the current affairs story was in place and seemed compelling. The 'plot' comprised, after all, kidnap, incarceration, torture, 'ransom', possible escape/release, even death. Arguably all this was already in the minds of the target audience. Alasdair Palmer's original treatment counted on exactly this. 'This is the story,' the first sentence reads, 'of how five men reacted to being kidnapped, chained to the floor, beaten, and held under the constant threat of death.' And then there was the additional connection to a wider debate about American and British foreign policy in the Middle East.

In the absence of well-known names and events, an historical or topical 'macro-story' can be hooked onto a lesser-known 'micro-story' (especially in pre-transmission publicity). *Fighting for Gemma* thus took its place in a long history of British television investigations of the nuclear fuel industry and its effects on the environment and on public health. In a standard docudrama ploy, the real life and real death of little Gemma D'Arcy was a *metonymic device* through which the dangers of nuclear power could be opened up for public debate. *Hostile Waters* presented its account of the saving of the world from nuclear holocaust by framing its story of a heroic submarine crew (a story allegedly suppressed in the West to the point of denial by the US military) with two 'master narratives' from twentieth-century history. The first (and older) one was the Cold War narrative of war game shadow-boxing by the Great Powers – of submarines trailing each other in the depths of the Atlantic, endlessly practising the moves of a nuclear endgame. The second narrative concerned the end-of-century (and pre-Fall of the Berlin Wall) story of the 1980s *rapprochement* between East and West. This story featured Reagan – the movie-President riding shotgun for the World – and Gorbachev, the 'modern' Soviet leader trying to move his nation beyond the time-warp of old-style communism.

Captions

Whether a docudrama's story is world-historical or local/national, whether it focuses on the personalities of the history books or those thrust into an unsought and unwished-for fame, whether the intended outcome is celebration or investigation, most docudramas deploy devices developed over a number of years that mark out the genre. Some derive from documentary, some from drama, and some from wider film and television custom and practice. Key conventions of the form cluster around the need for direct reference to real-life events. Such direct citation is often achieved by means of *captions* or *intertexts*, opening and closing films and linking individual scenes within them via still and rolling texts. Docudramas are routinely topped and tailed by captions, and as often as not lettering appears against a blank screen. In former times, the device of the news agency printer clattering out the latest news added urgency to information. As a verbal equivalent to the on-screen intertext, the *voice-over* announcement has been perennially useful. In former times, this was often a sepulchral male voice telling an audience that 'The Events You Are About To Witness Are True' (such voices habitually capitalised words).[2]

Captions in *Hostages* and *Fighting for Gemma* provide illustrations of the range of possibilities. In *Hostages*, of course, they were used to try to counter pre-transmission hostility. The *Hostages* pre-credits sequence is in many ways typical of the indispensable contextual-ising device that connects a film to its real-life referent through assertion, but untypical in its fending off of criticism. The very first film frame seen by the viewer contains white lettering centred on a black background. A classical film-music soundtrack builds, and the viewer sees/reads:

> Between 1984 and 1992 more than fifty
> Western citizens were held hostage in Beirut.
> This film dramatises incidents which illustrate
> what happened to some of them.

This opening caption, then, supplies time, place, indications about character focus ('Western citizens'), and the beginning of a dis-claimer (this dramatisation 'illustrates') which is to become quite detailed in this case. The visual and aural values are emphatically 'high concept' in that they are serious, cool in tone and well made.[3]

After about five seconds the caption starts to roll and the black background lightens, revealing the dawn scene of a bay with a town (Beirut) left of frame in the middle distance. The frame is carefully composed and the scene is both imposing and peaceful, an impres-sion reinforced by the strings-dominated music. Then, in deference to the real hostages' objections and the newspaper-inspired furore pre-transmission, the rolling captions extend both disclaimer and description of the 'illustration':

> Dialogue has been created based upon publicly
> available material, interviews with former hostages,
> their friends and relatives, diplomats and
> politicians from the United States, Europe and
> the Middle East.
> No endorsement has been sought or received
> from anyone depicted.

> To compress six years into two hours, chronology
> has been changed and some events have been
> amalgamated. The names of minor characters
> have also been altered.

Opening caption material often incorporates some kind of disclaimer like this one, acknowledging (as per television regulations) the partial nature of versions of events offered in dramatisation. But such a lengthy statement is rare (with the sentence about 'endorsement' being particularly interesting).

Whether brief or lengthy, this kind of disclaimer would be unthinkable in documentary and unnecessary in drama. Such captioning has been regarded with almost talismanic reverence in British television. Developed by Granada docudrama makers, it has been taken up by British regulators and policy makers (see again Chapter 2). Pioneered by Granada's current affairs series *World in Action* in the 1970s, the failsafe mechanism of 'labelling' is still widely recommended and used. Captioning, then, is multi-functional: it places the film historically; it sets the scene dramatically; it argues a representational case; it protects against legal action (see also, 'disclaimer', below). Many of these features are mirrored in closing captions. For example, the historical time-scale that looked backwards into the past at the beginning of the action, often tends to look forward at the film's conclusion. These captions classically tell the audience about outcomes (where known) and subsequent events in protagonists' lives. Docudrama is a form thus 'opened up' to historical time, its 'story-time' complicated by previous events, other contexts and future contingency.

The closing captions of *Fighting for Gemma* demonstrate both this convention and the extension of a disclaimer. It begins:

> Gemma D'Arcy died in September 1990,
> aged six.

> In October 1993, after an eight-month
> trial, a High Court judge decided that
> no link had been proved between a
> father's exposure to radiation and his
> child's cancer of the blood.

This caption fades, giving way to a second:

> British Nuclear Fuels, and its operations at
> Sellafield, were therefore not responsible,
> on the balance of probabilities, for the
> death of Elizabeth Reay's baby daughter or
> for Vivien Hope's illness.

After another fade, the third end-caption:

> Twelve days later, the government's Health
> and Safety Executive published a study
> indicating a possible link. The study showed
> the risk of illness to children in Seascale
> whose fathers worked at the plant before
> 1965 to be 14 times the national average.

Following this, the fourth and final caption appears:

> Martyn Day began re-assessing evidence
> of environmental exposure to radiation
> from the plant, for possible use in further
> cases against BNFL – including that of
> Gemma D'Arcy.

The whole sequence takes forty seconds of screen time. Its rhythm of presentation is solemn, the soundtrack silent, white lettering on black screen, each caption centred rather than rolled. Just before the final caption fades to give place to the rolling cast list and credits, Gemma's 'theme tune' for the film (Otis Redding's 'My Girl') poignantly breaks the silence. It fades in at about the time an average viewer might read as far as the last words on the final caption – Gemma's name. The cumulative effect is rather like reading an inscription on a gravestone (an appropriate model given the child-death of which the programme treats).

Legal as well as aesthetic considerations can be discerned in all this, helping editorially to angle the docudrama's conclusion. This not only maximises emotional impact, it also reduces BNFL's room for manoeuvre. The company's complicity in the death of children like Gemma was not proven so it was imperative to steer to the safe side of defamation. But the final captions of *Fighting for Gemma* can be read as *implying* a view about moral responsibility. In that sense it sides emotionally with the fight for Gemma outlined in the film, and undertaken historically by her parents and legal representative (the 'Martyn Day' of the final caption sequence, who led the legal team 'fighting for Gemma').

As they have become more and more hybrid, docudramas have increasingly featured actual protagonists as narrators or in voice-over. This variant has proved especially successful in examples like the 2003 film *Touching the Void*, and I shall say more about the implications of this development in the Chapter 8. The use of a protagonist as verbal caption was particularly striking in Oliver Hirschbiegel's 2004 film *Downfall* (German title: *Der Untergang*). About the last days of Adolf Hitler (and featuring a stunning impersonation of the Nazi dictator by Bruno Ganz), the film was partly based on a memoir by one of Hitler's wartime secretaries, Traudl Junge.[4] Junge appears at the beginning and end of the film. In the opening credit section, which lasts about a minute, her voice fades in as she recalls her wartime experience. The sequence ends with a freeze-frame on her 81-year-old face. This frame dissolves into a new frame showing the face of Alexandra Maria Lara, who plays her in the film, followed closely by a caption over action that gives time (November 1942) and place (Hitler's so-called 'Wolf's Lair' in East Prussia).

The closing credits are even more interesting from the point of view of codes and conventions. This sequence lasts a full four minutes. It begins with the final dramatic scene, where Lara-as-Junge escapes from Berlin. Four captions detailing historical information about the end of the Second World War follow (dates, statistics about total deaths and Jewish deaths in concentration camps). Then there is a lengthy sequence in which cast photographs are placed alongside written information about the historical characters they have played in the film. Twenty such individuals are presented. They include the usual suspects (Speer, Goering, Himmler, Bormann) as well as lesser known ones. Some of these – like SS man Rochus Misch – were still alive at the time of filming. The sequence culminates with Lara's photograph, in character as Junge. A reversal of the opening then occurs, with a sequence of the older, real, Junge in interview. She recounts how she came eventually to recognise her complicity with Nazism and its horrors. Passing a memorial to Sophie Scholl, she says, she noticed that they were the same age when Scholl was executed for opposing the Nazis in 1942. This was also the very year Junge herself started work as Hitler's secretary: 'At that moment I felt that being young was no excuse.'[5]

The essentially discursive nature of docudrama is well illustrated in these examples from 'high-concept' docudrama. In 'low-concept' films the tone of captions, as of much else, is much more varied. The potential for less solemnity was exploited to the full in the US network NBC's *Amy Fisher: My Story* (titled *Lethal Lolita* in the UK). The opening caption featured white italic writing on a black background and was underscored by a female voiceover reading the words for us in a markedly ironic tone:

> *This is Amy Fisher's story – her version*
> *of the truth. She says she had a partner*
> *in crime, the man she claims was*
> *her lover, Joey Buttafuoco.*
>
> *He has consistently denied any sexual*
> *involvement with her and any knowledge*
> *of the criminal activities you will see portrayed in this film.*

When this caption clears, the arch voice continues:

> Only they know what really happened.

The film's end-captions are similar; low-concept jokiness, reminiscent of tabloid prose, replaces high-concept seriousness.

As television formats have pushed at the margins between documentary and drama, captions have developed a rhetoric of their own. British playwright David Edgar once claimed, '[y]ou could chart the history of the docudrama by tracing its use of captions'.[6] Following *The Connection* case (see Chapter 2), documentary makers too began to be extra wary. *Shooters*, a 2000 film by Dan Reed for the *Cutting Edge* documentary series on Channel 4, offered this as its second and third on-screen captions:

> This film is based on original research.
> It tells a fictional story, set in these changing times.

> The scenes were improvised by
> non-actors, many of whom bring
> personal insight and experience
> to the parts they play.

The level of 'personal insight and experience' achieved by one of these 'non-actors' improvising scenes of inner city gun violence led to his face having to be pixelated in the film – 'for legal reasons', said a C4 continuity announcer pre-transmission.

Captions, then, set the scene, put the audience in touch with 'out-of-story' events and characters, negotiate representation codes, guard against legal repercussions and pitch claims for authenticity of varying kinds. Some of these functions are reiterated in the *disclaimer* – a rather more specialised kind of opening or closing caption. At one time in cinema history a standard rubric, such as 'No reference is intended to persons living or dead' or 'Based on a True Story', was sufficient. But films now often carry increasingly law-sensitive disclaimers. These are litigious times, and it is always worth watching all end-credits on reality-based feature films and television docudramas. Tim Robbins' 1995 *Dead Man Walking*, for example, ran this disclaimer caption before the credits:

> This film is inspired by the events in the life of
> Sister Helen Prejean, C.S.J., which she describes in
> her book *Dead man walking*. As a dramatization,
> composite and fictional characters and incidents
> have been used. Therefore no inference should be
> drawn from the events and characters presented
> here about any of the real persons connected
> with the life of Sister Helen Prejean, C.S.J.

The hand of the studio lawyer is evident in this meticulous stating of the obvious; there is all the difference in the (legal) world between Sister Helen Prejean, C.S.J., real-world individual and author of a book about her own life called *Dead Man Walking*, and 'Sister Helen Prejean, C.S.J.', a character played by actor Susan Sarandon in a feature film, also called *Dead Man Walking*.[7]

In addition to all this, *linking captions* are sometimes used to re-locate the narrative when a shift occurs in time and place. The narrative of *Hostile Waters* shuttles, often quite abruptly, between the virtually identical interiors of two submarines – the Russian K219 and the US *Aurora* – and their respective, identikit on-shore naval headquarters. The linking captions frequently needed to facilitate these shifts featured a teleprinter, its urgent sound and characteristic typography providing the equivalent of on-screen stage directions and enhancing dramatic tension. The hermetically sealed world of the submariner was also vividly evoked. Used to facilitate drama, this kind of device actually derives more from the codes of the documentary film than it does from drama (where stage directions are usually silent). Linking captions, then, can supply both a narrative and a dramatic function.

Voiceover and narration

The *voiceover* is another convention that docudrama shares with documentary film. It is true that some film dramas use character voiceover, but it tends to be seen as a rather antiquated device unless it can be used in ironically knowing ways.[8] Usually the device involves an unseen narrator addressing the audience directly. Voiceovers can be done by an actor-in-character from the docudrama, or by an established news anchor, or even by a real person from the pro-filmic events depicted. As the aural equivalent of the visual caption, the device has been used in the past to convey facts and information (see also Chapter 6), but today it tends to function as part of the dramatic *mise-en-scène*. In *Hostages*, for example, the voices of news reporters were used in the opening sequence to contextualise the conflict in Beirut and to add the note of urgency so prevalent in the voice of the on-the-spot reporter (see next section). In *Downfall*, as shown above, the individual who lived the experiences depicted appears in order to anchor the film's factuality.

The theoretical term *diegesis* covers all this. It refers to the method of narration employed in a film and is used to mark the degree to which necessary information is conveyed to an audience from *within* the story-world of the film. In realist film, information is mostly conveyed 'diegetically'. The audience receives it from the words of characters, from the *mise-en-scène* ('what is seen in the frame'), or from what the director, through their use of the camera, picks out for attention (depth of focus, angle of vision, camera movement etc. being crucial to this). In docudrama, captions are always 'non-diegetic' devices coming from *outside* the story-world. Voiceover too can be non-diegetic as described above. The function of these devices can be described as four-fold: to start us off with (or remind us of) the necessary prior knowledge of the non-story world (pre-story, as it were); to help the story take temporal and locational leaps within the unfolding narrative; to project us back into the real (non-story) world at the end of the film; and throughout to anchor story-in-history. Docudrama has a higher level of information to convey than most films and there is little choice but to mediate much of it non-diegetically. Here again, the docudrama is in the realm of documentary as much as it is in the realm of drama.

Documentary material

Use of *documentary material* is an important and distinctive convention of the part-fiction film that is docudrama. By this means information is supplied and credibility sought. Drawn from the same archives that supply news, current affairs and documentary, such material authenticates the docudrama as part-documentary, connecting it visibly to its documentary claims. Nowadays, this material rarely disrupts the narrative flow at a dramatic level, but it still provides vital contextualisation. Like captions, documentary material itself frequently has a dramatic function, setting the scene in time and place for the unfolding drama. Moreover, it plays a key role in drawing an audience into the docudrama through its rhetorical power as factual information. As Lipkin notes, the 'fusion' of documentary material with dramatic narratives 'makes docudrama particularly well suited to launch persuasive argument, when its narrative structure warrants the claims developing from documentary "data"' (2002: 55). Lipkin uses the verb 'warrant' a good deal in making his case for the modes of persuasion operating in docudrama. In its legalistic sense of 'guarantee[ing] as true', or making the attempt so to guarantee, it strikes me as highly apposite.[9]

Again *Hostages* provides an illustration. After the opening captions described above, the film cuts to a sequence that montages contemporary newsreel footage. The linking voiceover comprises fragments of news reports intercut with the images to establish the nature of the late 1980s conflict in Lebanon. The peace of the tranquil dawn-over-the-ocean opening shot is thus shattered in very specific ways by the documentary footage. Rocket launchers are shown firing right to left of frame (in viewing terms, towards the peaceful seaside town of the opening frames). The first newscaster voiceover is heard at this point: 'Lebanon is not the scene of one war but many ... '. The male voice has the urgent tones of the front-line television reporter and his voice fades to the next one in the montage. This is highly dramatic, and it 'hammocks' the film's credit sequence. Voices of Western newsreaders fade in and out with the jump cut visuals and a sense of urgency and danger is created. The scene is thereby set in two ways: there is literal scene-setting – in the visual form of real landscapes and places; and there is metaphorical (and historical) scene-setting in the form of voices intoning facts, information and moods about the Lebanon conflict. The joint visual and discursive mode is distinctive in the balance effected between pictures on screen and words on soundtrack.

The codes in this sequence are principally documentary: they function as non-diegetic captioning, but are 'semi-diegetic', to coin a word – they exist both *in* and *out* of the story-world. Although the footage is there to inform us directly about the historical situation in the Lebanon between 1984 and 1992 and to 'set the scene' (as a caption might), it is also used seamlessly within the dramatic action in order to progress the drama naturalistically. The first dramatic scenes in the opening section of *Hostages* are cut into the documentary news material in a rhythmical balance that, additionally, includes information about the cast. Killing several birds with one stone, the sequence seeks to draw its audience in with a blend of fact and fiction intended to be persuasive within documentary and drama terms. Modern credit sequences are often multi-layered in this way, to maximise the viewer's interest. In *Hostages* the first drama scene shows Jay O. Sanders as Terry Anderson, being snatched from the streets of Beirut by a Hezbollah kidnap squad. The second scene shows a similar fate happening to Josef Sommer as Tom Sutherland.

These dramatised scenes are confirmed by (simulated) news voiceovers identifying the victims and thus 'badging' the actors as their historical characters. In the first actual dialogue scene John McCarthy (played by Colin Firth) makes just such a news report. Ironically it is about Brian Keenan being taken hostage. In three neat dramatic steps we are presented with the four main players in the drama, the historical sequence of their abduction, and the general context of the conflict in Lebanon. That we are in the realm of drama on these occasions is obvious from the deliberate contrast in quality of the film stocks and shooting styles. The documentary footage reads as news – it has all the rough-and-ready hallmarks of being shot in natural light and under pressure (simple set-ups, lens flarings, occasional lack of focus, camera-shake, arbitrary framing). Whereas its quality as image is affected by circumstances when filmed and by being copied from archive sources, the drama footage is quite the opposite. Here we have multiple camera set-ups, conscious framings and focusing, and the smooth transitions of the continuity editing that is indispensable to realist film narrative. There are establishing shots of bombed-out streets; there is clear point-of-view identification of kidnappers and kidnapped through close-ups and eyeline matches. Dramatic depth is achieved in sequences such as the one in which Anderson is metonymically maltreated (his glasses knocked to the ground and shattered). Sutherland's point-of-view of the back of the limousine which will carry him into captivity has clarity of framing and focusing, but camera wobble conveys the naturalism of Sutherland's physical distress while simultaneously alluding to the documentary values of the previous newsreel footage.

In the docudrama these are mutually supporting camera rhetorics. As the sequences build, if there is an emphasis it is towards dramatic functioning. That which is forced on the news camera operator in the field – camera-shake (which has been seen authentically in the actuality montage) – is affected for dramatic purposes. Like the experienced speaker who uses the debating trick of putting facts and figures alongside an entertaining anecdote, the docudrama uses the continuous experience of viewing to fold two quite different techniques into one. The codes and conventions are mixed as a result of the development of the form, so that within a sequence such as this in a sophisticated modern docudrama they can scarcely be separated in analysis. The drama thus draws additional credibility from the documentary that has 'set the scene'.

In the first dialogue scene, a (fictional) news crew is shown in an establishing shot (with Firth/McCarthy centred in the frame). Firth/McCarthy gives us information about Keenan (whom we have yet to see) while the camera closes in on him. The camera finishes up in medium close-up on Firth/McCarthy's face. Around him the 'news crew' become part of the *mise-en-scène* establishing him as journalist-in-the-field. The factuality of this scene was challenged by Jill Morrell, who commented:

> It was weird seeing other people play us, but it all fell into perspective in the opening few minutes when John had been curiously transformed from producer to reporter. We all burst out laughing; it was simply incorrect. (McCarthy and Morrell, 1994: 616)

It was certainly possible to read this scene as a television reporter doing a piece-to-camera. Producer Sita Williams pointed out, however, that the camera set-up actually foregrounds the sound recordist's microphone and that there is no camera in sight – personnel wander about in a way that would not be possible for any piece-to-camera. Acknowledging that it was possible to mis-read the scene in the way that Morrell had, she refuted the idea that this had been the intention.[10]

Real and simulated news footage is used several times in *Hostages* and its primary function is the authentication evident in the opening sequence – it is used rhetorically and diegetically. Because it is used in this way slippage is always likely to occur and disputes like this one will occur at the (dramatic) edges of (documentary) truth claims. It is no wonder, then that the form is so hedged with disclaimers; no wonder, too, that it invites so readily rejections from participants. From an audience point of view, this can be destabilising, create doubt in viewers. Unfortunately for the makers, this was the ultimate effect on *Hostages*.

A further example of the use of documentary material is *Fighting for Gemma*, in which Britain's nuclear past is the focus for Scene 54 of the script. Here Martyn Day's legal team, in preparing their case, view actual 1950s newsreel footage about Windscale, the nuclear plant once supposed to be the solution to Britain's post-Second World War energy problems (a poor safety record led to its name being subsequently changed to Sellafield). By 1983, when Yorkshire Television made their documentary *Windscale – The Nuclear Laundry*, Sellafield too was being exposed as dangerous. This documentary on the problems associated with Sellafield's reprocessing plant is the one viewed by Day and his team in a scene in *Fighting for Gemma*. The use of this documentary material again has two main functions: documentarily, it helps the audience understand the 'backstory' of nuclear power (as above); dramatically, it enables the audience to share the legal team's learning curve on the whole complex issue. The mix of archive/library and acted reconstruction in the early part of *Hostages* is slightly different. Here it is more a *simulation of documentary material*, so closely are the actual and the fake newsreel intercut.

Increasingly, this technique has been used to develop character in the narrative, and dialogue sometimes occurs between figures in the drama and actual historical individuals, the two existing in different orders both of reality and representation. In *Hostages*, US President Ronald Reagan appears so often that his documentary image becomes a kind of character (a highly suitable role, perhaps, for the Hollywood President). First seen calling the Arabs 'barbarians' in the pre-credits sequence, he 'participates' directly in a scene depicting Terry Anderson's Christmas 1988 video message. The recorded message is such a faithful 'note for note' copy of Anderson's actual video that it is demonstrably a simulation. But whereas the scenes of the making of the video in Beirut, its transmission on US television and its reception in the home of his campaigning sister Peggy Say (Kathy Bates) are wholly acted, they are intercut with a documentary shot of Reagan's reaction at a White House press conference. With the actor Charlton Heston also in shot, Reagan gives his response to Anderson's video: 'I don't think that was Terry speaking. I think that was ... I think he had a script – that was given to him. When I was given a script, I always read the lines!' The sycophantic laughter that follows this shaft of wit underscores the film's theme of official muddle-headedness and collusion in keeping the hostages imprisoned for so long. A president-actor performing to camera does not get you out of a Beirut jail.

In *Fighting for Gemma*, the cutting together of footage from a Granada *Update* regional magazine programme with David Threlfall's performance as Martyn Day enables a similar 'virtual documentary' to be made out of Day's original *Update* dialogue with actual BNFL representatives. The makers were particularly pleased with this splice of the real and the performed. It sidestepped neatly BNFL's actual reluctance to have anything to do with the docudrama.[11] Another example is the 1988 *Shootdown* (about the downing of Korean Airlines Flight KAL 007 by Russian planes in 1983). Angela Lansbury (playing the mother of a victim) similarly 'participated' in an edition of the syndicated US television talk-show *Donahue*. Lansbury, like Threlfall, was simply called upon to replicate the words of the real mother, with Jerry Donahue responding through the original footage. We are not far in such scenes from the full-blown simulations of high-profile trials, like Sky News' daily re-enactments of the actual trial in their *The Michael Jackson Trial* (2005). Here, look-alikes of the principals performed repetitions of each day's hearing for evening transmission.[12]

The 'Long Island Lolita' trilogy, by contrast, was packed with openly simulated press conferences and journalistic ambushes of the principal protagonists using the stereotypes of film fiction. Broadcast and print journalists did indeed pursue the real protagonists in 1992, eagerly signing them up as soon as they could. In all three of the docudramas, they are portrayed by 'rent-a-media-mob' extras jostling hammily, thrusting out microphones and cameras. Their babble quietens quickly so that the story can be advanced via a scripted question. Such scenes could come from 1930s Hollywood; only popping flashbulbs are missing. 'Low-concept' docudrama needs such scenes purely as a narrative aid, not as an opportunity to add documentary credibility. The filmmakers offer enough for the drama and no more, and this is frequently the case in Hollywood-style docudrama. Conventions aim to knit together the documentary and the drama rhetorically, from within the parameters of film realism. News agencies' hounding of Amy Fisher and the others is recreated within the visual values of the made-for-TV movie not the documentary.

High-concept docudramas are much more likely to incorporate poor-quality (but 'dramatic' in a different sense) news images and devices. The presence of documentary material is in some ways a badge of quality. Sometimes docudramas provide an audience cue that such material is about to appear. *Hostages* uses a 'channel-zapping' visual/aural blip to assist the film's regular switches between archive and re-creation. This mimics the channel-surfing most audience members will have indulged in at some point in their viewing lives. Collaging in this way between different television stations and genres arguably promotes hybridity. The snow-and-static of the connective frame 'sutures' the polished frames of the drama to a documentary footage authenticated partly by its poor quality.[13] Reagan's comment on Anderson's performance is thus simultaneously within the drama (and is itself 'dramatic') and outside the drama (as a documentary image). Anderson's sister Peggy Say (Kathy Bates) comments as she watches her brother: '[the State Department] will say he was forced to read that.' A visual blip later and Reagan does just what she predicts. The docudrama narrative sequence is complete, the joins scarcely visible. The channel zapping convention is a direct acknowledgement of the continuum of mediations available in the world of television. All mediations, from news to cartoons are necessarily conventionalised, and the device is 'knowing' in the sense that it expects the audience to be media-literate enough to be able to see both with and through it. The device also betrays an anxiety, however: interrupting the dramatic diegesis is to be avoided at all costs in a media environment of short attention spans. In this early 1990s example, documentary functions actively within the drama. More recently, television has been more inventive in its use of documentary material in docudrama, more alive to the possibilities inherent in proclaiming its mixture of documentary and drama (see Chapter 8).

Drama conventions

Many of the other conventions of classic docudrama lie within the realm of *realist drama*. Modern practice in both television and film drama involves multiple camera set-ups on realistic sets or actual locations, 'key lighting', sound recorded for maximum clarity and narrative flow, continuity editing (minimising interruptions to narrative flow), non-diegetic music dubbed in post-production – in a word, the *gloss* of feature film. For performers the avoidance of direct address to camera is linked to believable physical behaviours reproducible to order. Most commonly scenes are filmed out of the narrative's chronological sequence, or *story-order*.[14] In casting broad resemblance to a real-world original can be an advantage and a 'low-key' acting style is often favoured. *Mise-en-scène*, so important in terms of information about character, is constrained in docudrama to replicate as far as possible real-world original interiors and exteriors. The general convention is for actors cast for resemblance to perform in recreated interiors.

In fact simulation of exterior scenes is sometimes nothing more than approximation. Alasdair Palmer did obtain some footage of the actual Beirut for *Hostages*, but most of the location filming was done, paradoxically, in Israel.[15] In *Goodbye My Love* there was some location work in the USA, mainly for house exteriors and car journey footage. By contrast, in a scene set in Portland International Airport, Oregon (Scene 183), the actual location was Manchester Airport. For most of the viewing public, perhaps, one airport is much like another. The routineness of real/fake exchanges at this level is rarely mentioned because it is so routinely accepted by most audiences. However, the town councillors of St Bees, a seaside resort in Cumbria, did object both to Granada and to their local MP, William Whitelaw, about a scene in *Fighting for Gemma*. They alleged that one particular scene showed tests for radiation levels being made on a beach recognisable as theirs. They argued that this could harm tourism. Such claims are perfectly understandable at a simple level of representation. The drama was using the beach metonymically – it stood for 'beaches tested for radiation'. But the councillors read the scene documentarily against the intentions of the filmmakers. In reception terms the recognition of somewhere one knows in a film drama is always more likely to cause alienation from the drama, puncturing the suspension of disbelief, rather than causing concern about what might be being said about that particular place. Such intrusion of the (unintended) documentary into drama as the St

Bees case was irritating for the filmmaker, but it came with the representational territory.

In early twenty-first century film and television, the use of small-scale metonyms for large subjects has increased. In Steven Spielberg's twenty-minute opening sequence for the 1998 film *Saving Private Ryan*, for example, the visceral visual style got the camera in close to the acted scene of GIs landing on Omaha beach in 1944. The dramatic effect of this foreshortening of perspective was to immerse the audience in the hectic and horrific view of the individual combat soldier. This 'witnessing' model was drawn consciously from Robert Capa's iconic action photographs taken at the time of the actual landing. A number of British films recalling and celebrating the final defeat of the Nazis and the 'Just War' have worked in a similar way. In *Dunkirk* (2001), *D-Day* (2004) and *D-Day to Berlin* (2005) archive (both black-and-white and colour footage) was mixed with recreated film scenes and, crucially, with personal testimony (see, again, Chapter 8). With a style that focuses on the small detail, all these films and mini-series were able advantageously to set scenes in miniature, as it were. A beach landing, a field in France, an operations room in an undesignated British country house or French chateau – all 'standing for' real historical locations seen in long view in archive footage. In *D-Day to Berlin*, the actor Nickolas Grace 'stood for' Field Marshal Montgomery in one scene, then the following scene presented the real, historical 'Monty' in newsreel fragment.

In the matter of casting, the convention for well-known public stories is often to go for a 'look-alike' performer, then to use the skills of actor, costumier and make-up artist to enhance resemblance. The created effect is sufficient for an audience to accept the simulated identity with no significant interruption to the suspension of disbelief that is a requirement for the enjoyment of realist drama. Nickolas Grace is a good example. He accurately mimicked Montgomery's characteristically retrusive 'r' which somehow sums up the real Field Marshal's peppery punctiliousness. In *Hostages* sufficient resemblance existed between, for example, actor Jay O. Sanders and Terry Anderson, and between Colin Firth and John McCarthy. In stories where protagonists are less well-known, such as the one told in *Fighting for Gemma*, or in stories where fame is so fleeting that the look-alike convention is not quite so urgent, such as the 'Long Island Lolita Triology', there is still some awareness that, in publicity at least, there may be advantages in being able to put performer and real person side by side. If anything, and perhaps inevitably, performers in drama in general are often slightly better looking than their real-life originals, and this often applies to docudrama too.

Two further drama conventions are often referred to in disclaimer captions. These are the *telescoping of events* and the creation of *composite characters*. Such devices point up the requirements that lurk undeclared behind the structuring in docudrama. The folding of real-world events and individuals into convenient dramatic units is done principally to achieve the economy needed for a good narrative dynamic. It is important that the story progresses at a rate suitable to a film's intended market slot (which might be a television or a cinema distribution network). This might mean that a series of complex events are summarised, or several individuals at the fringes of the real story are conflated. A basically fictional composite might even be given a real individual's name. Without these devices a story might be in real danger of becoming clogged with the kind of detail that exists in real life (where narratives tend not to be as tidy as they are in art) but is unsuitable in one or two hours of drama.

Hostages producer Sita Williams believed that one of the reasons for the relative failure of *Hostages* was because the team failed sufficiently to composite. The film did feature a large number of characters all with stories to tell. Williams felt in particular that the film 'undersold the women' (Keenan's two sisters, Jill Morrell and Anderson's sister Peggy Say). All, prominent in the actual story, are underdeveloped characters within the docudrama. Williams acknowledged that being 'properly ruthless' about these characters (i.e. 'drop[ping] them altogether') would have improved the film as drama because in docudrama it is necessary to 'filter out the number of characters so that the ideas and the issues are open through a limited number of characters whom the audience get to know and relate to'. But because the functions of the characters in the film duplicated their real-life roles (helpers to the heroes/hostages in the battle with the diplomats) the women could not be edited out completely; because they were relatively well-known in Britain and the USA (the film's principal markets) they could not easily be composited.

Detail of this kind might well be of interest, and might even be containable, in a documentary, but docudrama makers rightly fear it. Just as a film crew 'serve the camera' (see Chapter 1), documentary detail can only be justified in a docudrama while it 'serves the narrative'. The most obvious compositing in any docudrama tends to take place amongst antagonist characters, with whom an audience is not asked greatly to sympathise (much less empathise). In *Hostages* the presentation of the hostage-protagonists' Arab captor-antagonists and that of the politicians and diplomats who (so the film implies) prolonged their agony illustrates this. The politicians and (especially) the diplomats have such limited narrative functions – because they are at the margins of the experience being depicted – that they can only be dramatic stereotypes. By contrast, the Arab guards, while also recognisably stereotypical, are treated with a modicum of sympathy.[16]

Moments of *dramatic tension* and/or *dramatic irony*, the moments of disclosure, recognition and catharsis of classical drama, are part of docudrama plot construction. Actual situations are actively analysed and such moments highlighted in treatments of docudrama. In fiction film the need for such moments to be supplied regularly within a script has become programmed into screenwriters' courses and 'how to' books. The need to conform to the dominant structures of fiction film increases the temptation to invent dramatic tension and irony in docudramatic plotting if it does not already exist. But many real stories are easily structured in this way. In Alasdair Palmer's original treatment of the hostages' story, he highlights the key relationship between Keenan and McCarthy, a relationship of complementary opposites easily dramatised:

> If McCarthy saved Keenan from self-destructive rage, Keenan put steel into McCarthy's soul, and helped him to the strength he needed not to be scythed into submission by the guards and the dirt and degradation of his situation.

Palmer's treatment makes the moment when McCarthy and Keenan meet the dramatic climax to his proposed Part 1:

Without explanation, they are suddenly hurled, both naked and blind-folded, into the same pitch dark room. They say nothing for some time. Then McCarthy gradually slips down his blindfold, sees the stinking hirsute Keenan and says: 'Fuck me, it's Tom Gunn [*sic*]!' He then has to explain to Keenan who Tom Gunn is.[17]

This 'Treasure Island' moment did become Part 1's dramatic climax, and was the first appearance in the film of Ciaran Hinds playing Keenan. This relationship in the film is structured as the 'buddy movie' proposed by the treatment, and the narrative arc thus max-imises Keenan's significance. In drama's emotional trajectory ('hope and despair' following each other time and again in *Hostages*) the dramatic impact of the relationship between central characters is all-important. The separation of the two friends and fellow suffer-ers provides another dramatic cliff-hanger at the end of Part 2. In a film equivalent of the theatrical 'curtain line', Hinds/Keenan lifts his blindfold, finds himself alone in the cell and says: 'He'll be back. They'll not kill him. Just a few questions. He'll be back in a minute.' The docudrama again seeks a dramatic not documentary dynamic.

Editing out

The fear of losing an audience's attention often determines what factual material stays in and what is cut. Inevitably other kinds of factual material than people can be excessive in relation to the dynamics of drama. *Editing out* is thus unavoidable when plots are driven naturalistically. After many years of producing docudrama, Leslie Woodhead concluded that 'the most effective programmes satisfy almost Aristotelian rules of dramatic construction'. In his experience, he told me, 'the Aristotelian shape is an instinctive human impulse for narrative order rather than a planned strategy'. Sita Williams put it similarly, saying that it was necessary in docu-drama 'to – not simplify – but rationalise and structure in a more definite pattern than actually happens in reality'. For practical purposes, 'to rationalise and structure' dramatically means to follow the guiding principles of realist drama, cutting where necessary documentary material not crucial to the unfolding of the plot, the development of character.

Sometimes the sheer randomness inherent in the detail of real events and real lives is in danger of overwhelming docudrama. For example, in the story of *Fighting for Gemma* there is a lawyer called Martyn Day and a scientist called Philip Day. These two major figures are not related. No dramatist, however dedicated to realism, would write such a coincidence into their play for fear that the audience would ask irrelevant questions. In 1990, Peter Kosminsky's Yorkshire TV docudrama *Shoot to Kill* treated the events of the John Stalker inquiry into the Royal Ulster Constabulary's alleged policy of shooting to kill IRA suspects. Its writer Michael Eaton noted that he faced a huge problem in that all the main participants were called 'John'.[18] Required to stick to known facts as far as possible, only docudrama faces this difficulty, for in fiction a writer would always choose different names. The dramatic narrative of the contemporary docudrama being primarily one of character and relationships, documentary has a directly contrasting drive – to depict faithfully, and account for, events and their contexts.

The extra-textual

As sport on television features pre- and post-match analysis and discussion, so television docudrama is often preceded and followed by interview and discussion programmes. This marks the passage of a docudrama back into the public sphere. Sometimes such 'extra-textual' material is intended to supply the regulatory 'balance' or to conform to the codes of practice examined in Chapter 2. Jane Feuer calls these *extra-textual* elements 'nonstory materials' (1995: 35). The turbulence that results from screening a version of an anterior reality cannot be accommodated without further television talk (for this is what such TV programmes inevitably contain). This, then, is another convention of docudrama. In a similar way documentary theatre performances often trail in their wake such things as foyer displays of documentary material, extensive programme notes (even including facsimile documents), and post-performance discussion.[19] In television the extra-textual includes continuity announcements, talk-show appearances and discussion programmes. Newspaper campaigns, both for and against, can also be counted as part of docudrama's extra-textual. Cinema docudramas, too, sometimes provoke newspaper debate and increased television talk. Such events are as much a feature of the docudrama as the captions of their opening and closing sequences.

As part of the pre-publicity for *Hostages* in the USA, the real Tom Sutherland met his impersonator Josef Sommer on ABC's *Good Morning America* (16 February 1993) in front of an audience of nearly five million people. In contrast to this publicity-driven exercise, BBC2's arts magazine programme *The Late Show* offered a polarised debate (between those in favour of the docudrama and those against) on the night of the British transmission of *Hostages*. The framing question put by presenter Sarah Dunant was 'Is *Hostages* exploration of fact or exploitation through fiction?'. The tone was set by a news clip of Brian Keenan saying that Granada's film was not helping the hostages find 'a new bond of trust with the world'. Producer Alasdair Palmer faced a 'jury' of three, all of whom found the film wanting, and two charges: that *Hostages* was underdeveloped dramatically; and that its authority as fact was fatally undermined by the limitations of its form and the withdrawal of approval of the hostages themselves. This set-up condemned *Hostages* both as bad documentary and bad drama almost before the discussion started. The issues rehearsed included: individual privacy versus public interest, 'copyright' on personal experience, impartiality in broadcasters, and public trust in the inherent 'decency' of broadcasters.[20] As an indication of the way discussion of docudrama remains stuck in such grooves, consider television critic Paul Hoggart's view on *The Government Inspector* over a decade later in 2005. The docudrama, he claimed, 'relied overwhelmingly on our belief that we were being shown the inside story with meticulous accuracy. If we are then told that some of it is just dramatic interpretation ... this is completely undermined.' [21]

Another element of the extra-textual is the advertising of support-systems for victims and the traumatised. Following the screening of Granada's 1996 *Hillsborough* a continuity announcer voiced-over on-screen 'helpline' numbers thus:

> If you are distressed by this programme a helpline is now open [graphic for the 'Hillsborough Helpline' appears on screen] ... or if you have been

affected by the loss of a child and would like to talk to someone [graphic for 'The Child Death Helpline'].

In the northwest of England, the regional television morning discussion programme examined the trauma of the 1989 football stadium disaster further. The notion of police culpability, raised both in the campaign of the Hillsborough parents' group and in the film itself, focused the discussion. Websites too back up docudramas by deploying further information and when relevant furnishing the distressed with contacts (see Chapter 8 for more on this).

Both *Hostages* and *Hillsborough* caused media events. The negativity of the event for the former was a 'turn-off' factor. For the latter, a groundswell of public opinion carried the docudrama on a tide of sympathy towards a BAFTA television award in 1997. The actual case itself benefited from all this, for a judicial review was convened in 2000. More populist, and much more sympathetic, newspaper coverage reported the making of the film in the months leading up to transmission and in the days following. *The Daily Mirror* went as far as running a series of articles supporting the relatives' campaign, and reporters doorstepped the police officer many believed culpable. All this is an indication of the extent to which the extra-textual phenomenon can play a part in a docudrama's reception in the public sphere.[22]

Definitions

In docudrama, documentary's promise of 'privileged access' to information and to actuality is added to drama's promise of emotional understanding through 'second-order' experience. The camera accesses two different kinds of 'reality' – a record of external events (which still constitutes the basis of the documentary's appeal) and a simulated reality – that of acted events. The promise of the camera is to show events to an audience distant in place and time as though that audience were present (its documentary promise). This is extended, but only as a defining paradox, in the docudrama. The camera's promise cannot be fully delivered in actuality since there are places either where it cannot go or where it has missed its chance of going – its ubiquity is a convenient fiction rather than an actual fact. In the docudrama things that the camera has missed or that it can't get at (because 'the actual participants are dead or dutifully dumb', in Ian McBride's words) can still be shown – but only up to a point and at a price. Audiences who accept this extension of the camera's promise do so within the context of dramatic suspension of disbelief. There is also, perhaps, a general cultural need to believe the myth of the camera's universal access to be more than mythically true. Following transmission, and transformed by scepticism at the moment of reception, the form's bid for belief is as often *dis*abled by these factors as it is *en*abled. It is the docudrama's cultural fate to be believed and then disbelieved, so to speak.

The establishment of the broad conventions outlined above leads me to the task of definition. It is often the case in the arts that definition lags behind practice. But the difficulties peculiar to the docudrama have often been focused on the question of definition – as if clear categorisation would somehow solve the difficulties raised by the form. I do not believe this can happen. Definition alone can never hold back the tide of (mainly journalistic) unease and uncertainty about the form.[23] Historically, four key terms require definition, but I continue to hope that these definitions will serve primarily to provoke discussion and by so doing to increase understanding:

(1)   *Drama-documentary* uses the sequence of events from a real historical occurrence or situation and the identities of the principal protagonists to underpin a film script. A drama-documentary attempts to provoke debate about the significance of the events or occurrence. The resultant film usually follows and/or adapts a cinematic narrative structure and employs the standard naturalist or realist performance techniques of screen drama. If documentary material is directly presented at all, it is used in a way calculated to minimise disruption to the realist narrative. Substitute the adjective 'dramatised' for 'drama', remove the hyphen, and the term is perfectly clear: the film or play in question is a *documentary* that has been *dramatised* so that it *looks like a fiction film.*

(2)   *Documentary drama* uses an invented sequence of events and fictional protagonists to illustrate the salient features of real historical occurrences or situations. The film script may or

may not conform to a classic narrative structure; if it does not, documentary elements may be presented non-naturalistically and may actively disrupt the narrative. But 'documentary' in this form is just as likely to refer to style as to content and to be about the 'look' and 'sound' of documentary (hand-held cameras, location sound). A documentary drama in many cases is also structured as film realism. Assume 'documentary' to be an adjective rather than a noun and the term is perfectly clear: the film or play in question is a *drama* that *looks like a documentary*.

(3) *Faction* (a word once popular now little used) denotes a fiction that creates its basic structure using a real world template of events and characters. Factions rely on their audiences to connect with the 'out of story' factual template in reception, and do little within the work itself to effect this connection. Film naturalism is, almost inevitably, the staple dramatic means of representation.[24]

(4) *Dramadoc* and *docudrama* are contemporary shortened terms. The former describes television programmes that mainly follow the drama-documentary methodology. The latter is the more commonly used term in the cinema and in American television. I have argued on several occasions in this book that the two words are now used virtually interchangeably (thereby partly denying thirty years of practice) and that *docudrama* is now the more commonly used and most commonly understood term.

As I follow the historical development of docudrama in Chapters 5–8 I hope these definitions will clarify both how docudrama has evolved and how important it is to an understanding of the complex representations of real events available to screen media. First I shall trace some conceptual origins to this controversial form whose difficulties arise from its challenge to the limits of representation. Where, ultimately, has it come from? The answer to that question is very simple: it comes from a belief that truth can be established from evidence. Central to this belief is the almost mythic status of the camera as a provider of this commodity. The camera's power as witness is central to many cultural phenomena, the representational codes of the docudrama being one.

The camera's gaze

'Seeing is believing' became something of an article of faith for the twentieth century, along with the related idea that 'the camera cannot lie'. Towards the end of the century greater media sophistication in audiences in the developed world triggered doubts about both of these hoary aphorisms and the beliefs that lie behind them. The digital image, and the possibilities for fabrication inherent in digital technology, have eaten further into the faith in visible evidence (see Chapters 1 and 8). Although theorists began to demonstrate the constructed nature of all representation almost a generation ago, a belief in the evidential has proved difficult to shift and survives still in the public sphere – indeed, the public sphere could not survive without it. It is likely to continue to provide a basis at the very least for the archiving and use of the *document*, however defined. Since it would be difficult for societies of any kind to live without documents, there is a built-in guarantee for the continuance of the *documentary* too, perhaps.

In his history of the BBC, Asa Briggs observes that no one born after 1922 (when the BBC was formed) would really know what it was like to live in a world without broadcasting. This observation can be extended: no one born after 1945 will really know the pre-television world, and no one born after 1990 will really know the pre-digital world. There can be few people alive who have not spent much of their lives subjected to a variety of developing representational technologies. Even before initiation into the realm of language, infants are initiated into the realm of the camera's gaze, the 'being seen', by eager parents wishing to document first smiles, first steps, and so on, through the agency of the camera's lens. Indeed, it has become customary to document the very moment of birth. The Polaroid, the video, the digital camera and the mobile phone record the primal moment, technological midwives to the realm of representation into which humans are metaphorically thrust even as they are born. Major industries have grown up, and thrive, through the collective wish to record significant and insignificant life-moments. The same industries have democratised the ability to fulfil this desire through cheaper and cheaper routes to recording, processing and viewing.

The camera is one of the key inventions of the technological age. Like the internal combustion engine, the telephone and the computer, the camera was part of the twentieth century's transformation of time. Ways of being and seeing now accepted as the norm are actually part of a world created after the first Industrial Revolution, a world more individualised, less collective, than previous ones. The broad drift of civilised life since about 1850 can be summarised in Judith Williamson's succinct description of photography as 'a process developed historically alongside the modern bourgeois family' (1986: 125). Like so many of the great inventions of the last century and a half, the photographic and electronic cameras as developed by Western civilisations have been inexorably *privatising* instruments and those that have followed – the computer and the mobile phone – work similarly.

Faith in the image produced by the camera was grounded on two basic, and linked, premises that still patrol the boundaries between private and public experience. The first premise is that the camera will 'hold back time' (both private and public). This is the leap of faith made by all of us as we use our cameras in order to record those moments in our lives we wish to fix into memory – to record them for deferred contemplation and for memory. In photography they become, to use a paradoxical phrase, 'still moments' – they have no movement so are 'still', yet in fixing a moment they are enduring emblems of it.[25] Snatched from the flux of time they are 'still in' the former moment as we look at them again from times after them. Roland Barthes has referred to this as part of 'our mythic denial of an apprehension of death' (1993: 32). The camera's activities, in his word, 'puncture' our perception of the flow of time in unexpected ways. Within the unstudied detail to which it is always alert, he argues, lies the camera's power to fold time inwards (towards the past) and outwards (to the future). The camera is the indispensable pre-condition for what has become known as 'the postmodern' – that unfixing of linear, chronological, time that characterised the last twenty years of the twentieth century.[26]

As true for public as well as private moments, the 20:20 vision of hindsight will sometimes imbue a picture, still or moving, with a significance unimaginable to the actual recorder of the moment.

Consider, for example, the 'moment' of John F. Kennedy's death in 1963 as recorded by Abraham Zapruder, or the 'moment' when the first hijacked airliner hit the first of the Twin Towers on 9/11 in 2001. Both recorded a split second in which an event crossed-over into 'history'. Moments such as these are important enough to require representation beyond their time. Meanings must be made for them outside the specific, time-bound moment. Both sets of images have been endlessly re-run, and inserted into other film material documentary and dramatic, since the day the camera operators took them. As Bill Nichols has noted:

> The indexical bond of photochemical and electronic images to that which they represent, when framed by optical lenses that approximate the properties of the human eye, provides endless fascination and a seemingly irrefutable guarantee of authenticity. (1991: 149–50)

Access to moving images via the movie and video camera increases the paradox of the moment snatched from time, grounding memory not in lived reality but in re-produced photographic and electronic images which are not still like a photograph, but in motion every time those images are shown. In the realm of public affairs news footage takes on the role both of national historical family albums and of evidence. However, meaning is both revealed and concealed in iconic footage, the evidential status of which proves in most cases to be problematical. John F. Kennedy certainly dies again whenever the footage of his assassination is re-viewed, but do we understand this death any better? The 'absent-present' of the documentary image tantalises, and never more so than when we examine its promise of telling us what really happened on 22 November 1963 in Dallas, Texas.

The other major premise upon which the supremacy of the camera is built is that it will give us access to external events which otherwise would be lost except through the very different agency of *report*. The Zapruder footage is viewed again and again partly because it is always apparently more than an eyewitness report – it is a *record*. As such it ought to tell us more than a simple witness can, because the witness can only ever describe discursively what has passed before their eyes in the moment of its occurrence. Film taken from a camera that was really there ought to be able to say more – to solve the ongoing mystery of whether Kennedy was killed by more than one assassin, for example. This no-longer-innocent home movie has been scrutinised again and again; it has been subjected to fresh searches by new frame-by-frame analysis and by predictive computer technology. Yet, sphinx-like, it refuses all attempts to empty it of meaning. The more it is studied, the more it becomes evident that it is not, nor has it ever been, a transparent 'record' of the event it purports to depict.

In such moments as Kennedy's assassination if the camera does not lie then it riddles in paradoxical and inscrutable ways. As Art Simon has said, the footage haunts the history of the assassination:

> It is a history punctuated by faith in the film's revelatory power and by a crisis of interpretation. (1996: 35)

This was a moment fully as significant to a technological age, and subsequently as much mythologised as Oedipus's ancient discovery that taking filial relationships on trust and circumstantial evidence was potentially tragic. The emphasis has now shifted to the possibilities of construction and invention inherent in new post-production technologies, which threaten more and more the camera's potential as 'objective recorder' of pro-filmic events. Naive faith in direct access to events through the camera may have been challenged through theoretical debate, and may be under threat from new digital technology, but Western cultures continue to keep the faith because deferred promises of objective proof are historically grounded in ongoing technical advance.

There are many examples of this tendency to keep the faith despite intellectual scepticism. Technical progress, it was assumed, would always be making mediations somehow 'realer' than they were before. The record of an event, whether private or public, is always more authentic if it offers immediacy. But ultimately this immediacy – this authenticity – is dependent on *perception* rather than inherent in a *production*. Authenticity, like beauty, is in the eye of the beholder; it is easy to assert but more difficult to prove. As long ago as 1972 Nicholas Garnham pointed out that: 'the appearance of progress within [the documentary] aesthetic has been largely technical, the search for the Holy Grail of a totally transparent technique' (1972: 111). The search goes on, as witnessed by the late twentieth-century invention of the 'Steadicam' (a hydraulically balanced camera that allows its operator to move around during shooting without jerkiness resulting in the film image).

The search for transparency has developed sophisticated modes like the 'reflexive documentary', which shines a light on the work itself in order to reveal its constructed nature.[27] In Ross McElwee's *Sherman's March* (1986) or Michael Moore's *Roger and Me* (1989) the self-aware directors 'declare' their agency in constructing their films, making technique transparent in a provocative and amusing sense. Moore and McElwee act as *faux naif* reporters in their work, opening up the objective stance of the traditional documentary record by inflecting their reports with their personalities – anxious and neurotic in McElwee's case, ebullient and insouciant in Moore's. There is also the 'mock-documentary', like *The Blair Witch Project* (1999), which apes the conventions of the documentary in order both to satirise and to subvert them (see Roscoe and Hight, 2001).

Accepting convention

Docudrama's particular set of representational codes and conventions appeals to belief just like any kind of convention in representation, and the appeal to belief is anchored in a distinctively twentieth-century faith in images – especially moving ones – made by cameras. Conventions of any kind are, as Richard Sparkes has said, 'the condition on which the bargain of the suspension of disbelief is struck with the audience' (1992: 147). There is pleasure to be found in any set of conventions that are well understood and widely shared (but not yet ridiculed or despised). If, however, the conventions become out of date or difficult to give credence to, or if they have been trumped in some way by new forms, significant change must occur otherwise a form becomes obsolete. Conventions are always subject to a kind of 'Emperor's New Clothes' test, through which the majority of people will decline to question what they see most of the time on the majority of occasions. Indeed, acceptance of mediated forms in general depends on this. But the fable of the Emperor's New Clothes is also a warning. It is important sometimes to question what has been naturalised by convention. This is, of course, the very point of the fable: the unsophisticated child is so much more usefully critical than the sophisticated but sycophantic adult who cravenly kow-tows to the Emperor's vainglorious fantasy of importance.

The rise to prominence of television in the 1950s makes that its primal decade – the time of emergence for generic conventions of all kinds. It has been a gradual process for generic conventions to be questioned, both inside and outside the television industry, and then to be subtly altered over time. In the formative historical period of television, as John Corner has written:

> A primary factor in the formation of generic styles was the search for the distinctively 'televisual', which perhaps worked from cinematic, theatrical, radio, newspaper or music-hall precedents, but which then reshaped the material in ways which used the medium to the best possible advantage. (1991: 13)

The generic conventions inherent in docudrama are quintessentially *televisual.*[28]

Docudrama's continued prominence in television accounts in part for its becoming such a feature in cinema – the two industries being linked together like never before. The camera's apparent ability to go anywhere and see anything is both borrowed from documentary and current affairs on behalf of the drama, and extended by drama on behalf of documentary. They go together to increase the camera's truth-claim by denying its actual deficiency (it was not there in fact, but we can pretend it was in fiction). There is a disembodied air to the 'there-but-not-there' realm of the documentary record. Drama, by contrast, asserts an 'I-am-there-*now*' identificatory realm that counterbalances this. A several-bodied film crew has a hidden corporeal presence behind the camera lens in real time, but in television and/or cinema time (i.e. when we watch) there is only ever 'us alone' as we wrestle with the demands of evidence and belief. The desire to ratify emotionally what has been understood intellectually is a strong one. The camera's promise of complete seeing can only ever achieve completion if our emotions are stirred dramatically as well as our understanding increased intellectually. Docudrama's codes and conventions have been developed to try to achieve this if only we will believe. Perennially controversial, docudrama derives a kind of benefit in terms of conventions. The least remarked thing that any controversy in the arts does is to measure the degree of our willingness to accept conventions. The provenance of those conventions I have been discussing in this chapter can be clarified by examining some of the 'keywords' on which I have already been leaning heavily.

Notes

1   One of the few examples I have found in academic writing is Feuer (1995), where she talks of 'recent drama documentary films such as *Silkwood* (1983)' (41, footnote 2).
2   See also Paget (2000).
3   I am using here the terminology of Gary Edgerton's (1991) essay. His distinction relates to American 'high' and 'low concept' movies-of-the-week.
4   This book was written by Traudl Junge (1920–2002) and Melissa Müller and was published in Germany in 2002. Its English title is *Until the Final Hour*. Junge joined Hitler's staff in 1942, and was with him throughout the final days in the Berlin bunker. The book was written from notes made in 1946. In 2002 she was the subject of a German documentary, *Im toten Winkel* (English title: *Blind Spot*) directed by André Heller and Othmar Schmiderer). Interview footage from this film is seen in *Downfall*.
5   Junge's realisation that she could have seen through the iniquities of the Nazi regime as easily as Scholl came late, it may be felt, but better late than not at all. Scholl, her brother and a friend were members of a resistance group called the White Rose. They were executed for distributing anti-Nazi leaflets. Michael Verhoeven made a film on the subject, *The White Rose*, in 1982. Insdorf (1989) notes that the film ended with a caption pointing out that the Nazi state's verdicts on the group had never been put right by postwar governments in Germany, but that a public outcry had led to this being done (pp. 195–6).
6   David Edgar made this observation in his opening address to the 1996 'Reality Time' conference at the University of Birmingham.
7   When he makes docudrama Tim Robbins seems to take his responsibilities seriously. In his 1999 film *Cradle Will Rock* (which he scripted and directed) the opening captions give a very sharp potted history both of New Deal America and the 1930s international political scene that forms the backdrop to the film.
8   A good example of the 'knowing' voiceover in television is from the character Mary Alice (Brenda Strong) in the ABC's series *Desperate*

Housewives (2005–), shown on Channel 4 in the UK.

9 The dictionary definition is from the *Shorter Oxford English Dictionary* (1993 – 4th edn), vol. 2, p. 3626.

10 Williams also rejected the accusation that McCarthy's work in Beirut did not include direct reporting. McCarthy himself describes his work (as acting bureau chief for WTN) as: 'co-ordinat[ing] the activities of the camera crews and liais[ing] with London on the details of their coverage and the best means of shipping the cassettes', but Williams was adamant that occasional reporting tasks could and did occur. McCarthy partly corroborates this, writing in *Some Other Rainbow* about conducting interviews, accompanying the crews as they went about their work, and filing a report on Keenan's kidnapping (McCarthy and Morrell, 1994: 31–8).

11 Invited to put their perspective to Granada researchers, BNFL consistently demurred.

12 This show's star is Edward Moss who has made a living as a Michael Jackson look-alike for over a decade.

13 The theoretical term 'suture' usefully draws attention to the way the literal 'stitching together' of film frames by editing almost always guarantees a smooth narrative flow in realist film but can be discerned through analysis.

14 Some filmmakers – Ken Loach is one such – make a virtue of filming in story order to keep actors on their toes (see Chapter 6).

15 Sita Williams tells an instructive anecdote about this strange situation. One day the Israeli crew removed Marlboro cigarette packets from the Arab captors' table on the set, believing that these men would not buy a product made by a 'Great Satan' American company. In fact, this detail had been very carefully researched. The cigarette packets were duly reinstated.

16 Both Keenan and McCarthy present much bleaker pictures of their guards in their memoirs.

17 This is very 'accurate' in terms of the published memoirs – see McCarthy and Morrell (1994: 101) and Keenan (1992: 91) – apart from the mistake about the Robert Louis Stevenson character (Ben, not 'Tom', Gunn). Palmer was possibly thinking of the American poet. His treatment shows, too, how necessary it is to have an awareness of advertising breaks when writing for commercial television.

18 Michael Eaton was speaking at the 1996 'Reality Time' conference.

19 One celebrated American example was Donald Freed's 1970 play *Inquest*, which even had documentary material displayed in the street outside the New York theatre it was playing – see D. Freed (1970: 17).

20 The 'jury' comprised Peter Kosminsky, a maker of docudrama; Roger Bolton, maker of documentaries such as Thames TV's *Death on the Rock*; and broadcaster Mark Lawson, then television critic for the *Independent*.

21 *The Times*, Section 2, 18 March 2005: 23.

22 This officer had by now taken early retirement on health grounds. Some of the *Mirror*'s zeal may have derived from its fierce rivalry with the *Sun*,

a newspaper that had been spectacularly offensive about the actual Hillsborough incident. Alleging that Liverpudlian hooligans caused the disaster in the first place, and then robbed corpses, the paper is still shunned in Liverpool to some degree. In January 2007, at a game against Arsenal, the crowd organised a protest against former *Sun* editor Kelvin MacKenzie's continued assertion that fans had behaved badly, indeed criminally, at Hillsborough in 1989.

23 See, for example, Lynne Truss's remark in her *Times* review of *Killing Me Softly* (a dramadoc about Sara Thornton, a woman who was jailed for killing her husband then released after a campaign): 'With docudrama, two types of reality fight it out, and neither wins' (8 July 1996).

24 In a similar way to 'faction', 'theatre of fact' was once a popular alternative term for 'documentary theatre'.

25 John Corner's phrase 'captured moment', introduced in a fascinating essay on convergences between documentary painting, photography and film, conveys a similarly paradoxical conceptual reach (2007: 11).

26 Hutcheon (1988) is a useful introduction to this difficult area of theoretical debate.

27 Bill Nichols offers 'six modes of representation that function something like sub-genres of documentary' (2001: 99). The full list is: 'poetic, expository, participatory, observational, reflexive, performative'. His Chapter 6 discusses the characteristics of each.

28 Commentators from Caryl Doncaster in 1956 to David Edgar in 1981 have made this point; the docudrama (like the talk-show, the sit-com, the soap-opera, and the news broadcast) is a television form; there is nothing quite like it in other visual media.

4

Keywords, key debates

Wordsearch

When the eminent British cultural theorist Raymond Williams published *Keywords* in 1976, he intended an 'inquiry into a *vocabulary*' (1988: 15 – his emphasis).[1] Williams took language fundamentally as a thing of *use* – shaped by the people who speak it, in the context of the living cultures within which language is embedded and the societies in which people live. He traced slippages in meanings in commonly used words, noting the important nuances generated thereby. 'Keywords', he argued, acquire cultural resonances partly because the very commonness of their usage leads to an unquestioning acceptance that their meaning can be taken for granted. Wherever he found what he took to be 'unquestioning acceptance' he cast his forensic light. His analysis illuminated the process by which meanings have been, are being, and will go on being contested and changed. Cultures are living things, condensing around 'key words'. Such words mark out points of interest, contestation and anxiety. They offer insights into how cultures work.

This chapter is inspired by this great theorist's example. I want to scrutinise further the provisional definitions offered in Chapter 3 and through this to demonstrate the parameters of change within the docudrama form. The sheer proliferation of words and phases coined to categorise forms that mix drama and documentary is in itself remarkable. Phrases, compound nouns and noun coinages have been drawn mainly from four root words, all of which have cultural histories. The words are *documentary, drama, fact,* and *fiction* and I will group them under three combinative categories:

(1) Combinations using *documentary* and *drama* that either begin

with documentary, or use a corruption or derivative of that word, or that modify documentary with a prefix of some kind. Hence:

- *semi-documentary*
- *documentary-style*
- *documentary drama* (also *documentary-drama*, and *documentary/drama*)
- *docudrama* (also *docu-drama*, *docu/drama*)
- *docutainment* (also *infotainment*)
- *docu-soap*

The last two coinages lead to the heart of a cultural dilemma that is focused as much on the information/entertainment binary as on the fact/fiction one, but I am arguing that each coinage signals an intention both to inform (documentary) and to entertain (drama). Marking a development that has taken place since the first edition of this book, I am adding two more coinages to this group:

- *docu-opera*
- *docu-musical*

In Chapter 8 I shall further discuss these examples of 'inter-generic hybridisation'[2], but it is worth remarking here that their structures are fundamentally dramatic – as, of course, are those of the operas and musicals 'proper' to which they allude in practice.

(2) Combinations that lead with 'drama', or a derivative of that word:

- *dramatised documentary*
- *dramatic documentary*
- *drama documentary* (also *drama-documentary* and *drama/documentary*)
- *dramadoc* (*drama-doc* and *drama/doc*)
- *dramatic reconstruction*

While the latter more commonly refers to segments within television programmes, I incorporate it into this list because the notion of 'reconstruction' clearly identifies a documentary claim.

(3) Noun-coinages and phrases based around the idea of fact or truth and either using or implying the word fiction:

- *faction*
- *fact-based drama*
- *fact-fiction drama (fact/fiction drama)*
- *Based on Fact* – as in 'made-for-TV movie based on fact', or 'drama based on fact'. This phrase tends to come with capitals, as does:
- *Based on a True Story*

The last two phrases in this category are more often used of cinema features, and I shall examine the reasons for this further in Chapters 6 and 7.

The 'wordsearch' for a phrase that will tie docudrama down has been going on since television in particular became culturally important. Other phrases that fall outside my categories but which I find useful have come from Carveth (1993), Feuer (1995), and Kerr (1990). 'Headline docudrama' (Carveth) and 'trauma drama' (Feuer) give due attention both to docudrama's tabloid sensationalism and its interest in the realm of the psycho-social, while Kerr's abbreviation 'DD' – the initial letters of the two most popular coinages 'documentary drama' and 'drama documentary'– is tempting.[3] But usage of these terms is sporadic compared to the originary words above that have fed the most common coinages.

From such a proliferation of terms, it is of course possible to argue either that the genre is sick or that it is healthy. In my view it indicates something more interesting: that docudrama marks a point of cultural turbulence made up in almost equal parts of fascination and uncertainty (amounting sometimes to anxiety). This phenomenon is part of a generalised cultural and social concern about truth and reality. The form and its debates highlight questions about the nature of the real and the limits of representation, about film and television and the access offered through screenings of all kinds to social reality. Television's very ubiquity lies at the heart of the problem and marks it as a more important medium than film in a social sense. This most popular and accessible of media has provoked worry in governments of all political persuasions in all nation states, with the idea of regulation and legal intervention never very far away. John Caughie put this succinctly when he remarked 'it is an uncertainty as to what can and cannot be shown which creates nervous reactions within institutional control' (1981: 329). Political 'nervous reactions' are exacerbated by this *mass* medium. The effects of any kind of mediation may be a cause for concern, but minority mediations – *avant garde* theatre, for example – are more widely tolerated by the authorities, less often regarded as threatening, and therefore allowed to exist relatively free of regulation. In many respects the histories of television's development both internationally and nationally have been about the ways populations would be permitted to talk about themselves and to each other and about how they would negotiate within those permissions. Television has raised more difficulties for the common culture than the older mass media. The docudrama was born to television out of early cinema (see Chapters 6 and 7 on this); in a medium subject to high levels of surveillance and control it should be no surprise that this is a much scrutinised programme category (as I tried to show in Chapter 2).

'Pure' documentary films have been (and still are) routinely described as 'dramatic' if they are made coherent through narrative structuring and the foregrounding of character, but such a claim has not been contentious in quite the same way as when it is reversed and the 'documentary' claim is made by mixed-form drama. It was mainly in television that the terms listed above became the focus for real discussion, because television developed mixed forms more systematically than either theatre or film. It did this for two main reasons, one philosophical the other technological: firstly, television's dual mission to instruct and to entertain a mass audience in their own homes determined matters of content and form; secondly, its need to overcome the early inadequacies of electronic reproduction led programme makers to 'reconstruct' almost as a reflex (see Chapter 6). So, although coinages were evident from the moment John Grierson adapted the French term '*documentaire*' and talked for the first time about 'documentary' film, it is to television one must look for evidence of attempts to categorise and define.

Of all the words and word coinages listed, 'documentary drama', 'drama documentary', and the shortened forms 'docudrama' and 'dramadoc' are the most common. The minor adaptations signalled by linkages (hyphens, slashes and the like) are revealing. They enact conceptual confusion, uncertainty and anxiety at the level of typography. They are typographical nervous ticks. The adjective-noun combination is turned into a compound noun by means of these grammatical umbilical cords. The kind of visual balanced equality found between two keywords is that which practitioners have pleaded, and critics found lacking, for over half a century. However they appear, typographically the weight of the phrases is always tipped towards the second word. Thus, just as 'dramatic' in the phrase 'dramatic documentary' acts as an adjective modifying the noun 'documentary', so 'drama documentary' is a documentary treated dramatically. 'Drama-documentary' has the appearance at least of a balance in which both will be equally present.

Following the same logic, 'documentary drama', a drama treated 'documentarily', also has a balance. But definitional problems have not gone away so easily. Consider, for example, what is different if 'historical' is substituted for 'documentary'. 'Historical drama' tells us immediately that we are to expect a play based on known history (or, more precisely 'History' – an academic subject with which most people will be familiar). The phrase makes a statement primarily about the *origins* of the filmmakers' narrative material. 'Documentary drama', however, is just as likely to tell us about the *style* in which a film is made as it is about its basis in 'documents', however defined.

Unfortunately, and confusingly, both the drama-documentary and documentary drama terms are often used as if there were no difference between them. They have become routinely interchangeable even within the same book. The excellent 1986 collection *All Our Yesterdays*, for example, describes the 1966 television film *Cathy Come Home* as a 'documentary-drama' on page 95, while a still from the film on page 199 has the caption 'the Ken Loach/Tony Garnett drama documentary' (Barr, 1986). Neither has shortening the terms improved clarity. 'Dramadoc' and 'docudrama' are frequently used (at least in British journalism and academic writing) and appear on the surface to be corruptions of the original compound nouns 'drama documentary' and 'documentary drama'. But these words, too, are used interchangeably in Britain. So, for example, *Killing Me Softly* (transmitted on ITV in 1996) was reviewed by Lynne Truss in *The Times* as a 'docudrama' on 8 July of that year, while Allison Pearson in the *Observer* six days later called it a 'drama-documentary'.

This is not simply lazy usage: it marks the condensation of a cultural crux around language. Once American and British industrial practice began to synergise in the last quarter of the twentieth century, 'docudrama' gradually became the favoured term. It is principally in Britain that 'drama-documentary' and 'drama-doc' has currency and continues to be used. As with all shortened forms, these corruptions are highly convenient, especially in speech. Shortened forms began to creep into use in the 1960s, by which time television had been around long enough to be both familiar and to be treated in some quarters with elitist contempt. 'Drama' is a difficult word to shorten, but 'documentary' (four syllables if pronounced 'doc-u-men-t'ry', and five if fully enunciated – 'doc-u-ment-a-ry') almost begs to be reduced to the 'doc' or 'docu' stub. Docudrama is sometimes seen as a form that deviates from some notionally 'pure' documentary norm, and the shortening of the word may contribute to this view. Less serious, more likely to be frivolously entertaining at some level, docudrama has been treated with critical suspicion in which 'drama' contaminates 'documentary'. The implication that a documentary would be a more serious and more honourable treatment of the events in the external world to which a film alludes is a common critical move. Dramas that 'protect the innocent' by changing names and locations (what I am calling 'documentary dramas') are sometimes perceived as more honourable in this regard, but they are still tarred with the brush of an inaccuracy and frivolity which, in obscuring and exaggerating for dramatic purposes, can distort serious subjects. Ongoing attempts to negotiate a path amongst competing terms have resulted in a confusion that can only be untangled by a review of the history of both practice and usage of each term. Raymond Williams' remark about his own 'keywords' is salutary here:

> Every word which I have included has at some time, in the course of some argument, virtually forced itself on my attention because the problems of its meanings seemed to me inextricably bound up with the problems it was being used to discuss. (1976: 15)

In general, writing about docudrama has a similar tendency.

Barbara Foley defines the documentary novel as 'near the border' between factual and fictional discourses but asserts that 'it does not propose an *eradication* of the border' (1986: 25 – my emphasis).[4] This, in a nutshell, is my view of the docudrama. The practical and theoretical traversing of the border between documentary and drama, fact and fiction, is of the utmost importance culturally, but a border is the necessary condition for the act of crossing. Documentary's declared links with pro-filmic reality still give it a sharper evidential quality and claim than fiction, and the docudrama continues to borrow this. Drama continues to have a grasp on the popular Imaginary. The mixed form in film and television has consistently mapped the shifting nature of the border between two important cultural impulses. As Goodwin and Kerr once put it: '[t]elevision "drama-documentary" is not a programme category, it is a debate. And that debate has ranged so widely across programme forms that it is very difficult indeed to pin down' (1983: 1). Kerr found it difficult to go beyond this notion six years later. It is 'not so much a distinct genre,' he writes (1990: 76), 'as a debate about genre distinctions'.

This academic view is endorsed by practitioners such as McBride and Woodhead. The latter told me he prefers to think of the form as a 'spectrum':

> with all the blurry edges that implies. I can appreciate the value to your students of having access to a more defined taxonomy, but as a practitioner of this odd trade, I'm only too conscious of adapting the form anew for every dramadoc I'm involved with.

Practitioners, then, are almost as troubled about definition as academics (though it should be noted that, in common with most people who have worked for Granada, 'dramadoc' remains

Woodhead's preferred term). Two things keep the 'debate' going and keep fuelling the effort to define as well as describe. The first is a continued demand for clear definition (if not taxonomy) on the part of students, non-academic commentators and, not least, ordinary viewers. This fire is continually stoked by print journalists. Television journalists and programme makers believe the reason for this is that newspapers feel threatened by the investigative power of television, and see the docudrama as a weak point. Ian McBride's view is representative of the professional practitioner:

> It makes a good story to 'flam up' the row about drama-documentary. For the newspapers, there's what I would describe as a needle factor in all this – you're either treading on their territory or you're stealing their clothes. That ignores the fact that most of the substantial investigative journalism in the last five years, maybe in the last decade, has been on television.

If that last sentence reads as *hubris* it is worth noting that, following the furore about Carlton Television's *The Connection*, the then editor of the *Guardian* newspaper Alan Rusbridger (who was also the prime mover in his newspaper's investigation of the fakery in that television documentary) greeted the ITC's judgement on the programme with a degree of triumphalism. The punitive fine was, he claimed, 'a wake-up call to the whole [television] industry' (5 December 1998 – and see again the discussion of this case in the Introduction).

Secondly, as John Hartley has remarked, the inherent institutional conservatism of television leaves it 'characterised by a will to limit its own excess, to settle its significations into established, taken-for-granted, common senses' (1992: 37). There is a common desire in broadcasters themselves, in other words, for what Hartley calls 'clean' boundaries in television. 'Dirty' forms complicate this, and it suits an industry reliant on combinations of governmental and commercial goodwill to argue that it can regulate itself. The effort to be precise acknowledges a kind of responsibility towards content fundamental to the contract that broadcasters have with their audiences. Proliferation of 'guidelines on practice', an increase in the pressures around legalling, and the shift in emphasis in regulation following digitalisation all indicate continuing pressure, as I argued in Chapter 2.

The occasional nature of docudrama and the rows it even more occasionally creates cause further difficulty. Mixtures of drama and documentary do not constitute a genre in quite the same way as, for example, soaps, or sit-coms, or the police/hospital series, all of which are regular features of television programming. Whether terrestrial or non-terrestrial, these genres are ever-present in schedules. They are found at least once a week and are regularly updated stylistically to suit new demands. But the television docudrama is more usually a response to a very particular situation. Because it is occasional, arguments about it do not tend to progress; they are simply revisited again and again. In an effort to unpick the confusions I shall now examine my keywords in order to trace the way in which the different phrasal configurations have come to be as they are. I will work with easily accessible dictionary definitions (the two-volume *Shorter Oxford English Dictionary* – henceforth *SOED* – 1993). For terms not in the dictionary I shall cite critical writing.

Keyword 1 – 'Drama'

I start with the word 'drama' rather than the word 'documentary', yet it is almost always a film's moral and ethical right to the designation 'documentary' that provokes debate when mixed forms are under discussion. While people are happy on the whole to assume common understanding of 'drama', they want to know the basis for any documentary claim. Whenever mixed forms have been defined or described there has always tended to be a concentration on the word 'documentary' in the compound noun and a taking-for-granted of 'drama'. This is partly why I am starting with this word; but also, it happens to be the word with the longest history.

It is relatively easy to agree on what constitutes 'drama'. With 'drama', an expressive and aesthetical basis for understanding is usually sufficient. Moral and ethical considerations are not absent when drama is under discussion, but they only become contentious in relation to content. But even the briefest survey of the etymology of 'drama' demonstrates that it is not without its anomalies. The dictionary takes us first to a late Latin word derived from the earlier Greek word *dran*, 'to do' (*SOED* 1, 1993: 743). This word for a kind of action entered English in the early sixteenth century via a French word, *drame*. In the Elizabethan and Jacobean periods, the institution of 'theatre' – and the practice of 'drama' therein – staked out its cultural importance as a representation of actions, and this has become established and accepted. The earliest recorded meanings of drama refer to 'plays', or dialogue compositions in verse and prose, that have 'high emotional content'. Their 'composition and presentation' has often been termed 'the Drama' (the capitalised usage dating from the early seventeenth century – when plays began to be part of an industry).

This explanation ignores the fact that 'the Drama', like any human activity, is always situated in history and as such subject to different inflections at different times. Even drama as apparently universal in its depiction of human motives, feelings and emotions as the plays of William Shakespeare was an important ground for contemporary discussion of essentially social and political matters. If it were not so, the real historical Ben Jonson would not have been imprisoned as a result of his part in the writing of the contentious 1597 play *The Isle of Dogs*, and Shakespeare himself would not have been summoned to Star Chamber to explain why his company had been so willing to perform his play about regicide (*Richard II*) to an audience of rebels the very day before an attempted rebellion against Elizabeth I (Essex's Rebellion, 1601). These plays were *dangerous* in their time. Even with much contemporary theatre trying hard to relate the Jonson and Shakespeare it produces to current events, it is hard to imagine such an outcome in the twenty-first century.[5]

Metaphorical use of the word derives from these meanings. Thus something described as a 'drama' covers happenings of 'high emotional content' that occur in the real world. This usage has proliferated with news media from the nineteenth century onwards. Similarly, notions of 'narrative', 'plot' and 'character' have been transposed into common usage for descriptions of actual occurrences as 'story' acquired its news resonances. Psychological identification with 'protagonists' (main characters), dislike of 'antagonists' (opposers of main characters), and even the presence of 'catharsis' (or emotional release) have been imported wholesale into current affairs and news coverage, making for more vivid copy for the journalist.[6] The end result is that everyday events are now routinely described as 'dramatic' when they exhibit, or seem to exhibit, the contrived structural elements of the staged drama. Narrative completion, another structural notion deriving from the early eighteenth century, has also been important to the development of this usage. A derivative of the concept of narrative completion, 'closure', crossed over into popular psychology (and thence critical terminology) at the end of the twentieth century.

Conversely, resemblances to 'real life' are a frequent feature of the definitions of 'drama' in non-specialist dictionaries and in ordinary conversation. Thus a mid-twentieth-century inflection created the meaning: 'dramatic quality; interest, excitement', indicating that the presence of 'drama' in an action fictional or otherwise will infallibly spice it up. This is the very stuff of tabloid journalism in both print and television. It helps make television news simultaneously informative and entertaining and guarantees it to its audience as both understandable and watchable. It ensures high audience figures for news programming and, ultimately, the profitability of specialist organisations like CNN. It is responsible for the 'Reality TV' strand that has so dominated the beginning of the twenty-first century and that began with such programmes as America's *Rescue 911*, and Britain's *Crimewatch UK*.

In summary: we currently have notions of 'drama' whose history in the English language goes back more than four hundred years. There are two quite distinct resonances to the word: 'Drama', which is the practice of a representation in some way 'staged'; and 'drama', the affective quality inherent in actions of all kinds, including those in the real world. 'Drama' itself, then, comes down to us clothed in elements both factual and fictional that are more complex than they look. But it is worth insisting that in grammatical terms the word is a *noun*, whose function is to *name* or *designate*. The adjective form of this noun is 'dramatic', and this word applies the attributes of the noun to another noun entity.

'Dramatic' is the word Raymond Williams chose to examine in *Keywords*. He makes the important point that all examples in the drama word group 'belong to a traceable habit of mind in which life is seen, or is claimed to be seen, *through art*' (1976: 109–10 –

my emphasis). It is this 'habit of mind' and its documentary mirror image – the seeing of art in life – that established the dominance of the naturalist/realist dramatic form in the twentieth century. It also established the documentary impulse as a kind of equal-but-opposite means to the expressive dramatic one of understanding the phenomenal world. The secondary experiential dimension to art-works is folded back into our 'real', ongoing, sometimes incomprehensible, primary experience of life. If experience of life can be construed within art-work paradigms in this way, a further level of sophistication arrives when those paradigms themselves begin to define primary experiences.

This is of great importance to television, a medium that John Corner sees as having both 'centrifugal' and 'centripetal' tendencies (1995: 5). Through the former, he says, television has a 'powerful capacity ... to draw towards itself and incorporate (in the process, transforming) broader aspects of the culture'; through the latter, 'television seem[s] to project its images, character types, catch-phrases and latest creations to the widest edges of the culture, per-meating if not dominating the conduct of other cultural affairs'. In this way, television's construction of 'drama' has extended well beyond the remit of the fictional. Operating centrifugally it has drawn in the categories of news, current affairs and documentary to the extent that they are perceived as dramas. The 'pushing out' of re-formed images, character types, and so on (the centripetal part of the operation) validates television's power within culture.

The new medium has indeed added to a general cultural tendency to shape life through art. This has a very long history indeed. It is partly what leads Alan Rosenthal to reassure a would-be screen-play writer that: '[t]he elements of drama are universal and exist as much, if not more, in real life than in fiction' (1995: 53). As I pointed out in Chapter 3, it also led producer Leslie Woodhead to believe that 'almost Aristotelian rules' govern the best kinds of prac-tice in docudrama as in drama. Such assumptions are the result of both centrifugal and centripetal tendencies, the former drawing in that which seems to work often enough for 'universal' qualities to be claimed, the latter pushing out the notion that there really is no other way for any story to be told *dramatically*. As Woodhead's comment on Aristotle indirectly demonstrates, Western civilisation has an acute awareness of precedent in drama that stretches far beyond the four centuries of usage in the English language. There exists both a solid body of practice in drama going back to the Greek playwright Aeschylus in the fifth century BC and an equally solid body of dramatic theory going back to his fellow Greek Aristotle in the third century BC. Since Aristotle wrote his *Poetics*, writers have regularly engaged with the formal and theoretical tasks of definition and speculation about drama in the abstract, basing their explorations on observed practice and their sense of an 'ideal' drama.

Dramatists and writers from Sir Philip Sidney in the sixteenth century through Diderot in the eighteenth and Brecht and Artaud in the twentieth to the academic semioticians of the present day, have continued to ponder and theorise drama's capacity to produce a perspective on human behaviour and history unavailable to other kinds of artistic endeavour. There is, so to speak, a track record on drama that can make it seem unproblematical. In our own inexorably realist times, we know we have to pretend most drama is real to get anything from it. In such a climate it is no wonder that claiming closeness to fact came to seem an advantage when making a film or teleplay. But this very claim of 'closeness to fact' brings the argument within range of the apparently equal-but-opposite term 'documentary' in the specialist category 'docudrama'.

Keyword 2 – 'Documentary'

In NBC's 1950s cop show *Dragnet* the main character, Sergeant Joe Friday, proclaimed over the introductory music and credits: 'The story you are about to see is true; the names have been changed to protect the innocent.'[7] This became a popular catch-phrase, but it had a point: the series took its stories from Los Angeles police files and thus has a claim to the label 'documentary drama' as I defined it earlier. The generality of docudrama as currently practised has more in common with my definition of the drama-documentary, in that the truth-claim is taken one stage further. Real-world namings and the resultant claim on 'documentary' results in a presentation that is always more than just 'drama'.

Etymologically, 'documentary' is much a more recent word than 'drama' – its history really begins in the nineteenth century (*SOED* 1, 1993: 719). Although it may be a relatively less theorised concept historically, it generated a high level of definitional activity in the twentieth century as a result of its identification with the camera. Its usage coincides with early film history. The considerable anxiety within anglophone (and other) cultural communities about 'documentary' shows nowhere better than in the frequent attempts to define it. The first recorded usages of the adjective 'documentary' in English are from the early nineteenth century and can be linked to a post-Enlightenment faith in positivist science and rationality. The word developed from a much earlier noun, 'document', that had been in use from around 1400 and that is clearly connected to the invention of the printing press and the resultant production of paper records of events and transactions. A verb, 'to document', was in use by the middle of the seventeenth century as a print culture took hold in Europe.

Latin rather than Greek was the language of origin for both these words, and the law, heavily dependent upon Latin models of practice, was the active source of their use. Importantly, these words are connected from the earliest times with 'evidence' and the 'evidential'. The 'document' and the action of 'documenting' constituted a means of 'objectifying' evidence that could then be produced and accepted as 'objective' proof positive in courts of law. Evidence in the cause of social change is prominent in this history. The social reformer Jeremy Bentham was an early user of 'documentary' as an adjective deriving from the noun and verb. He used the phrase 'documentary evidence' when writing on the law in 1827. Thomas Carlyle, another secular 'thinker/leader' in a very nineteenth-century sense, used the word in his book *Sartor Resartus* (1831), again as an adjective denoting proof of a material, rather than conceptual, kind. The notion of evidence was also instrumental in grounding the modern study of history; Lord Macauley uses 'documentary evidence' in his *History of England* (1855). These kinds of writing contributed to the innate worthiness and seriousness that continue to hover around the idea of the documentary.

The use of 'documentary' as *noun* came much later, with the new arts and technologies of the early twentieth century. Camera-based media of still photography and film were prominent in this development, each medium making evidential claims as both witness and recorder of the real. These claims resided partly in the belief that these modes of representation were inherently superior to those possible in other, older media. Accordingly, dictionaries tend to take from books on film their examples of documentary as noun. Other coinages such as 'documentarian' and 'documentarist' come also from the mid-twentieth-century, and derive from the media (including television – see *SOED* 1, 1993: 719). Boleslaw Matuszewski, an early filmmaker from Poland, is frequently cited as the first individual to assert the power of the cinema to document. In the pamphlet *Une nouvelle source de l'histoire*, published in Paris in 1898, he remarked 'one could wish that other historical documents could have the same degree of accuracy of evidence and certainty' as he felt were evident in 'cinematic documents' (Macdonald and Cousins, 1996: 14).[8]

In 1926 the (for some) Father of the Documentary John Grierson wrote in a review of Robert Flaherty's *Moana* that the film had 'documentary value' (Hardy, 1979: 11). But it was 1933 before he composed, almost as an afterthought, his celebrated definitional phrase 'the creative treatment of actuality'.[9] This marked an important moment in which a genre could be said to have been born. Its discursive priorities included the affective as well as the evidential. Many writers claim (as I did in Chapter 1) that it is the point of reception that actually secures the categorisation for any genre; the proof of the pudding, so to speak, is in its acceptance by the spectator. About documentary Brian Winston says, '[t]he claim on "truth" necessary for the documentary exactly depends on spectators "constructed" by the genre to have that prior faith in it' (1995: 104). This 'construction' began in the 1920s and was secured by1930s practices before becoming a widespread phenomenon.[10]

There are now strong traditions of documentary practice in film, radio and television from which to work in discussions about the form. These too are not without theoretical dispute, and the label 'documentary' could hardly be said to be uncontentious. But no one would deny that the 'documentary' has a place in understandings of the media both specialist and general. If nothing else, the term serves as an indexical indicator – it 'points to' a kind of film that claims (and, more importantly, an audience knows it claims) directly to access the external world. Theoreticians may argue that we cannot trust what we see, and this is a valuable message to receive insofar as it makes us ask questions and positions us as sophisticated spectators. But fundamentally, both the sophisticated and the naïve spectator start from a basic position of acceptance – that the documentary, however reflexive, offers a declared engagement with unrehearsed reality rather than the simulated one of rehearsed drama.

Historically, the attraction of early documentary was its seemingly unstructured, 'unconstructed' nature – in comparison with the drama's inherently structured and constructed nature. A wish to hold on to this notion of the unstructured led the American 'direct cinema' practitioners of the 1960s to base their claim to authenticity on a 'found' quality of unpremeditated, discovered unfolding. Although the equally 'artful' nature of the documentary is now well established, a widespread faith in the form remains. As the Beirut hostages specifically noted in their letter to the newspapers of 21 September 1992, a documentary treatment of their experiences would have been acceptable to them in a way that Granada's docudrama was not. When it appears in the schedules, 'documentary' offers first and foremost a guarantee to its audience that the profilmic is closer to its surface than it can possibly be in any drama. The credibility of this claim has been somewhat undermined by a variety of eventualities: documentary's own codes and conventions have been worked over by filmmakers; they have come under the harder scrutiny of audiences more media-literate than those of the past; and of course filmmakers have come under more and more pressure to deliver a commercially viable product. The status of the documentary as 'fact' is less certain than it once was. This is borne out by the emergence of a mock-documentary form both on television and in the cinema that relies on common understandings of the codes and conventions of the documentary proper (see Roscoe and Hight, 2001).

Keyword 3 – 'Fact'

'Fact' has come a long way from its late fifteenth-century meanings of 'an action' or 'a deed', deriving from the Latin *facere* – to
do (*SOED* 1, 1993: 903). It first picked up the inflection of 'truth;
reality' in the sixteenth century. The antithesis with 'fiction' began
to develop in this period also, as did its connection with 'document'
and 'evidence'. These connections appear inevitable in our own
time, but they are the result of cultural imperatives – in particular
those relating to property rights. In the seventeenth century a 'fact'
began to mark the notion of the legally verifiable – the dictionary
uses the phrase 'a datum of experience'. This again was useful in
the emergent institutions of the law and in the rise of the 'private
citizen' owning property. This resonance in turn facilitated the shift
in the rationalist eighteenth century to the legalistic phrases 'basis
for inference' and 'interpretation'. Such phraseology enabled courts
of law to accept verbal and other evidence of occurrences as admis-
sible to their processes.

All these meanings fed the pervasive twentieth-century Western
democratic notion that there is an essential factual level to things
that is:

• prior to interpretation;
• 'unbiased' and thus free of ideology; and
• to be respected and protected as originary and disinterested.

The quasi-religious level to which 'fact' had risen by the early twentieth century is epitomised by the 1926 dictum of the *Manchester
Guardian*'s editor C. P. Scott: 'Comment is free, facts are sacred.' In
the twentieth century, derivatives such as 'facticity' and 'factuality'
(*SOED* 1, 1993: 903–4) are indicators of the kind of tinkering with
terms that attempts greater exactitude and that would have 'fact'
itself floating free as an ideal term. And yet suspicion and scepticism remain, encouraged by the post-industrial alienation of populations accustomed to mistrusting authority. Who is offering these
facts to us? How can we be sure we have been given all the facts?
Are other facts being suppressed? If so, by whose agency, by what
mechanisms and to what purpose? Can we trust facts given, or are
there others, equally credible, that will come to light later? An all-

too human desire to trust in something is often undermined by an equally human suspicion that *something* is missing (even if we are not sure what).

Docudrama's truth-claim, based as it is on 'fact' and derived from the linkage of the documentary with systems of incontrovertible facts, is frequently wrecked on the rocks of such scepticism. And the more the photographic and electronic media claim the fact, paradoxically the more their audience have tended to grow in doubt. The suspicion that facts are never what they seem is now so endemic in Western and other media-literate societies that it amounts almost to a creed ('Don't believe everything you see!'). 'Seeing is believing' is countered by a suspicion bordering on certainty that mediation will always obscure as much as it reveals. The new age of digital manipulation of images has, of course, exacerbated the sceptical turn.[11]

Keyword 4 – 'Fiction'

The Latin root of 'fiction' is *fingere*, to fashion; so fourteenth- and fifteenth-century Anglicisation of Old French produced the verb 'to feign' (*SOED* 1, 1993: 941). Although 'feigned' implied an untruth of a kind, it was a weak implication – rather like 'pretending'. It was certainly not a word as morally loaded as 'faking' is today. 'Feigning' denoted an imaginative, even idealised, activity and was not perceived with the kind of moral outrage implied in the notion of an outright lie. It is salutary to consider here how sophisticated the early modern period was in this reasoning. Its sophistication was unlike our own, of course, but in an age when language itself was excitingly volatile the skill of imaginative *apprehension* was often valued above that of more rational *comprehension*. So in Elizabethan times poets like Sir Philip Sidney leapt to poetry's defence, claiming that in its 'feigning' it produced higher, purer, more ideal versions of truth than less imaginative forms of writing. In *A Midsummer Night's Dream*, written in the late 1590s, Shakespeare's Theseus observes that 'shaping fantasies ... apprehend/More than cool reason ever comprehends' (V. I: 5–6) – he is disapproving of this, but he is a character in a play that challenges this disapproval.

Sidney's 1580 defence of his art, *The Apologie for Poetrie*, marked the emergence of the imaginative, the fictional, into English culture's classificatory system. The written output of narratives derived from the imagination solidified in later centuries around the composition and production of stories and novels in particular. By the nineteenth century, the prose 'novel' (see *SOED* 2, 1993: 1948–9) had become the dominant cultural form with a reach well beyond a middle-class readership thanks to industrial printing processes and the circulating library. Insofar as film and television inherited a popular storytelling function from the nineteenth-century novel, their dramatic products have also become classifiable as 'fictions', and are routinely described by the adjective 'fictional' (a nineteenth-century coinage itself dependent upon the emergent novel).[12]

By the early twentieth century the category 'non-fiction' makes its appearance in the lexicon as an opposite to the factual. Williams calls this a 'curious ... back-formation ... at times made equivalent to "serious" reading'. It depends, he says, upon 'the conventional (and *artificial*) contrast between fiction and fact'(1976: 134 – my emphasis). Nothing could better illustrate the cultural distinctions routinely made between words that have come to symbolise the serious and the frivolous, the sacred and the profane. This binary divide bedevils discussion of the docudrama still; indeed it bedevils the very study of culture. The level of seriousness inherent in the fact, the document and the evidential inform the concept and category of 'non-fiction'. The 'documentary' film and television programme exists historically within this category and this reasoning.[13]

The 'documentary', then, descends to us trailing clouds of seriousness acquired through contact with terminology opposed to the frivolous and the entertaining. Through its supposed access to the phenomenal world, it holds the promise of a special kind of insight into and control of the external world. The control is inherent in the knowledge and information made available; herein lies the instructional and educational thrust of the documentary impulse. 'Fiction' and 'drama', on the other hand, come to us separated from seriousness by a nineteenth-century cultural shift that has resulted in a perception that these are peripheral activities, associated with leisure and 'non-serious' aspects of life. They may be fun, but they are not real, not fact. Inherently they are fabrications, a species of lying –

thus runs this line of argument. The American comedian George Burns once remarked the importance to the actor of sincerity: 'Once you can fake that you can do anything!' Like a good many jokes, his one-liner lays bare a cultural crux. Overt performance, by its very nature, can never be trusted completely. Yet the emotional dimension of the drama promises another kind of understanding that audiences continue to seek. Drama may be simulation, but the desire for emotional knowledge fuels a different kind of seeking and a different kind of final 'truth'.

It is as well at this point to remind ourselves that 'drama' and 'documentary' do not automatically map on to 'fiction' and 'fact'. Andrew Goodwin notes that the first two words refer to 'practices [which] ... overlap considerably' while the latter pair of words 'are not ... mutually exclusive' (1986:11). Andrew Higson, in his turn, warns that the 'powerful differentiation ... between "realism" and "escapism" ... is not ... reducible to a distinction between "fact" and "fiction"' (1986: 81). Whenever the debate over docudrama raises its head, it is often as a direct result of a determination to regard all these categories as separable when they are demonstrably not so, whether in history, in theory or in practice. The wish to separate is perfectly understandable at one level: a 'fully-fashioned imaginative reality' originating in the mind of an author or authors is different from an anterior reality, if only in the sense that the anterior reality is doubly accessible – through both the research material (when recoverable) and the resultant constructed work. The 'fully-fashioned' version, meanwhile, is a thing of autobiographical fragments, of half-remembered and mis-remembered moments, of fantasy and imagination – in a word, of *apprehension*. Harder to pin down, it is thus easier to mystify. David Hare has vividly described the conscious/sub-conscious genesis of his 1978 play (subsequently a successful 1985 film) *Plenty* set during and after the Second World War. Hare recalled: 'I had originally been attracted by a statistic, *which I now cannot place*, that 75 per cent of the women flown behind the lines for the Special Operations Executive were subsequently divorced after the war' (1984: 15 – my emphasis). Nothing could better exemplify the distance between documentary and drama in practice; nor could anything better exemplify the difference between a documentary play and a 'history play' (Hare's preferred designation for his work). A documentary play, for whatever medium, had better be able to show whence its information comes.

Coinages and compound nouns

Dictionaries have increasingly been forced to take note of the coinages and compound nouns forged from 'drama', 'documentary', 'fact' and 'fiction'. To take coinages first, 'Docudrama' is categorised in the *SOED* as a 'M20' (middle of the twentieth century) word. It is explained in terms of its constituent elements, which are then (somewhat bizarrely) turned round: '[f. DOCUMENTARY + DRAMA] = DRAMA-documentary'. The word is accorded a separate entry from 'documentary', as is the very recent coinage 'docutainment' ('L20 ... documentary film or programme designed as entertainment' – all three words: *SOED* 1, 1993: 719). It is interesting to note how readily the editors of *SOED* reverse the words on either side of the equals sign. Compilers of dictionaries are as much recorders of usage as readers of critical theory, so the problematical nature of the reversal does not concern them.

Not even this kind of minimal definition is offered for 'drama-doc'. The noun coinage and its definition are simply appended to the other meanings of drama, and no date is given: '*Comb*: **drama-doc** *slang*, **drama-documentary** a film (esp. for television) dramatising or based on real events' (*SOED* 1, 1993: 743). The dictionary, then, proposes equivalence between the two compound nouns and their corruptions – effectively, they are one and the same. Meanwhile, the crucial coinage from 'fact' and 'fiction' – 'faction' – has its own entry even though the term is no longer much used: 'M20 [Blend of FACT and FICTION *n*.] Fiction based on real events or characters, documentary fiction; an example of this' (*SOED* 1, 1993: 904).

The two really important compound noun keywords – 'documentary drama' and 'drama-documentary' – are, of course, what have given rise to the shortened 'docudrama' and 'dramadoc'. 'Documentary drama' has a well-established history, which is complicated by the fact that its early models are drawn from the theatre not television or film. 'Documentary drama' and 'documentary theatre' derive from oppositional European theatre practices of the period between the two world wars. Beginning as an adjective + noun combination, by the time of certain celebrated stage plays of the 1960s the separate words comprising the term had acquired a kind of equal status. Particularly in the work of the German theatre director Erwin Piscator in West Berlin between 1950 and 1965, documentary drama came to mean dramatisations that utilised technological features (such as slide projections and loudspeakers) to relay facts to an audience and to signify a dramatic method-ology that diverged from the dominant naturalism/social realism to include two-dimensional 'characters' who could represent abstrac-tions (rather like the creations of medieval religious drama).

Piscator's post-war practice actually harked back to the 1920s and 1930s, when Russian and German communist troupes and the US Federal Theatre Project's journalistic 'Living Newspaper Unit' extended the reach of non-naturalistic theatre styles. This connec-tion with European left-wing politics proved the undoing of early American theatrical experiment. The war years and the McCarthy period virtually expunged that type of theatre in the USA, and the continuity was partially lost in Europe too. This history is more clearly rendered in the term 'documentary theatre'. The resur-gence of this form in the 1960s saw a great many serious issues investigated and not just in Piscator's productions. The theatrical style pioneered by Piscator and by Bertolt Brecht was in a sense re-discovered after the Second World War. When published, the texts of these 1960s plays were labelled 'documentary dramas'. One example, Rolf Hochhuth's 1963 play *The Representative*, was about the Holocaust. Its documentary element was mainly to be found in lengthy published 'stage directions' (which were in effect footnotes), but other documentary dramas openly displayed their factual basis in the manner of Piscator's earlier work in Weimar Germany. In Britain somewhat similar work was produced by Joan Littlewood and Theatre Workshop – the 1963 play *Oh What a Lovely War* – and in 1965 Peter Brook and the Royal Shakespeare Company produced a play about the Vietnam war called *U.S.*. These plays were labelled 'theatre of fact' at the time. American plays like Father Daniel Berrigan's 1968 *The Trial of the Catonsville Nine* (about

Vietnam 'draft dodgers') and Donald Freed's 1970 *Inquest* (about the Rosenberg trial) were similarly designated.[14]

Specialist reference books on theatre and drama tend to follow either theatrical or television traditions of usage but usually fail to make clear which and rarely attempt to explain both. The *Batsford Dictionary of Drama*, for example, defines 'documentary drama' as 'a drama which deals with contemporary social problems, usually in a direct and naturalistic way' (Hodgson, 1988: 100). Naturalism, however, can only be inferred from some of types of play, and to exclude others flies in the face of dramatic history. The Batsford definition relies more on the *Cathy Come Home* type of television play than on theatre plays such as *The Representative* (a play written in blank verse) or Theatre Workshop's *Oh What a Lovely War* or Arthur Kopit's 1968 *Indians* (both of which incorporate non-naturalistic styles). I have described documentary dramas as 'plays with a close relationship to their factual base ... a twentieth-century extension of historical drama or the *pièce à these* where the factual basis gives the action its credibility' (see Chambers, 2002: 214). The 'close relationship' can mean that the documentary material that inspired the play in the first place can be directly exhibited in the performance and can 'show through' the fiction in a variety of ways – the 'extension' is inherent in the technological means of presentation.

Normally, documentary material is included in dramas that have a *polemical* purpose – the company and/or writer(s) wishing to argue a case forcefully, and generally in opposition to an established point of view. So Hochhuth wished to point an accusatory finger at the Vatican in terms of its wartime failure to stand against Nazi Holocaust policies; the Theatre Workshop company wished to challenge received wisdoms about the First World War, and Arthur Kopit sought to set the record straight regarding the US military's treatment of Native Americans in the 'frontier' years. 'Documents' as evidence of facts are either quoted or shown directly to the audience in the Piscatorian theatre tradition. In the television tradition they are embedded in a predominantly naturalistic playing style via voiceover, documentary footage and visuals. It must be stressed, however, that 'docudrama' has little or no connection with a theatrical tradition that endures to this day as a weapon of opposition in the

Third World. It has also enjoyed a resurgence in recent years in the UK and the USA.[15] But documentary film and television does share the campaigning aim of theatre in the Piscatorian/Brechtian tradition. Documentary productions in all media are often put together rather in the way a prosecuting counsel might assemble a case, with governments or their institutions as the 'accused'.[16]

Ian McBride's view is representative of television professionals: 'I don't think most viewers, or most people, can handle the distinction between "documentary drama" and "drama-documentary". I think the distinction is completely lost.' Docudrama is now a form, in Daniel Dayan and Elihu Katz's phrase, 'preoccupied less with the factual than with the meaningful' (see Smith 1995: 185). Its relationship with drama, perhaps, is clearer than its relationship to documentary in contemporary practice. The worth of individual docudramas is still judged in both aesthetic and informational senses, but much discussion is indistinguishable from that related to other kinds of television drama. On television screens and in the multiplexes alike, similar visual and dramatic values are in play.

If common usage is blind to distinctions, the easiest way forward is to say that in most docudrama, the dramatic element controls the documentary. It diverts the film into structures and rhetorics associated with naturalist/realist drama, such as:

- rehearsed and 'staged' action;
- recognisable '3D' characters;
- plots coherent in terms of time and space;
- dialogue-based scenes that illustrate character and develop plot;
- mix of studio and location setting;
- camera shots suited to 'clean' narrative; and
- clear and directed sound.

In some examples of documentary drama, on the other hand, the documentary element exerts more control and diverts the film more clearly into documentary structures and rhetorics. Here, formal features have included:

- some improvisation in scripting and acting (use of non-actors);
- voiceover commentary;
- real locations – indoors and out;

- 'wildtrack' and/or live sound;
- improvised hand-held camera work; and
- plentiful captioning and other documentary visuals (graphs, charts, etc.).

I was wrong, in 1998, to take the view that 'documentary drama' was a variant that existed only briefly and that it was unlikely to re-emerge. It has made a triumphant comeback in the early 2000s. 'What if' docudramas in particular have re-emerged on British television. In classic docudrama, too, the formally disruptive is once more spicing up the dominant fictional mode. A 'documentary style' in a film or television drama, however, will still often refer to style as much as content.[17]

Phrases incorporating the words 'drama' and 'documentary' have been used loosely, to say the least – as have 'dramadoc' and 'docudrama'. But the two commonest terms deriving from the history of the mixed form – 'drama-documentary' and 'documentary drama' – are still potentially useful critical tools. The persistence of such phrases in critical writing has meant that it has become axiomatic to define them in two particular ways – either to call attention to the institutional base for a programme (linking it to the discursive priorities of an entertainment/drama or a news/documentary department) or to analyse a programme's formal properties (locating them in modes of address emanating from, and comparable to, drama or documentary 'pure'). Thus, a news and current affairs department of a television company, making journalistic use of dramatic structures and techniques to 'get where the camera can't go' produces a drama-documentary. John Corner's insistence on the phrase 'dramatised documentary' makes this construction of adjective-modifying-a-noun clearer, and draws attention to the likely processes of production (1995: 92).

Meanwhile, a drama department, making use of various kinds of documentary 'look', produces a documentary drama – again taking 'documentary' as an adjective modifying the noun 'drama'. Leslie Woodhead made this similar-but-different process even clearer when he used the phrase *'documented* drama' in his BFI/*Guardian* Lecture in 1981 (my emphasis). Alan Rosenthal remarked to me that putting 'documentary-style' before the word 'drama' would be clearer still.[18]

Television drama departments have made this move in the past to bring a qualitatively different level of seriousness to their entertainments at the point of production. And at the point of reception audiences have often been prepared to acknowledge the seriousness of the documentary as a manifest contribution to the drama (as, for example, in the case of the 1966 *Cathy Come Home* – see Chapter 7). In performance a drama-documentary will tend to use the names and identities of real historical individuals, and its plot will stay close to the pattern of (relatively) verifiable real-life events. Its use of these elements will be, perhaps, closer to its surface. A documentary drama, on the other hand, will tend to use fictional constructs, such as an invented plot and characters composited from several real-life originals. Its factual base will be, like the mass of an iceberg, located below the surface of its action, in the research that has informed it. Within the essentially fictional structure, complex elements of verifiable factual precursors and real-life situations may be incorporated, however, and may 'show through' as in a palimpsest. It is to some extent a matter of available structures – in drama-documentary, the drama diverts the documentary element into dramatic structuring; in documentary drama, the documentary diverts the drama into documentary structures.

Both forms make use of the visible and audible evidence that audiences associate with the 'authentic' documentary – news and current affairs footage, still photography, the visual rhetoric of graphs, charts and statistics, the aural rhetoric of location sound, voiceover commentary and interview/witness statement. But in the drama-documentary the use of this kind of evidential material is always likely to be incorporated within the parameters of naturalistic believability in performance.

John Corner is surely correct in saying that, as a means of categorisation, the two terms 'documentary drama' and 'drama-documentary' usefully mark out 'clusterings of work with *a sufficient level of internal commonality*' (1996: 31 – my emphasis). It is equally true, however, that we have become accustomed to certain kinds of performance on our cinema and television screens – audiences have become 'acculturated' through repetition, in television and film dramas, to an acting style that covers a relatively small range of predominantly naturalistic techniques. 'Serious' styles contrast quite markedly with the more melodramatic styles of the soap and the series, which are more heightened but usually just as naturalistic. The acting styles found in single play drama on television seem to be 'realer' if only because they are, so to speak, ratcheted down in terms of performative display. They are more like movies. For the actor, the claim to be representing the real is secured by doing less, not more, on screen. This tendency is intensified by the inherent minimalism of film dialogue.

The academic debate

In this book's first edition, I suggested that both the academic debate about docudrama and the history of the form itself could be split into two traditions – a British and an American one. In the American academy, as Rosenthal has pointed out, the docudrama was 'virtually ignored' for many years (1988: 16). Comment in book form mainly occurred either within writing on the documentary proper or in writing on the institutional bases of American television. In this tradition the docudrama's claim to documentary status was often challenged and frequently dismissed. However, the very different British critical tradition has acknowledged the cultural importance of the investigative drama-documentary – the 'drama-doc' of my original subtitle. Andrew Goodwin's two collections for the BFI on the subject (1983 – co-edited by Paul Kerr, and 1986) and John Corner's investigations both of 'public drama' (1995) and of documentary (1996), and the first edition of this book have all been central to an historical account and a theorisation of the form that was not replicated in the United States until the publication of Lipkin's important 2002 monograph (see again the Introduction).

The efforts of practitioners to define and describe their activities pre-date the entry of academics into the debate, but both have had to face the fact that drama with a 'D' (rehearsed and performed drama) is always excessive in comparison to drama with a 'd' (real-world drama). By 'excessive' I mean that the pro-filmic is different in both degree and kind in acted performance when compared to documentary proper. In docudrama, whether factual material is in the foreground or (as is more usual now) the background, the performed docudrama will always be an 'excess' if only because it has been added to what happened. The justification for the added element constitutes the theoretical battleground of proponents and opponents alike. This notion of 'excess' in fiction film derives from Bill Nichols' contribution to Michael Renov's influential 1993 collection *Theorising Documentary*. Nichols makes distinctions between what happens when real historical individuals 'perform' for the cameras on newsreel footage and in documentary proper, and what occurs when the imitators of real individuals reconstruct on location and in the studio for the docudrama. He talks of 'a body too many' and 'a body too few' in his explication of the differences between documentary and fiction film (1993: 177). In fictional representation of historical events, he claims, we find 'a body too many'; in documentary representation, there is always 'a body too few'. In the body of the actor, then, a kind of *excess* is enacted; in non-fiction representation, a kind of *dearth* is apparent. This matters not only to makers of films (directors, crew, performers) but also to viewers. If the protagonist in a documentary can be said to be performing him or herself, 'the submergence of self', in John Freeman's phrase, 'is a defining trait of acting' (2002: 98–9).

Critics of the form, especially in newspapers, tend to pick up on this excess/dearth paradigm and construct it as a fissure, as a cause for loss of credibility. They have focused on and opposed the drama's attempt to be more-than-just-fictional. Journalists have habitually preferred, and continue to prefer, to find docudramas either bad documentary or bad drama, or both; and some academic commentators have chosen this path too. Both Ken Loach and Tony Garnett tend to try to deflect criticism by refusing the docudrama label. Garnett told me in 1996, 'I don't make docudramas, I make fiction!' Both became tired of the repetitive nature of the debate about the form. A director in many ways their heir, Peter Kosminsky, said to me in 2005:

> If they've tired of it I can quite understand it because I'm sick and tired of it! I first encountered [the debate] 15 years ago and I still seem to be answering the same questions.

The notion that documentary is, somehow, more honest, is there sub-textually in Sylvia Plath's daughter Frieda Hughes' remark to those who wanted her to meet Gwyneth Paltrow during the making of *Sylvia*, the 2003 film about her mother in which Paltrow played Plath. 'What am I supposed to call her?' asked Hughes caustically, "Mummy"?'[19] The belief that protagonists and audience alike are manipulated and/or misled through the drama in docudrama is still, and is likely to remain, a feature of industry sensitivity, newspaper commentary, and academic critique.

But academic writing has at least exhibited a growing awareness that audiences are not necessarily passive sponges soaking up the flow of televisual activity. Audiences, at whatever individual intellectual level, can and do negotiate meaning *actively*, as some recent studies have shown. Audience research in media studies has burgeoned in recent years. In the twenty-first century academics are basing their arguments less often on the notion of an easily duped audience and working more towards finding out the how and the why of audience involvement.[20] There have, of course, been famous occasions when audiences have been duped, and these seem to have influenced commentators well beyond their sell-by date. Orson Welles' radio adaptation of *The War of the Worlds* in 1938 is the example most often quoted, creating as it did widespread panic in America.

Such occasions are rare and have, in almost every case, depended upon acts of bad faith on the part of broadcasters. The bad faith involved codes and conventions being imported from one broadcasting area to another *without warning*. Sometimes this has had a comic outcome, at other times it was rather more serious. In each case, it resulted from artistic overreaching rather than any conspiracy to defraud. And the only really serious case happened a very long time ago. If these examples demonstrate anything, they show very clearly that broadcasters cry wolf at serious peril of forfeiting the credibility essential to their medium.

Acceptance of codes and conventions is hard-won at the levels both of production and reception. A wish to regulate, and legislate for, the docudrama in part reinforces this – the mere suggestion of confusion induces a knee-jerk reaction that is inevitably conservative. Andrew Goodwin points out that 'clashes and connections ... between television's factual and fictional discourses' are part of the representational territory (1990: 8). In the 'debate' as Goodwin and Kerr saw it in 1983, a clash and/or connection was the single most important feature in the development of docudrama. Periodic rejection of connection between the two discourses has sometimes reduced docudrama's access to the handling of serious issues, has sometimes diminished the form's claims as documentary, but most of all has lead to a circularity in debate that partly explains Kosminsky's irritation. Docudrama does seem at times a form condemned endlessly to push the same arguments up the hill of the same objections in a task that would have intimidated Sisyphus.

When the British drama-documentary first became a media event in the 1960s there was a good deal of effort to understand what was happening conceptually. The English writer Paul Ableman, for example, expressed a representative ethical view: 'for television to remain a force for mental expansion and greater understanding, it is vital for the distinction between the real and the simulated to be kept sharp and clear' (1972: 48). Worth noting here is the optimistic post-war tone of the belief that 'mental expansion and greater understanding' are even *possibilities* in the growth of a mass medium. One can hear and read this view still, though the pessimistic notions that television executives are all exploiters and the viewing public active agents in their own 'dumbing down' are far more common. In general, an awareness that the bleeding into each other of the real and the simulated is now a fact of post-modern (mediated) life is far advanced into the public consciousness.

Early reflections on the British dramadoc include practitioner Jerry Kuehl's influential essay of 1978. Like Ableman, Kuehl was uncomfortable with the ethics of the exercise, feeling that 'factual claims ... are compromised by the very existence of the dramatic elements' (1978: 3). But he acknowledged a 'legitimate province' for the form in subjects which 'resist exploration by the methods of classic documentary film-making'. His answer to the problem of dramatisation was prescient if we consider the legal situation discussed in Chapter 2. He advocated what amounts to a footnoting methodology, suggesting that 'precise descriptions of the sources for each scene and each line of dialogue' be made available, which 'do not necessarily have to be transmitted' (1978: 7). Returning to the debate a few years later in *Sight and Sound*, however, he had become less sanguine, saying the form's 'inauthenticity is inescapable' (1981: 274).

In the USA, Bill Nichols' books (see Nichols 1981, 1991, 2001) have been especially influential in defining and describing the nature of the documentary mode, but all included brief, almost parenthetical, observations on the docudrama. Nichols has been consistent in his view that the form exists *outside* what he calls the 'discourse of sobriety' (1991: 160). A particular kind of seriousness, inscribed within documentary, stands in contradistinction to fictional discourses of entertainment. In 2001 he acknowledged the extent to which the seriousness of documentary's discourse has been transformed by new modes, and that variant discourses rather than a single discourse now obtain. He has 'taken some pains,' he remarks, to demonstrate that 'the domain of documentary exhibits permeable borders and a chameleon-like appearance' (2001: 35). Defining docudrama in an earlier book as 'stories based on fact but performed by actors and scripted from both documents and conjecture', he suggested it lacked even a subjective documentary's grip on real-world pro-filmic events (1991: 160). The docudrama must ultimately be located, he said, in an 'essentially fictional domain'. But in 2001 he was ready to acknowledge that the form 'has a complex and even more fascinating history in Britain than in the United States' (p. xvi). Part of this complexity, of course, is docudrama's affinities (methodologically, institutionally and stylistically) with documentary.

Thus docudrama shares its excess with the biopic and the historical drama, and it can be located on a fact-based spectrum with these forms. Working through the 'body too many' of the actor, films on this spectrum are manifestly beyond the realm of the histories they set out to depict. In reconstruction, says Nichols, a film 'trade[s] documentary authenticity for fictional identification' (1991: 249–50). I find 'trade' an interesting word here, and see in its use both a connection to the Griersonian suspicion about Hollywood commercialism and an Old Left belief that trade means gain for someone or something and equal and opposite loss for someone or something else. For Nichols in 1991, American docudrama was nothing more than contemporary-historical fiction, its claim on documentary muted to say the least. Another prominent American theorist, Michael Renov, concurs with this view saying: 'At the level of the sign, it is the differing historical status of the referent that distinguishes documentary from its fictional counterpart' (1993: 2). However in 2001 Nichols acknowledged the underlying challenge of the form, and its different (and more complex) configuration in Britain, and its dramatic focus on 'emotional intensities' and a 'high degree of constructedness' (2001: 23).

Some American theorists have followed practitioners in making an approach through function and purpose. Richard Barsam follows the line taken by filmmakers like Willard Van Dyke, claiming: 'The documentary is distinguished from the factual film by its socio-political purpose, its "message"' (1974: 369). Such a view is echoed by William Guynn, who claims that documentary films 'seek to account for actual occurrences in the phenomenal world' (1990: 13), and by Paula Rabinowitz, who says that 'the implicit meaning of documentary is not only to record but to change the world' (1994: 102). Scholar/practitioner Alan Rosenthal set more modest (though perhaps more realisable and verifiable) aspirations: 'the function of the documentary is to clarify choices, interpret history and promote human understanding' (1980: 1). Use value can be argued for both the explanatory or informational and the agitating or campaigning aspects of documentary, irrespective of the status of the reality depicted. It is here that the British dramadoc has had an advantage over the American docudrama tradition. It has generally achieved a good ethical fit with the documentary's claim to be an agitational and campaigning form. If its reality status can only ever be under challenge, its bids over the years to intervene in historical situations have given it credentials drawn from the discourse of sobriety. As the opening paragraph of ITV Network Centre's 1994 *Statement of Best Practice* proclaimed:

> ITV is proud of its record in factual drama. Programmes such as *Who Bombed Birmingham, Shoot to Kill, The Life of Phillip Knight* and *Fighting for Gemma* have used journalistic methods and drama techniques to bring important issues of public policy to the widest audiences. Series such as *Crime Story* and *In Suspicious Circumstances* in part fulfil a docu-

mentary tradition of throwing light on the human condition, as well as presenting popular programming. (Corner and Harvey, 1996: 253–4)

The British investigative dramadoc is seen here as a full partner in 'a documentary tradition', a bold claim far less unlikely to come from an American network.

Discussion of docudrama, then, has been dominated more by questions about its claim on documentary than by questioning of its use of drama. In the UK, the late 1970s and early 1980s saw the real academic debate about the form begin. Distinctions between documentary, drama-documentary and documentary drama became important to academics and even to practitioners. A seminal article by John Caughie in *Screen* contributed to the growing theorisation of the two dominant forms, which Caughie labelled 'dramatised documentary' and 'documentary drama' (1981: 9–33). The article was framed also by a current debate about 'progressive drama'. This discussion was focused on the question as to whether any fictional representations could ever lead to political change (or even sharpened awareness) in the popular audience.[21] Caughie's two categories separated out rationalist/documentary (essentially films exhibiting Nichol's 'discourse of sobriety') and aesthetic/dramatic ('discourse of entertainment') strands. These tended to be mapped onto the ideology of the broadcast institution department out of which programmes or films emerged. Discursive origins were, Caughie contended, evident formally in the cinematic 'looks' mobilised in the finished product, and could then be read off the product. Drama-documentary, in the Caughie taxonomy, was a convergent form based on an investigative, journalistic imperative; its audience was encouraged to see itself moving towards the truth of a specific situation. Documentary drama, meanwhile, was a divergent (and inherently more progressive) form, with its audience encouraged to move outwards from a representative fiction – in the direction of generalisable, but still in one sense 'documentary', truth. Both forms as employed by British media institutions could be shown to be campaigning forms, and therefore shared a seriousness of purpose with documentary. Caughie concluded that practice that was *formally* disruptive was more likely to lead to questioning responses in the audience. Overly naturalistic styles, he argued, were more likely to lead to passivity in the audience and acceptance of the *status quo*. The argument derived, in part, from Brecht's theatrical theory, aimed at producing the 'active spectator' through a performance that enacted – indeed embodied – Marxist theory.[22]

The view that docudrama 'blurred boundaries' emerged in the 1980s as much through critical writing as new institutional practice. Bennett *et al.*'s 1981 view, for example, can stand as representative:

> While the broadcasting institutions would strictly demarcate between documentary series and drama, this distinction has recently been blurred by various hybrids of drama-documentary, which lay claim to greater historical accuracy because the sequence of events depicted (and, in some cases, the dialogue spoken) is in some fashion authenticated by archive sources. (1981: 285)

The British tradition regarded facts and information as some kind of key to unlock closed social situations – leading to action in the wider political world. This is Oliver Goodenough's 'fact-rich British tradition' (see Chapter 2). American writers of the same period, subject to similar theoretical justifications, tended to endorse the view that British practice was grounded more on investigative documentary terms. Bruce Crowther, for example, pointed to the presence of British personnel on the 1983 Anglo-US co-production series *Kennedy*, and commented that it brought a 'detachment' to proceedings which helped to make it 'the most thorough examination of the Kennedy era so far brought to the screen' (1984: 160–7). British confusion between 'documentary drama' and 'drama-documentary', however, is on the whole absent in American circles. The term 'docudrama' is consistently to be found in American writing and has a long history. Robert Musburger quotes a definition of docudrama that goes back to 1951: '"a program presenting information or exploring an issue in a dramatic fashion, with story emphasis usually on the social significance of the problem"' (1985: 93).[23]

As this quotation indicates, there has been less emphasis in general on the 'fact-rich' approach in the American tradition. From the very beginning in 1924, Grierson himself had been struck by the American journalistic penchant for the 'story' over the 'report' (see

Winston, 1995: 99) and the force of individualised narrative has always been in evidence in the docudrama. Hoffer *et al.*, for example, describe them as 'accurate re-creations of events in the lives of actual persons' (see Rose, 1985: 182). This definition leaves out completely the issues of 'public policy' on which the British tradition has rested. Todd Gitlin, too, offers a discourse of entertainment provenance for fact-based television drama, calling it: 'melodrama whose stereotypes ... sometimes disclose the point of view of historical victims' (1994: 162). The point about melodrama is an important one and has been comprehensively developed in Lipkin (2002). Amongst much else, Lipkin notes that the 'lens of melodrama' can bring 'a moral clarity' (p. 7) and that:

> Proximity to the factual ... attempts to root artistic vision within the sober ground of historical actuality, suggesting at the same time that good has come out of suffering, that justice has prevailed, that as it must in melodrama, some order has been restored to a chaotic universe. (2002: 11)

Lipkin identifies qualities here that are so central to theatrical history that they are indeed almost Aristotelian.

The American documentary tradition, in film and theatre, has made much greater use of the human face, so to speak. The concept of the 'Little Man' witness to and victim of history has always been close to the heart of the best American drama. Social concerns were individualised from a very early stage in the 'Living Newspaper' theatre productions of the 1930s New Deal era, for example. These plays used a character directly identified as 'The Little Man' to demonstrate the vulnerability of the 'ordinary citizen' to failures in social, economic and governmental systems with primary duties of care.[24] Gitlin notes the similarities between the docudrama and another liberal American cultural phenomenon, 'the social problem movies that Warner Brothers produced in the thirties and forties' (1994: 170). Willy Loman, in Arthur Miller's 1949 *Death of a Salesman*, might stand as the tragic apogee of the Little Man figure. All this is part, perhaps, of a national cultural trait towards individualising issues of social and political debate, displacing them into tropes of victim and villain, hero and antagonist, crisis and rescue, and seeking the consolation of emotional closure. The movie-of-the-week 'trauma drama' of the 1980s was, in Jane Feuer's words: 'The eighties version of the "sociological film" or "public service drama" [which] resolved the traumas of the American family in a rejuvenation of public institutions by the people' (1995: 13). More sombrely it was, she went on to say, 'the same promise that got Reagan elected'. Gitlin sees a psycho-social function in the docudrama: 'it exists not to comprehend but to document, to authenticate the validity of surface detail, to establish that this really happened' (1994: 162). Feuer, by contrast, takes the view that the trauma drama is American public service television's endgame, denoting a 'massive loss of faith by individuals in [public] institutions' (1995: 18). The trauma drama is thus part of society's ongoing testing out of reality – the attempt to find what can and cannot be represented and thus deemed true-in-the-way-of-belief. It gives expression to a popular belief that society's major institutions will do you down – unless you stand your ground and fight. The trope of the 'Little Man' was extended through 1980s trauma drama to encompass the challenges faced by the 'Little Woman', demonstrating television's ability to move (eventually) with the feminist times. The resultant movies, however, still structure their narratives insistently through individual-in-crisis, against-the-odds, melodramatic stories (see also Chapter 7).

Paula Rabinowitz believes that docudrama as a form is dependent upon documentary cinema in one further respect. She sees both documentary and docudrama 'pictur[ing] history through vivid characters who live in families' (1994: 137). To an extent, the primary American myth of the white European family hacking out 'civilised' territory from the wild (in opposition to wild peoples who live in primitive tribes rather than families) lives on. The new frontier is in a quotidian reality of citizens routinely failed by institutions set up to 'look after' them, and reliant instead on themselves and truncated but more individualised communities. The late capitalist world of privatisation thus inscribed itself indelibly upon its (factual) fictions. In re-living 'trauma', the dramas offer comfort and hope, but little in the way of overt practical assistance other than post-transmission helplines. They do not, on the whole, believe in the idea of facts as keys to locked doors; in this tradition, the facts of a situation provide templates to confirm the possibility of individual action.

The British playwright and essayist David Edgar set out the basic rules of engagement for the docudrama in a series of important contributions to this subject in the 1980s. 'What sets drama-documentary apart from the mass of public plays,' he said in 1980, 'is not the employment of facts but the theatrical use to which those facts are put' (1988: 52). 'Theatrical' is possibly the most important word here; his notion was that 'credibility' in the performance was enhanced by facts.[25] Edgar is one of the very few commentators to take account seriously of the role of drama in the mixed form. His highlighting of 'credibility' (rather than 'believability' or 'truth-to-life') is crucial. In invoking the 'documentary' in their dramas, whatever the order of the two words, writers and filmmakers seek more-than-just-dramatic justification for belief. Only audiences can ultimately judge the success of the claim. More recently Edgar has observed:

> In drama-documentary, our interest is in the rights and wrongs of what is being represented … , or the credibility of the argument … In documentary drama, on the other hand, the doc is merely a means to the dram; specific events are used as a source for treatment of general questions, in the same way as Shakespeare drew on real history, historical myth and his own imagination for plays that dealt with essentially similar themes. (1989: 13)

Like Nichols, he places one form in the realm of the historical fiction; unlike Nichols, he retains space for a form that has the *potential* to intervene historically, whatever its provenance. Essentially, this is still the Caughie position on progressive television drama.

Caughie himself returned to the debate in 2000. Still a proponent of formal innovation as a means towards critical response, still favouring Brechtian collision montage over the integration montage of high naturalism, he returns to *Up the Junction* and *Cathy Come Home* in order to make the following point:

> It is [the] absence of a strongly marked hierarchy between the documentary figures and the narrative figures, the documentary gaze and the dramatic look – a kind of reversibility of story-telling between drama and documentary – which greatly confuses the expectations of the narrative order, and makes the form so full of possibilities. (2000: 119)

Crucially, Caughie takes the articulation of these 'possibilities' to be oriented towards avant-garde film rather than television, and he alleges:

> The aspirations and desires of television to be filmic [in the period of *Cathy Come Home*] begin the process which leads to the death of television – or at least to the death of the televisual in television drama. (2000: 124)

The growing synergies from the 1960s onwards between the industrial worlds of television and film in many ways bear out Caughie's view. It is certainly the case that many television workers behind the camera and microphone aspire to work in film. The docudrama was certainly closely connected with the documentary film movement in its earliest phase of development, and it is to this history that I will now turn.

Notes

1 In 2005 Williams' book was updated as *New Keywords: A Revised Vocabulary of Culture and Society*, edited by Tony Bennett, Lawrence Grossberg and Meaghan Morris. I have, however, continued to refer to the edition Williams himself revised first in 1983 for two reasons: firstly because its original publication in the 1970s is so close to the cultural shifts that produced the categories of 'documentary drama' and 'drama-documentary'; and secondly because amongst the words excluded from the 2005 edition are 'dramatic' (pp. 109–10, the nearest Williams gets to 'drama') and 'fiction' (pp. 134–5) – i.e. two out of my own four 'keywords' have not in any case been updated. Significantly, *New Keywords* is not, nor could it be easily imagined to be, a single-authored work. The editors remark in their Introduction on the 'shift to a collective and more international mode of production' (p. xxi) made inevitable by the 'changed contexts of "general" discussion which people inhabit today' (p. xix).

2 See Introduction, note 5. For the full reference to this phrase of John Corner's see Corner (1997).

3 For more on 'headline docudrama' and 'trauma drama', see Chapters 6 and 7. In relation to Kerr's shorthand, I acknowledge my own tendency to write 'dd' when making notes. In general, however, this is not a common usage.

4 The documentary novel, too, is a burgeoning form. I believe that Truman Capote's 1966 *In Cold Blood* was crucial to the history of this genre; he certainly claimed it as the first 'non-fiction novel'. Thomas Keneally's 1982 *Schindler's Ark* marked a point at which the docudrama and the docu-

novel coalesced (through the precedent of Spielberg's 1993 film *Schindler's List*). To trace this particular history would take up too much space here, but the number of modern novels that have 'Historical Footnote' sections, select bibliographies of source material and so on is remarkable. Barbara Kingsolver's 1998 novel *The Poisonwood Bible*, for example, has a two-page Bibliography (Kingsolver, 2000: 615-6), and in her 'Author's Note' (ix-x) acknowledges that her account of her fictional family's life in the Congo/ Zaire relied totally on 'the diversity and value of these sources' since she had never visited the Congo/Zaire (ix). In addition, many writers are using biography creatively – in the so-called 'bio-novel'. For example, David Lodge's *Author, Author* is a biographical novel about Henry James, which has five pages of 'Acknowledgements etc.' (Lodge, 2005: 385–9). This book also has a Preface which states, *inter alia*, 'Nearly everything that happens in this story is based on factual sources'. Lodge acknowledges (p. 387) the help of Kathy Chater, the writer of books on research whom I quoted in Chapter 1. All this is yet another indication of that current fascination with, and investment in, the real that I discussed in the Introduction.

5 Aside from libel, the most likely causes of court action in Britain and the USA are allegations of gross indecency or the offending of religious beliefs (in the context of the performing arts on stage and screen).

6 For useful definitions of all these dramaturgical terms see Hodgson (1988).

7 *Dragnet* ran in primetime from 1952 to 1959 with Jack Webb as Joe Friday. It was 'probably the most successful police series in the history of television' (Brooks and Marsh, 1999: 282). NBC essayed a rather poor revival in 1969–70.

8 See also Winston (1995: 8) – note his trenchant observation that had Matuszewski not been a Pole writing in French he might now be credited as 'documentary's Adam'. Note also Matuszewski's term for film itself: *'la photographie animée'*.

9 The phrase, offered parenthetically, is actually in Grierson (1933: 8). See also Chapter 5, where I discuss this phrase again.

10 See Ellis (1989) on documentary films in developed and undeveloped nations.

11 Again, see Winston (1995), in particular pp. 5–7.

12 The epic German television series *Heimat*, for example, has been described by its writer/director Edgar Reitz as 'a television novel'.

13 Though writers as eminent as Erik Barnouw have preferred 'non-fiction' to 'documentary' (see Barnouw, 1975).

14 See Chapters 2 and 3 of Paget (1990) on the techniques and significance of 'documentary theatre' and 'theatre of fact'. See also my entry 'documentary' in *The Continuum Companion to Twentieth Century Theatre* (Chambers, 2002: 214–15) and on 'documentary drama and theatre' in *The Oxford Encyclopedia of Theatre and Performance* (Kennedy, 2003, vol. 1: 379–80).

15 The history of documentary theatre demonstrates that the form lacks

continuity, being essentially a 'guerrilla' form. Although a 1946 play, *Documentary Drama*, indicated that techniques were already well known in Britain by the mid-1940s, the new generation of 1960s playwrights had virtually to re-learn them. Van Erven (1988; 1992) shows that, while Third World practitioners often have some knowledge of Brecht, for example, they also tend to find documentary theatrical techniques out of pure political necessity. Among several publications on the subject of recent 'Verbatim' and 'Tribunal' theatre in the UK and USA, see especially A. Forsyth and C. Megson (eds.) (2009), *Get Real: Documentary Theatre Past and Present*, Basingstoke and New York: Palgrave Macmillan.

16   This intention is visible in, for example, Peter Kosminsky's 2005 *The Government Inspector* – one of a number of television programmes that took to task the Blair government's handling of the Iraq War.

17   See Chapter 8 for more on these new developments.

18   Rosenthal's email of 23 November 1998.

19   Hughes' telling, even bitter, remark was quoted by Libby Purves in *The Times* 'Thunderer' column on 6 November 2003.

20   The industry, too, is taking more and more interest in finding out about audiences – it has to in the current broadcasting ecology, or risk declining numbers.

21   Caughie's article was reprinted in both Bennett *et al.* (1981), and Goodwin and Kerr (1983). Amongst others, Colin McCabe was one of the foremost of Caughie's interlocutors in the *Screen* debate (which took place between 1975 and 1980) about what was and what was not 'progressive' in television drama. See McCabe's collection *High Theory/Low Culture* (1986). See also Caughie's account of the debate in Caughie (2000: 105ff).

22   The most useful accounts of Brecht's theories are in two books edited by John Willett (1984; 1986).

23   He references the quotation to Willis (1951: 101).

24   For more detail on Federal Theatre and the 'Living Newspaper', see O'Connor and Brown (1980).

25   Edgar's essay began as a radio talk, 'Acting Out Facts' (BBC Radio 3, 28 December 1980), and has been much anthologised. It is most conveniently found in Edgar (1988). Interestingly, the headline of the version of his essay which appeared in the British entertainment trade paper *The Stage* (16 April 1981) was 'Why We Must Save the Documentary Drama', even though Edgar consistently refers to 'drama-documentary' throughout his article.

5

Histories: antecedents and first phase

Documentary film and its 'judicious fictions'

Docudrama has its roots in a documentary film tradition that was always prepared to use fictional means to tell a factual story. The implication is there in Grierson's defining phrase 'the creative treatment of actuality'. The phrase has often been misquoted, with US Judge Pollack's ruling in the case of the film *Missing* (mentioned in Chapter 2) just one example. More than once 'creative' has become 'imaginative'; 'treatment' has turned into 'interpretation' or 'use'; and 'actuality' is sometimes rendered 'reality'. Even specialists have garbled the phrase. Kevin Macdonald and Mark Cousins, editors of a standard work (*Imagining Reality: The Faber Book of Documentary*), do it. 'Grierson', they remark, 'famously defined the documentary film as "the creative use of actuality", a phrase so broad it is almost meaningless' (1996: 93). Sometimes Grierson's own colleagues added to the confusion.[1]

It could be countered that the phrase might be more meaningful if quoted correctly, of course, but vagueness has intensified its gnomic quality. The words first appeared in *Cinema Quarterly*, an Edinburgh-based periodical edited by Grierson himself in the 1930s. In an article about the role of the producer in documentary film, it was, as I remarked in Chapter 4, almost an afterthought. 'Documentary, or the creative treatment of actuality,' he writes, 'is a new art with no such background in the story and the stage as the studio product so glibly possesses' (1933: 8). The paradox of the full sentence is that Grierson simultaneously sets his 'new *art*' (my emphasis) up against not only the 'old' arts of novel and stage but the 'new' art of

commercial film. His lofty proclamation is that commercial cinema
in particular is inferior because 'glib'. An implicit new honesty is
balanced against an old fakery. The use of 'creative' and of 'art',
however, is so key to both his conception and his polemic that, as Bill
Nichols has astutely observed, 'Documentary, like the avant-garde,
begins in *response to fiction*' (2001: 137 – my emphasis).

Griersonian documentary actively embraced an artfulness always
likely to be at odds with the recording of 'actuality'. The apparent
rejection of 'story' is countermanded in his iconic phrase via the
force of 'interpretation'. All these words imply *agency*, without
which there can be no art. The definition thus celebrates documentary's formal splitting-off from fiction while simultaneously binding
documentary *practice* to invention. This quasi-philosophical move
legitimised the technologically inevitable. There was little practical
choice *but* to reconstruct in the 1930s and 1940s, given the nature
of the camera and microphone technologies available to the Empire,
the GPO Film Unit and the Crown Film Unit, and their clones in
other countries. Fictionalisation was an indispensable approach to
the documentary subject for crews wrestling with primitive cameras
and lacking location sound resources. In the following issue of
Cinema Quarterly producer H. Bruce Woolfe took the issue further,
directly advocating the use of fiction in documentary. He wrote: 'I
believe that the addition of *judicious fiction* may increase both the
aesthetic value and the point of a film that in the main deals with a
non-fictional subject' (1933: 96 – my emphasis).

The 1938 film *North Sea*, sometimes described as a 'semi-
documentary', is a good example of the mix of fact and fiction that
the pre-war British documentary movement bequeathed to post-
war British television and the international documentary movement. And American filmmakers in the Second World War, most
of them with Hollywood backgrounds, skewed documentary even
more towards fiction. As Ian Aitken says, the integration of 'documentary techniques and methods into a format derived from the feature film' was widely influential as documentary developed (1990:
145). Brian Winston makes a convincing case that the liberal/non-
interventionist politics of the documentarians made for a practice
just as formally conservative as realist film. Griersonian film, he

argues, was always somewhat compromised in terms of its effects in the public sphere.[2] Always prepared to compromise politically, the new documentarians leant more heavily towards Hollywood than they were ever prepared to let on. Even Joris Ivens, a filmmaker Winston regards highly, did not eschew the 'semi-documentary' approach, using eloquently judicious fiction in his 1933 film *Borinage*. In this film, which examined police violence during a miners' strike in Belgium, the original miner protagonists recreated their brutalised demonstration.

The narrative turn taken very early on by the emergent cinema looks inevitable at this distance in time, but its synergy with nine-teenth-century realist 'ways of seeing' in the arts must be stressed. This mode tended to make all new screen forms reactive to a domi-nant narrative feature tradition associated with between-the-wars Hollywood. Realist movies went about their business of entertain-ing through the interaction, in more or less linear plots with pre-dominantly three-act structures, of key characters with whom the spectator was encouraged to identify. The dominant film tradition encouraged in audiences that suspension of disbelief which is a default mechanism. As has been often noted in film theory, the key indications were realist *mise-en-scène*, continuity editing in sound and vision, dialogue that often would not have been out of place in a realist novel, and naturalistic acting. In such fictionalisations, the believable in acted performance constituted, and continues to consti-tute, the credible in terms of reception. The dominant techniques for filming these performances encouraged, and continues to encourage what Noel Carroll calls 'spectator scanning', which is 'taken to be more like our normal perceptual behaviour than our reaction to the composition in alternate styles' (1996: 243 – original emphasis). The view centred by Hollywood realism has its greatest affinities, as Carroll also points out, with 'preexisting cultural practices and concerns' (p. 244).[3]

What would now be called 'faking', then, was not originally so much an aesthetic choice or an avoidance of an ethical imperative, much less a 'playing' with genre conventions – it was a necessity if anything was to be presented on film at all. Equipment that denied access required alternative approaches, and fiction was the most convenient. Robert Flaherty, the Griersonians' American role model, routinely faked action in all his influential works. As Carl Plantinga has said, 'if Flaherty were to make his films within the context of today's media institutions' – a vital and telling 'if' – 'we would almost certainly not call them documentaries, but docudramas or "dramatic documentaries"' (1997: 35). For Grierson's own 1929 film *Drifters* the ship's interior was mocked up; in the GPO Film Unit's 1935 *Night Mail*, a mail-truck interior was constructed in the studio, leaving one side open to the camera. A mechanism allowed these 'sets' to be rocked to simulate the movement of ship and mail train. The realities of both were profoundly inaccessible to camera and microphone. A studio set meant in its turn that a script had to be written. In this regard, these sets were different in degree but not in kind from the elaborate studio sets to be found in contemporary docudrama production – the kind I described in Chapter 1.[4]

When the documentary movement went into wartime service, its exploitation of the feature film's 'look' went hand-in-hand with a pre-Loach underplayed acting style. Andrew Higson calls the style of the Crown Film Unit 'a particular *de-dramatised* naturalistic form' (1986: 76 – my emphasis). Restraint in performance in these films sorted well, perhaps, with a generally stoical British wartime mood. The films produced by the Griersonians and funded by the Ministry of Information, were more often than not, as Higson points out, 'documentary-dramas' (p. 79 – note the hyphen). In America the style was more directly Hollywood because directors like Frank Capra, William Wyler and John Huston made them (see Barnouw, 1993: 155–64). But their style, too, was relatively restrained. The appeal to identification with characters worked just as usefully in the fiction feature as in the documentary at a time when stark contrasts between life and death constituted the day-to-day reality for many people. The Griersonian documentary moved steadily away from its early espousal of montage. 'Collision' editing, the formal style of Soviet Russian filmmakers, may have been admired, and the styles and values of the American-dominated film industry labelled 'glib', but actual practice differed from theory.[5]

Two contrasting examples of character-led wartime documentary will illustrate these points about British and American filmmaking:

their use of judicious fiction, and their influence on subsequent docudrama history. Harry Watt's 1941 *Target for Tonight* and the original *Memphis Belle*, directed by Hollywood's William Wyler in 1943, were both 'windows on the world' of the long-distance bomber mission over Germany. Watt always preferred what he called 'dramatisation of reality' over the Griersonian creed. His 'source books' were pilots' flight logs, which he used to underpin his script. The cast of his film were actual bomber crews, with assumed names. They acted insofar as they were asked to 'repeat their roles for the benefit of the camera' (just like participants in post-war British television's 'Built OBs' – see below).[6] These non-actors now seem stilted and impossibly 'stiff-upper-lip', but their performance was probably read at the time as understated and restrained – brave, in a word, in a very British way. However their performance is read, 'characterisation' is a major signifying technique in a film that uses a great deal of actuality filmed by equally brave camera crews.

All this is true of *Memphis Belle*, which reads today less stiltedly owing to a more relaxed demotic in the commentary and to its slicker film style. Writing of directors of American war films like Wyler, Bruce Crowther notes that 'most settled for the small unit which represented all the other small units which made up the whole' (1984: 134). Wyler's bomber crew are thus presented as a metonymic representation of the Great American Nation. In *Memphis Belle* the crew of the eponymous B-17 Flying Fortress come from all over (white) America. The voiceover draws attention directly to this by listing hometowns as the crew are introduced. *Target for Tonight*'s bomber crew 'characters' are similarly regionalised, but only through accent. *Memphis Belle* needed only a romantic plot to be developed into the full-on fiction made by David Puttnam in 1990. In pace and style *Target for Tonight* takes its lead from 1930s documentary. As a result, it is close to being unwatchable for a modern audience; *Memphis Belle*, though also dated, mobilises sufficient current cinematic codes and conventions to be potentially much more acceptable.[7] Both films' mixture of fact and fiction, their blurring of boundaries, caused no heart-searching back then. In Eric Barnouw's words: 'There was little public discussion about the validity of such techniques' in the 1930s and during the Second World War (1975: 131).

Griersonian television

The shadow of the Griersonian documentary can be discerned in post-war British television, partly because Grierson himself and some of his former colleagues worked in television after the Second World War. In the USA, too, documentary film personnel were recruited to staff the news and current affairs departments of post-war television networks. It should be no surprise, then, to find that a defining principle of early film documentary (reconstruction is permissible because unavoidable) became the enabling rubric of the new television service. Television at the time was just as hamstrung technologically as early film had been. Thus documentary films' willingness to dramatise was imported into fledgling television documentary. With the market for cinema documentary having attenuated post-war, personnel in Britain and the USA who drifted into television came in from the cinematic cold, so to speak.

It must be stressed that 'documentary' was still a contested notion. As documentary film became culturally more visible in the 1930s and 1940s, various institutional bodies had tried to describe and define it. From a distance, this looks like a doomed effort to limit the parameters of the faking in which filmmakers were already constrained to indulge. The grandly titled 'World Union of Documentary', for example, was formed post-war and its 1948 conference in Czechoslovakia formally agreed that documentary had to be permitted a certain amount of 'sincere and justifiable reconstruction'. It also acknowledged that appeals 'either to reason or emotion' were equally necessary:

> for the purpose of stimulating the desire for, and the widening of human knowledge and understanding, and of truthfully posing problems and their solutions in the spheres of economics, culture and human relations. (see Barsam, 1974: 366)

'Sincere and justifiable reconstruction', like 'judicious fiction', is a phrase that eloquently indicates the dependence of 1940s filmmakers on something beyond raw actuality. The level of this dependence changed as camera technology improved. In television, however, it continued to be the operational rule in the making of documentary for at least the following decade. Cumbersome 1950s television equipment was the norm just at a time when film itself was beginning to break free of technological constraints. Pre-war cinema and post-war television were developing media trying hard to 'go with the flow' of events but still largely thwarted in that desire (now so surfeited with CCTV images, webcams and camera phones that it is taken almost for granted).

In Britain the synergy achieved through the Griersonian inheritance can be illustrated clearly and indeed personally: Paul Rotha, a Grierson protégé, was put in charge of a 'Documentary Unit' at the BBC in the 1950s. Dedicated to film, Rotha was 'less than enthusiastic at the conventional mixture of studio-reconstruction and film-inserts' upon which the television documentary magazine programmes of the time depended, as Norman Swallow was later to recall (1982: 87). During his short tenure at the BBC (1953–56) Rotha was especially irked by unavoidably drama-based solutions to technical deficiency. He yearned for the world of film he had left, where there was a growing direct access to reality as portable sound and vision equipment developed. Reconstruction could, it began to seem, be eliminated altogether by these means, and he believed this could not fail to increase the social impact of documentary. For Rotha, as with many others who were forced to leave film for television, however 'sincere and justified' the reconstruction of events was, it only ever came a poor second to the Holy Grail of capturing actuality.

His disenchantment with television was especially evident when he noted his BBC staff's 'envy of the professional skill already attained by film people which television in its infancy ha[d] yet to acquire' (Rotha, 1956: 13). Whatever his negative instincts about the new medium, Rotha had a symbolic importance for his young BBC staffers. Norman Swallow, a key figure in post-war British television documentary, recalled thirty years later 'the sense of excitement that followed the announcement that Paul Rotha was to become the Head of our new Documentary Department' (1982: 86). Elaine Bell observes that 'all Unit members had seen documentary films, were enthusiastic about their integral social conscience, and assumed that television could – or must – perform a similar role' (1986: 71). Kenneth Adam, Director of BBC Television in the immediate post-war period, reflected:

> After the war there was nothing left for the documentary film-makers
> but amiable and diffused sponsorship to which the survivors attached
> themselves. It was left to television to pick up the pieces and to assume
> the social responsibility. (see Swallow 1966: 86)

This remark is a fair reflection of the actual destination of the 'documentary conscience' post-war.[8]

The interpenetration of documentary film by fictional rhetorics can be read in almost all contemporary industrial pronouncements on documentary. The acceptance that existed at a technical level as a necessity was sufficient philosophically as far as most practitioners were concerned. It was vital, as it had been for cinema practitioners in the earlier period, for television documentary to distinguish itself from both film newsreel and television news broadcast. So practitioners made space in their work for 'judicious fiction' and 'sincere and justifiable reconstruction' whenever they had to. Even Academy Awards rules on documentary reflected this:

> Documentary films are defined as those dealing with significant histori-
> cal, social, scientific, or economic subjects, whether photographed in
> actual occurrence or re-enacted, and where the emphasis is more on
> factual content than entertainment. (Jacobs 1971: 276)

Playing with purpose

Its proponents often bolster their claim that documentary film differs from fiction film by appeals to a purity of purpose. The purity unachievable technically was and is often finessed into arguments for a special relationship with ethical notions of intention and purpose. This tendency was especially marked amongst the pioneers. Basil Wright, for example,claimed: 'documentary is not this or that type of film, but simply a method of approach to public information' (Barsam, 1974: 367). His colleague Stuart Legg contended that documentary 'is an instrument of information, of propaganda' (Sussex, 1975: 203). Grierson's own preference was for the 'instructional and educational type of film', or so Harry Watt observed in 1983 when interviewed for BBC2's *Arena* programme. The playing of purpose against representational shortcoming has proved a useful trope in justifying the documentary ethically. When this ethical stance was allied to an artistic rhetoric of restraint it produced the best films that constitute the Grierson legacy. The historical role of the documentary film – however much equivocation its makers indulged in – was to function as the conscience of a capitalist film industry all too prone to exploitation politically, economically, socially and sexually. This conscience transferred readily to post-war television.

Dai Vaughan, with the twin perspective of theorist and practitioner, has perhaps best summed up the double-bind of the documentarist's wished for one-to-one relationship with reality and their actual, inevitable, relative position to it. Documentary is, he says, 'one of those terms which refer not to an entity which may be definitively described but to an *ideal*, attainable or otherwise, perhaps even self-contradictory, to whose fulfilment we aspire in our specific uses of it' (1976: 1 – my emphasis). Many concepts of value (and much that is valuable) are like this – ideal rather than real. The modern academy has had trouble with almost all of them in the period of High Theory. 'Objectivity' and 'truth' are other examples of terms that resist definition but which represent notions that can ill be spared. As rhetorical aspiration, such concepts have a significant part to play in the history of a form that has consistently claimed that its ends justify its means.[9] 'Self-contradictory' claims to the real can be relatively easily defended because, as Vaughan adds: '[c]ommon to all forms so designated has been the appeal to an anterior truth' (1976: 1). This appeal, present from the outset, has provided documentary and its derivative forms with their most significant and permanent stock-in-trade.

As with the historical play, the appeal to 'an anterior truth' and to 'a prior referent' is, at the very least, a useful means of drawing attention to a piece of work, and alerting potential audiences to its 'known-ness', its existence in the realm of the actual rather than the imaginative. This has often been a matter of assertion: for example, the filmmaker Lindsay Anderson baldly stated:

> It isn't a question of technique, it is a question of the material. If the material is actual, then it is documentary. If the material is invented, then it is not documentary' (Lewin, 1971: 66).

There has always been an acknowledgement that 'documentary' simply designated a means of representation. W. H. Auden, who supplied the famous verses he himself read in voiceover in *Night Mail*, said:

> The only genuine meaning of the word "documentary" is true-to-life. Any gesture, any expression, any dialogue or sound effect, any scenery that strikes the audience as true-to-life is documentary, whether obtained in the studio or on location. (Mendelson, 1977: 355).

Between the pro-filmic event and the set of codes and conventions that help an audience to accept a piece of film as 'true-to-life' lies documentary's continued claim for attention. This claim is borrowed every time the rubric 'based on a true story', every time the designation 'docudrama', is used – with varying degrees of justification. The claim is in the background throughout the different stages of the form's development.

Docudrama's four phases – the developmental model

In 1998 I suggested a developmental model for the histories of British dramadoc and American docudrama. I argued that these histories needed to be understood first as separate but related stories, then as the story of gradual convergence. I split docudrama history into three phases:

- the immediate post-war period 1946–60 – in which each national television system had *points of comparison* but also idiosyncratic differences;
- the Cold War period (1960–80) – in which film technology and the film industry itself impacted profoundly on the two television systems, and had far-reaching consequences to the docudrama form. In this phase convergence began to be a factor;
- the period of Détente, including an interregnum following the collapse of Eastern European communist states (*ca* 1980–*ca* 1996). In this period production co-operation between US and United Kingdom film and television companies began to ensure that the docudrama, American-style, became formally dominant, but the fact-rich British tradition continued to inflect the docudrama.

To some extent, these phases can be mapped onto John Ellis's 'three eras' of television. He defines these as: 'scarcity' – 'which lasted for most countries until the late 1970s or early 1980s', 'availability' – including the onset of 'more competition in the shape of cable or satellite services', and finally 'plenty' – 'an era in which television programmes ... w[ould] be accessible through a variety of technologies' (Ellis, 2000: 39).[10]

Revising at the end of the first decade of the twenty-first century I find it necessary to propose a fourth phase. By the end of the 1990s a new dispensation had emerged which was unclear to me in the mid-1990s. It is, of course, part product of new geopolitical realities in which the USA has adopted a militaristic 'World Police' role.[11] From the screen industries' point of view, this period is one of technological convergences and sophistication. In this new dispensation factual television forms have burgeoned and have influenced film. Docudrama has a key presence in this new dispensation, this changed ecology. In this new edition I will give a more hopeful account than I did in 1998 of such developments, in which media converge and focus anew issues of access, representation and referentiality. I have moved from a critical position in which old forms were being mourned to one in which I believe new forms should be celebrated (see Chapter 8 for detail on this).

In what follows, I shall argue that in the first phase of development documentary was the important element. In the era of 'Griersonian television', documentary's probity and sobriety were little doubted by audiences relatively unschooled in understandings of representation. In this pioneering phase, British television's synergy with contemporary theatre and its debt to the legacy of Grierson was at its strongest. American television had a not dissimilar debt to Broadway and to New Deal documentary. In both cultures mixtures of drama and documentary were effected principally for technical, operational reasons. As a result their visual style leant further towards documentary than drama.

During the second phase specific practices consolidated to a point where the specific programme category 'docudrama' began to be recognised. Even if definition was problematical, and the form of words used in descriptions variable, the idea of the docudrama would be broadly recognised for the rest of the century. At this point a new fluidity, the result of accelerating technical innovation, increased experimentation with form. Two traditions of practice emerged, with differing documentary and dramatic priorities, the results of markedly different cultures and institutions on both sides of the Atlantic (as I hope to show). By the second phase the debate about form 'tended ... to concentrate more on the "doc" than the "dram"' (Edgar, 1988: 23). It was at this point that the documentary claim within docudrama began to be doubted and interrogated.

The third phase concerns saw the 'dram' becoming ever more important in practice, ensuring increased critical suspicion still founded as it was on considerations of 'doc' value. A form that started out as a response to real-world events located in documentary practices gradually became a response to a public situation articulated principally through the codes and conventions of film and television drama. An aspect of development between 1980 and the mid-1990s was that the American tradition became dominant, but 'public-service' British dramadoc continued to have influence. The values of the fiction film became dominant, as it were, but did not necessarily prevail. David Edgar was moved in 2003 to remark on 'the battering that traditional dramadoc has suffered in the post-documentary world of fissiparous format borders'. He noted that:

> The great sweep of the fact-based drama story from predominantly 'doc' to predominantly 'dram' has changed not only how these products are written but also *how they are read.*[12]

A more media-literate set of makers and viewers, a new set of technological possibilities, a television service battling with other providers for audiences have had the effect of expanding the reach and grasp of fourth-phase docudrama. It is possible to discern in this development *dialogical exchange* between the United Kindom and the USA rather than the blanket imposition of a cultural imperialist hegemony – or so I will be arguing.

In a 1997 article, I called the third phase rather disapprovingly the 'Drift towards Hollywood'.[13] But over time the developments of this period have resulted in a variety of forms that I did not anticipate. Some would argue that the inherent power of the documentary has been attenuated in the process and that this loss overrides all other considerations. I respect this view, but it is not mine. Take the issue of the public service remit. Historically British television has always had a more developed public service role than American television. As late as 1994 Brian Winston was able to argue that over its long history the BBC had on the whole sailed successfully between 'the Charybdis of American commercialism' on the one hand and 'the Scylla of ... Western European state control' on the other (1994: 38). However, the technological revolution of cable and satellite television have reconstituted this essentially European institution, born of the liberal state, and thrown it into a confusion from which it has emerged to become a global player. The American system has always dominated economically, while the British system has acted as a model for responsible, non-commercial broadcasting in any state prepared to take it up. Many commentators see the death agony of public service television in all this, but I take a more optimistic view.[14]

Historically the USA has 'lacked even a cultural reservation, an institutional home (like the BBC or a national theater) for a segment of popular culture empowered to owe allegiance to standards beyond the marketplace,' as Todd Gitlin has said (1994: 29). PBS (the 'Public Broadcasting Service') has survived only by trying to adapt to the commercial environment (to which it was partly abandoned in the 1970s). Many fear that this is the route that beckons for British public service broadcasting. It is important, however, not to claim simplistically that American television lacks a public service imperative altogether. Les Brown observes that the networks themselves have provided 'a unique and valued service as the central meeting place for the nation', as well as an 'influence, for better or worse ... throughout the world' (1995: 259, 284). PBS, too, has not been without influence, and who could have predicted the élitist but highly successful appeal of the cable channel HBO?

The lack of a dedicated public service network can be attributed to the USA's status as the major capitalist nation of the twentieth century. To read accounts of the wheeling and dealing which brought first radio then television to American households is to marvel at the ingenuity of the capitalist mind (or – and it comes to the same thing

– to marvel at the lengths some people will go to make a buck).[15] The cultural difference can be illustrated by looking at the leaders of the early television services – big personalities with distinctive national characteristics. British broadcasting culture had Lord Reith as its founding father – sober, responsible, suspicious of popular taste, repressed; a colonial-style, elitist administrator suspicious of the talents and abilities of the subaltern classes. The fact that he was Scottish rather than English merely underscores the extent to which the old British Empire was dependent on subaltern nations and cultures.

David Sarnoff is an equivalent American figure. Head of NBC in its early years he was known within the company as 'The General'. At once industrialist, entrepreneur, populist and visionary exploiter of new technologies, his honorific military rank was jealously guarded once conferred. It is a suitable badge for his militant commercialism. The national American predilection for entrepreneurial activity ensured that broadcasting would, like other human endeavours in America, be commercially orientated. The facts of the two individuals' lives, the differences in their ideologies and temperaments, make it all the more remarkable that it was actually Sarnoff and not Reith who dreamed up the idea that broadcasting had the triple duties to 'inform, educate, and entertain', as Reith's daughter Marista Leishman revealed in her 2006 memoir *My Father: Reith of the BBC*. Sarnoff, naturally, put entertainment first not last; Reith, typically, 'just turned [the phrase] around' according to his daughter.[16]

First-phase United Kingdom – the 'dramatised story documentary'

In the two national television systems of the UK and USA the key post-war determinants that shaped the initial development of British dramadoc and American docudrama were economic, historical, cultural and political. They followed templates already laid down in other media, indeed in other industries. What Hoffer, Musburger and Nelson say about the roots of American docudrama is equally true of British modes of the late 1940s and early 1950s: the uses of drama-in-documentary and documentary-in-drama are to be found 'in theater, motion pictures, radio, newspapers, and books' earlier in the century (1985: 183). Founding practitioners, too, were drawn from these areas. For example, the 'dramatised story documentary' of the 1940s (the phrase coined by producer Caryl Doncaster) was the first factual drama development in British television. Programmes were based on the journalistic practices of pre-war BBC radio, which already had a reputation for mediating factual material through drama.[17] The department known as 'Features' in the 1930s used documentary material in dramatised form in order to make subjects of public interest accessible.[18] BBC television's post-war dramatised story documentaries were built upon the twin foundations of this radio work and documentary film. Dramatised story documentaries in the late 1940s and early 1950s were essentially 'documentary dramas' according to my definition in Chapter 4. They explored a documentary subject dramatically and were focused either on some public service institution – hospitals, the police, the probation service – or on individuals and their professional status within such institutions.

In the late 1940s television personnel may have shared intellectual reach with colleagues in radio and film, but television's technical grasp lagged far behind the older media. Radio and film had the advantage of a twenty-five-year start in technical development. Getting the television cameras of the time outside a studio required the kind of logistics once needed to get medieval armies on the march. Set-piece outside broadcasts (mainly sporting and royal occasions) occurred, with the Coronation of Queen Elizabeth II in 1953 a triumphant example of what could be achieved. But in general studio-based approximations were the necessary norm for most documentary and current affairs programmes. In the early, innocent, period, such approximations were embraced by the industry and, in the absence of any real alternative, readily accepted by audiences. As a result, rehearsed re-enactments and simulations of situations based on research regularly took the place of actuality filming. Only with technical advance was actuality to become the natural element of television's coverage of the everyday and the 'live'.

To educate the audience documentarily about some matter

of public interest '[t]he cameras stayed put while the actors and researchers went out into the world to gather a faithful record that could be recreated in the studio' (Goodwin, 1986: 3). Illustrative film sequences were then inserted into live studio action as a means of providing authenticating documentary and as a visual escape from studio action. For contemporary writer/producer Arthur Swinson, the difference between television and film was between 'a "live" as opposed to a recorded medium' (1963: 28). For audiences, the novelty of a new kind of seeing (taking place in the private space of their living rooms) vastly outweighed any ethical questions about the means of representation, or any doubts about the status of the reality being shown. The main difference when comparing this work to the kind of reconstruction used by radio features was that a realist *mise-en-scène* was now required. The 'look' of reality inevitably became an issue for a medium that has always, in one sense, been less free in imaginative terms than radio.

The BBC's key personnel in this enterprise included a former journalist (Robert Barr), a former filmmaker (Duncan Ross), a former theatre worker (Michael Barry), and a former teacher (Doncaster). Barr's 1948 dramatised story documentary *It's Your Money They're After* was based on research but entirely acted. Norman Swallow describes it as the 'first ever [television] "documentary series"' (1982: 86). Doncaster picks out the 1950–51 *The Course of Justice* as the series that set the agenda.[19] She claims that Ross 'found a method of translating complex social problems into human terms' in this programme (1956: 44). In many ways this is the classic defence for mixing documentary and drama: in the dramatisation of documentary material you both humanise it and sweeten the bitter pill of fact, allowing audience identification (which makes for something entertaining). Some would have difficulty regarding these programmes as documentary at all. But the pioneers did not see dramatisation as a second-best alternative to location filming: this was the perspective of a later phase that enjoyed greater technical freedom. Instead, they saw dramatisation as their means of controlling the documentary material both editorially and technically. In other words, because their focus was on the documentary not the drama, they seem to have been blind to the representational shifts inevitable when something is rehearsed and acted rather than filmed as it happened.

In a 1951 memo Barr could even write to his head of department Cecil McGiven: 'Documentary is concerned with ... the dramatization of facts, reconstruction of events, *and it uses any dramatic device to make its point*' (see Briggs, 1995: IV, 705 – my emphasis). The willingness to dramatise at virtually any cost to the documentary could hardly be more evident. Nor could the Grierson link be plainer. 'The facts of life so [dramatically] presented', Doncaster believed, 'get across to a much wider section of the public than the straight talk ... One appeals to the intellect, the other to the emotions' (1956: 44). This very 'common-sense' approach is still close enough to the beliefs of many people – programme makers and audiences alike – to be a default position even now. The 'keywords' of Chapter 4, with their cultural assumptions about works of the head and of the heart, can be traced behind these quotations. Doncaster's 'straight talk' is a less attractive proposition in this taxonomy, even if accompanied by illustrative visual material. A major concern articulated by Ofcom in 2004 in their survey of the state of British television was the apparent diminution of the public taste for documentary programming in the new digital ecology – an indication, perhaps, that the factual is still inherently less attractive.[20]

Doncaster is clear that, in spite of the emotional appeal deriving from drama, the dramatised story documentary differed both in degree and kind from 'straight drama'. She was even prepared to concede it to be less-than-drama in certain respects. Writers must discipline themselves, she observed, to cope with inevitable restrictions on their freedom of expression that resulted from the finding of any programme's research base. The necessity for documentary objectivity (this was clearly a given for her) could easily produce 'unwieldy intractable material'. She warned of the 'temptation for the writer ... to include too many facts in the draft dialogue' (1956: 46). Her advice – when in doubt to cut the facts and go for the drama – remains a classic formulation. In her own *Return to Living* (1954 – about the re-entry into the outside world of ten prisoners) Doncaster's start-point was 'an outline giving the progression of action, number and type of characters, sets and film sequences required.' She submitted this outline (effectively, her 'treatment') 'to all interested parties so that minor inaccuracies of fact or emphasis [could] be corrected and any major points of disagreement thrashed out'. A dramatic skeleton of 'action' and 'characters' then provided a narrative structure that was agreed as factually representative. A script was developed from the outline and, after minor amendments, became the rehearsal script (Doncaster, 1956: 45ff). Importantly, no real historical individual was named in the programme. Called a 'dramatised story documentary' by its maker, it seems to have most resembled a documentary drama rather than a drama-documentary.

The writing process, unlike the usual one for drama, was clearly subjected to a rigorous regime of interrogation, yet Doncaster talked, just as producers do today, of her particular relish of 'the characters ... coming to life' during the polishing of the dialogue script. The enabling conventions of the dramatised story documentary were emphatically dramatic – and naturalist/social realist at that: this was a given of post-war practice. 'Television drama,' as J. L. Styan sagely remarked, 'leans hard on characterisation in the naturalistic vein: the age of Freud and the Method is ripe for this medium' (1962: 189). The programmes made by Doncaster and her colleagues in the 1950s, with their composite characters and invented plots, were *documentary dramas* (see Chapter 3). At the level of information a position of authority was established by research, but at the level of performance the credibility of the action was the all-important element.

Doncaster felt the actor in this kind of programme should not just underplay (already perceived as a necessity for television in comparison to theatre): they must, she states flatly, '"be" the person [they are] portraying'. For his role in *Return to Living* Thomas Heathcote (a well-known British character actor of the 1950s) 'spent many hours talking to an ex-inmate of Dartmoor to get the feel of his character,' she remarks, 'so that he might *stop acting and become an ex-prisoner himself*' (Doncaster, 1956: 45ff – my emphasis). Folding the identity of an actor into that of a character is a frequent feature of Method-inflected screen acting. Over the years this seriousness of attention to real-life models has proved powerfully reassuring to makers, writers and actors of docudrama. It is a symptom of anxiety at the level of dramatic credibility made inevitable by a documentary absence. The mantra-like claim of equivalence based on research is neurotically necessary at audience level too. Acted performance, after all, is only ever based upon conventions to which an audience can assent or not by believing or disbelieving. Any kind of naturalistic acting is, at best, a leap in the dark, justified by the hope or belief that audience endorsement will follow. The fusing of actor and real-life protagonist is as much as anything a rhetorical appeal to belief made in the hope of an affirmative response.

A mix of drama and documentary is, and always has been, more vulnerable to audience doubt than any other form of realist drama. Despite their best efforts at research, actors as well as filmmakers and writers rely on their audience to square the circle during trans-mission or performance. As a result, pre-publicity for the docudrama tends to assert equivalence between real-world experience and its reconstruction, and it always has done. Doncaster's observation that Thomas Heathcote talked to his real-life model for 'many hours' is a classic example. Why 'many' hours? Because to say this is more than simply to say he 'talked to' the ex-Dartmoor man, or that he 'met him'. The rhetorical insistence, the indexical gesture (*this* man – not any man) is part of a claim to authenticity that can only be secured ultimately by audience belief. But actively to solicit that belief prior to the event of performance is a must.

More recently, Colin Firth talked at the press preview for *Hostages* about the scene in which his character is mummified in packing tape and put in a 'coffin' underneath a lorry (*Daily Mirror,* 19 September 1992). This method of transportation around Beirut was employed by John McCarthy's captors and was central to the traumas suffered by the hostages. In Alasdair Palmer's treatment for the film, 'cam-era tape and suffocation' is mentioned seventh in seventeen key 'ele-ments in the story'. 'It was an appalling experience,' Firth is quoted as saying, 'even though we were trussed up like that for just a couple of hours.' In the metonymic relation of his 'couple of hours' to the repeated experience of his real-world model lies the rhetorical claim of the docudrama at the level of performance. It was no different in the film *Blind Flight,* endorsed by Keenan and McCarthy and released in 2004. The camera tape and suffocation scene was still a marker for pre-publicity claims for authenticity. Doubts about what anything is 'really like' may haunt the realist mode, but they bedevil the fact-based drama to the extent that such simulation becomes *de rigeur*.[21]

It is also worth considering the place of Doncaster's 'experts' and their right of factual veto. These people were called in for the final few days of rehearsal of the dramatised story documentary. For *Return to Living*, she recalled: 'I contented myself with a Home Office official and a representative "ex-lag" – whom we invited to visit us on different days!' There is no mention of a lawyer's involvement. As I argued in Chapter 2, the increased level of such input today is an index of increased cultural doubt and anxiety and an emblem for fears about television's increased social power. It is also a marker for the more litigious turn taken by late capitalist societies. Doncaster's trust in the figure of the 'expert' is a vivid blast from a relatively innocent past. Her confidence in the notion of documentary authenticity was underwritten by research and the approval of experts. There is an implicit deference to these experts, and an implicit appeal to documentary 'objectivity'. These factors not only guarded against drama's excess but also constituted an implicitly superior status for facts and information. One can detect a culturally learned deference towards 'straight' drama, too. It is implied, for example, in: 'I am not suggesting ... that the production of a story documentary is more difficult than that of a drama', and present when she says revealingly: 'These productions are popular with actors because they often graduate from them to drama *proper*' (Doncaster, 1956: 47–8 – my italics).

It is easy to see why Doncaster's somewhat clumsy construction 'dramatised story documentary' did not subsequently gain currency, but it does have the virtue of precision: it describes a 'documentary' (category of origin) made for television by 'dramatising' (methodology) a 'story' (a journalistic, rather than literary, product). Pressure of usage in the United Kingdom shortened this by degrees: to 'dramatised documentary', then 'drama documentary', and finally to 'dramadoc'. But I am forced to argue that this 1940/50s form is better termed 'documentary drama' so that it does not become confused with very different second–phase practices. At the time, as now, both phrases were routinely used in the industry.

Duncan Ross, for example, used 'documentary drama' about the same programmes Doncaster calls 'dramatised story documentary' when he was writing in the *BBC Quarterly* in 1950 (see Goodwin and Kerr, 1983: 12).

Arthur Swinson, another early practitioner, wrote a book about the process and methodology of these programmes. His *Writing for Television* was first published in 1955, with a second edition in 1960, and a partially re-written third edition, *Writing for Television Today*, in 1963. In the earlier editions, he used Doncaster's term 'dramatized documentary' (1955: 78; 1960: 80). In a new chapter ('Present trends') in the second edition, he noted: 'The dramatized documentary has moved closer to the play; and the actuality documentary has moved closer to the dramatized form' (1960: 138). In 1963 he significantly replaced 'dramatized documentary' in every instance with 'drama-documentary'. This does not prevent him continuing to refer to Barr, Ross, and Michael Barry as 'the three men who evolved the dramatized documentary' (1963: 116). Amongst other significant shifts of emphasis, he altered the earlier advice that all documentary programmes 'need several stories and one theme' (1955: 87) to make space for the developing emphasis on the single story in the late 1950s (1963: 123). Over the eight-year period of these books the industrial trend to single story drama-documentary, and the shifts in terminology, can be plainly seen.

Swinson defined three kinds of documentary production in his books: 'dramatized documentary'/'drama-documentary', 'actuality documentary', and 'magazine documentary'. He sub-divided the first category into studio-based programmes and what he called 'the built O. B.', ('built Outside Broadcast'). About the former, he wrote:

(a) It is played by actors who give, as far as possible an accurate interpretation of the people they represent.
(b) It is produced 'live' in the studio, with the help of film sequences.
(c) The locations in which the action takes place in life are copied and reproduced in the studio.
(d) The stories are true in the sense that they are taken from life with as little modification as possible, bearing in mind the demands of the medium. (1955: 80; 1963: 118–19).

Once again, the innocence inherent in the confident proposal of so many questionable notions ('accurate interpretation', 'locations ... copied and reproduced', 'as little modification as possible') should not blind us to the fact that these rubrics are still in use. They are alive and well, if re-phased somewhat, in the disclaimer function I talked about in Chapter 3. What has changed, arguably, is the willingness of an audience now to agree to, and become complicit with, such proposals of equivalence between art and life.

The 'built O.B.' did not feature actors, the participants were: 'acting the parts they played in real life and in the real setting' – a bit like Harry Watt's bomber crew in *Target for Tonight*. The 'thoroughly scripted and rehearsed' built O.B. had its cast 'speaking lines they had learned by heart and performing movements worked out by the producer' (1963: 120). In his earlier book Swinson said: 'The technique of getting people to "act" their own jobs is becoming so well established that in television the gap between an actor playing a surgeon and a surgeon playing himself is being considerably narrowed' (1955: 53). The restraint of British documentary's underplayed style, so well known to all the television workers, narrowed this gap further. The technique caused the first questioning of the ethics of mixed forms. Its days of innocence might even be said to have ended when Maurice Wiggin, respected television critic of the *Sunday Times*, used a 1954 built O.B. about the health service (*House Surgeon*) as a stick with which to beat the dramatised story documentary. He compared studio work (which he found stilted) to what he took to be the greater documentary authenticity of *House Surgeon* (see Swinson, 1955: 82–3; 1963: 120–1). But Wiggin 'did not, as he imagined, see "the real thing" at all; what he saw was a reality created by artifice,' Swinson pointed out. Producer Bill Duncalf had extended the remit of the dramatised story documentary, arguing: 'that if interviews could be rehearsed, then dialogue could be rehearsed, as in a dramatic programme using actors.' The worries about duping the audience, now endemic in newspaper criticism of fact-based drama, can be traced back to this early experience, when (as Swinson innocently acknowledged) Wiggin 'was deceived' about *House Surgeon* (1963: 207).

Deceit was perhaps more excusable in these early days because of television's profound need for the real at a time when it was establishing its social *bona fides*. Audiences were gradually becoming accustomed to television as a major source of both information and entertainment, and we can speculate that in this case they completed the communication circuit willingly enough. But doubts were opening up between programme makers and the audience's self-appointed spokesperson the newspaper television critic. The presence of this doubt can probably never now be avoided, however great the search for new means of claiming a one-to-one relationship with the Real. At times of controversy it is precisely this gap that continues to be exploited and finessed (especially by journalists and politicians).

By the time of ITV's Annual Report for 1959/60 both *Emergency – Ward 10* and *Probation Officer* are being described as 'two established documentary drama series' (see Goodwin and Kerr, 1983: 3). Although these programmes were, in effect, nearer to soap opera, Antony Kearey (producer of the former) was proud of the research that went into his hospital series: 'A panel of special advisers is permanently on call' (n.d. *ca* 1958: 7), he notes. The ITV Report even included in its list of 'documentary drama series' the programme destined to become British television's longest running soap opera, Granada's *Coronation Street* (first transmitted 1960). It is hard now to imagine 'Corrie' as in any way documentary, but early episodes certainly had a realist, 'kitchen sink' quality derived from contemporary theatre and film. The character Ken Barlow (played then as now by William Roache) started out as a Jimmy Porter-style 'angry young man' returning to his Northern roots from a university education that fitted him poorly for re-entry into his region and class.[22]

At the end of the 1950s the BBC was also searching for grittily realistic contemporary drama. It developed the police series *Z Cars* which (again relatively speaking) provided a new take on police work in the suddenly fashionable north of England. One of *Z Cars'* original writers, Allan Prior, is clear that the makers of dramatised story documentaries 'virtually invented the Studio Play: they were making documentaries but the techniques were to remain the same to this day ... These men's names may be half-forgotten now, but they made the rules of television-drama, rules that remain, even now, in place' (1996: 5–6). Although he does not mention names, Prior might have noted that Robert Barr, in his own drift from journalism to drama, also contributed to Z *Cars*.[23] The documentary aspect of such programmes as these lay in two related areas: first, there was a socially realistic *look*, very fashionable at the time; and second there was a new social extension in subject matter. In retrospect, this can be seen as all of a piece with the late 1950s drive to make space for new voices and for regional locales in British culture (other, that is, than received pronunciation and the Home Counties). All this was made increasingly possible during the 1960s by new, portable sound and image recording equipment.[24]

First-phase USA – the 'documentary-drama'

The different imperatives of American television also produced fact-based programming in the first phase of US development. The staple mode was different from British 'dramatised story documentary'. It was a mode much more influenced both formally and institutionally by the film industry. It used the narrative practices, and on occasions the personnel, of Hollywood feature film. Institutionally, the 1948 Paramount judgement heralded a reconfiguration of the film industry designed to eliminate the monopolistic practices of the old studio system. The reformed film industry was to have a profound influence on the development of television in the USA. In the area of fact-based drama, the influence of the film industry became almost total because of the way the remaining studios diversified and made the most of opportunities in the newer medium.[25]

The documentary movement of the pre-war years had its influence here too. And yet Robert Flaherty, Pare Lorentz and Willard Van Dyke were not key to US television history in the way that the likes of Grierson and Rotha were in the United Kingdom. American journalism's pioneering of the 'photo journal', through which actuality photographs were turned into a popular art form, was much more influential. From the founding of *Time* magazine in 1923, US journalism's address of the real had been dominated by the still camera lens. The photo-journalist's ability to capture the *zeitgeist* of Depression America fuelled American filmmakers' approach to the real, and the synergies between journalism, film and broadcasting were many.[26] When NBC and CBS radio expanded their drama output during 1928–29 the connection was very direct: some of the new programming was actually sponsored by photo-journals, with *Time* magazine leading the way.

Time Inc. developed the long-running series *The March of Time* for NBC, first for radio (from 1931) then for film (from 1935). From the outset the radio version used actors; their voices provided further illustrative input to a mode that was essentially narrated in direct address to the audience. Impersonation by actors of real-world individuals was a staple technique. Competitor network CBS had *True Story*, a drama series sponsored by Macfadden Publications to boost sales of a magazine of the same name. This drama series was: 'Based on magazine stories, neatly bowdlerized and dressed with strangely literate dialogue and philosophizing.' Eric Barnouw called it 'both lurid and respectable enough to be a smashing 1928–29 success' (Barnouw, 1966: I, 224). The lineaments of the modern American docudrama can be clearly discerned in these early journalistic reshapings of the American documentary project. When *The March of Time* turned to film in 1935 it was a newsreel with a difference. It was first in the field for the illustrative 're-enactment' now so beloved especially by crime-based 'Reality TV'. William Bluem remarks that in the radio version the enforced absence of any authorising image made it a technique easy to absorb at the point of reception, as well as simple to organise at the point of production. It enabled editors to make a key decision: to use fewer stories than competitor newsreels, but to treat those stories in more depth and *dramatically* (1979: 36).[27] This, too, is a classic claim for the docudrama. As British filmmaker Paul Greengrass remarked before the screening of *Omagh*, his account of the 1998 'Real IRA' bombing in which 29 people died in Northern Ireland:

> Storytelling is very limited in documentary. Drama offered more texture, a fuller picture, so in a way I like to think *Bloody Sunday* and *Stephen Lawrence* give much fuller pictures than if I'd just made them as documentaries.[28]

The concept of the 'fuller picture' draws the belief that *feeling* is a crucial component to *knowing* for a popular audience.

About the fuller picture of *The March of Time*'s mix of drama with actuality Bluem notes:

> This expansion of time in the reporting process was important chiefly because it permitted a journalistic style in which emphasis was divided between the inherent drama of an event and a dramatic technique of presentation. (Bluem, 1979: 36)

The March of Time plotted its news items, enabling a structure that 'mov[ed] toward a dramatic climax which, in turn, dictated a unified continuity' (Bluem, 1979: 36). These are the terms of classic Hollywood realism, indeed of realist drama. Like in modern docudrama, a socially responsible dimension to the project was sought: 'The journalistic documentary was designed to inform great audiences of the immediate conflicts and crises of the age,' notes Bluem (1979: 40). Raymond Fielding, in his 1978 study of *The March of Time*, points out that the team avoided the word 'documentary' wherever possible. Louis de Rochemont and Roy Larsen, founders of the series, preferred the term 'pictorial journalism' (1978: 75). The format was eminently exportable, and production offices opened in Canada and the UK. British editions included local material and were produced from 1935. Prominent Griersonians were involved (Edgar Anstey, Harry Watt, Len Lye, Maurice Lancaster and Arthur Elton, for example – see Fielding, 1978: 93, 156).[29]

The 1950s are often cited as the 'Golden Age' for a particular kind of American television drama: the live 'dramatic anthology series'. Plays for anthology programmes such as *Philco Television Playhouse, Goodyear Television Playhouse* and *Kraft Television Theater* were produced from a large New York studio. And for the first time people could and did achieve reputations as *television* workers. Dramatist Paddy Chayefsky was a key example, his 1953 play *Marty* being the first really famous television play. As he noted in 'The Big Deal: Television Craft' (an essay first published in 1955), the essence of the new dramatic art was 'every day crises' and the avoidance of 'excessive theatricality.' 'Television has a camera, and the audience expects the camera to show it something real,' he sharply observed (1995: 133–4). As well as new writers like Chayefsky there was a plentiful supply of cheap new acting talent available, often fresh from Lee Strasberg's Actors' Studio (one such, Rod Steiger, was television's Marty). Famous names, too, were happy to take roles in the increasingly prestigious drama series that proliferated in 1950s America. Tino Balio notes that in the 1953–56 heyday 'the networks broadcast 20 such programs a week' (1990: 17).

The speciality of NBC's anthology series *Armstrong Circle Theatre*, in which the likes of John Cassavetes, Robert Duvall and Telly Savalas made their television debuts, was fact-based drama. The series began basing its dramas on factual material in 1955. The year is a crucial one because this was the point at which movie studios started selling off their back catalogues to television networks following the Paramount Decree. RKO (the weakest of the 'Big Five' pre-war film studios) did this in 1955 as part of what became a complete withdrawal from film production.[30] Emergent television network ABC made an agreement with Warner Brothers in the same year. The agreement was a prelude to Warners' gradual participation in television drama production. With film fictions past (back catalogues) and present (from new production companies) about to flood the market, and with anthology dramas under pressure to move with the rest of American television from the East to the West Coast, the producers of *Armstrong Circle Theatre* elected to stay in New York and to move into original, fact-based, teleplays. This enabled them, briefly, to create a market niche.

Armstrong Circle Theatre used docudrama because, then as now, it was relatively cheap to make and, to repeat the Lipkin mantra, 'rootable, relatable and promotable'. Contemporary factual material was also unlikely to form part of a Hollywood studio back catalogue because of film's longer lead-in time. Hollywood, with some exceptions, was in any case notorious for its tentative approach to contentious subjects. The television docudramas, 'pre-sold' to their audience through the news media, aimed to be socially responsible in terms of content. They can be contrasted with British 'dramatised story documentaries' of the same period in two significant respects: firstly their strategic objective was commercial; secondly their production priorities leaned much more towards the dramatic. About *Armstrong Circle Theatre*'s producer Robert Costello, Bluem comments:

> [he] worked toward a format which offered two basic methods of drama-
> tisation. In certain cases it was found advantageous to deal directly with
> a real person, and in others it was found best to create a purely fictional
> character which represented several real people or a shared attitude.
> (1979: 193)

Costello's commitment to a concept of public service should not be
undervalued. Bluem quotes him saying: 'We can't use an idea only
or a news story only, we must also be able to present some potential solution, some hope for our citizens to consider, to think about'
(1979: 193).

The team producing the series came mainly from drama backgrounds, but the programme makers had a similar faith in expert
consultants to subsequent makers of docudrama. Producers
employed these experts to establish the documentary base for their
dramas (see Hoffer *et al.*, 1985: 182). In presentation, a journalist/
narrator supplied narrative continuity in direct address voiceover,
as is the case in many modern docudramas. *Armstrong Circle Theatre*
made its reputation through 'specializ[ing] in dramatizations of
actual events' (McNeil 1991: 53). Bluem, and others, label the teleplays from this anthology series 'documentary-dramas' and this
term (along with 'docudrama') were certainly in use in the 1950s
(see Musburger, 1985). Dropped by NBC in 1957 *Armstrong Circle
Theatre* was immediately taken up by CBS, remaining in production until 1963. In the CBS years its shift away from documentary
towards drama became still more marked. In 1961 CBS 'eliminated
Douglas Edwards from the narrator's role', thus bringing the series
into line with the kind of filmed dramas that were beginning to
dominate the networks (Bluem, 1979: 165). Bluem concludes that
the demise of the series was due to a perception that the documentary-drama form as developed by *Armstrong Circle Theatre* was:

> neither fish nor fowl ... its commitment to the faithful duplication of
> events and people limited its freedom as drama ... [but] the use of actors
> and theatrical conventions deprived it of any validity as documentary.
> (Bluem, 1979: 193)

This succinct summary of the problems of the form favoured by the series could stand today. It was nothing less than the prototype for that branch of the 'made-for-TV movie' that specialises in the fact-based drama – 'movie-of-the-week docudrama'.

A good example of an *Armstrong Circle Theatre* teleplay based on fact is *Freedom Fighters of Hungary*, transmitted by NBC on 22 January 1957 in prime time (9.30–10.30 p.m.).[31] Written by Art Wallace and produced by Costello, the play is a treatment of the 1956 Hungarian uprising. The programme was fronted by the series' link-man, well known television personality/news anchor John Cameron Swayze. His introduction is delivered from a newsroom set and provides an ideological frame for the story. Swayze tells the audience that the historical event of the uprising is evidence of 'the complete brutality and inhumanity of Soviet oppression'. An archive sequence follows these words, showing footage of Soviet tanks in the streets of Budapest. This brief opening is followed abruptly (and rather startlingly for a British viewer) by an advertisement break. In the common practice of the time, the sponsor Armstrong required maximum exposure for its products in the programme that bore its name (the advertisements in all anthology series were, of course, solely those of the sponsor).

Freedom Fighters of Hungary mixed archive newsreel exteriors with acted studio set interiors. The latter sequences were very similar to the British dramatised story documentary. There were representative characters: an 'ordinary' family celebrating their son's twelfth birth-day; an officer in the Hungarian army and his girlfriend; her father, a pavement café owner; a group of young students; the grandfather of one student. The latter character gives contextualising 'backstory' about Hungary's proud and independent past. With just a few sets, the camerawork is mostly one- and two-shot arrangements. The *mise-en-scène* is basic compared to the practices analysed in Chapter 1. Because both studio and newsreel footage was in black-and-white, the frequent cutting from (photographic) documentary to (elec-tronic) drama works fairly seamlessly. The studio lighting helps, with greater use of chiaroscuro effects than is common today. So, when a sequence following the first advertising break mixes street fighting archive material with the actors-as-students taking cover behind café tables in the studio, it would be difficult to read it as a Brechtian 'interruption' to the story.

Swayze's voiceover sets and re-sets the scene frequently, giving dates and times, recapping situations previously shown in newsreel footage. The drama, meanwhile, illustrates the human dimension of this classic Cold War event. Father and son die in the uprising, as does the army officer's girlfriend and one of the students. The mother (Anna), her son, the remaining students and the officer finish up in Anna's flat, defiantly continuing to fight the perfidious Russians. Viewed today, the acting appears overstated in its theatricality but could conceivably be read as underplayed by an audience half a century ago. The writing telegraphs its main points and makes self-consciously theatrical repetitions but, again, is dominantly realist. Repetitions serve, for example, to signify the collectivity of the Hungarian people against their oppressor. One repeated question–answer sequence follows Sandor (the army captain) asking another character: 'Do you know how to handle a gun?' All reply: 'I can learn.' This mantra is repeated with the girl student, the twelve-year-old boy, and the boy's mother. On each occasion someone has died and therefore relinquished a gun (a male student, the father, the boy). The exchange signifies metonymically the necessity for heroic continuity in the struggle. The doubly-bereaved Anna speaks the line as the final words of the play.

As a further, documentary, dimension in the casting, Eva Soreny, playing Anna, is billed as 'the First Lady of the Hungarian National Theatre', and announced as such by Swayze. The programme's final extra-textual word on this great twentieth-century historical moment is Soreny's piece-to-camera, delivered out of character. She speaks with her own real authority – that of someone who has actually lived through the days from 23 October 1956 – when the first demonstrators took to the streets in Budapest – to 4 November, when the insurrection was finally crushed. She has the additional authority of someone who then escaped to the USA. In her own person, she speaks briefly but movingly of the 'spirit of Hungary', which she herself thus represents both in and out of the action. The emotional effect of this for a contemporary audience would almost certainly have been heightened by the play's transmission only two months after the historical events depicted.

Armstrong Circle Theatre was not the only exponent of documentary drama on 1950s American television. The series *You Are There* used a newscast format that allowed modern reporters to 'go to', audiences to 'be at' historical events. This format did not allow, of course, for the kind of contemporary subject that *Armstrong Circle Theatre* treated. But the format was copied by the BBC in Britain, particularly at Second World War anniversary points like D-Day (around 6 June 2004, current newsreaders presented the news as if on the day in history). Codes and conventions familiar to popular audiences from their nightly news can bring historical events closer, and animate personalities behind them, as *You Are There* proved in the 1950s. Their reporters 'interviewed' actors playing historical figures such as John Dillinger (22 February 1953), Cortes (5 April 1953) and Mata Hari (9 May 1954); they investigated events such as 'The Sailing of the Mayflower' (22 November 1953), 'The Vote That Made Jefferson President' (27 June 1954) and 'The Triumph of Alexander the Great' (27 March 1955). Like many another history programme, the nearest *You Are There* got to contemporary affairs was events from the previous decade (there was an episode in 1953, for example, about Rudolf Hess's 1941 flight to Scotland). This CBS show ran in an early evening slot from 1953 to 1957, with the great Walter Cronkite himself as anchor.[32]

Like *The March of Time*, *You Are There* emerged from an earlier radio series (1947–50) and had sponsorship from capitalist companies. This is ironic since, although the subjects may not have been obviously political, all the *You Are There* shows referred to above were written by writers blacklisted by the House Un-American Activities Committee (HUAC) – Abraham Polonsky (Cortes, Alexander), Walter Bernstein (Dillinger, Jefferson), and Arnold Manoff (Mayflower, Mata Hari). Bernstein explicitly makes the connection between the plays and contemporary events:

> History served us well. We had no need to invent conflicts to serve our purpose ... In that shameful time of McCarthyite terror ... we were able to do shows about civil liberties, civil rights, artistic freedom.[33]

As with other anthology series, *You Are There* was a training ground for directors and actors as well as writers (James Dean, John Frankenheimer, Sidney Lumet, Paul Newman).

In the first phase of docudrama, then, there were important differences between British and American traditions and practices in fact-based drama. These developed over time into what I defined as the 'documentary drama' and 'drama-documentary' approaches. Both approaches mix dramatic and factual/editorial priorities in slightly different ways, which become more obvious in the next phase of development.

Notes

1 Paul Rotha, for example, used the following formula as subtitle for his book *Documentary Film* (first published in 1936): 'The use of the film medium to interpret creatively and in social terms the life of the people as it exists in reality'.

2 Winston offers a trenchant critique of a school and history of filmmaking that he accuses of constantly 'running away from social meaning' (1995: 35ff).

3 See also the entry on 'classic Hollywood cinema/classic narrative cinema' in Susan Hayward's *Cinema Studies: the Key Concepts* (2006: 82–5). See also Bill Nichols on the effects of continuity editing (1981: 70–92).

4 Winston (1995) gives details about the artfulness of the pre-war documentarians' use of drama – see especially pp. 99–103, on Flaherty's 1922 *Nanook of the North*. See also Barnouw (1993: 33–51).

5 Eisenstein's film *Battleship Potemkin* (1925) was a particularly important film for Grierson, who prepared English subtitles for the first US showing of the film in 1926 (see Aitken, 1990: 75). Its influence on *Drifters* is easy to see, but this was the only film that Grierson actually made.

6 Watt used the first phrase in an interview for the BBC2 *Arena* programme (1983). The second phrase is taken from the notes on the Imperial War Museum video version of *Target for Tonight* (1992).

7 Showing the two films in class over a number of years, I have found this to be true for student audiences at least.

8 *The Documentary Conscience*, the title of Alan Rosenthal's 1980 book, captures eloquently the social rooting of the documentary impulse.

9 Lipkin (2002) is especially interesting on this aspect of the docudrama's unique mode of persuasive discourse. See also Chapter 8.

10 The difference between us is that Ellis is looking at a whole *system* of representation whereas I am looking at one *form* of representation within that system. Ellis draws attention to fundamental shifts in the ecology of television, while I am concerned with a form that responds over time in

'phases' to the seismic shifts noted in Ellis's analysis of 'eras'.

11 In this period there has been a sharp re-focusing of notions of a Western 'Us' and an Eastern 'Them' as a result of the events of 9/11.

12 David Edgar was speaking at the 'Visible Evidence XI' conference in Bristol in 2003, on the panel 'Docudrama – Evidence of What?'

13 See Paget (1997).

14 See Briggs (1995) on the history of the BBC; on European public service broadcasting, see Smith (1995: 62–91).

15 See Barnouw (1966) on the history of American network television.

16 Leishman also recounted the Sarnoff story during BBC1's *Imagine ...* ('And Then There Was Television', 19 December 2006). The predilection of American entrepreneurs for self-awarded military status is a fascinating one. Elvis Presley's huckster manager 'Colonel' Tom Parker was another such individual: not only was he *not* a colonel, he was not even American. Of Dutch origin, he assumed the name 'Tom Parker' as well as his military rank. The capitalist reflex to cover one's tracks is writ large in such individual re-inventings. It is not unusual, of course, for companies too to re-name themselves following bad publicity – the North Sea ferry company Townsend Thoresen was rebranded as P&O following the 6 March 1987 Zeebrugge disaster. The ship that capsized was the arrogantly named 'Herald of Free Enterprise'.

17 When she left the BBC in the mid-1950s, Doncaster went on to be Executive Producer of Documentaries for ITV franchise holder Rediffusion (see Finch, 2003: 202).

18 See Scannell (1986: 1–26).

19 Arthur Swinson gives an earlier date, citing two 1946 programmes: *Germany Under Control* (Robert Barr) and *I Want To Be An Actor* (Duncan Ross).

20 Ofcom's April 2004 report noted an *average* audience share drop of minus 44% for 'serious programmes' in multi-channel homes in the United Kingdom (*Guardian*, 22 April 2004, p. 9).

21 To be fair to Firth, he also remarked: 'I know it always sounds terribly precious when an actor talks like this ... But it gave me a clue. And you apply your imagination ... ' (*Elle Magazine* September 1992, p. 40).

22 Roache is the only original cast member left in Coronation Street.

23 Prior talks of the show emerging from 'the BBC's Drama Documentary Unit' (1996: 7). In the past it has usually been called the 'Documentary-Drama Group' (Goodwin and Kerr, 1983: 3); indeed Corner (1996: 38) argues a special significance in the slippage from the 'Dramatized Documentary Unit' of the early 1950s. The original writing team also included Troy Kennedy Martin and John Hopkins, as well as Allan Prior and Robert Barr. John McGrath and Ken Loach were two other significant figures who cut their creative teeth on *Z Cars*.

24 See Laing (1986) for more on this period and its television. Some research

into the output of television journalist/dramatist Tony Parker is much needed to expand our understanding of the mixed form during this early period. Irene Shubik makes much of him in her book *Play for Today: The Evolution of Television Drama* (first published 1975; second edition 2000 – see especially pp. 78–86 in the latter). In August 2006, thanks to BBC archivist Andy O'Dwyer, I saw *Without Love*, a teleplay of Parker's from 1956 about prostitution. Essentially, it is a studio-based *Cathy Come Home*, a fictionalised working of detailed research material. Its visual values are, of course, different, having been made almost entirely in the studio.

25 See Balio (1990: 3–40) on the actual (rather than the desired) effects of the Paramount Decree.

26 See Stott (1973) for more detail.

27 I have used the 1979 reprint of Bluem's book, which was first published in 1965. His important account of 'first phase' developments should be seen as the American equivalent of the British account offered by Swinson.

28 See Simon Hattenstone's interview with Greengrass ('A lot of factual drama is crap', *Guardian 2*, 20 May 2004, pp. 8–9). Greengrass refers in this quotation to two of his other docudramas (discussed elsewhere in this book).

29 As well as working on the series in London, Anstey was also based in New York in 1937–38 as Foreign Editor for *The March of Time*.

30 RKO still exists (see the company's website www.rko.com), but the original company was effectively wound up in 1959.

31 I watched this teleplay on video at the Museum of Broadcast Communication in Chicago in 1997. The *Armstrong Circle Theatre* programmes are part of its David Susskind Collection.

32 The show was briefly revived by CBS in 1971–72.

33 Quoted in Schultheiss and Schaubert's edition of ten Polonsky teleplays written for *You Are There* (Polonsky, 1997), which contains a reprint of the script for 'Cortes Conquers Mexico'. His treatment of the Cortes story, for example, bears the quotation out, being clearly focused on the notion of imperialist exploitation.

6

Histories: second-phase developments

'Public goods' (USA) versus 'public good' (UK)

In my account of docudrama's second phase I will argue that different-but-related broadcasting cultures in the USA and the UK were gradually drawing together during this period. In America, broadcasting served a variety of needs (which, of course, centred on the all important selling of *goods* to the *public* – hence my coinage 'public goods'). In the UK this period was still marked by a robust concept of public service (hence 'public good'). But from this point on the market place became an ever more noticeable factor. In the USA the docudramatic branch of the 'made-for-TV movie' and the 'faction' drama series developed from the previous *documentary-in-drama* approach. In the UK the *drama-in-documentary* approach took its colour primarily from investigative journalism. This led Granada's current affairs programme *World in Action* to develop 'dramadoc', a form clearly derived from the 'dramatised story documentary' of the 1950s. There was also some *documentary-in-drama* in several important social-realist dramas of the second phase (see next section). In the USA, synergy between the film and television industries gradually amplified the dramatic priorities of industries more focused on entertainment. As Lipkin (2002) shows in his analysis of what he calls 'semi-documentaries', Twentieth-Century Fox led the way with a series of post-war film docudramas that utilised melodramatic tropes to 'warrant' their claims. Where the film industry had led, the made-for-TV movie followed. In Britain, a weak film industry could (and did) influence visual styles, but the journalistic link between television documentary and drama continued to endorse factual claims more assertively.

The history of factual drama replays in microcosm the essential differences in emphases between the British and American television systems. In 'public goods' television and its docudrama, public *wants* tend to be uppermost at the point of production, in terms of the advertisers to whom the filmmakers are beholden, of the entertainment values endorsed, and, more importantly, of the stories characteristically sought for dramatisation. Conversely, judgements about public *needs* are uppermost where 'public good' is the consideration. In the words of Vance Keply Jr: 'advertiser-supported commercial television is an example of a public goods industry ... [in which] the public good label refers only to the industry's economic qualities' (1990: 42–3). Thus the maximising of a product's sales potential is a key consideration for the American broadcaster; it must come before everything else. The made-for-TV movie, emerging in the mid-1960s, was an ideal vehicle for such a scale of priorities. By contrast, British dramadoc in the same period was more high-mindedly conscious of social and political purpose.

British dramadoc – projecting truth

In the second phase live studio drama was being superseded by location-based filming developed following technological change. It is generally accepted that new technology turned television drama away from the theatre and television studio, and towards the look and sound of cinema. This had implications not only for television drama departments but also for political or current affairs, and arts and science departments too. In this period both 'documentary drama' and 'drama-documentary' practices developed in parallel, with some departments leaning towards informational, documentary priorities, others towards recreational, dramatic ones. And it was not necessarily the case that the more informational a department's remit, the more documentary its method. BBC Science and Arts Departments, for example, responded to the pressing need to explain things by using more and more dramatic devices and structures. In Roger Silverstone's succinct phrase, the

BBC Science Department habitually used 'non-scientific narratives to legitimate itself' for lay audiences (1986: 82). He calls attention to the generally 'agonistic', dramatic, nature of BBC's science series *Horizon*'s presentations in particular. Drama's dialogical framework provided a ready made intellectual 'other' – representing as often as not those regressive forces that perennially doubt and oppose the advances of science. This doubting figure played antagonist to progressive scientific protagonists in many productions. *Horizon* (1964–) routinely used and still uses docudrama, its narratives close to structures of, for example, detective film and biopic. And in arts programming too, the innovative protagonist met oppositional figures in strands like *Monitor* (1958–65). Ken Russell, for example, explored famous musicians' careers (Bartók, Berlioz, Debussy, Elgar) through his often formally inventive films.[1]

The work of another director who was to become famous, Ken Loach, provides an illustration of the contrasting potential for documentary styles in second phase UK television. A crucial factor in British culture has always been the bringing in from the margins of radical commentaries through the direct agency of the liberal state. This kind of radical stance has often utilised the documentary because factual material can so directly critique, oppose, and indeed accuse the social *status quo*. Using contemporary material – the 'only-just past' – documentary drama as practised at the BBC by Loach, producer Tony Garnett, and writers such as Jim Allen, Nell Dunn and Jeremy Sandford, was classically issue-based and politically oppositional. Over the years, Loach has acquired a deserved reputation for films that mix documentary and dramatic styles, and that use information from the real world as their basis for making polemical points. As he himself has said, his aim is to 'cut through the glass wall that separates fiction from fact' (Hood, 1994: 199). In this sense, all his work could be categorised as 'documentary drama' according to my Chapter 3 definitions.

Loach's current status as *auteur* director is the result of a string of successful feature films during the past two decades – from *Land and Freedom* (1995) to *Looking for Eric* (2009). These have secured his international reputation, but during the 1980s he became such a controversial figure politically that for a time he could not get his work screened anywhere (see A. Hayward, 2005). Whether his subject is contemporary society, as in *Carla's Song* (1996), or past betrayals of the socialism he so believes in, as in *The Wind That Shakes the Barley* (2006), he has always probed capitalism's failures of social duty and celebrated the struggles of the organised working-class. His television documentary dramas of the 1960s set up this reputation for opposition to the *status quo*. *Up the Junction* (1965), *Cathy Come Home* (1966) and *In Two Minds* (1968), were all made for the BBC and set a benchmark for the factually-based teleplay.[2] Programmed in the anthology series *The Wednesday Play* (1964–69 – the brainchild of Canadian producer Sydney Newman), the series was conceived as television's contribution to a new contemporary taste for realistic social drama.[3] Newman's resonant phrase for what he wanted in his drama series was 'agitational contemporaneity' (see Sendall and Potter, 1982: I, 338), a phrase that even today could describe Loach's work.

Loach's 1960s films bore trademark features that almost define second phase British docudrama: a pronounced social critique at the level of content (usually focused through 'underdog' protagonists); filming techniques that placed a premium on immediacy (from which a documentary authenticity could be readily inferred); and acting styles that stressed underplaying and appeared improvised (even when they were not). Performances and film style alike eschewed the theatrical. Loach has often used non-professional actors in order to access an unselfconscious quality in performance that sometimes cause difficulties for professional actors. *Ae Fond Kiss* (2004), for example, has a centrepiece relationship between Catholic music teacher Roisin and Cassim, a Muslim DJ. Through these characters, Loach examines the pleasures and pains of love across religious and cultural divides in contemporary Glasgow. He paired as his contemporary Juliet and Romeo a professional (Eva Birthistle) and a non-professional (Atta Yaqub).[4] His favoured professional performers have to possess that unstudied quality on screen that is the ultimate refinement of Strasbergian focus on the moment. Compare the central performances of Carol White in *Cathy Come Home* (1966) with Chrissy Rock in *Ladybird, Ladybird* (1994) and the continuity is evident across three decades.

Loach's major preoccupation, 'to give a voice to those who are often denied it', is the democratic ideal that animates all his films.[5] His working practice is to use real locations and to shoot a film in story-order (i.e. chronologically and not for logistical convenience). Actors are deliberately kept guessing because they are denied any overview of the script; Loach reveals the plot, so to speak, a page at a time. He seeks through these means to preserve an unaffected authenticity in performance. His methods, like those of Mike Leigh (another British film director with the kind of *vérité* style that asks actors to be consistently 'in the moment') are often warmly endorsed by actors because they counter the danger of 'playing the result'. This phrase describes the jumping or eliding of the psychological stage between the experience of an event by a character and its behavioural manifestation. As well as damaging the dramatic moment, this has consequences for what follows in a character's development and is an occupational hazard that tends to worry actors. Finding directors who actively help you deal with the problem, like Loach and Leigh, is something they value. If you stay 'in the moment', and forget (or better still do not know) where the story arc is taking you, if you are encouraged to improvise, the performance has more chance of staying 'real' and 'true' – or so many actors believe. Robert Carlyle, the male protagonist in *Carla's Song*, told an interviewer: 'Ken makes it easier to become real ... You're not projecting a character, you're projecting a truth' (*Guardian*, 31 January 1997).[6]

The Loach-directed *Cathy Come Home* is the prime example of second-phase documentary drama from British television's own 'Golden Age'. It is still widely regarded not only as 'a representatively "classic" piece of British television', but also as '"essential television"' (Corner, 1996: 90). In some ways, *Cathy* was simply a film whose time was right. Loach himself has taken a more critical view of his early classic as time has gone on; he has said, for example, that it was 'by and large approved because even Tory politicians got on the bandwagon and said: this is helping to solve the problems of the homeless' (Hood, 1994: 196–7). But the film did give prominence to a 'public good' by attacking an iniquitous social situation regarding housing. It unquestionably stirred the public conscience in the mid-1960s. *Cathy Come Home* is also that rare thing, a television programme that is not, as most television is, ephemeral. It registered with audiences at the time, and continues to register, on both the documentary and the drama scales. Even today, I have found that student groups still respond to Cathy's human dilemma, and are more than willing to connect the film to continuing problems with social housing. The British charity 'Shelter' continued to use the film as a consciousness-raiser long after the particular facts embedded within it became out of date. The late Carol White's face (in role as Cathy) can still sometimes be seen illustrating articles about both housing and serious British television drama. One of the most repeated dramas on British television, *Cathy* remains iconic.[7]

There has been some critical debate about whether *Cathy* is documentary drama or drama-documentary. I take view that it is the former because, in John Corner's felicitous phrase, the film 'opens up *documentary space* around the storyline' (my emphasis). This 'space' encouraged the viewer to think about the actual social problem that the fictitious Cathy faced. *Cathy Come Home*'s impact was later seen by its makers as somewhat fortuitous. Jeremy Sandford told me, 'Perhaps *Cathy* could only be done once. It was part of TV's "Age of Innocence".' In 1994 Loach said something similar: '*Cathy Come Home* had quite a strong impact because the audience were much more innocent at that time.'[8] This was a fiction film produced within a drama department, but possessing a strong documentary element that manifested itself in both content and form: the script was the result of demonstrable research, and the film-style echoed contemporary non-fictional works reliant on new camera technology.[9] The two elements ensured its sharp social criticism and its cutting edge. Producer Tony Garnett's achievement in smuggling contentious subject matter through an institution always prone, like any other, to be resistant to challenging ideas was remarkable. In Garnett's view – thirty years later – the film happened 'despite the powers that be rather than because of them'.[10]

Cathy Come Home also transcended the docudrama classification so compromised by troubled institutional and cultural histories. It is this quality that ensures it will be cited, in the UK at any rate, for as long as mixtures of drama and factual material are found problematical, and as long as television drama is celebrated. What *Cathy* possesses, even seen many years after its first transmission, is what Garnett calls 'life in the frame'. It had and still has a level of authenticity conferred by a style of film making that appears (like the acting) to take the audience into events as-they-happen. The immediacy of this style, based on hand-held techniques of 1960s documentary, was sometimes derided as 'wobblyscope' by camera operators schooled to aim for technically perfect images. The documentary element of Loach's directorial style was made possible by equipment already widely used in both documentary and anthropological film-making but new to drama. It was born, in summary, of a combination of the naturalism favoured by post-Jimmy Porter theatre, the 'new realism' of *Wednesday Play* television drama, and the access to the real promised by new technology.

The new technology was crucial to the documentary element of *Cathy Come Home*. The film utilises a sophisticated series of looks and sounds that offer to the audience a variety of spectator positions. Sometimes the operative verb is 'to witness' – the audience being offered an omniscient, surveillant, 'objective' point of view. At other times there is an emphasis on the emotional and the visceral – especially when the point of view is centred on Cathy herself.[11] The documentary and the drama of *Cathy Come Home* pull us to different angles of vision that are complementary. They enable a focus on an officialdom that is not exactly malign, but neither is it particularly competent nor disposed to be sympathetic in the face of human misery. The consistency of Loach's style makes his new work no different in some ways from this summary of the generality of 'the slice-of-life drama':

> never better received than when it is written and presented in the mood of topicality, when we are aware of the camera following the actors a little raggedly, when the actor is spotted groping for a word, and when there is a *commedia dell'arte* spirit of improvisation in the studio. (Styan, 1962: 188–9)

Generally, the look of fiction film contrasts very obviously with the *Cathy* kind of film. In fiction film the visual element is generally uncluttered and clear; action is 'staged' and technically orchestrated

– it is glossy in a way rigorously avoided by documentary drama. The 'natural' clutter and confusion of documentary filming are second-phase documentary drama's guarantee of authenticity. On one side 'perfection in the frame'; on the other 'life in the frame'. Spectators drawn into Loach's world could (and still can) see their experience as part of a continuum that includes action in the real, phenomenal, world. This kind of experience is, importantly, not just entertainment; there is a seriousness – Nichols' 'sobriety' indeed – that both authenticates the drama and validates the pleasure offered to a viewer. Loach's films, humorous as they can sometimes be, are fundamentally serious films for serious people.

Made-for-TV-movies – a very American genre

In the USA the second-phase shift to the docudrama 'made-for-TV' contrasts culturally, institutionally and formally with British documentary drama. The politics and aesthetics of the American form tended to produce films more accepting, perhaps, of the world as it was. While the best of the British form earnestly questioned and challenged the world of the 1960s through provocative experiment and subject matter, the American equivalent worked off a more commercial, but honourable tradition of socially-conscious films that reached back into the period between the World Wars. As Lipkin notes, the series of influential post-war Twentieth Century-Fox social problem *films noirs* were rooted in Darryl F. Zanuck's pre-war 'predilection for actuality-based story material' in his pre-war work with Warner Brothers (2002: 14). The progenitors of the US television docudrama – as both Lipkin and Custen have shown – are to be found in the Hollywood 'biopic' and in Warner Brothers and Twentieth Century-Fox fiction film about social subjects.[12]

If the American fact-based drama on television ended its initial developmental phase with the demise of *Armstrong Circle Theatre*, the made-for-TV movie re-configured the form. By common consent the forms that the old-fashioned Hollywood studio system (dead by around 1960) had so assiduously developed percolated into the new medium into which studios were diversifying. Gary Edgerton (1985) proposed docudrama as one of his three categories in the

new television genre 'Made-for-TV movie'.[13] They tended to capitalise, he remarks, on 'the intrinsic topicality of the television medium
itself'. Films drew their form and structure from social problems, the
headlines of newspapers, the stories in the news. Edgerton emphasises that the made-for-TV docudrama 'blend(s) essential aspects of
both the fictional and the documentary film', but he notes that 'the
narrative form has usually dominated' (1985: 152). The 'story', in
other words, was all-important in the USA. However, the proposal
of public issues qualifies the post-war made-for-TV docudrama as a
development of public service drama US-style.

In contrast to Edgerton, Todd Gitlin comments acerbically:
'Television docudrama abhors what it considers polemic, didacti-
cism, speechifying. Convention clamps a tight frame round the story.
It doesn't want the larger public world leaking in' (1994: 175).
British filmmakers like Loach have always more actively sought such
'leakage', but in my view it not as absent in American docudrama
as Gitlin asserts. It is, however, 'a very American genre' in the way it
tends to avoid a direct relationship with abstract political ideas and
contentious subject matter. Elayne Rapping noted in 1987 that US
docudramas rely on 'actors, staged settings and dramatically written
scripts' (p. 142).[14] But in seeking socially relevant themes, movie-
of-the-week docudrama also entered the 'duty space' of public service. Gitlin's obvious dislike of the mode has perhaps blinded him to
this. The mode has delivered public issues to the popular audience
via individually focused stories. The generic dependence upon the
actor and the dramatist has led many American scholars to allege
that the made-for-TV movie docudrama is, lineally, the descendant
of the often despised B-movie of the 1940s and 1950s. This, too, has
not helped its critical cause.[15]

Edgerton believes that it is not so much the link with film that
should concern us as the development in television. And within
the context of the television institution itself the emergence in the
1960s of a production system for made-for-TV movies of all kinds,
as Edgerton contends, has had cultural benefits. He sees in such films
what he calls 'the "televisionization" of contemporary American
interests, affectations, and obsessions' (p. 167). The cultural landscape of middle America can be discerned quite clearly, especially

in 'high-concept' docudrama (his useful 1991 categorisation).[16] The seriousness of purpose in high-concept docudrama makes it dangerous to dismiss, and I share Edgerton's more generous view of the importance of the made-for-TV movie. He argues that the form as a whole has always been allowed greater latitude by the networks' Broadcasting Standards Departments (which we encountered in Chapter 3). A 'greater freedom in [the] handling of controversial topics,' he says, has come about through the genre's 'noncontinuous format and because of the TV movie's special quality and higher status within the sphere of nighttime programming' (1991: 124). US docudrama, like British docudrama, is *occasional* and has impact benefits that accrue from this factor. As a form that can literally and metaphorically 'follow the news' it has its advantages over feature film.

The first 'made-for-TV'/'movie-of-the-week' docudramas emerged in the early 1970s. By the mid-1970s, the three major US networks of the time were regularly screening made-for-TV movies and the 'docudrama' was being recognised as a sub-division of the new genre (see Gomery, 1983: 126). Hoffer *et al.* (1980) claim ABC's *Brian's Song* (1971) as the first purpose-made docudrama, while Edgerton (1985) cites *The Weekend Nun* (1972). The former is the story of a football star's battle with cancer. It used real names, and verifiable places and events. The latter film, 'based on' the life of the nun Joyce Duco, was rather less successful. *Brian's Song* was not only hugely popular on first transmission, it was much repeated and even achieved cinema release.[17] Both films offer a serious treatment of a serious subject; both films use a realist film-style; both films are labelled 'docudramas' by American writers.

American practice branched out further in the 1970s with the so-called 'faction'. The cultural reasons for this demonstrate what might be called a 'bicentennial mind-set'.[18] An almost valedictory attempt is discernible in the American nation as a whole to get to grips with its past and present, in order to gauge possibilities for its future.[19] Key docudramatic examples of this tendency can be seen in ABC's 1974 *The Missiles of October* (a docudrama on the Cuban Missile Crisis of 1962)[20]; ABC's 1977 *Roots*, one of the most successful network series of all time (which explored the history of

Black America); and Paramount's 1977 *Washington: Behind Closed Doors* (a 'faction' probing the 'Watergate' latter days of the Nixon Administration). By 1979 the docudrama was sufficiently well established in American network programming for a symposium on it to be held by the Academy of Television Arts and Sciences. The publicity potential of the 'fact' continued to be a powerful persuader for the adoption of the mixed form at this time and was borne out by significant success with audiences. Free trails from already existing news and current affairs sources, both inside and outside the television institution, were already a trump card.

James Monaco summarises:

> Trading on the striking identity between fiction and reality that characterizes the television experience, program executives developed the so-called 'docudrama', a made-for-TV film based more or less loosely in current events and history, dealing with subjects already well know to viewers and thus in a sense presold. (Monaco, 1977: 380)

Relatively cheap to make, American docudrama also had what the industry calls 'long legs', enjoying multiple repeats, especially across local channels, over long periods of time. The docudrama has a real advantage across time in that folk-memory is easy to trigger when associated with some events and individuals caught in difficult and unusual situations. Journalistic, theme-based docudramas tied, like the daily papers and news broadcasts, to iconic 'stories' can parlay this to advantage.[21] In a more and more competitive market it remains one of docudrama's trump cards.

Granada dramadoc – a very British genre

By 1980, the 'dramadoc' had become as well established on British television as the docudrama had on American. Granada provided this development through its *World in Action* current affairs programme. *World in Action* began mixing dramatic reconstructions with documentary footage almost from its inception in 1963 in a practice which links back to *The March of Time* and forward to *America's Most Wanted* (1988–) and *Crimewatch* (which began as *Crimewatch UK* in 1984). Its founder-producer Tim Hewat made programmes on the Portland Spy Trial of 1961 and the Great Train Robbery of 1963. Leslie Woodhead says these were 'dumb show' dramatisations in which look-alike figures re-enacted in brief fragments of illustrative film which were accompanied by voice-over commentary.[22] Jeremy Wallington, a former journalist on the *Sunday Times* who came to Granada in 1967, was a key influence in the search for what Woodhead calls 'visual equivalents for that torrent of verbal information you got in [*Sunday Times*] "Insight" features'. Woodhead had come to *World in Action* primarily as a filmmaker. He was 'very engaged' by the work of Ken Loach, liking especially 'the documentary stillness with which he framed things'. Peter Watkins' 1964 BBC film *Culloden*, with its news broadcast dynamic and *cinéma vérité* aesthetics, also influenced him, as did the Leacock/Drew *vérité* documentaries of the early 1960s.[23] He was, he acknowledged to me, less aware of the British line of development from the Doncaster/Swinson dramatised story documentaries of the 1950s.

Woodhead's 1970 *The Man Who Wouldn't Keep Quiet* is often cited as the first Granada drama-documentary though Woodhead himself believes it was Mike Murphy's *The Pueblo Affair* (transmitted earlier the same year). For Woodhead's film, Russian dissident Major-General Pyotr Grigorenko provided the 'document'. His diary had been smuggled out of the Soviet Union in the early 1970s, and Woodhead describes this source as being 'nurtured and matured inside the *World in Action* set-up' (see Goodwin and Kerr, 1983: 25). His attitude to the dramatisation of documentary source was, he says, 'very careful and rather puritanical'. He believes in a very particular set of responsibilities to audiences that can only be fulfilled by scrupulous adherence to documents and careful declaration of the provenance of dramatic action via captioning.[24] He also believes that film crews with documentary backgrounds were indispensable in ensuring the 'visual understatement' that he values to this day. David Plowright (later Granada's managing director) talks of the conscious effort made at Granada to 'weld ... together the skills of the investigative journalists and the filmmakers' (Goodwin and Kerr, 1983: 26).

The 'special responsibilities' incurred when 'impersonating

living individuals' can only be fulfilled, Woodhead believes, through research on the one hand and skilled performance on the other. He offered me the example of the actor Leslie Sands, playing Edward Gierek, the Polish Communist Party's First Secretary in the 1976 *Three Days in Szczecin*. Sands prepared for the role 'by detailed study of film of Gierek', learning an important speech 'under the watchful eye of a photograph of the real Mr. Gierek pinned on his study wall' (Goodwin and Kerr, 1983: 28). Woodhead, like many dramadoc personnel, was and is highly sceptical about formal dramatic experiment. In common with many people who worked on these formative dramadocs, he places special emphasis instead on captions and voiceover supplying details about the provenance of information used in the films. These are vital elements, he believes, in securing an audience's trust and belief and he asserts a 'passionate obligation [for] labelling' focused on 'telling the audience what game we were playing ... let[ting] them know at the outset that this [film] was not a *conventional* documentary' (my emphasis). At the beginning of his 1981 film *Strike* (about the Polish Solidarity union and its challenge to the Soviet empire) there is a lengthy factual exposition which he himself narrates. 'These days,' he said to me, 'that would be regarded as an Andean barrier to audience sympathy!'

By 1980, the techniques of the Granada dramadoc were well enough established for fellow producer David Boulton to describe them as the 'Woodhead Doctrine', which aimed:

> to recreate as accurately as possible history as it happened. No invented characters, no invented names, no dramatic devices owing more to the writer's (or director's) creative imagination than to the implacable record of what actually happened.

Crucially, he added: 'For us, the dramatised documentary is an exercise in journalism, not dramatic art' (see Goodwin and Kerr, 1983: 29). This rooting in current events gave *World in Action*'s 'Iron Curtain' dramadocs a campaigning edge.[25] Paul Kerr has characterised second-phase docudrama as based on 'reporter inaccessibility', the most famous examples based on events in a Soviet bloc unavailable to Western news and documentary television crews right up until the Velvet Revolutions of the late 1980s (1990: 82). In retrospect, films like 1980's *Invasion* (about the destruction by the Soviets of the Czech Communist Party's 1968 'Prague Spring') can be seen as the first chinks in the collapse of the Soviet system. The films were welcomed by Western political establishments and applauded by Western audiences.[26] As Ian McBride observed to me: 'Nobody ever argued that dramadoc was a deeply flawed and suspicious form when we were in shipyards in Gdansk, or psychiatric hospitals in the Soviet Union!'

By the end of the second phase, docudrama had shown an additional potential to become a 'media event' by being controversial as well as worthy. If 'Woodhead Doctrine' drama-documentaries about the Soviet bloc were perceived as usefully critical of communist regimes, then documentary dramas such as Peter Watkins' anti-nuclear film *The War Game* (BBC, 1965), Loach/Garnett's *Days of Hope* (BBC1, 1976) and Antony Thomas's *Death of a Princess* (ATV, 1980) were more contentious. Watkins' controversial film was banned, and remained untransmitted for twenty years; *Death of a Princess* caused widespread panic in terms of the UK's diplomatic relations with an important ally and trading partner – Saudi Arabia.[27] These films illustrate the fact that controversy usually results from issues about content not form. When factual treatments stray into areas of political tension and anxiety, problems occur, as they did with Antony Thomas's treatment of the gap between Middle Eastern and Western societies. *Death of a Princess* was self-reflexive in its foregrounding of the difficulty of accessing 'the truth' of any situation. Thomas dramatised his own search for the truth about the 1978 execution of a Saudi princess by placing himself in the film, thinly disguised as the character 'Christopher Ryder'. Situating his audience within this subject position he hoped to clarify the essentially illusory nature of any documentary claim to objectivity.[28]

The self-conscious attempt to make points about the nature of representation marks a kind of 'coming-of-age' for the docudrama, and this is partly why I choose 1980 as a rough cut-off date for the second phase. *Death of a Princess* is the televisual equivalent of modernist 'metatheatre' and 'metafiction' (plays and novels that embed discussion of the making of theatre or fiction within their construction). It also illustrates how little such a formal strategy protects against the catapulting of a television programme into 'media event' controversy. This is the price paid when the outer public world has yet to come to terms with *content*, irrespective of the intentions of film and programme makers. As McBride cautions: 'When you're dealing with something which has got a political resonance ... that's when these kinds of arguments take off.' The docudrama became established in the second phase simultaneously as an important means of representing the public world, but also as a suspect mode of doing so. By the end of this phase, both the US Academy of Television Arts and Sciences (in 1979), and the British Film Institute (in 1981) were each in a position where debate about docudrama's characteristics and terms of reference was deemed necessary. There were now enough examples of significant practice for the form's legitimacy to begin to come into question.

Trauma drama

In marked contrast to Granada dramadocs, American docudramas around this time were beginning to focus more and more on the personal and the tabloid. Disdain for this low-concept docudrama unites critics like Gitlin and practitioners like Woodhead. Gitlin sees 'a kind of self-censorship' among docudramatists that was acquired 'simply by accepting the conventions of their form' (1994: 175). Woodhead sees them as traducing the purity of his own concept. Gitlin's line of argument is a familiar and not unreasonable one: sensational stories about individuals, coupled with the tele-realism used to tell them, destroy any potential for social or political analysis; the concentration on personalised 'story arcs' and 'three act' plot structures ratchet up ethical dangers; and increase the resemblance of some docudrama to tabloid journalism. To what extent, if any, it seemed fair to ask, was the suffering of individuals being exploited? To what extent, if any, were the issues raised by their stories being sidelined in order to hack out a jeopardy plot, a love story, or a forensic thriller? Was the price being paid for easy recognition and instant involvement by the popular audience too much?

Jane Feuer usefully warns against readings of popular culture that 'proceed from thin description to condemnation' (1995: 147).

She argues that, although low-concept docudrama rarely offers solutions at a macro-societal level, it still articulates 'social discontent' and circulates debate about that discontent. Her term for these docudramas – 'trauma drama' – describes 'domestic melodramas in which private ills are centred in the family' (1995: 31). These films, she argues, came to prominence in the 1980s and voice publicly doubts and suspicions about social and political institutions. Trauma drama is not culturally dumb, she claims, even if some critics label it so. It focuses on an extreme situation experienced by an ordinary member of the public (ordinary, that is, until they suffer their particular trauma). Plots often feature serious illness (hence the term 'disease-of-the-week'), violent crime, race-hatred and so on. Feuer argues that the trauma drama is interesting precisely because it offers a metonym for a widespread social frustration, instantly recognisable to a popular audience through news coverage and its own experience. Clustering around 1980, and indicating a shift in the development of docudrama, these films coincide more importantly with a growing frustration with, and distrust of, social agencies.

Feuer takes the docudrama *Friendly Fire* (ABC, 1979) as a key example. The film is about ordinary American parents forced to investigate their son's death while serving in Vietnam. Officially his death is recorded as 'accidental'; he was killed in error by so-called 'friendly fire'– a victim of his own side. His parents Peg and Gene Mullen of La Porte City, Iowa, set out to investigate how and why he died. The film explores their journey of discovery, in which personal grief sits alongside the mealy-mouthed 'explanations' of official discourse. This kind of popular docudrama presents a real challenge to academic opinion, for academics are particularly vulnerable through temperament and training to rejection of 'low art' of any kind. Robert Sklar, for example, saw the protagonists as 'universalize[d]' by the style of the film ('universal' signalling outright condemnation in the academy of the 1980s). He sees the Mullens as 'neutralize[d]' characters, helpless in the face of the situation as dramatised (1980: 187). Feuer's approach to the film, by contrast, is to analyse the ethical implications of using the actual experiences of individuals. In particular she examines the film's portrayal of the way they are forced to act on their own to uncover the reality behind the military's information-management systems. This, she argues, enacts the agency that Sklar finds lacking. Crucially, the film's approach is more likely to work with popular audiences, who will identify with the Mullens, than it is with media academics. The very title of the film isolates an early point in the history of official oxymoron, and the phrase 'friendly fire' is thus thrown back at its military originators. If nothing else, the film has a place in a cultural history of the ghastly newspeak of the modern military.[29]

Feuer identifies eight structural points in the narrative of trauma dramas. Opening scenes often depict 'the ideal and norm of happy American family life'. The next structural node sees trauma affecting the family and fracturing its normality – the stable is destabilised, so to speak. The suffering family then look for help in their distress to official institutions. Although these institutions have a democratic duty of care, says Feuer, they 'are shown to be totally inadequate'. The protagonists decide in the plot developments that follow to 'take matters into their own hands'. Sometimes they seek the help of a grass-roots, *samizdat*, organisation of some kind that has grown up in part recognition of officialdom's past failures of care. Sometimes individual 'helpers' are found who can uncover the lies of institutions for them. The tactics of such organisations and individuals are then shown to work to some degree, even occasionally effecting change in official practices. Closure follows, as Feuer eloquently has it, 'however inadequately' (see 1995: 25–6). She draws attention here to the fact that closure is difficult at the best of times in docudrama (hence captions dealing with events-beyond-the-text), but the impossibility of complete resolution remains unlikely given wider social circumstances. Trauma dramas focus dramatically, and read sympathetically they critique, the very self-help individualism touted by Ronald Reagan in the run-up to his victory in the 1980 Presidential election. The trauma drama 'opens up documentary space', in John Corner's phrase, and exposes official inadequacy at a human level. The mendacity of authorities who use phrases like 'friendly fire' to gloss over deaths from failures of care is held up for scrutiny through individual action by protagonists who have been affected directly and through whom popular audiences can identify. The cases treated, of course, acquire further public attention through their depiction in docudramas. It is within this classic 'faceless official *versus* recognisable individual' trope that the trauma drama operates. The fragility of a trauma drama's closure can be read as the clearest evidence of the profound ambiguity at the heart of this cultural enterprise. Such ambiguity arguably marks the difficulties inherent in squaring ethical circles, for 'solutions' to the problems raised are almost always beyond the capacity of the individuals depicted. In a culture accustomed in its drama to promote the idea that stories can be 'closed' at all, the troubled moment of closure in made-for-TV docudrama often illustrates, as Feuer herself says, that 'the stability of family life is fragile indeed' (1995: 34).

Towards a third phase – merging the two traditions

While American docudrama looked inwards in order to look outwards, so to speak, a new flowering of the form in the UK in the late 1980s renewed docudrama's potential for controversy. The focus in the films of this period shifted from the Communist East to the Democratic West. Societies under threat from shadowy 'terrorist' organisations offered new templates for the docudramas that eventually fuelled 1990s 'co-pros' of interest to audiences on both sides of the Atlantic. These became a staple of the third phase (see Chapter 7). Docudramas were becoming progressively detached by the end of the second phase from bases in informational television departments like Current Affairs, becoming instead 'stand-alone' dramas that most resembled either the old 'single drama' of television's 'Golden Age' or the cinema 'issue film' or 'biopic'. By this means the two traditions – American docudrama and British journalistic dramadoc – began to fuse through the economics of co-production. Transatlantic co-operation was not a new thing, of course. *The March of Time* had a London office in the 1930s and *World in Action* had a fully staffed New York office 'from the mid-1960s', according to Leslie Woodhead.[30] *Death of a Princess*, too, was a co-production involving Britain's ATV, WGBH of Boston, Telepictures (Holland), Seven Network (Australia), and Eastern Media (New Zealand). The losses and gains of such arrangements can be gauged through a comparison between Granada and HBO – two of the major players in co-production from about 1990 onwards.

What the two players brought to co-production from the second phase was quite distinctive. Granada brought the British dramadoc tradition and HBO brought the recognition that US television was ready for a niche-marketed, high-concept drama output that would include serious docudrama. Leslie Halliwell once waspishly described Granada as 'more intellectual than the other ITV companies' (1986: 326). It is the lone 'original' franchise-holder in British commercial television, a status obtained partly because from the time it won a place in the system in 1955 it has demonstrated public service awareness. This is at least on a par with the BBC, but with a difference: Granada has always had a more populist orientation. The company's location in Manchester is important to this history; the city has had a particularly independent voice in British national affairs ever since the nineteenth century. Granada's first executives built on this pre-existing local tradition of populist radicalism. Founded by Sidney Bernstein in 1955, from 1964 its managing director was Denis Forman. Interestingly, both men had connections with the earlier Griersonian documentary film movement. Bernstein was in the 'Films Division' of the Ministry of Information during the Second World War; Forman was a staffer at the pre-war GPO Film Unit.

Between them these men 'introduced Grierson's ideas into the heart of the contemporary media establishment' (Aitken, 1990: 4). Granada's characteristic commitment to 'social purpose' was spearheaded by its current affairs magazine series *World in Action* (Sendall and Potter, 1982: I, 346). *World in Action* followed a reformist political line from 1963 until it was controversially taken off the air in 2001. As I remarked above, *World in Action*'s house-style always favoured drama because its staff knew the impact it could have on a popular audience. Granada personnel believed strongly that issues were made accessible by personalising them, and that drama could facilitate this. Forman himself acknowledged as much in 1966, noting that experts 'are seldom interesting unless they disagree emotionally. Intellectual disagreement is generally better expressed in the written word' (see Swallow, 1966: 217). The belief that access to information will lead to general societal improvement still exists in

British television, but it is the weaker without programmes like *World in Action*.[31]

HBO, in contrast, is an ultra-modern cable television network that launched in America in 1972. It became a division of corporate media giant Time Warner Entertainment in 1989. By 1994, 18 million people were subscribing to HBO in the USA and it had subsidiaries in South America, Asia, Scandinavia, Turkey and Eastern Europe. It was active in making production agreements with national television companies, network subsidiaries and independents. By 2005, HBO International was claiming 16 million subscribers in 50 countries *outside* the USA.[32] Gitlin's earlier view that 'pay cable, dominated by Home Box Office, seems most interested in circulating Hollywood movies and their derivative forms' (1994: 329) has given way to a widespread recognition that HBO is actually a serious, 'quality', player in the global television market. This reputation has been won partly through its documentary output, its drama, and its drama series. It was the first cable company to win an Oscar for a documentary, *Down and Out in America* (1987), and has attracted Emmy awards regularly. The company's commitment to the high-concept docudrama began with its very first film, *The Terry Fox Story* (1983).[33] It can be seen too in films such as *The Simon Wiesenthal Story* (a 1989 film about the famed Nazi-hunter who brought Adolf Eichmann and other Nazis to trial), and in the much-repeated 1993 AIDS epidemic docudrama *And the Band Played On*. Significantly, HBO 'took over th[is] project after NBC rejected it' (see Horenstein *et al.*, 1994: 156). The company made films about the Kennedy assassination and the Vietnam War, both crucial markers of seriousness in American popular culture and history. When HBO struck a deal in 1990 with Granada International, it was one of HBO's most extensive co-production arrangements at that point in its history. Eight co-productions were planned for HBO's high-concept *Showcase* slot.[34]

At Granada in the late 1980s, Ray Fitzwalter remarked to me, 'we believed we could do more popular subjects ... and tougher subjects'. This became more possible with an international co-funder on board. Resources had tightened domestically, and the co-production deal facilitated their aspirations even as the industry itself reconfigured.[35] Co-production with an American partner meant more drama, less documentary in terms of approach. As early as 1993, dramatist and writer David Edgar was challenging the official line that docudrama depended fundamentally on the documentary element:

> I have some doubts about the Granada team's insistence that [their films] are, in fact, not plays but works of journalism carried on by other means. This could be taken to imply that journalism operates in the realm of pure and objective fact, as opposed to the supposed vagaries and subjectivities of drama, which seems to give television journalism a credit that almost no journalism is due. More profoundly, it also implies that people read drama-docs as docs rather than as dramas, whereas it seems to me that the power of the drama-documentary is in what precedes rather than follows the hyphen.

Edgar's point is borne out by the fact that, while Granada personnel involved in docudrama production in earlier phases of development tended to share a journalistic background, a drama background became increasingly important.

Practitioners who began in documentary were drawn more and more to drama. Directors such as Peter Kosminsky and Paul Greengrass, for example, demonstrate in their careers the shift in emphasis in third-phase docudrama towards drama. Sita Williams, producer of both *Hostages* and *Fighting for Gemma*, had a drama training and background.[36] As a result, she always tended to focus on the importance of the drama in docudrama:

> Essentially what you are striving to do is present something on the screen which is dramatically coherent, and is a story told through character... You can't make drama-documentary just with the journalists – people suggest all sorts of stories to me, and they're good stories, but there has to be a key. Not every good journalistic story can be translated into a piece of drama.

Docudrama may start, she noted, 'in news broadcasts ... in the public domain', but it has to find 'something new and different to say'. The 'drama legs', as she put it, 'justify [docudrama's] existence'. In interview, she listed five key questions she sought to resolve as a producer of docudrama, and the balance of documentary and drama is a suggestive one:

1 Is it a viable [journalistic] story?
2 Can it be created out of the available material?
3 Is there documentary/is there drama?
4 Will simplifying produce a legal problem?
5 Will the amount of information produce a problem for the audience?

The concept of 'the available material' highlights producers' practical role as editorial controllers and researchers as well as production co-ordinators (see again Chapter 1). The fourth question highlights docudrama's legal sensitivity (see again Chapter 2). The last question focuses an aesthetical realm that became altogether more important in the new co-production dispensation. The shift to filmic discourse carried with it the danger of edging out the distinctive discursive elements of documentary 'proper' that had been so much a feature of the Woodhead doctrine. The account of *Hostages* which follows in Chapter 7 aims to illustrate the third-phase shift towards drama – and the opportunities and difficulties this brought with it.[37]

Notes

1 His *Elgar* was broadcast as *Monitor*'s 100th edition on 11 November 1962 (Vahimagi, 1996: 73). Russell has revealed that *Monitor*'s editor Huw Wheldon and influential BBC staffers Norman Swallow and Humphrey Burton were all at the time very much against drama entering into the programme's generally documentary discourse (see Tibbetts, 2005: 41).

2 Peter Collinson made a much inferior film version of *Up the Junction* in 1967; Loach himself filmed David Mercer's *Family Life* in 1971.

3 The period of the 'Angry Young Man' and 'Kitchen Sink' drama is generally dated from the first production of John Osborne's *Look Back in Anger* at London's Royal Court Theatre in 1956.

4 Loach has filmed in Glasgow more than once; it seems to attract him as a city where working-class cultures are still both current and vibrant. Yaqub, it should be said, had some experience of performance, insofar as he had done modelling work part-time.

5 He made this remark on BBC2's *Face to Face* on 19 September 1994.

6 Phil Davis, one of Mike Leigh's regular actors, said in interview for the AHRC 'Acting with Facts' project: 'Just working with Mike and inventing a character from scratch ... the *detail* of inventing a fictional character [...] I really found that revelatory and I apply all manner of principles from that

work when I'm doing scripted drama' (23 June 2008).

7 *Cathy Come Home* has been transmitted on British network television many times – in 1966, 1967, 1968, 1976, 1993 and 2006. The last transmission on the digital BBC4 channel coincided with the dual 40th anniversary both of the founding of the charity Shelter and of the film's first transmission. *Cathy Come Home* is now also available on DVD.

8 Although Sandford described *Cathy* as 'dramatised documentary' in a 1973 article, he was using the phrase then current in the television industry. His part of a 1973 *Theatre Quarterly* dialogue with the critic Paul Ableman (who opposed the form) is reprinted in Goodwin and Kerr (1983). A journalist by trade, Sandford's early experience was in radio rather than television. *Cathy Come Home* was preceded by a radio feature, *Homeless Families*. This 1960 programme was part of *In the South-East*, a daily radio news feature. It provided most of the research base for *Cathy* and even some of the 'wildtrack' sound included on the soundtrack. I interviewed Jeremy Sandford twice (on 24 November 1995 and 4 October 1996), and corresponded with him many times before his death in 2003.

9 Over the years, some caveats grew up not only about the reliability of Sandford's research in *Cathy* but also about his reliability in general. I believe these caveats traduce his memory. The cause – in the academy at any rate – was academics' excessive reliance on Irene Shubik's 1975 memoir *Play For Today: The Evolution of Television Drama*. My article about all this in *New Theatre Quarterly* (Paget, 1999) attempts to show the ways in which I believe Shubik to be untrustworthy on *Cathy* (her book's 2000 reprint unfortunately perpetuates most of her own inaccuracies). It also argues that Shubik-inspired academic commentary has tended to play up the myth of Sandford's inaccuracy. See also Paget (2003), my Preface to the new edition of the script of *Cathy Come Home*.

10 Interview with Tony Garnett (London, 7 November 1996).

11 My argument here follows Chapter 5 of Corner (1996), which contains a detailed analysis of shifting points-of-view within *Cathy Come Home*. Corner lays particular emphasis (pp. 94–5) on a scene where Cathy is interviewed by a board of middle-class officials in charge of a homeless people's hostel. He argues that the positioning of the camera behind the officials, and the actress's direct look at it at one point in the scene, make the audience a 'secondary addressee' of Cathy's angry accusation that the board do not really care about her situation.

12 See Lipkin (2002, Chapter 2) for a discussion of Twentieth Century-Fox *films noirs* and their relation to made-for-TV docudrama. He analyses such films as *13 Rue Madeleine* (1947), *The House on 92nd Street* (1945) and *Call Northside 777* (1948). Louis de Rochemont, legendary originator of the docudramatic newsreel *The March of Time*, was producer on the first two films. Custen (1992) traces the tradition of life-story films as far back as Sarah Bernhardt's 1912 film *Queen Elizabeth* (1992: 5). His Appendix

D – 'Biopics by Profession' – demonstrate how the form burgeoned in Hollywood from the 1920s onwards.

13   Edgerton's other categories are 'the telefeature' and 'the miniseries'. The latter, of course, is often docudramatic too.

14   Rapping's observation that the docudramas 'never use actual footage of historical events and interviews with real people' is interesting, given that this is not the case now (see Chapter 8).

15   See, for example, Gomery (1983). It is fair to say that such a lineage proves to many commentators that the docudrama can be safely ignored in terms of seriousness of purpose.

16   See Edgerton, 1991.

17   This was not so successful – possibly because so many people had already seen the film on television.

18   Throughout the early 1970s, culminating on 4 July 1976, the USA engaged in events in celebration of two hundred years of nationhood.

19   This can be compared to similar cultural attempts to take stock in Britain in the 1960s, though this was more to do with an end-of-Empire national awareness of fading international influence and pressing national problems.

20   The writer called this film 'a "Theater of Fact" production' (Auster, 1990: 164).

21   HBO was still repeating the 1990 'co-pro' *The Tragedy of Flight 103: The Inside Story* (known in Britain as *Why Lockerbie?*) as late as 1997 – partly because the original incident was again newsworthy, with the trial taking place of the Libyans alleged to have perpetrated the air crash.

22   In Finch (2003), Hewat remarks (p. 198), 'For those who know film history, the shape of our reports harked back to *The March of Time* of the 1930s but was absolutely new to television'.

23   For an account of Drew/Leacock's work, see Ellis (1989).

24   John Wyver for one disputes Woodhead's own complete adherence to this methodology. His 1980 *Invasion*, according to Wyver, goes against 'the producers' statements of rigid asceticism' (1983: 33). It seems to me that the claim for purity has an unacknowledged rhetorical value. Woodhead's belief in the power of the document can be paralleled to the late British theatre director Peter Cheeseman, whose musical documentaries at the Victoria Theatre, Stoke-on-Trent, similarly put an emphasis on primary documentation in the same period. See his Introduction to *The Knotty*, London, Methuen, 1970 where he states: 'If there is no primary source material available on a particular topic, no scene can be made about it' (p. xiv). [REF: Cheeseman, P. (1970), *The Knotty*, London: Methuen.] For an American take on this theatrical movement, see Favorini (1995).

25   Kilborn and Izod (1997: 243) list six 'Iron Curtain' dramadocs (transmitted in the period 1972–80).

26   In 1990 *World in Action* showed *Invasion* to Alexander Dubček him-

self, lately emerged from obscurity thanks to the 'Velvet Revolution'. He movingly embraced Julian Glover – his impersonator in the drama – at the transmission's end.

27 Corner (1996: 40) classifies *The War Game* as 'imitation documentary'. It generated a furious and well-documented controversy. See, for example, Aubrey (1982). *Days of Hope* was debated extensively in *Screen* in 1979. *Death of a Princess* was broadcast on PBS in the USA in 1980. Accounts of the 'media events' surrounding all these films can be found in Goodwin and Kerr (1983); see also Paget (1990: 97–105). For more on recent developments in 'imitation documentaries', and other new-form docudrama, see Chapter 8.

28 Cumings (1992: 121) actually refers to this as 'a documentary', saying PBS's screening of it was a 'highlight' of US television's 1979–80 'scrutiny' of Saudi Arabia.

29 Military euphemisms are a product of late twentieth-century wars. A less ready acceptance of casualties by populations supplying troops to conflicts leads directly to the language of 'body counts', 'pacification programmes' and 'collateral damage' as well as 'friendly fire'. A cultural history of such terminology might explore the histories and contexts behind first uses of such terms in the 'real world' of the military's interface with politics and foreign policy. This might assist informed consideration of the aesthetical and ethical implications of such terminology in representation of all kinds.

30 Even then, he observed, its American crew 'had a much more free-wheeling approach' to the idea of documentary than crews at Granada's home-base in Manchester.

31 Stephen Heath and Gillian Skirrow began the debate about the implications of Granada's populist methodology in *Screen* as long ago as 1977 (see McArthur, 1980: 14–15). In her excellent 'Introduction' to Finch (2003), Julia Hallam writes (p. 19) that the title *World in Action* was in fact bought for £100 from Grierson himself and that the programme's style 'was modelled on "Mirrorscope" the serious four-page fold-in which the *Daily Mirror* produced for several years'.

32 See the HBO corporate website www.hbo.com for updates on these figures, and for information on the network's output past and present.

33 This film was a classic docudrama which told the story of the eponymous Canadian hero, who lost a leg to cancer then ran 'The Marathon of Hope' in 1980, raising in the process $20 million dollars for cancer charity. Again, see the HBO website for details.

34 *Screen International* (no. 978, 7–13 October 1994: 37–8, 40) ran a special issue on HBO at a time when its market penetration was just taking off.

35 Interview with Ray Fitzwalter (Manchester, 14 March 1996). This kind of reconfiguration resulted from the changes brought about by the 1990 Broadcasting Act. The move to networks-as-publishers affected people like Fitzwalter, who left Granada to become an independent producer.

36 Williams' subsequent career has been in drama rather than docudrama, with Granada/PBS's two *Forsyte Saga* series (2002 and 2004) being examples of the kind of 'quality' drama production with which she is now principally associated.

37 I refer readers again to my justification in the Introduction for continuing to present this 'failure' docudrama as a case study, and to material on the process of its production in Chapter 1.

7

Histories: third-phase 'co-pros'

'Cultural collision'

The first collaboration between HBO and Granada was in 1987 with *Tailspin* (US title)/*Coded Hostile* (UK). This treatment of the 1983 shooting down of Korean Airlines Flight KAL 007 was described by Leslie Woodhead as 'very ritzily made. High-profile actors, driving score'. The Hollywood influence was obvious, and continued to be for third-phase co-pros. The kinds of genre rules that have accrued from fiction filmmaking added a further dimension to docudrama's rooting in news and current affairs. *Tailspin*/*Coded Hostile* nevertheless subscribed to 'all the journalistic priorities' of previous docudramas, according to Woodhead. Granada/HBO co-pros went on to set a high standard, especially in the case of the deservedly famous *Who Bombed Birmingham?* (1989 – HBO title: *Investigation: Inside a Terrorist Bombing*). The campaign for the release of the 'Birmingham Six', six Northern Irishmen jailed in the UK in 1974 for allegedly perpetrating the 1973 Birmingham bombings on behalf of the IRA, became something of a *cause célèbre* at Granada. *World in Action* used the research of Labour MP Chris Mullin in 1985, and the docudrama built on a layer of serious investigative journalism.[1]

The British Court of Appeal eventually sanctioned the release of the 'Birmingham Six' in late 1990. The campaign that led to this outcome took many forms, but the docudrama was a distinctive and high-profile part of it. Ian McBride, editor of *World in Action* at the time of the 1985 documentary, was himself impersonated in the film by actor Martin Shaw, an unusual occurrence for someone from 'behind the scenes'.[2] The grateful members of the Birmingham Six signed a poster for the film as a gift to McBride. It is an emblem of the wider potential significance of docudrama. As material in culture such artefacts can and do enter the public sphere. Those who made *Who Bombed Birmingham?* have just cause to believe in the power of television to achieve change in society. Docudrama investigating miscarriages of justice constitutes a veritable sub-division of the form. Whenever termination of a case in the real world leads to subsequent doubts about the 'safety' of the conviction, a docudrama will often follow. If doubts grow, there follow repeat transmissions, even a celebratory reprise when innocent victims of the law are released. This is exactly what happened with the Birmingham Six.[3]

Richard Kilborn (1994), John Corner (1995 and 1996), and Julian Petley (1996) have all drawn attention in their analyses of docudrama to the structuring of the form during this period. The use of templates drawn from fiction film gathered pace in the third phase. Structures like the 'international thriller' and 'disaster movie', for example, were evident in *Why Lockerbie?* (1990) and *Disaster at Valdez* (1991) – US titles for the former *The Tragedy of Flight 103: The Inside Story*, and for the latter *Dead Ahead: The Exxon Valdez Disaster*. My phase-three example *Hostages* could be called both a 'political thriller' and a 'buddy-movie'. There was, however, a difference – when the film was being made nobody knew the outcome of the thriller, and whether the buddies (Keenan and McCarthy) would survive. The BBC used genre-familiarity to advertise its own co-pro, *Hostile Waters*, at a press preview in 1997, describing the film as 'a submarine action thriller, inspired by a true story' (the 1990 film *Hunt for Red October* being one of several possible intertexts here). McBride and Williams acknowledged to me their awareness of both the film *JFK* and the television series *LA Law* when *Fighting for Gemma* was being made (its storyline of a lawyer and his legal firm campaigning against the agencies of the status quo make these obvious intertexts). British 'golden-age' documentary dramas (*The War Game*, *Cathy Come Home*, *Days of Hope*, *Death of a Princess*) and drama-documentaries (*Invasion*, *Strike*) alike may also have had filmic 'looks', but it was documentary film to which they primarily aspired and with which they can be compared. By the mid-1990s, fiction film genres were driving British dramadoc towards the values of the American docudrama like never before, and Granada's link to

HBO provided a context for this transformation.

Looking back on the early co-pro period Leslie Woodhead took the view that HBO had been 'positive and revitalising' as a partner in production: 'They've surprised me by being even more demonic about information and scripts than we are.' While acknowledging the vast difference in filmic 'look' over the decade between *Three Days in Szczecin* and *Why Lockerbie?*, Woodhead regarded tapping into other associations than those of factual or current affairs programming as part of a new television ecology:

> Where there is a collision between journalistic values and dramatic values, journalism has to win. If the priority is to bring these things to the attention of a mass audience, to collide with territories of the twentieth century that they wouldn't otherwise collide with, then it doesn't matter if the play's bad.[4]

Woodhead described to me the different emphases given in Britain and the USA to the final, tragic, section of *Why Lockerbie?/The Tragedy of Flight 103*. In the British ending, as the Pan Am jumbo goes down over Lockerbie, the dot symbolising its existence disappears off the flight controller's radar screen. After a sombre cut to roses on the graves in Lockerbie churchyard, shots of the victims' memorial service follow. The American producers, according to Woodhead, found this 'too muted':

> They didn't want bodies tumbling out of the sky, but they wanted to feel something about what had been done, so they went for about a minute of archive of blazing rooftops and fire brigades and policemen rushing round in the night in Lockerbie village. It's not a sleazy ending, just a different one, and was a very interesting difference of reading of what their audience wanted. It's a kind of *cultural collision*, where we can cope with the interiorising of our feelings but they feel like they're being short-changed [my emphasis].

Perhaps Leslie Woodhead cannot be accounted an impartial observer, but his argument about the playing of emotion for different national audiences is fundamental to my argument about the 'two traditions' of docudrama.

Such divergent adjustments are not uncommon, whatever the

convergences occasioned by a shared language. The 2005 film adaptation of Jane Austen's *Pride and Prejudice*, for example, had an alternative ending for the US market that added a couple of minutes to the film. It portrayed Darcy and Lizzie (Colin Firth and Jennifer Ehle), nightwear-clad, in a clinch on a romantic moonlit balcony. Not for the US audience it would seem, the chaste kiss in broad daylight (following Lizzie's acceptance of Darcy's proposal) that was deemed most appropriate for the British audience.[5] A case study of the 1992 co-pro *Hostages* offers an opportunity to chart such differences in reception between the two audiences.

Hostages – a third-phase case study

The news story behind *Hostages* had been around for a while by the time Granada/HBO's co-production reached television screens in the UK and the USA, in 1992 and 1993 respectively. Centring as it did on captives from both nations, there was every reason to expect the film to strike a chord with British and American audiences. It dealt with an issue at the forefront of public debate then as now: the perennially troubled Middle East. The notion of 'ordinary' citizens being taken as unwilling representatives of their governments touched a very real fear in Western populations at the time: a fear that has grown rather than diminished. At root was and still is a fear of an Eastern 'Other'. Iraq and Afghan wars, and fears about 'terrorist organisations' such as Al-Qaeda from 2001 onwards have exacerbated this fear. The drawn out attempted pacifications of those countries are part of a continuing *zeitgeist*. The initial rash of 1980s hostage-taking looks in hindsight like the beginning of a new international political era.

Such a high-profile international subject undoubtedly suited both parties in the *Hostages* co-production. Colin Callendar, HBO's executive in charge of the project, said of the arrangement with Granada: 'We have never told Granada what they should make, or how they should make it. They come to us with a list of things they are going to do, we invest in the things we think are right for us'.[6] Ray Fitzwalter commented to me that at this time making docudrama in Britain 'was less expensive' for the American company: 'All they provided was half the finance and some editorial expertise.' HBO finance offered additional flexibility, but Fitzwalter observed that 'making a drama-documentary was still about four times the cost of an equivalent documentary on the same subject', so it was something of a prestige operation for both companies.

Although television programmes should not be expected to change the course of history, there was no reason why *Hostages* should not have taken its place in the mostly honourable tradition of British television docudrama. At one stage in pre-production, pretty well everyone directly involved in trying to get the Anglo-American hostages out of the Lebanon was agreed that the film offered at the very least potentially useful publicity that would put pressure on Western governments. The then US President Ronald Reagan was inclined, like his UK opposite number Premier Thatcher, to try to deny the 'oxygen of publicity' to terrorists, and direct negotiation with extremist groups was not something either regime was willing openly to do. But *World in Action* was well used to crusades for public information against the tendency of twentieth-century governments to be 'economical with the truth'. Like *Friendly Fire*, *Hostages* had a focus on officials and institutions, their policies, their failures, and the effects of these on ordinary individuals caught up in history.

In Sita Williams' words, '*Hostages* started out as a campaigning film to get [the hostages] out of Beirut'. Ethical considerations were always present, say its producers. Ian McBride told me that early on such concerns led to the project going into abeyance:

> it became clear that [the film] might well be misunderstood by those holding [the hostages], and cause immense anguish and perhaps continued incarceration. So we put the whole thing to one side, with the occasional piece of 'care and maintenance'.

It was Alasdair Palmer's idea at the outset, and Williams recalled that he did 'all the initial research'. He wrote a four-page treatment in 1990, the essence of which was a character-based drama focusing especially on the English friends. His inspiration was Brian Keenan's post-release press conference in Damascus in 1990. Like many people, Palmer had been struck by its inherent drama. He kept a file as hostages continued to be released, but the project was effectively on hold until December 1991, by which time Terry Anderson had been released.

Palmer went to Granada after graduating from Cambridge in 1987. His work on *World in Action* led him in time to be the researcher for *Why Lockerbie?* and to a docudrama specialism. In 1990 an article in the *Guardian* convinced him that

> it was a natural thing, to write about this relationship between Brian Keenan and John McCarthy. And you couldn't do it as a documentary, you had to do it as a drama because John was still in captivity.

The main problem was dramatising the situation the hostages were in; they spent much of their time in darkness and boredom, with, literally, nothing to do. The initial question that troubled everyone at Granada was, in Palmer's words, 'How do you make two hours of darkness viable?' His answer came from the research process itself. Denied access to McCarthy (still in captivity) and to Keenan (because of his antipathy to the project), Palmer wanted to 'come outside, where the women were doing this incredible work'. Different plot-lines allowed the hostages, captors and Middle East plot to be mirrored in a relatives and home governments parallel plot. Action by the relatives, and their on-going struggles with officialdom, supplied contrasts and, crucially, female characters.

Eventually Granada executives felt there was enough potential in the *Hostages* project in terms of 'bedrock' docudrama appeal. This is summarised by Williams:

> *Hostages* is not only the story of John McCarthy, Brian Keenan, Terry Anderson, Tom Sutherland and Frank Reed. It is also the story of how their friends and families fought to bring their plight to the attention of the world. And their fight was not principally against the hostage takers, theirs was a fight against governments who, like the British Government, said: 'We do not negotiate with terrorists' and did not; the American Government who said they would not negotiate and then were found to be trading 'Arms for *Hostages*' and in the case of Brian Keenan the Irish Government, the least powerful, and probably because of it, the most successful in negotiating his earlier release. (Williams, 1994: 209)

In the research period Palmer and Williams consulted widely over what she describes as 'eighteen months of painstaking research' (1994: 212). In addition to assistance from the normal agencies

Palmer had help from the Irish Foreign Office, which facilitated a meeting with the Iranian ambassador in Bonn – the man responsible for the release of Brian Keenan. He also met the Lebanese negotiator who arranged the release of French hostages one of whom, Jean-Paul Kauffman, had already appeared in a *This Week* documentary in 1988.[7]

In addition, Palmer met groups of campaigning relatives (of which there were several by this stage). A British group was led by Jill Morrell (McCarthy's girlfriend at the time), Terry Anderson's sister Peggy Say headed another in the USA, and Brian Keenan's sisters Elaine Spence and Brenda Gillham organised one in Ireland. In 1990 all could see the advantages of participating actively in the project. Reed and Keenan had been released by then, but Sutherland, McCarthy and Anderson (and others like Terry Waite) were still in captivity. Palmer's recollection of the 'Friends of John McCarthy' was affectionate: 'I had to make a presentation to them. They were wonderful. Very dedicated people.' Palmer says Jill Morrell herself then approached Keenan's agent, who was also interested initially. Keenan, however, was firmly against and his opposition was a vital factor. It emerged that he and McCarthy had discussed what they would do if and when they were released and resolved that they wanted control over how their story was to be told.

Palmer's meeting in late 1990 with Frank Reed in Boston takes us to the heart of some of the difficulties encountered when anchoring a drama in portrayals of real people:

> Frank was half an hour early for the meeting, arranged by his agent, and we talked ... Then the agent arrived, and said, 'Hold on, switch off the tape recorder, we've got to do the deal first!'. I explained it was for a television drama-documentary, and that Jill Morrell wanted to do it, and that we could buy Frank's time but no more than that – I mean we just don't buy people's stories [at Granada], that's not what we're about. The agent said, we're looking at bids in excess of $1 million for this story. So that was the end of the meeting![8]

Something similar happened to Palmer with almost everyone else involved and the situation was exacerbated as the hostage crisis moved towards its complicated conclusion. With the historical process itself bearing down on the individual protagonists of this world-historical drama, everyone was being drawn into a situation where their (bitter) experience was ironically becoming a major asset. The protagonists' wholly understandable protection of this asset gradually forced *Hostages* out of the space of the campaigning film and into a more controversial space – that of privacy rights.

Eventually all the protagonists acquired agents for their stories. Peggy Say, to whom Palmer talked in Washington, was again initially helpful – then her book was commissioned. Palmer 'ran into the same problems with her agent, too'. But the key difficulties for the project occurred after McCarthy's release in August 1991. Jill Morrell facilitated a meeting with Palmer in London in December of that year: '[McCarthy] talked very freely and openly and so did Jill ... It was great to meet him and get a sense of him.' To Palmer, both McCarthy and Morrell were clear that they were not in favour of the film but would not oppose it. McCarthy's agent Mark Lucas, however, moved to try to halt transmission by threatening legal action (see again Chapter 2). He sought and obtained disclaimers from the very 'Friends of John McCarthy' who had already spoken to Palmer and went to the press with the story. Palmer found these developments 'very unpleasant, because I knew and liked these people'.

By now *Hostages* was locked economically into a co-production deal. On the payroll were a writer (busy drafting scripts) and a director, and the casting process was under way. From the point of view of the people mainly concerned with the project, two years' work was at stake and resources were committed. The only thing that could stop it now was executive intervention. In industrial terms, the project was beyond the point of no return. Palmer continued with the research, had another meeting with Frank Reed in America, and a four-hour interview with Tom Sutherland in Scotland during New Year 1992:

> He was just out. It was like someone who had just had enormous pressure taken off him. In a way he was the most helpful of all because the experience was very fresh and he'd been with all of them, and he was one of the last to be released.

McCarthy, understanding all too well the post-release strain, worried about his fellow ex-hostage:

> I was ... very disappointed when Tom, eager to accommodate all-comers, spoke to Granada, after all. I was deeply troubled that he was taking the attention and adulation too much to heart. I tried to explain to him that while all the warmth and affection was quite genuine, it wasn't based on who we really were, but on the symbolic value which we seemed to have acquired. (McCarthy and Morrell, 1994: 613)

Writer Bernard MacLaverty incorporated Palmer's Sutherland material into his final script draft, and the actors met for a read-through in Manchester at the end of March 1992.[9]

An impressive cast – one impossible to contemplate without HBO finance – had been assembled. American actors Kathy Bates ('Oscar-winner Kathy Bates', as the Anglo-American tabloids tended to refer to her, played Peggy Say), Harry Dean Stanton (Reed), Josef Sommer (Sutherland), and Jay O. Sanders (Anderson) joined equally prominent British actors Ciaran Hinds (Keenan), Colin Firth (McCarthy) and the late Natasha Richardson (Jill Morrell). The cast represented the very best in Anglo-American film acting. Hinds had already worked for the Granada team, playing Birmingham Six member Richard McIllkenny in the 1989 *Who Bombed Birmingham?*. Firth too was familiar with portraying living people, having played Robert Lawrence in the Charles Wood's film about the Falklands War (*Tumbledown*, BBC, 1987). Williams reflected:

> The scales between cinema and television are quite different ... I wouldn't have got Kathy Bates and Harry Dean Stanton for the kind of fee I did if *Hostages* had been a feature film.

Hostages cost in the region of £1.5 million to make in 1992.

After rehearsal over a seven-day period in March and April, filming in Manchester and Israel took place between 7 April and 12 May 1992. Post-production continued through the summer and the programme was transmitted in the UK in September 1992 and in the USA in February 1993. McCarthy's agent Mark Lucas 'never let up' in his efforts first to halt then to discredit the film, but Palmer 'could understand why he was doing it – it was financially driven.

He thought, I can't sell the film rights to this book if they've done a film without [those rights].' Lucas, meanwhile, told the *Sunday Times*: 'It's been a cynical, fiscal exercise by Granada in getting the story before anyone else, doing its own version and not paying anyone for it' (20 September 1992). McCarthy sent a letter to Granada requesting withdrawal of the film and told the *Daily Telegraph*: 'I have made my opposition clear to Granada and I am saddened they are still going ahead' (19 September 1992). McCarthy had actually gone public with his opposition as early as 2 February 1992. An article in the *Sunday Times* (headline: '"Exploited" McCarthy seeks ban on TV hostage drama') quoted agent Antony Howard as saying that his client Brian Keenan was also 'uncomfortable and unhappy' with Granada. He claimed that Granada's Mike Beckham (producer-director of *Why Lockerbie?* and involved in the initial stages of the *Hostages* project) had falsely stated that Keenan had already co-operated on the project. Beckham denied this. In the same piece, Ray Fitzwalter rejected the suggestion that the project lacked credibility because of this opposition: 'We have done a great deal of work over many months and are entitled to bring it to conclusion ... We have had the co-operation of a vast number of people.'[10]

The controversy culminated in the letter quoted in Chapter 1, with McCarthy, Keenan, Waite and Anderson accusing Granada of 'grossly misleading the public'. Their major contention was that: 'Of the six hostages portrayed in the film Granada has spoken to just two, Frank Reed and Tom Sutherland.' There could therefore be no 'legitimate basis on which to claim that they have a "full story for the first time".' The letter made one emotional and one somewhat naïve but ostensibly rational appeal. First, the signatories wondered 'how Granada and HBO can think they have the right to produce a story, reporting [*sic*] to be true, before those at the centre of it have come to terms with it themselves.' Second, they made a distinction between a researched/factual story and a 'true' story, calling *Hostages* 'only partly factual':

> We feel Granada and their American co-producers must explain this to their audiences and also make plain that we four have no part in the film's production.[11]

There is, perhaps, one further aspect to a crisis like the one involving the Beirut hostages. Just as individuals find themselves in a 'slowed down' state after a traumatic event, like a traffic accident for example, so something similar seems to occur in a national collective consciousness after an event that cannot be readily assimilated or comprehended. Docudramas are sometimes the visible evidence of this state in a culture. All docudrama, by this definition, is 'trauma drama' – through which collective guilt, paranoia and vicarious suffering is picked over and examined, and anxiety either mitigated or cranked up. This may explain why *Hostages*, however briefly and even for those who did not watch it, became such a *cause célèbre*.

UK reaction – 'Drama out of suffering'

Some of the evidence for a television drama playing into a public context lies in initial reactions to it. These are expressed through reviews and comments in a variety of media. In the UK the adverse pre-publicity outlined above had a direct effect on reception. British newspapers carried the story of the hostages' opposition to *Hostages* during the very week of its transmission. The *Independent* (19 September), for example, summarised the fundamental ethical challenge:

> The moral question: should McCarthy's life have been seized again by Granada TV for the purposes of entertainment?

In many ways this dilemma is the key to discussion of third-phase docudrama. All the national newspapers that week wrestled with it. On 22 September the same newspaper went as far as condemning the television company in a leader article 'Drama out of suffering'. The leader accused Granada of being at the very least 'guilty of distressing insensitivity'. Tabloid newspapers raised the same issue, but were less censorious. In the *Daily Mirror* on the day of transmission, for example:

> Some may think [*Hostages*] simply turns the victims' dreadful experience into entertainment. Judge for yourselves.

On 23 September the Granada production team (Palmer, Williams,

McBride and Fitzwalter) fought back in the *Guardian*. Much of their letter in reply was taken up with refutation at the level of fact – there was, for example, no evidence that Reed and Sutherland were misled ('as Mr. Reed's lawyer ... can confirm'); most of the factual material had already 'entered the public record'; the disclaimer demanded by the hostages was there in the film. The team counter-claimed that they had never stated that *Hostages* was the 'true story'.[12] They concluded with their own questions:

> The issue is: exactly which account will be the 'true' or 'full' story? Will it be Brian Keenan's, to be published the day after our film is transmitted? John McCarthy's? Terry Anderson's? Terry Waite's? Who will reconcile the inevitable differences? And how? Could any account, written from a specific standpoint, be the 'full' story?

It is interesting, incidentally, that it should be the producers (not the writer or the director) who took responsibility for defending the film – a demonstration if one were needed of the locus of power in television.

As might be expected of someone with a good deal of experience of re-presenting living people in performance, Colin Firth had some interesting reflections on these matters. English newspapers of the week of transmission quoted extensively from his remarks following a fairly hostile press preview. Firth defended the film, the *Daily Express* (19 September 1992) quoting him saying:

> I think John McCarthy has become something of a folk hero ... He captured the public imagination, because a man who emerges from a horror with such immense charm is inspirational to thousands of people.

The film was actually 'the most balanced account of the events,' he claimed, 'because we're independent collectors of information'. In the *Daily Telegraph* of the same day he demonstrated an awareness of the political context, saying: 'We are dealing with a very interesting and public story which in a way held us all to ransom, and we want to understand its effect on us.'

The furore caused the same edition of the *Daily Telegraph* to say elsewhere: 'The row will undoubtedly boost audience figures.' The facts were to be counter-intuitive. Ian McBride's general assertion that docudrama's 'power is to do with whether the audience are attracted to the subject' was borne out negatively in this case; the audience was not attracted. The producers' view is that low audience figures were the result both of the real hostages' intervention and of the resulting furore. Alasdair Palmer reflected:

> The effect was very much to stop people watching it. We were all very disappointed in the viewing figures. I think it was two things: partly the 'anti' campaign, also something to do with it being very tough viewing in midweek.

Sita Williams recalled: 'there was a huge amount of press interest ... I've never worked on a programme which created more press and media interest. I was never off the phone'. However, she became convinced that this publicity would not work in the film's favour. It was, she felt, ultimately 'a turn-off factor' for the audience at which the producers were aiming. *Hostages* was watched by an average UK audience of 6.7 million (with an audience share of 29%). By contrast, the more low-profile 'local/national' *Fighting for Gemma* (shown a year later in the same *World in Action* slot – Wednesday, 8.00–10.00 p.m.) got an average audience of 8 million and a share of 35%. Hardly surprising, then, that Williams and Palmer believe their achievement in *Hostages* was undermined by pre-transmission publicity. Williams observes that American press and media reaction was 'entirely different ... to the mealy-mouthed knocking we got [in the UK]'.[13]

US reaction – 'Struggles ... in a larger context'

Hostages' mainly negative pre-publicity, however, was perhaps not as important as the fact that the British hostages were known to be against it. In this sense it fell foul of the third element of the Lipkin 'mantra' of 'relatabilty, rootablility and promotability'. Its promotability was heavily compromised by the way the British public were denied a chance to empathise with Keenan and McCarthy in the docudrama without feeling guilty about it. By contrast, *Hostages* was received in the USA with interest, some enthusiasm, and only muted concern about issues of media intrusion and exploitation. Only Jeff

Jarvis of *TV Guide* (20–26 February 1993) took any account of the furore that was so dominating the British press. He noted mildly that *Hostages* 'is not the authorized story of any single hostage'. After its first transmission by HBO on 20 February 1993 (a Saturday) there were six repeats during the following three weeks of February and March. February is an important month in US television, for one of the yearly 'sweeps', in which ratings are calculated, takes place then. Networks often seek to boost their viewing numbers by screening programmes with known rating value, or ones easy to publicise. *USA Today* welcomed the film as 'an HBO specialty: the investigative docudrama' (19 February 1993). And whereas four hostages had condemned the film in the UK, HBO found two to endorse it. Tom Sutherland was widely quoted in the American press, making remarks like: 'The movie is stark and realistic' (*USA Today*, 19 February 1993) and 'It comes as close as is humanly possible to showing what we went through' (*Boston Herald*, 19 February 1993). In the *Fort Lauderdale Sun-Sentinel* on the same day he went further:

> Frankly I was kind of shocked at the reality of it. I watched in amazement. To see somebody re-creating what we had been through so vividly and so accurately, I was kind of blown away.

Terry Anderson, a co-signatory of the hostages' letter, also approved, or so Sutherland claimed in an interview with the *Cleveland Plain Dealer* (20 February):

> When I saw this movie, I thought, 'My God, that's really well done.' So I called [Anderson] and said, 'Have you seen it?' He said no, so I sent him a copy and called back. He said, 'I just talked to my agent at NBC a couple of minutes ago and told them, 'You guys have to come up with a good movie because you've got a damn good one to beat here.'

Elsewhere Sutherland did temper this praise somewhat, noting that the requirement of compression increased the drama to a level which was not present in the real situation (the experience was mainly 'just boring and frustrating as hell'). However, his general support for the film is clear enough in media reports of the time.[14]

There were some critical voices: the *Seattle Post-Intelligencer*'s John Engstom wrote that the film 'falls short ... because it follows so many characters through so many years' (19 February 1993). The under-written nature of the women's roles was also remarked upon in *USA Today* and in *Entertainment Weekly* (the latter rightly calling Bates's and Richardson's characters 'peripheral figures'). Many American reviews during the week of transmission, however, exhibited a fascination with form wholly absent from British reviews. Reviewers were taken especially with the documentary values of the film. The British press's obsession with the idea of drama contaminating documentary purity, with 'blurred boundaries', just did not feature. *USA Today*'s coverage could be taken as representative. Their reviewer praised the film's 'astringent objectivity'. The *Seattle Post-Intelligencer*'s critic (19 February 1993) admired the 'careful, ethical approach'. In a lengthy article for *New York Newsday* (18 February 1993) Diane Werts contrasted the film directly and favourably with the generality of America docudrama. While American network television, she said, 'might try hard to personalize the situation – using long scenes among the hostages to have us identify with one or more of them', the Granada film 'goes a more complex route':

> Instead of a few expansively telling moments, we're given hundreds of brief snapshots with which to piece together our own understanding of the situation.

John J. O'Connor in the *New York Times* echoed this praise, noting the care with which the script 'keeps placing the struggles of the hostages *in the larger context* of Mideast and world politics' (19 February 1993 – my emphasis). In *Weekly Variety* Todd Everett found a cryptic tabloid formulation: 'The gripping production cleverly mixes news footage with topflight thesping' (17 February 1993). HBO's perspicacity in spotting the potential for high-concept docudrama in the USA 'cashes out' in such comments.

American tabloids tended to approach the film through reference to the cast's recent movies or their established drawing potential (McBride's 'marquee names' – see Chapter 1). *Entertainment Weekly* described Harry Dean Stanton (Reed) as a 'veteran character actor ... able to communicate more with his back to the camera than many actors can in several pages of script' (14 February 1993). Other tabloids connected variously: Kathy Bates to her

Oscar-winning role in *Misery* (1990); Jay O. Sanders to the film *JFK* (1991); Josef Sommer to *Witness* (1985); Ciaran Hinds to *The Cook, the Thief, his Wife and her Lover* (1989); Colin Firth to *Valmont* (1989); Natasha Richardson to *The Comfort of Strangers* (1990). Even supporting player Conrad Asquith, who gives the briefest of Terry Waite cameos in the film, was connected to the movie *White Hunter, Black Heart* (1990). The Hollywood connection, one might say, was much more central to American critical comment.

Judgement of the success or failure of *Hostages*, then, has to take account of the fault lines between the two cultures. McCarthy's and Keenan's opposition to the making of *Hostages* stands in marked contrast to Sutherland's enthusiasm. In popular culture on both sides of the Atlantic these men were contemporary heroes/martyrs. Their published personal experiences (part historical record, part personal therapy) were received with a degree almost of reverence in the UK, but more robustly in the USA. Hence Firth's respectful – even quasi-religious – attitude to his real life Other:

> I thought about getting in touch with John but it boiled down to asking for some sort of *absolution*. (*Daily Telegraph*, 19 September 1992 – my emphasis)

The hostages' own published accounts were vivid documents in very contrasting ways. Keenan's eloquent 1992 book *An Evil Cradling* maintained his general silence about *Hostages*. McCarthy, however, gave an account of his responses in *Some Other Rainbow* (1994 – co-authored with Jill Morrell). He implies that Keenan's opposition virtually compelled his own (McCarthy and Morrell, 1994: 585). After their release he and Keenan still needed each other's support emotionally. 'I wasn't coping as well as he was,' remarks McCarthy, but Keenan's opposition to the film also proved to him 'I wasn't the only one with worries'. Opposition to the film was one way he could demonstrate solidarity. There was also the 'decision we had all made in captivity ... not [to] get involved in any dramatic representations of our years as hostages until we were all free'. For McCarthy the most painful part of all this was the fact that Morrell and Chris Pearson (of the 'Friends of John McCarthy') had already approved the project. McCarthy was troubled by this: 'I was trying desperately hard to reconcile the world I now lived in with the world I had lived in as a hostage, yet my greatest friends from those two worlds were divided by a misunderstanding.' For McCarthy, then, the film became 'a recurring irritation' (1994: 612).

Morrell, meanwhile, used her section of their book to acknowledge the role she played in early plans for the film, but remarks:

> When John was released ... I believed that the situation had changed so dramatically that the film would be redundant. Chris [Pearson] told Granada that we would no longer be involved, and we believed that the film would not go ahead. (1994: 616)

She also, of course, implicitly discredits the film by criticising the way McCarthy is 'curiously transformed from producer to reporter' (see Chapter 3, note 10). Morrell's difficulty with the film – indeed the whole 'inner circle' view of it – is probably best summed up by her disarmingly frank acknowledgement:

> I felt guilty that I had contributed to something that was putting [John] under such strain; our correspondence with Granada, the stories in the press and the prospect of the programme itself cast a shadow over us until the film was shown. (1994: 616)

On Granada's side there was no such 'guilt'. The producers held to their view that the film was 'a dramatisation of events which illustrate[d] circumstances and attitudes and show[ed] context' and that it still had a part to play in public understanding of the Hostage crisis. Williams asserted: 'No one has an exclusive right to a story which is in the public domain' (Williams 1994: 210, 212). Both these points are part of Granada's classic 'public interest' defence of docudrama.

By contrast, in July 1992 a play called *Someone Who'll Watch Over Me* by the Irish playwright Frank McGuinness opened at the Hampstead Theatre Club in London. Set in an unnamed but clearly Middle Eastern country, the play depicts three men, Michael, Edward and Adam – the Englishman, Irishman and American of popular joke and mythology – chained to the walls of an undifferentiated cell. This fictional treatment of hostage incarceration was strongly, even emotionally, endorsed by Keenan in an Introduction to the published text. Its link to the Beirut hostages could not have been more evident and, like *Hostages*, marketing when it transferred into London's West End played upon its proximity to real recent events. Before the play was produced at the Abbey Theatre, Dublin, it was reprinted apparently to incorporate Keenan's Introduction. The former hostage, clearly moved by McGuinness's treatment, remarked: 'Though [McGuinness] had no information on which to base his play, I could see that he had the touchstones of emotional truth' (1992b, 1). The prose of Keenan's Introduction to *Someone Who'll Watch Over Me* – like the writing in his own memoir – positively blazes. Although he never mentions *Hostages* by name, Keenan endorses 'emotional truth' over 'information' and admires the way that the play 'touched wellsprings that moved the drama out of its vague topicality and sang to Everyman'. The implicit value judgement could not be clearer (1992b, 2).

The essence of the Granada claim to the hostage story, however, was that an overview of events was unavailable to those directly involved in the hostage crisis. From the outset the *Hostages* team had tried conscientiously to cover a wider angle than the simply personal. As early in the process as his treatment, Alasdair Palmer examined the *general* context, writing on the first page:

> The aim [of the film] is not only to depict the culture of terrorism. It is also to provide insight into an alien but crucially important aspect of Muslim/Iranian psychology – an aspect the people and governments of Britain and America have so far totally failed to comprehend.

This aspiration was picked up in the more successful climate the film inhabited in America. In post-9/11 hindsight, too, these remarks resonate. Bill Nichols has noted that: 'If excess tends to be that which is beyond narrative in fiction films, excess in documentary is that which stands beyond the reach of both narrative and exposition' (1991: 142). The production team's own admission that the documentary claims of multiple-narrative interfered with the potential of the drama demonstrates, perhaps, that *Hostages* struggled with excess in both genres – there was too much to deal with in terms of emotional and historical truths. The history itself exceeded representation precisely because contemporary history is not, as postmodernism would have us believe, simply narrative; it is (or was in this case) heated dispute.

The reaction to *Hostages* in Britain caused by the exchange of letters of 21 and 22 September 1992 had the effect of locating the film within a cultural discourse about the right of privacy. The campaigning film of the producers' intentions became instead a film that exploited the hostages' privacy. Its promise of insight into the 'evil cradling' that Keenan pictured as the reality of hostage-taking was superseded in its truth claim by the witness-discourse of the hostages themselves. Some of this complexity can be discerned in Hugh Hebert's review of the film in the *Guardian* (24 September). First Hebert praises the programme's conscientious setting of the hostage crisis in its political context and notes that this aspect 'was almost totally lost in the emotional bonfires lit by the carefully graduated release of the captives'. But he goes on to claim that it 'misses on what television drama ought to be able to do, get inside the heads of its characters. The more you stick to known facts, the more difficult that becomes.' This view was echoed elsewhere in the broadsheet British press's responses to the film. The critical move that sees docudrama as bad documentary, bad drama, or both is, Williams believes, generally less prevalent in the tabloid press. This was not altogether borne out in reviews of *Hostages*. In the *Sun*, for example, Garry Bushell wrote that it was 'more than a play but too full of guesswork to stand as documentary'(24 September 1992).

In the case of *Hostages* there was, perhaps, a 'presenting problem', as family doctors say, and a less obvious underlying one. The presenting problem in the news media of the day was whether McCarthy/Keenan should have been portrayed in a television film against their wishes. The real underlying problem was about the nature of public sacrifice on a political stage by private citizens. Taken as hostages for political purposes by the proponents of one side of a global ideological argument and isolated as part of the rejection of this tactic by their own side, these individuals became modern martyrs in a global village where anyone might be called to account at any time for the wider actions of the society of which they are a part. As Paula Rabinowitz has pertinently noted: 'The invention of the individual witness whose personal story serves as a template for history has been crucial to twentieth-century Western accounts of atrocity and war' (1994: 107–8). The hostage crisis of the 1980s and 1990s was, as it turned out, part of a war that has still not ended, and the hostages paradigm – private individuals held to account for the actions of their political masters – turns out to be a defining one for the millennial period.

No wonder, then, no one dared to criticise these secular martyrs at the time – at least in the UK. The quasi-religious idea that only they could tell us about the pain of their experience, and set that pain in an existential context, was stronger than the wider representational claims of any docudrama. All the protagonists represented in Granada's film tried to articulate these things in their subsequent memoirs. By common critical consent, Keenan's book *An Evil Cradling* in particular succeeded to an extraordinary degree.[15] What was difficult for all the ex-hostages, however, was setting their experience in contexts beyond the purely personal. *Hostages* thrust some unarticulated questions about these matters into the public domain in 1992 and gave offence when it might easily have been hailed as a campaigning film had transmission occurred a year earlier. Watching the film in the UK in 1992 became like a violation, a metaphorical thrusting of hands into the martyrs' open wounds. Watching the film years later, it seems an unlikely source of such controversy, being rather doggedly worthy and certainly over-plotted and over-populated with characters.

The relativities involved in the complex reception process associated with *Hostages* give it a special significance for this study of docudrama. For a start it shows that proximity to contemporary events and recent history can be a weakness as well as a strength. Teams making docudrama as well as audiences are drawn to the contemporary material precisely because immediacy and possible controversy are inherent, but there are dangers in this proximity. Co-pro films on international subjects seek a leverage beyond what was possible to national networks and filmmakers in previous phases of development, and this marks an advance. At the level of politics and ethics, such projects claim moral justification, so are weakened if this is forfeited. At the economic level, the 'pre-sold' element is a continuing draw for producers, but it can have an unexpected price. The additional promise of the co-pro is that audiences might be persuaded to accept the angle of vision offered by the docudrama – so long as they can clearly see that the ends justify the means.

But – and this was the case with *Hostages* – when the complexities of events in the real, historical, world create problems at the point of transmission and reception, then results can be unpredictable to say the least. Relatively successful (and often repeated) in the USA, transmission in the UK was once and once only. In the UK in 1992 circumstances conspired fatally to disable reception, whatever the intentions of its makers, whatever the film's diligence in acquiring facts, whatever the excellence (or not) of the production. This is only in part because popular dramatic genres and formats, in seeking to make films more accessible to audiences, can and do complicate documentary claims. The 'tidying up' of plots and compositing of characters demonstrate the incapacity of third-phase docudrama to accommodate to at least some of the complexities of 'real history', but it is when real history bites back that docudramas really hit trouble. The encounter with real history experienced by *Hostages* in its reception in the UK tells us more in its relative failure during this early period of co-pro development than we can learn from a generally agreed success like *Who Bombed Birmingham?*.

Traumas and headlines

In the first edition I tried to make out a case for the usefulness of the humble made-for-TV/movie-of-the-week docudrama as well as for the high-concept film. Where the prestige co-pro was a new departure, this kind of film represented a kind of staple in the spectrum of docudrama production. My argument in 1998 was that the drama-doc (especially Granada-style investigative drama-documentary) was a very British and a very masculine genre, the docudrama (especially movie-of-the-week docudrama) a very American, very feminised one. The level of convergence that has now taken place ensures that elements of these two traditions are now evident in a good deal of docudrama production across the board. Docudrama's capacity to work close to current events (especially in television) and to pro-

vide a platform for exploiting new technologies (internet back-ups
to docudrama information), combined with film studios' renewed
use of the form has seen a resurgence in docudrama production that
leads me to assert that a fourth phase of development is now evident.
And in this phase, in some cases, the strengths of the overlooked and
disregarded movie-of-the-week docudrama have merged in astonish-
ing ways with those of the traditional dramadoc to produce exciting
and challenging new hybrids (which I will discuss more fully in
Chapter 8).

I have argued that the major element of the third phase was an
increased accommodation to the trajectories of dramatic presentation. This ensured that the person-centred drama began to account
for a considerable portion of docudramatic output. In 1993 Rod
Carveth classified American docudrama into two basic forms. The
older form is 'the historical docudrama, a fictionalized re-telling of a
period of history', which 'benefit[s] from the perspective of time passage' (in that events depicted within it are widely known). This form
looked back to Hollywood's long tradition of historical film and
biopic. The newer form he calls 'headline docudrama' (Carveth,
1993: 121).[16] This is 'based on events that have occurred much
closer to their airing' ('usually within five years of the events they
portray', according to Carveth). In the third phase, headline docudramas concentrated on 'tales of adversity' and 'tales of crime',
mimicking tabloid headline stories (their principal source).

Everyone who writes on the form comments on the dangers of
this kind of docudramatic response to news (see in particular
Rosenthal, 1995: 3, 10–11). Carveth adduces three kinds of ethical
danger: headline docudramas 'may compromise the legal positions
of the principals'; they may 'ignore the social and political forces
surrounding an event'; and 'the act of adapting an event to standard narrative formulas changes reality in the process'. In addition,
he points to the dangers of producers 'moving more quickly to
secure rights' and indulging in what has become known as cheque-
book journalism (1993: 121, 123–5). Producers protect themselves
legally, of course, by this 'optioning' process, and by using real-
world protagonists as 'consultants' at the point of production. Thus
they buy the rights to a point of view, rather than subscribing to a

journalistic notion of an objective or investigative account. Both television and film now routinely follow this path, the difference being that if you can parlay your story to moviemakers, you stand to make more out of it.

A good illustration of this 'exploitation of subject power' is Frank Abagnale Jr's masterly use of his story as a con-artist – or rather his extension of con-artistry into the film optioning process. The main protagonist of Steven Spielberg's 2002 *Catch Me If You Can* first produced a book (with the same title) about his exploits with ghost writer Stan Redding in 1980. He then:

> option[ed] his rights half a dozen times to a succession of producers, earning himself a tidy $20,000 with each option renewal. As scams go, this one was perfectly legal. 'It was the biggest racket in the world,' Abagnale later told a *Newsday* reporter. 'I thought, I've got to keep this up!' Ultimately, Abagnale cashed in by selling his story outright for a cool $250,000. (Vankin and Whalen, 2005: 6)[17]

The case of the 'Long Island Lolita' films is the best exemplar of 'low-concept' docudrama's optioning processes in the 1990s. All the main protagonists were able to obtain a piece of the economic action. NBC paid Amy Fisher's bail for collaboration on their film; CBS financed Joey Buttafuoco and his wife to get their 'angle'; and ABC used trial transcripts for their take on the saga. The result was three films offering a multiple perspective on this headline story. David Edgar called this an exercise in 'competitive fictions'.[18] The ideal of objective Truth, of course, was arguably not so important to network producers as the tabloid 'urban tragedy/sensation' news value of the story.

Ultimately, the headline screen docudrama is an eloquent demonstration of the late capitalist principle that the personal is first and foremost the economical. Personal experience, elevated to public notice by news coverage, is sufficient guarantee of audience interest to get producers optioning and even to put docudramas into production. As early as 1993, US television executives were openly acknowledging this fact. Mark Sennett, for example, noted that there was an inherent attraction in 'stories of people who've been through everybody's nightmare.' John Matoian, then a CBS executive in charge of made-for-TV movies and mini-series, commented: 'I suppose these are as hard and difficult times as ever, and people are looking for windows into behaviour.'[19] Ian McBride calls these kinds of story 'journalism of the first resort'. The trend towards the 'people story' has not diminished. By the mid-1990s Alan Rosenthal noted that 43 out of 115 movies shown in the first season of 1992 in the USA, and seven out of the top ten made-for-TV movies of 1991, fitted the category (Rosenthal, 1995: 10). Steven N. Lipkin remarks on the high visibility of headline stories in an increasingly competitive American market (Lipkin, 2002: 56). An Appendix to his book surveys docudramas transmitted during the all-important 'sweeps' period on US networks, noting a pretty steady percentage proportion (at 10–15%) of docudramas aired as 'movies-of-the-week' (p. 143). Confirmation, if this were needed, came from a network executive, Victoria Sterling, interviewed by him in 1997. 'Docudramas', she told him, 'are a lot easier to sell a movie audience.' They 'have really proliferated,' she adds, 'because they fit *new operational circumstances* so well' (p. 59 – my emphasis).

Docudrama desires and pleasures

By the fourth phase, from the late 1990s onwards, the desires and pleasures available to the viewer of docudrama had been exploited and developed to a new and sophisticated level. In the best examples of the new practice, the fundamental originary appeal of docudrama was not lost, as I shall argue in Chapter 8. Michael Eaton's remark at the 'Reality Time' conference in 1996, is still the best summation of this perennial appeal: 'You can throw light into dark places, he said, 'and show large audiences the way power is exercised.' Even trauma/headline docudramas have turned to some big subjects as new developments have taken the form further. An audience may not even need to be convinced that a film shows *exactly* 'how it was' to be convinced of their newly privileged access to information about events in the public sphere. If they are drawn to docudramas in the first place, and even partially convinced by the 'new light' claim, then by the very act of watching they enter ongoing public debate.

It is, of course, always more difficult to make a critical case at the low end of any market. The sneering notion persists that the pleasures of the made-for-TV/movie-of-the-week in *all* its forms are those of a 'woman's genre', through which anything serious is first domesticated then trivialised. As early as 1990 Laurie Schulze pointed to the mostly male critical move that shifts from a negative critique of value to a condescending comment on the taste of (presumed) female consumers. 'A female audience', she remarked, 'is taken to task by popular criticism to strike another blow against what is perceived to be a nonaesthetic and morally defective form of popular culture' (in Balio, 1990: 355). In 1998, I suggested that such a critical move (which sees documentary as always and inevitably more important and more serious than drama) will always construct high-concept docudrama as a 'masculinised' form, with a greater inherent value than forms easily characterised as 'entertainments' – like movie-of-the-week docudrama.[20] I shared and still share Schulze's view that docudrama was 'capable of pushing at the limits of the controversial *without losing its audience'* (Schulze, 1990: 364 – my emphases). The ethics of docudrama (though many commentators would argue that this very phrase is an oxymoron) exist in a spectrum: at one end there is a feminised 'ethics of care' that can be best understood emotionally; at the other a masculinised 'ethics of rights and duties' that can be best appreciated rationally. I believe the most effective docudramas negotiate inventively between these positions, producing a teasing amalgam of two modes of thought – a mixture, in short, of challenges to apprehension and comprehension in the viewer.

In his foundational study of documentary Bill Nichols noted that documentary had: 'kinship with ... other nonfictional systems – [s]cience, economics, politics, foreign policy, education, religion, welfare' (1991: 3–4). Elizabeth Cowie quotes this list, but adds, pertinently, 'the law' (1997: 2). Nichols' 'discourse[s] of sobriety', manifestly serious knowledge systems, have what he believes is a natural antipathy towards '"make-believe" characters, events, or entire worlds (unless they serve as pragmatically useful simulations of the "real" one)'. Note his bracketed caveat: it provides the rubric under which rests docudrama's documentary claim. In all cases where there is 'no other (documentary) way to tell it', dramatised forms fill the vacuum. Although the discourse of sobriety 'operates where the reality-attentive ego and superego live', Nichols in common with many writers on documentary is rather reticent on what part *desire* might play in, and what *pleasure* might inhere in, his 'sober discourses'. Michael Renov, however, touches on this territory when he comments that the documentary conscience of ego and superego expresses 'an explicit "documentary desire"' when it seeks special knowledge or understanding (1993: 5). In a more recent study Nichols goes some way to try to accommodate to the evidence provided by the 'artistic proof'. 'In his *Rhetoric*,' says Nichols, 'Aristotle divided artistic proofs into three types … ':

- ethical: generating an impression of good moral character or credibility;
- emotional: appealing to an audience's emotions to produce the desired disposition; putting the audience in the right mood or establishing a fame of mind favorable to a particular view;
- demonstrative: using real or apparent reasoning or demonstration; proving, or giving the impression of proving, the case. (Nichols, 2001: 50)

These proofs are the territory of the docudrama as much as the documentary, given that the docudrama is always already more overtly 'artistic' and focused on the ethical, emotional and demonstrative. The case of the first artistic proof is the case of the high concept film – the exemplar that convinces audiences of its 'good moral character', partly because it will often exhibit more clearly its documentary provenance. But all docudrama tries to activate the quite different desires and pleasures associated with imitation, simulation and impersonation resulting from drama – the imitation of an action. Drama allows an audience to move in and out of belief-in-the-illusion, even while the illusion unfolds. The pleasure that follows derives from an imaginative response to the claim to the 'life-like' and a recognition of second-order experience – it is not *my* experience, but I can make it mine by *believing*. This is an outrageous claim, when all is said and done, but one which retains a formidable psychic power still evident in the regular 'willing suspension of disbelief' necessary in any encounter with film and stage fictions.

Mixed with documentary, as Stella Bruzzi has observed, 'the role of performance is, paradoxically, to draw the audience into the reality of the situations being dramatised, to authenticate the fictionalisation' (2000: 153).

John Ellis once characterised television viewing as based on the 'glance' rather than the 'gaze' of film (1992: 128).[21] He argued that attention to the television screen is more likely to be fractured by domestic and other claims, whereas the fact that the spectator has gone specifically to look in the cinema ensures more focused attention. In his recent work, Ellis has gone further, talking of television as primarily a mode of *witnessing* for audiences. This, he says, is 'a particular modality of the experience of recorded images *and sounds*, rather than an inherent quality to be found within those images' (2000:14 – my emphasis) and thus defining further the difference between cinema and television. Audience 'witnessing' carries with it a subject-position 'safe but also powerless, able to over-look but under-act' (p. 15). Small-screen spectatorship is now a more or less continuous process of self-reflexive questioning and reality-testing, as rewinding and reviewing has joined domestic interruption in fracturing continuous viewing. Ellis regards fact-based television drama especially as offering an opportunity for a Freudian 'working through' of problems at many levels:

> The TV movie provides a form in which social issues can be worked through explicitly, often in the form of dramas based on real life stories. The *Movie of the Week* form on American television plays exactly this role, dealing easily with issues such as rape, AIDS, paederasty, petty crime, senility and so on, issues which the Hollywood feature film finds it almost impossible to address within its entertainment formats. (2000: 122)

The attentive (and inattentive) ear should not be forgotten in any discussion of docudrama. When analysing present practice in Chapter 1, I remarked that an essentially un-realistic sound technique now formed the basis of the hearing through which we engage with distance shots. The radio microphone, which allows audiences to hear the conversations of distant figures in a landscape (hearing them as if, metaphorically, at their shoulder), was imported from television news and current affairs programming, where its miniaturisation offered additional flexibility to reporters. It is a technological device that underscores television's historic drive to *hear* as well as to see, and this issue is one to which I will return in Chapter 8. In television drama, sound technologies paradoxically support the visual aesthetics of the real, even though they are inherently unrealistic. In this sense they too are part of the continued technological quest for access to the real.[22]

My view, then, is that the docudrama offers pleasures beyond those of the documentary and the drama in its dramatising of anterior realities. It offers the pleasure of hearing as well as seeing – 'eavesdropping' as well as witnessing. Far from being disconnected entirely from the documentary, it offers a potentially unique dual perspective on the phenomenal world. The work of the eye and ear are equalised in television docudrama, and words as well as looks have their weight. To repeat my earlier formula, the ideal spectator for docudrama seeks to ratify emotionally what they already know (or suspect) intellectually. The spectator is both the witness/looker-on of documentary (looking with a socio-anthropological, scientific, gaze) and the voyeur-eavesdropper of the fiction film (looking from a position of privileged identification). The docudrama's ideal spectator is both over-look-er and over-hear-er.

By the end of the 1990s docudrama as a form had acquired a mixed reputation amongst makers and users alike. In a review of the first edition of this book Leslie Woodhead himself noted and deplored 'the inexorable drift of television dramatised documentary from information to entertainment' (*Times Higher*, 19 June 1998: 21). He was unhappy, too, with my defence of the made-for-TV movie. Discussing two BBC programmes on a case of so-called 'cot death' – one a documentary, the other a docudrama – Mark Lawson observed '[the docudrama] never suggests that drama can improve on fact', demonstrating that he too doubted the helpfulness of the cultural drift towards drama.[23] But I believe that the form has acquired new potential thanks to the fourth and latest phase of its development, in which the modes available have expanded in particularly interesting ways – as I hope now to show.

Notes

1 *World in Action*'s documentary on the subject was transmitted in 1985. Mullin went on to write his book, *Error of Judgement*, published by Chatto and Windus in 1986.

2 Chris Mullin was played by the actor John Hurt in the film.

3 There have been other successful cases: in 1993 the BBC film *Bad Company* explored the 'Bridgewater case' convictions (four men convicted of murdering a newspaper delivery boy). After the release of the three living protagonists in this real-life drama in 1996, the film was transmitted again in 1997, with a final caption updating the story. In 2004 the BBC's docudrama *Cherished* explored a 'cot death' case. Angela Cannings was convicted of killing her baby in 2002, released on appeal in 2003. She and several other women had been convicted largely on the evidence of leading British paediatrician Professor Sir Roy Meadow. Following public campaigns by the various women's supporter groups, appeal cases and the docudrama, Professor Meadow himself was tried by the Medical Council in 2005 and his expert testimony discredited – leading to the women's release. Meadow himself was initially struck off by the Medical Council, but was reinstated on appeal in 2006. Such mini-histories illustrate the way in which the docudrama is embedded deeply in events in the public sphere (see also Chapter 8, note 12).

4 Woodhead often says – as he told me – that he does not mind making bad drama in a documentary cause (Corner, 1996:41, quotes another example); but he began to feel in the late 1990s that his emphasis on the journalistic over the dramatic was becoming harder to sustain.

5 However, such was the demand in the UK for a sight of this that the producers, Working Title, were persuaded to add the US ending to the DVD version of their film on sale in the UK. See *The Week*, 19 November 2005, p. 27 – the story was originally reported in *The Times* by Chris Ayres and Jack Malvern.

6 He made this remark in an interview with *The Times* (22 September 1992). Callendar is now President of HBO Films Division. An Englishman and ex-Granada staffer, he has taken HBO down a road of high-quality drama that has made serious docudrama something of an HBO speciality. John Ellis notes HBO's high art commitment to the 'creative vision of a single artist working through large-scale production teams' (2007: 15).

7 This programme also contained a reconstruction scene of the 'mummifying' method of transporting the hostages around the Lebanon that can be compared to the scenes in both *Hostages* and in *Blind Flight* (2004 – see note 10 below).

8 Palmer consoled himself with the fact that he had 'got a lot of interesting stuff about Brian and John, and about Frank's relationship with John' from the meeting.

9 Bernard MacLaverty was already a well-known Northern Irish writer when

he took on the screenplay for *Hostages*. For example, his 1983 novel *Cal* was filmed in 1984 by David Puttnam's Enigma company. He is also the likely originator of the popular phrase 'the elephant in the room'. He used the idea of an elephant in a room in his 1978 children's book *A Man in Search of a Pet* and it was picked up by the director Alan Clarke who used *Elephant* as the title of his bleak 1989 television film depicting an almost dialogue free sequence of sectarian murders in Belfast. Marcel Berlins' column in the *Guardian* (*G2*, 20 September 2006, p. 5) quotes an email from MacLaverty: 'I was asked what it was like to live in Northern Ireland during the troubles. My reply was that it was like living in a room with an elephant and trying to ignore it.'

10 The film that McCarthy and Keenan backed, *Blind Flight*, was finally released in 2004. The twelve-year time lag between this film and *Hostages* bears out to some extent their agents' original misgivings about the Granada docudrama.

11 In this section of the letter can be found the genesis of the defensive opening caption of *Hostages* discussed in Chapter 3.

12 Unfortunately for Granada this claim was made in a trailer on Thames Television – something that the *Hostages* team, they all told me, deeply regretted.

13 Although it is true that *Hostages* got a lot of publicity, the bulk of press attention in the UK went to Lynda La Plante's BBC drama series *Civvies*, about de-mobilised paratroopers. 'Based on fact', *Civvies* provoked controversy because of the peculiar place the 'Paras' occupy in the British popular imagination (following such events as Arnhem in 1944, 'Bloody Sunday' in Northern Ireland in 1972 and the 1982 Falklands War). The series' unusual 'take' on the emotional lives of these hyper-macho men caused widespread complaint from a variety of institutions (not least from the Paras themselves). In the tabloids especially, *Civvies* took far greater precedence.

14 He willingly gave the film his 'blessing', using this word in a *Washington Post* piece (17 February 1993).

15 It was reprinted (and re-titled) to coincide with the release of *Blind Justice*.

16 I prefer this term on the whole as less apparently judgemental than 'trauma drama' (and certainly less so than 'disease-of-the-week'). It is not that I wish to avoid value judgements of docudrama – some docudramas are indeed crass. However, I do feel that in an account of *development* a measure of neutrality is appropriate.

17 *Catch Me If You Can* is, of course, part of the kind of fourth-phase convergence I discuss in Chapter 8, with docudramas appearing across media. I use it here as an example of the increasing sophistication of the use of 'story rights'.

18 David Edgar made these points to me in a note of April 1997. One of the source books for the trilogy was *People* journalist Maria Eftimiades' *Letha*

Lolita: a True Story of Sex, Scandal and Deadly Obsession (1992). The 'Long Island Lolita' saga continued to produce drama into the new century. Joey Buttafuoco relocated to California but was later jailed for gun crime. Meanwhile, the released Amy Fisher became a journalist and champion of prison reform. The three original protagonists even appeared together on American television in 2006. Fisher's book *If I Knew Then ...* was published in 2004.

19 Quoted in the *Sunday Telegraph* on 2 January 1993.

20 In trying to offer a corrective to this view, I followed Carol Gilligan's (1982) use of 'masculine' and 'feminine' to: 'highlight a distinction between two modes of thought and ... focus a problem of interpretation' (1982: 2). As Gilligan says, these gender terms are not intended to 'represent a generalisation about either sex' – it is the cultural roles commonly associated with these terms that are of interest to me.

21 The theory of the 'gaze' is based on psychoanalytic theory. It is highly complex and has always seemed to me to overvalue looking over listening in the viewing experience. I have found Turner (2006) to be the most readable introduction to this area of film theory.

22 Veteran producer of documentaries John Willis, in 'What's up, docs?'(*Guardian*, 6 October 1997), argued that 'small DVC cameras have reduced both crew sizes and costs, opening up the potential for greater intimacy as well as more flexibility.' Digital cameras have developed even further, with 2005's Panasonic AJ-HDC27 camera blurring even further the definitional differences between video and film. Sound quality on the new cameras, too, is better than it was in the 1990s.

23 *Guardian G2*, 21 February 2005, p. 17.

Histories: fourth-phase hybridisation

A 'varied and robust ecology'

'Authenticating detail' in television drama, as Robin Nelson has observed, can supply 'a sense of conviction' (1997: 109). Docudrama's stock-in-trade – the pro-filmic reality that lies behind dramatic performance – is intended to 'authenticate', or to warrant, its dramatic representation-cum-speculation. And in general, the more detail the better. But there is an overarching problem of *fidelity* to the reality dramatised. This problem has continued to focus discussion in a fourth phase of development characterised by genre hybridisation. A similar issue of fidelity often bedevils discussion of screen adaptation of the novel. Adaptation of a (prior) literary text and docudrama's transformation of facts and information have this issue in common. It is often hard to move discussions of adaptation away from the common-sense argument that finds a screen adaptation 'not a bit like the novel'. It can be just as hard to shift the notion that docudrama will inevitably play fast and loose with facts. The contention that a docudrama has not been, or might not be, 'true to the facts' is thus endemic to discussion of docudrama. The 'fidelity argument', then, tends to resonate in discussion both of screen adaptations and docudramas well beyond television transmission or film release.

In literary adaptation, the argument tends not to be heard so stridently when the author under discussion is, say, Frederick Forsyth or John Grisham. The adapted works of 'classic' writers like Jane Austen or William Shakespeare, however, are very different matters. In screen adaptation of classic novels and plays the canonical written text is more often than not the privileged one. In docudrama the greater authority is often ceded to a documentary covering the same subject matter – hence the 'not as good as the documentary' argument (or even the argument that 'it would have been better to make a documentary').

In his book on literary adaptation Brian McFarlane tried to cut through the fog of assertion and counter-assertion by proposing a notion of 'relative transferability' between literary texts and their adaptations in other media (1996: 13–15).[1] I want to extend this idea to the docudrama, which after all shares the need to transfer narrative from one kind of representation to another, very different, kind.

'Relatively transferable' in the case of docudrama, then, are what I would describe as the *essential* elements of a prior event in the real world. Without these elements any subsequent screen drama would just not be recognised as being in any sense 'documentary'. Names, places, dates, particular events – all these stack up to provide material which is *structural* to the representation. 'Documents' of various kinds back up these essential elements – newspaper reports, witness statements, court records, tape and video recordings, and so on. Some of these enter docudramatic representation, some remain in the background. All have the potential to give added detail, colour and depth to the film. The dramatic narrative within which such 'transferable' documentary elements are 'relatively' embedded is a different matter, however. In this 'enunciation' of the narrative lies the interpretative challenge for maker and viewer alike. The narrativisation of the essential story elements, the 'showing through' of the prior text and its documents into a newly-fashioned dramatic text – this is what *presents* the prior referent to an audience. A sufficient showing through of prior referents in presentation is what ensures the 'doc' label, just as the character names and plot events are what makes a 1999 film called *Mansfield Park* recognisable as an adaptation of a Jane Austen novel first published in 1814.[2]

No novel is invalidated by adaptation (though it may well be criminally reduced in some people's eyes). Neither is a real-world event completely erased in docudramatic performance. An area of intertextual reference is *ipso facto* proposed, and a cultural space thus created within which society's 'conflicts and fault-lines' are exposed (Schulze, 1990: 371). Intertextuality will always call representation into question but it can never invalidate it, demanding only that audiences make connections and consider their significance. With questions thus posed about what we take to be real, there is a case for a 'both documentary and drama' argument rather than the more common reflex 'either/or' opposition.[3] It is at the point of reception, in the vast collective memory of talk about theatre, television and film that intertextual forms resonate, cause argument, and give pleasure. In the docudrama, contrasting pleasures of rational 'separation' and of empathetic 'attachment' are evident. Carol Gilligan has used these terms to describe different, but balancing, ethical positions: 'separation is justified,' she says, 'by an ethic of rights while attachment is supported by an ethic of care' (1982: 163–4).[4] The 'ethic of rights' was arguably one of the strongest elements of twentieth-century public service broadcasting. Like all ethical inclinations it was double-edged: in one sense, it was (and remains despite commercial depredations) profoundly democratic and libertarian, concerned with the creation of the responsible citizen competent to join in the collective business of living in, and deciding the direction of, a society through rational means. In another sense, and just as profoundly, it created subaltern groups dependent upon intellectual elites to facilitate (or, more dangerously, to manage) understanding, to pre-structure (or, more dangerously, distort) information, and in general to lead.

No institution can entirely escape its history, and it is likely that future understandings of television will continue to be intimately linked to the continuing, but much re-shaped, mission to inform and entertain. Docudrama has a unique place here, as Janet Staiger notes:

> The mixture, the blurred boundaries among the conventions [of docudrama], and the public discussions caused by these blurrings and mixings, remain central to any full understanding of the practices and the roles of television in contemporary society. (Staiger, 1997: 517)

Documentary's place in Western cultures seems assured while any kind of faith in facts obtains. A distinctively rationalist/forensic cultural imperative, an integral part of Western philosophical as well as cultural history, is satisfied in important ways in the intertext of the docudrama. In the twenty-first century the place for an 'ethic of care', in societies tending to overvalue 'rights', has become a matter of urgent debate. The social value of the empathetic, altogether more problematical politically, is foregrounded frequently in docu-drama and its variants on television and on film. This is one reason, I believe, for the burgeoning of the form.

Although the docudrama is still occasional in television sched-ules (although 'more occasional', as it were, than formerly) it has achieved a permanent place in television culture as a result of its use over several decades as a response to important social and politi-cal situations.[5] Through just the kind of relative transferability argued above, the 1996 Granada dramadoc *Hillsborough* established itself within a wider public campaign to revisit a 1989 tragedy – the disaster at an English football ground in which over a hundred people were crushed to death. This classic campaigning film, writ-ten by Jimmy McGovern, one of the best and most successful tele-vision dramatists of his generation, argued that people died at the Hillsborough football ground in Sheffield as a result of police incom-petence in marshalling the crowd gathered to watch an FA Cup semi-final. The film further implied that this incompetence was covered up by the authorities in the aftermath of the tragedy. In making the film McGovern was partly expressing his solidarity with the Hillsborough Family Support Group and their campaign for justice – indeed, he worked with and had their support in his preparation for the film.[6]

Hillsborough crucially offered new evidence in its contribution to the wider public debate on the disaster. Specifically, it refuted an earlier police claim that a security camera's malfunction pre-vented the availability to subsequent legal process of video evidence of the crowd 'pen' in which the majority of casualties occurred. Transmission of *Hillsborough* renewed the debate about culpability and compensation for victims' families by challenging this. Ministers of State were lobbied, there were discussions on radio and television and in the newspapers, and the whole issue was again prominent years after the event. The film made a major contribution to this climate of opinion, providing a focus and an occasion for the kind of discussion that can influence opinion, even change the course of events, in the public sphere. Following the 1997 general election, the new British government agreed to a fresh inquiry into the events of 1989. Newspaper accounts on the day the new inquiry was announced (29 June 1997) certainly saw *Hillsborough* as a significant element in the families' campaign.[7]

This kind of docudrama was – and is – special. Docudrama was defended by Ian McBride when I first interviewed him in 1994 as being an integral part of television's public service mandate: 'useful when conventional means of telling a story are denied – usually when the actual participants are either dead or dutifully dumb'. When I interviewed him again in 2003 the form was, he remarked, 'alive and well and as strong and high-voltage as it ever was'. In fact, he saw – as I do – a new richness emerging:

> I think that the programme makers and – critically – the broadcasters have learned good lessons over the last nine or ten years. Particularly about the positioning of these kinds of projects. Whether it's something like *Bloody Sunday* at one end of the scale which is significant and contentious or whether further along the scale something is being made which is a good drama – though it doesn't necessarily carry a message – like *Danielle Cable: Eyewitness* [which was] good journalism but not a campaign film – but very honourably in that tradition of taking the camera where it can't go. We've got a very varied and robust ecology.[8]

A film like *Hillsborough* constitutes something of a refutation of Margaret Thatcher's epoch-marking one-liner about society. The film shows that working together, working for a common rather than an individual good, *can* work – at least insofar as the film helped the Hillsborough families continue to assert their dissatisfaction with the official version of the tragedy that had taken away their loved ones. In the kind of political context that still obtains in the late-capitalist West, the docudrama thrives and continues to exercise (or at any rate to claim) the historic function of a 'public service' broadcasting institution – the duty of keeping people informed, even when the authorities are trying to draw a line under events.

All this depends in large part on there being a social 'market place', in the form of a network broadcaster, in which and through which such discussions can achieve prominence. The continued need for such a forum is, I believe, at least as likely as scenarios in which television's digitalisation creates a multi-form ecology incapable of delivering anything other than niche-market audiences to advertisers. Greater choice, in which 'niche marketing' of programmes is a stock-in-trade, will not *necessarily* mean the elimination of mixed programming on national networks designed for large, collective, audiences. If developed societies are to hold together at all in the future, it will be through such social 'glue' as this. And even if docudrama is constrained to fit into 'narrowcast' programming (and, manifestly, an occasional form is not strong enough to sustain its own cable outlet) companies like Discovery and the History Channel, drama/entertainment ones like HBO and UK Gold, and public broadcasters' own digital channels will always find space for re-runs of past docudrama successes – like both *Cathy Come Home* and *Hillsborough*.[9]

The US industry mantra for docudrama (see again Lipkin, 2002) – that it is 'rootable' (in terms of current events and history), 'relatable' (in terms of potential for audience involvement), and 'promotable' (in terms of their easy access to publicity) – virtually guarantees its continuance. The form is now also more attractive to filmmakers thanks in part to industrial convergences between American film and television over the past two decades. It seems to me also that the future of the form is tied to the very inventiveness evident in recent hybridisation.[10] With the factual back-up to individual docudramas now more available to the public through the internet (this being not so much of an untapped resource as it was when the first edition of this book appeared) social utility is being enhanced in the present conjuncture. Research for a docudrama lies like the bulk of an iceberg below the surface of a film, and in the best examples adds moral and ethical weight to dramatisation. Exploitation of the information uncovered in high-concept docudramas, via internet publication, has reclaimed some of the journalistic virtues of the old-style British dramadoc, virtues I feared for in the late 1990s. The various websites for the 'Bloody Sunday' films, for example, uncovered a good deal of their well-researched factual base. And these sites did not shirk contentious issues (either of fact or of representation). One even presented contrasting views from two prominent academic historians of the Northern Ireland conflict, Professors Paul Arthur and Keith Jeffery of the University of Ulster.[11]

When a docudrama is linked to an ongoing public campaign, websites associated with the film can constitute a further exploitable resource in the cause of making oppositional arguments visible. While no production team has yet made available what the *Guardian* television critic Mark Lawson once asked for – an online annotated script – there is still a good deal of information now available to answer the question 'How true to the facts is this docudrama?'. If production companies did respond to this excellent idea, of course, the screen docudrama would connect across time with documentary dramatic forms of the past. In the 1930s the US Federal Theatre Project's 'Living Newspaper Unit' did publish its scripts. All were fully footnoted, thus making the factual material available for the kind of close attention that Lawson had in mind.[12] But websites have nevertheless gone a long way towards making good some of the informational deficiencies of the third phase of development (when questioning of the form's right to claim the real was at its most vigorous). Post-transmission debates, too, are now entered more directly (and more judiciously) into the post-transmission arena than was formerly the case. I drew attention in 1998 to the 'extra-textual' dimension of docudrama, and it is pleasing to note that this area has developed. It continues an honourable tradition, that of making links with direct action in the real world through factual forms in drama. The British investigative tradition, then, has not faded away, as some commentators feared; it has adapted to new times and extended its reach into a new phase.

The famous libel case in which the hamburger chain McDonalds took two British environmental activists to court offered a case study in the late 1990s that now seems prophetic. A docudrama based on John Vidal's 1997 book *McLibel – Burger Culture on Trial* was broadcast over two nights (18 and 19 May 1997) on Channel 4. *McLibel* was basically a re-enactment of the trial, linked by a studio talking head. Around the same time Franny Armstrong made *McLibel – Two Worlds Collide*, which was mainly documentary, with drama inserts in which the real defendants Helen Steel and Dave Morris re-enacted scenes with actors (and there was a continuity with docu-

drama tradition provided by the famous director of these scenes
– Ken Loach). Armstrong's film was linked to a 'grass-roots' environ-
mentalist campaign against a particularly litigious corporate giant.
The 'McSpotlight' website, as Vidal himself pointed out (*Guardian*,
16 May 1997), had in excess of 14 million 'hits' for the film – 'a
figure any mainstream television executive would love'. The original 'McLibel case' ended in June 1997 in a hollow legal 'victory' for
McDonalds. But Steel and Morris continued their struggle for justice,
aided by the further circulation of Armstrong's campaigning film.
They emerged triumphant in February 2005 when the European
court overturned the original judgement. Armstrong's updated
film was then transmitted on BBC Four in April 2005. This kind of
mixed-mode approach to a social issue has been exploited further in
fourth-phase docudrama.[13]

'Persuasive practice' – American docudrama in the fourth-phase

In its third phase docudrama demonstrated an accommodation to film aesthetics and structures that many found worrying.
Specifically, 'fiction film values' seemed to be threatening, indeed
driving out, the values of documentary – hence the concerns of
media lawyers to which I drew attention in Chapter 2. But convergences both industrial and aesthetical have marked out fourth-phase
docudrama as something altogether different. New levels of synergy
with movies, new creativity, new adaptations of basic generic structures on television, all have offered new ways of making sense of
a new world. HBO's success in the early 1990s in finding a market
for high concept docudrama in the USA led the way to some extent.
An indication of HBO's achievement in becoming a 'big hitter' in
the entertainment industry was the 2001 *Band of Brothers*. This
docudrama mini-series, with the BBC as its co-producer, dramatised
historian Stephen E. Ambrose's 1992 book about 'Easy Company',
a unit in the US Army's 101st Airborne Division. His narrative followed the company from their initial training, through the 1944
Normandy landings to the end of the Second World War. The series
is a benchmark for what is possible through co-production at the

top end of the financial scale. Ian McBride observed to me that 'HBO and any quality-niche American broadcaster have marquee-name requirements'. Just like the feature film from which it grew (*Saving Private Ryan*), the series boasted the 'marquee names' of Steven Spielberg and Tom Hanks. Such names mean movie-style finance in production (a huge budget in television terms of $120 million), audience appeal in reception, and a noticeable cultural impact.[14]

HBO was not the only player in the docudrama market in the 1990s, but its success with a key professional American demographic had profound knock-on effects in the movement of docudrama into the cinema. The burgeoning of cinema docudrama also coincides with the shift of the television 'co-pro' towards 'historical-event television'. This is at once an industrial and a formal development that has thrust docudramatic representation into a fourth phase of its history. As Lipkin astutely notes:

> The recurrence of film and television docudrama indicates the extent to which the mode has become an important means of presenting persuasive argument in [US] culture. The very prominence, if not notoriety, of docudrama titles in the 1990s shows that these are works that tell stories that we need, works that, as their label indicates, make compelling arguments because they bring documents to life. (Lipkin, 2002: xiii)

One major route, Lipkin points out, to 'bringing documents to life' for American film and television has been melodrama, which has classically offered 'alternatives to the kid of sober discourse about history that would be the province of documentary' (p. 10). The appeal of B-movie and low-concept, movie-of-the-week melodrama is pinpointed by Marcia Landy: 'As the lifeblood of commonsensical thinking,' she says, 'melodrama is an essential ingredient of consensus' (1996: 16). Docudrama's grasp on the popular imaginary – a powerful cocktail of factual content and melodramatic structure – has been successfully parlayed by the twenty-first-century film industry into the kinds of film docudrama I listed in Chapter 1.[15]

While 'classic' docudrama has become a staple of the film industry, new mixed forms have crowded into the television market place in this fourth period. As Peter Kosminsky remarked to me:

> Even straight documentaries [on television] these days seem to have dramatic reconstruction that was the province of the occasional *Panorama* a few years ago – some of it really bad. But the whole thing of giving people factual information in dramatised form seems to be mushrooming.

As Kosminsky remarks, some reconstruction seems to add very little. However, in the better examples I hope to show that something else is happening. There are certainly no longer any easy assumptions to be made about the ways the media represent reality, nor about the ways audiences deal with these representations. Television, yesteryear's 'window on the world', is now routinely questioned even by the (supposedly dumb) popular audience.[16] Jean Baudrillard's provocative observation at the time of the Gulf War – that the event was nothing but a media 'simulation', its available meanings driven as much by previous mediations of war as the promise of information – has become something of an orthodoxy. Seeing may once have meant believing, but no longer.[17]

A backlog of past media representations, trailing memories, intervenes in current understandings of events, especially during traumatic moments in the histories of sophisticated, media-reliant societies. When the hijacked planes crashed into the World Trade Center on 11 September 2001 many witnesses could only relate what they had seen to conventions of representation with which they were familiar. Perhaps understandably, many eye-witnesses fell back on their experience of the disaster movie in traumatic reaction. What was happening before disbelieving eyes was, as people often said, 'unreal'– and there was an almost routine link made between the real happening and movies. In his article 'In the Ruins of the Future', novelist Don DeLillo wrote:

> When we say something is unreal, we mean it is too real, a phenomenon so unaccountable and yet so bound to the power of objective fact that we can't tilt it to the slant of our perceptions.[18]

The jolting power of the images was too much initially, claimed DeLillo, 'to set into the frame of our *practised response*' (my emphasis). Inevitably this power was reduced by multiple repetitions over the hours, indeed days, that followed. Perhaps this in itself was part of a cultural effort to 'tilt' what had happened to 'the slant of our perceptions', and to enable 'our practised response'. New docu-dramatic representations try to take account of the 'double bluffs' of contemporary perceptions of what is real and what is fake, and to utilise that ability to 'see through' representation possessed by media-literate audiences.

Back to the documentary future – the new television docudrama

I was drawn originally to Leslie Woodhead's phrase 'no other way to tell it' because it signifies so well the basic drive of docudrama to compensate for otherwise denied *access* to aspects of social and historical reality. But in 1998 I found myself asking whether the situation then obtaining was one in which there really was 'only one way to tell it' – the way of the Hollywood fiction film towards which 1990s docudrama seemed so inexorably to be drifting. With American companies so dominating the co-production aesthetics of television docudrama in the 1990s, it began to seem so. The use of naturalism and social realism to represent events originally unavailable to cameras was endemic, the borrowing of fiction film genre characteristics so widespread, and documentary in some instances so shrunk to introductory and closing captions that I saw, and disapproved of, this 'drift towards Hollywood'. But the creativity exhibited in the following decade has been remarkable. To appreciate this, it is necessary to put on hold the perception that cynical film and programme makers are just out to exploit ignorant and gullible audiences, a view popular with media pundits and academics alike. Although I can see its logic, I no longer share this view. I believe that some of the new hybrid forms of documentary I shall describe below are not so much distorting mirrors for the times but more ingenious means of throwing mean times into critical relief. All the new forms I shall examine use performative methods to open up spaces both documentary and dramatic, and in doing so they enhance the docudrama. They introduce into the public sphere new combinations of established modes of perception. At one and the same time they alert audiences both to issues *and* their representation – at least potentially.

The 'radical dispersal' (Corner, 2002) undergone by documentary itself during recent times in part accounts for this. There has been a concomitant resurgence for documentary itself in the film, television, and indeed in the new media, industries, much of the new work of a 'light' kind driven by hybridisation with such genres as the game show, the travelogue, and so on. Increasingly the oldest hybrid form – the 'docudrama proper', as it were – begins to look the most respectable of the (some would say) mongrels on offer. These new hybrids challenge audiences to adjust their views of fundamental ways of making sense of the world, of organising knowledges of self and other, and of self and the external world. Instead of this amounting to a dangerous 'blurring' of boundaries, I want instead to propose the concept of 'porosity', and to suggest that porous rather than blurred borders mark an *opening up* of both documentary and drama spaces.

The idea of porosity comes from Walter Benjamin, who used it describe his sense of the freedoms available in a between-the-wars Naples able to sidestep what he calls 'the stamp of the definitive'.[19] The idea of categories becoming unfixed and unstable in certain presentations (if a city can be described as a 'presentation') simultaneously disturbed and excited him in his encounters with the unusual urban culture and landscape of Naples. It struck me that many commentators on the current media landscape long for a 'stamp of the definitive' now mourned as lost. It is easy to forget that definitions mostly lag behind practices, and that practices are always contingent. If borders themselves are considered from the point of view of beginnings and endings, about change instead of demarcation, then more exciting prospects are revealed.[20] By using the idea of the porous rather than the 'blurred' boundary I hope to avoid the more-than hint of the pejorative in the more popular phrase.[21] The notion of a porous border enables a countervailing argument to the one that says things are only ever getting worse. Docudramatic innovation calls attention particularly to the nature of the transformations that can occur in representation. Porosity at boundaries, then, can potentially be celebrated as exploration of something excitingly different from the norm – as Benjamin does in his view of Naples.

One point of convergence both industrial and aesthetical was marked by the Spielberg/Hanks film and television productions *Saving Private Ryan* (1998) and *Band of Brothers* (2001). These works demonstrated the extent of the film and television industries' reliance on each other by the end of the century. This reliance led to an increase in the extent of aesthetic porosity – both film and television values entering the mix with a degree of equality. Their utilisation of features I analyse in more detail below (such as witness statement) was extended elsewhere in high-end film production, for example in the multi-award winning film about mountaineering *Touching the Void* (Kevin Macdonald, 2003).[22] Such films as these were at the forefront of the surge in production of docudrama, especially in film, that I outlined in the Introduction.

Television docudrama has continued its revisiting of events from history in the fourth phase, but has utilised new means to its memorialising ends. Historical docudrama has always been ready to employ the rubric of the anniversary to justify itself and to attract audiences. 'D-Day' 1944, for example, was docudrama-ed in 2004, Hiroshima (the first A-bomb was dropped in 1945) in 2005. In terms of more recent events, in 2006 the historical sore of 9 September 2001 was picked at both on television (in co-pros such as *9/11: The Twin Towers*, the mini-series *The Path to 9/11*, and *9/11: The Flight That Fought Back* – all shown by a variety of broadcasters worldwide) and on film (Paul Greengrass's *United 93* and Oliver Stone's *World Trade Center*). Politics of the past continue to featured, with the histories of Suez and Hungary 1956 re-visited televisually in the UK fifty years on. As I remarked in the Introduction, contemporary theatre too has evinced a renewed interest in the power of the documentary (with 'verbatim theatre' and 'tribunal plays' investigating current political and social issues). Docudrama, in adjusting to all this, has – at the 'high end' of the market at least – rediscovered its former seriousness of purpose. Underwriting this seriousness has been both a new investigative energy and a new readiness to introduce performed elements to the structural mix.

All this activity leads to my claim that the 'porous' boundary between documentary and drama has produced highly creative treatments of the serious and the social, the historical and the public, the personal and the collective. Styles used can be traced not only to

British and American docudramatic traditions but also to Hollywood bio-pic and 'issue' film and to boundaries newly made porous (with, for example, the musical – see below). The importing into docudrama of direct witness testimony – as used in news and documentary – has been particularly evident in what German producer Guido Knopp labelled 'historical-event television'. In the Germany reunited after the fall of the Berlin Wall in 1989, docudrama has demonstrated the form's enduring capacity to deal with the complexities of history. In Tobias Ebbrecht's words, '[a] new temporal distance has allowed emotional empathy between grandchildren and grandparents' (2007: 2). This has facilitated new understandings of Germany's Second World War history. Docudrama has opened up debate, and released new consideration of a past repressed in the decades immediately following the Second World War.[23]

The need for representation of this troubled period in German history is made more urgent as the number of living eye witnesses to the Nazi era diminishes year by year. New treatments have been facilitated, as Ebbrecht observes, by a rising generation questioning its parents' received versions of history, and demanding explanations of their role in history from its grandparents. A cross-generational collision has fuelled a burgeoning of historical-event docudrama in Germany. From British television docudrama practice, I want to illustrate something of this with reference first to *Hiroshima* (2005). Like many co-pros, this was a complex affair involving a partnership between the BBC, TF1 (France), ZDF (Germany), and the Discovery Channel. There was additional credited involvement from the Tokyo Broadcasting System and CBC (the Canadian Broadcasting Corporation). Directed by Paul Wilmshurst (who co-wrote the script with Clare Saxby) this film included the kind of formal mix that characterises the new docudrama: archive footage, acted reconstruction, witness testimony, voiceover (supplying context via the familiar voice of John Hurt), and CGI 'recreation' of historical events. The breakthrough with CGI has meant that images can now be fashioned where none existed through computer programmes. This has extended docudrama's ability to show (or claim to show) 'how it was' or 'how it might have been'. Red Vision, a Bristol-based company, won a BAFTA for their CGI work in *Hiroshima*. CGI and on-screen witness testimony (both also features, of course, of *Band of Brothers*) add new factual dimensions to the palette of the docudrama.[24] In *Hiroshima*, for example, the late Paul Tibbets (he died in 2007) talks about his experience as a young man piloting *Enola Gay*, the B-29 Superfortress (named for his wife) that dropped the world's first atom bomb on the Japanese city of Hiroshima on 5 August 1945. His testimony is juxtaposed both with acted scenes (in which Ian Shaw plays his younger self) and with archive footage of actual plane and crew. The audience, then, sees three representations of a significant historical figure. Equally significant, Hiroshima survivor Akiko Takakura, now an old woman, contributes her testimony, reflecting affectingly on her experience as a teenager. She, too, is portrayed as that teenager by Haruka Kuroda in reconstructed scenes, all juxtaposed once again with newsreel footage – this time of the devastated Hiroshima and its appallingly maimed citizens. All this is, to say the least, a powerful mixture and a vindication of borders in television representation newly made porous.

The use of witnesses within the discourse of the new docudrama is an especially telling one. The idea of 'witness' carries two relevant connotations for the new hybrids. There is the legal and quasi-legal sense of someone providing 'authenticating detail' in relation to an event. Legalistic testimony is intended to ratify, to provide evidence. It can also, as in this case, serve to validate that within which it is embedded. A witness assures an addressee that something did indeed happen, and in *this* way. The words of witnesses carry, as often as not, an emotional as well as an evidential weight. Witness discourse is, by its very nature, subject to the vagaries of memory, and the possible distortions that follow intent, but whatever doubt might inhere in the notion of witness it has become an important element in millennial culture. This is possibly because there is also a sense of witness as used in religious discourse – especially in the cultures of Protestant Northern Europe and nations influenced in their sense-making by Northern European history and culture (the USA, countries of the former British Empire in particular). What is validated here is not so much the 'truth' of the content of the witness's words but 'belief' that what is remembered was as remembered. A witness's articulation of a powerful experience – their 'bearing witness' to it in religious terms – carries a powerful emotional charge. This is the case with Takakura's testimony in *Hiroshima*. If the legalistic witnessing has claims to objectivity and rationality, the latter is emphatically subjective and emotional. Both these elements of witness are to be found in the testimonies of the new docudrama. Tibbets and Takakura assert in their different ways presence at an historical event, their words marking them as both witness and participant. They are also cast in role for the history and the drama as perpetrator (Tibbets) and victim (Takakura). Tibbets, in one section of testimony defends the bombing, thus bearing defiant witness to a belief in the ultimate efficacy of actions some abhor. He articulates his unswerving belief that dropping the A-bomb was the right thing to do in the circumstances that obtained. Takakura, on the other hand, bears the physical and mental stigmata of her experience as a twentieth-century secular martyr – she was and remains part of a civilian *sacrifice* to twentieth-century warfare. At a time in Western societies when so many serious discourses have became suspect and discredited (politics and religion in particular) the bearing of witness in art has acquired a new pre-eminence.[25]

My second example is the 2006 co-pro *9/11: The Twin Towers*, made by Dangerous Films and Blakeway Productions for the BBC, ATL, France 2 and Discovery. This too mixes acted scenes, archive, witness statement in order to memorialise, and to console as well as to explain. Dangerous Films' Richard Dale has made a speciality of historical-event docudrama, his 2004 *D-Day: 6.6.1944* winning an RTS award (see Chapter 3). The breakthrough signalled by this kind of hybrid is a canny capitalisation on the fact that television has many more ways of telling stories than film. The very different formal methodologies that feed in from programming across the spectrum of the schedule effect a kind of triangulation between archive, reconstruction (acted and CGI), witness and didactic direct address (the actor supplying voiceover in this case being Terence Stamp). With this variety of input it becomes possible to take a bearing on both documentary and dramatic means of representation. In a real sense, one can think *about* and *through* what is being offered. With internet back-up for information, the possibility of new kinds of engagement with, and questioning of, the factual base of docudramas is greatly enhanced. Websites offer meaningful *extension* to the docudrama's extra-textual dimension. The potential for viewer–film interactivity is enhanced and the pleasures offered by docudrama broadened. A multiplicity of discursive modes increases the possibility of engagement with the issues that lie beyond the docudrama.

The second style evident in the new docudrama is actually a 'back to the future' development. It involves the 'conditional (or 'subjunctive') tense' documentary drama first seen in such programming as the 1953–57 American television series *You Are There*, the 1963 film *It Happened Here* and the BBC's *The War Game* (1965). The style's renaissance coincides with current political and cultural anxieties. Films in this 'What If?' mode explore mostly future scenarios, their very titles reflecting fears and anxieties that, try as they may, politicians cannot calm. For example, the fear of terrorist attack using chemical and biological weapons in crowded urban areas increased in the early part of the twenty-first century, even before 9/11. In 2001, the BBC screened both *Gas Attack* and *Smallpox 2002*. The urban scenarios of both films exploited what had already happened on 20 March 1995 in the Tokyo underground. The second film was broadcast again in 2002, when it tapped into the post-9/11 anthrax scare. *Dirty War* in 2004 examined that great current metropolitan dread, the 'dirty bomb'. *The Day Britain Stopped* (2003) provides a useful example of the way these docudramas dramatise millennial anxiety through hypothetical scenarios. The film projected a Christmas disaster in London in 2004 (in which year, ironically, it was shown again). In this imagined future, a plane crash near London creates gridlock on the M25. This problem is exacerbated by a national train strike. As if this were not enough, the film piles on further chaos resulting from a simultaneous, but unrelated, terrorist attack in the City. So three disaster scenarios are enacted in one docudrama. In this docudramatic speculation, emergency services that would be stretched to the limit in any one of these extreme situations, are shown buckling under the combined pressure with horrific results. Their (acted) officers reflect after the event, as in a conventional documentary, direct to camera in 'witness statement'. The techniques used to explore the hypothetical situation are again eclectic: acted reconstruction, newsreel, CCTV and documentary footage, CGI, and voiceover contextualisation.

The real key to this particular hybrid is the actor – their skill in the frequent simulated interview sections is paramount. For a start, it is vital that none of the performers has a recognisable face that can be easily associated with previous dramatic performance. The 'unknown' actor finds a place in such docudramas because they can more easily pass for the ordinary people they simulate. Gabriel Range and Simon Finch have made a speciality of these docudramas. As well as *The Day Britain Stopped* they also made 2006's controversial *Death of a President*, a film which depicts the assassination of George W. Bush, projecting it forward in time to October 2007. The witness interview is, of course, the very staple of documentary and news filming but, as Range notes, in docudrama this feature is 'unforgiving of an actor's performance'. In their training, actors may well use 'hot seating' improvisations to *explore* character as part of their preparation, but they are rarely asked in normal performance conditions to sustain such an unsupported role. Range continues:

> In a conventional TV drama, the audience is engaged by a world in which everyone is acting. What we're watching is not life but a highly stylised representation of it. In a documentary, there's no similar suspension of disbelief ... Actors couldn't simply learn their lines, to get the spontaneity and the feel of a real interview, they would need to inhabit the world of their characters, learn every aspect of their lives and their role ... and then improvise answers to genuine interview questions.[26]

Actors in 'What If?' docudrama cannot count on the 'benefit of the doubt' accorded to obviously acted performance, nor (being unknowns) can they count on the actor's equivalent of 'brand loyalty' – the recognition factor that draws audiences to well-known actors.

This kind of docudrama proved so popular in the UK that it moved into series form in 2004 with the first of several series organised around the word 'If'. Amongst the millennial anxieties explored were: a power crisis projected for 2010 (*If ... The Lights Go Out*); a 2024 revolt by a debt-ridden younger generation against well-off retired baby boomers (*If ... the Generations Fall Out*); and, projected to occur in 2020, a post-feminist world with women dominant in all public realms and men reduced to second-class citizens (*If ... It Was a Woman's World*). The series returned in 2005 with a whole crop of new anxieties (cloning, urban violence, drugs), and there have also been 'one-off' dramas (including an *If ... on* so-called 'charity fatigue'). Some 'What If?s' have explored the less obviously dramatic situation of economic disaster, as in Range and Finch's *The Man Who Broke Britain* (BBC, 2004). Again, an actorly voiceover (in this case, Tim Piggot-Smith) served as a kind of informational Master of Ceremonies; again documentary credibility was buttressed by unknown actors; again simulated news and documentary footage supported the factual 'feel' of the film. *The Man Who Broke Britain* also utilised the device to which I drew attention in the discussion of *Hostages*, the cutting of news footage to fit a fictional scenario. In this case, Tony Blair and Gordon Brown are shown *apparently* responding in news interviews to the film's fictional financial crisis. Simon Finch told the *Radio Times* that these inserts:

> do have a shock value ... They're there to underline the authenticity, but I can't claim that I attempted to clear either of them via Number Ten or the Treasury ... [27]

The makers used a City company for action shots of a financial trading floor. IFX Group's offices supplied an authentic *mise-en-scène* and their traders became extras in the film. An executive, Edmond Warner, writing in the *Guardian*, thought that the film conveyed very well 'the feeling of individual and collective powerlessness that major events in world markets can engender'.[28]

Documentary hybrids of opera and musical

As a final illustration of the way 'radical dispersal' and resultant 'porosity' have made the idea of blurring irrelevant in the face of creative work, I want to draw attention to the merger of musical and factual forms in the 'documusical' and the 'docuopera'.[29] Docuopera is closely linked in style to classic opera. A docuopera composed specifically for television was *When She Died ... : The Death of A Princess*. Shown on Channel 4 on 25 August 2002 (the fifth anniversary of Princess Diana's death – so in a sense also historical-event television) this docuopera examined popular cultural reactions to the death of the so-called 'People's Princess'.[30] Most significant in this sub-genre is the opera-house work of the contemporary American composer John Adams, some of which has been adapted for the screen.

Adams' first docuopera, *Nixon in China*, premièred in 1987. This work, which earned Adams an international reputation in the world of serious music, transformed the historic 'East meets West' 1972 meeting between President Nixon and Chairman Mao Zedong into opera. His librettist, the late Alice Goodman, used documents from the period of this watershed in US–Sino relations to shape often hilarious psychological studies of the major participants. Much of the libretto is verbatim or near-verbatim. Adams wrote his second, *Prix Italia*-winning, docuopera, *The Death of Klinghoffer* – again with Goodman as librettist – in 1991.[31] This work is a treatment of the 1985 *Achille Lauro* incident in which a group of armed Palestinian militants, discovered on board an Italian cruise ship, hijacked it and subsequently killed a passenger. The opera explains in exemplary early choruses the historical provenance of an Arab–Israeli conflict that led directly to the tragedy of the Jewish-American Leon Klinghoffer's death. The fact that Klinghoffer was also wheelchair-bound added a dimension to Anglo-American reporting of the incident. The opera features arias sung by gunmen and victims alike. About a hijack that further cranked up the demonising of Palestinian militancy in Western reportage, *The Death of Klinghoffer* is a careful meditation on the complexity of the situation. Nonetheless, Adams found himself criticised in some quarters for an even-handedness that attempted to set out both Palestinian and Israeli accounts of the origins and history of an ongoing Middle Eastern conflict. Although it is performed around the world, in the USA 'opera companies just won't risk it,' Adams has said, adding:

> What upset people who didn't like it was that I gave both sides a voice ... I think that the subject matter that Klinghoffer deals with is very much at the root of much of [Middle East] misunderstanding and hatred. But Americans are just implacable in their viewpoint.[32]

In 2003 Adams worked with British film director Penny Woolcock to make a film version of this docuopera. Again, Woolcock's imaginative dramatisation did not please all critics. Her use of real locations (including an actual cruise ship) and archive footage brought further documentary hybridity to the opera. The film's methods were similar to those of the historical-event television discussed in the last section. In particular the big Choruses at the opening of the docuopera underscore very different Palestinian and Israeli takes on the formation of the state of Israel in the late 1940s. Archive and acted footage added an extra dimension to the libretto's historical and political points. The film was helped, too, by the recent general turn to realistic performance in opera itself. This move has seen a number of famous theatre directors producing operas that aim to convince in terms of acting as well as being excellently sung. The performances in the film *Klinghoffer* are in this new realist tradition. In 2005, Adams wrote a further docuopera, *Dr. Atomic* (2005), about atom scientist J. Robert Oppenheimer. The libretto was by Peter Sellars, or rather it was compiled from a variety of sources somewhat in the manner of Documentary Theatre. Sellars also directed the first performance.[33]

There are more British than American examples of documusical, but, as might be expected, HBO co-produced one (with Cinemax) for their 'America Undercover' series. *Showgirls: Glitz and Angst* (2003, director: Kirby Dick) explored the onstage and backstage lives of Las Vegas showgirls and featured music and song, both in rehearsal and performance. There was also Bullfrog Films' *The American Ruling Class* (2005, director: John Kirby). This examination of power in the USA was fronted by former *Harper's Magazine* editor Lewis Lapham. It included interviews with such luminaries as former politicians James Baker and Harold Brown, and the (then) President of Harvard University Larry Summers.[34] In the UK, Brian Hill has an impressive track record in documusical, with his company Century Films producing the first one, *Drinking for England*, in 1998. The BAFTA-winning *Feltham Sings* followed in 2002, *Pornography the Musical* in 2003, then *Songbirds* in 2005. These films represent the continuing strengths of the British television industry in innovative documentary and documentary-related productions.

When arias in operas and songs in musicals occur, dramatic action is simultaneously suspended at the level of plot but allowed to operate at a kind of 'beyond story' level. This often permits a psychical state to be explored through song, offering that potential for heightened emotion inevitably excluded from naturalistic performance with its heavy emphasis on the believable, accessed through underplaying. Arias in docuopera and songs in documusical are inevitably highly theatrical, and 'make strange' both dramatic moments and the characters inhabiting them. This, clearly, marks a heightening beyond the scope of conventional documentary or naturalistic drama. An especially provocative shift in spectator-position occurs at the moments when participants in the Hill's documusicals, for example, shift from documentary interviewee to musical performer, from 'real person' to performer. At such production nodes audiences have the possibility to cut themselves free from conventionalised points-of-audition and points-of-view drawn from either documentary or drama. The subjects of Hill's documusicals escape the 'victim' status often accorded in documentary, and become active in a different way from actors in drama.

Soundtracks in the sub-genres of docuopera and documusical are, of course, fundamental both to the viewing experience and to the documentary information offered. Simon Boswell is a composer who has worked on several of Hill's documusicals). He describes the songs as 'a short cut to [a] real emotional hub ... because of that combination in singing of being vulnerable and showing bravery.' Hill's documusicals have benefited from Boswell's facility with different musical styles, and from the lyrics of the British poet Simon Armitage (who has worked on all the films). Armitage listens to the subjects' characteristic intonation patterns and vocabularies (accessed through interview recordings – he seldom meets them face to face) and incorporates these into the lyrics. He tries:

> to be simple and clear, to get out of the poetry mindset when I'm writing lyrics ... I offer the stuff to [the composer] as fabric, really. I don't see it as fixed and unchangeable like my poetry.[35]

Feltham Sings, for example, is about the Feltham Young Offenders Institution near London's Heathrow Airport. Armitage wrote the rap-style song 'On Road' with the composer Errol Francis (aka 'DJ Dextrous'). This is young offender Terell's song. Armitage shaped the lyric around Terell's distinctive speech filler 'what-not' (Terell used this in interview in the way others might use 'blah blah blah'). Armitage and Dextrous converted the phrase so that it functions as a rhythmic underpinning to Terell's song. The lyric centres on what Terell calls his 'business' – car crime – and his fantasy of himself as an 'operator'. He sees himself as a businessman, and the song offers an opportunity for him to show a kind of pride in who he is. We see a different Terell from the 'banged-up' victim of social circumstances that might be a more characteristic documentary approach to the car-thief. Of course, hearing the words becomes important in docu-musical, it is as logocentric as documentary tends to be. Documusical capitalises on speech mannerism and demotic language to add a dimension to character.[36]

Writing about Reality TV, Jane Roscoe has drawn attention to revelatory moments she calls 'flickers of authenticity', in which the mask of performance falls away from the Reality TV contestant/participant and they are revealed as the person they are trying to conceal. Her phrase deliberately recalls Barthes' notion of the 'punctum' and her analysis echoes Brecht's 'alienation effect'. The 'event of the song' in documusical, however, produces a kind of obverse effect to the flicker of authenticity. The abrupt breaking away from the conventions of documentary and acceleration *into*, rather than *out of*, performance emphasises the essential falsity of a song. But this falsity does not necessarily constitute an untruth; instead it can be revelatory, as it is on many occasions in Hill's docu-musicals. The 'flicker' in documusical signals a new kind of life-in-the-frame. In effect, the spectator encounters an individual newly enabled in a triumphant burst of performed activity.[37]

To take another example from Hill's first documusical *Drinking for England* (about alcoholics), the first song occurs some fourteen minutes into the film and on first encounter it certainly had the shock of the new going for it. Forty-year-old Tony, previously seen in conventional 'talking head' interview, suddenly bursts into song. The film style shifts, and he stands, glass of beer in hand, in front of a closed-down inner-city shop, singing jauntily:

Thinking's a beautiful thing for a man,
Thinks from a bottle, thinks from a can.[38]

The lyric goes on to explore the sheer personal confidence he gets from his drinking. The visuals shift from the graffiti-ed urban backdrop to Tony's favourite pub where an MTV-style fish-eye lens thrusts the singer forward from his working-class fellow drinkers. The visual aesthetics of music video shift the piece away from conventional documentary, but Hill never loses touch completely with documentary because it is there in the lyric of the song. Tony's move into performance for the camera does not serve to hide a 'real' self; rather, it enables-in-enacting a version of himself he seems comfortable to own – a version that would probably be denied to conventional documentary representation. The self-mockery of the song's words means he performs his drink addiction with a self-knowledge and self-confidence that are, to say the least, unexpected. This tends in its turn to lift his subsequent conventional pieces-to-camera to new levels. The space Hill creates through the device of song in these examples is a reminder that constructing people as victims can sometimes say more about makers and watchers than it does about subjects. Any documentary on drinking almost has to disapprove of this (anti-)social activity, but the documusical celebrates through song (without diminishing a sense of the seriousness of the problem in the abstract). The pleasure induced in an audience when someone manages to do something well, like sing a song, punctures documentary's tendency towards the solemn. Hill's documusicals reverse conventional audience expectations of documentary through the shift into song.

In 2003 *Feltham Sings* won the prestigious BAFTA (British Academy of Film and Television Art) Flaherty Award, named for that doyen of the documentary Robert Flaherty. Hill's 2005 *Songbirds* was featured at several film festivals, including Sundance in 2006. The documusicals contain plenty that is classic documentary – voiceover and interview, captions, 'inquisitive' fly-on-the-wall camerawork and 'wildtrack' sound. But they expand the potential of witness statement through the form and content of the songs, enabling individual documentary subjects to go beyond what can be revealed in face-to-face-interview. Another layer of self, as it were, is peeled away as they participate in a challenging rhetoric altogether new to documentary and not part of any previous docudramatic practice (unless a bio-pic protagonist was a singer, of course). As protagonists do in plays through the device of soliloquy, as characters do when they shift into song in musicals, as opera singers do in arias, documentary subjects become larger than life in documusical.

Second-order experience, 'second looking' and the 'immiscibility' of fact and fiction

Added to their offer of the resemblance between themselves and an anterior reality, the new docudramatic forms, then, have developed a reflexivity. Hybridisation has promoted intertextual relationships with a variety of different sense-making factual and fictional entertainments. They capitalise on television's enduring hold on history, news and current affairs but continue to rely on levels of intimacy and immediacy at the level of consumption not always associated with the more public media of theatre and film. The new docudrama hybrids are part of the repertoire of late capitalist cultures with populations not only highly dependent upon television for knowledges, attitudes, beliefs and memories but also highly aware of television's modes of production. Audiences drawn to docudrama are necessarily alert to that-which-is-pointed-to (or at). A kind of palimpsestic 'second looking' takes place in which audiences can look *past* (or *through*) any current representations to previous ones, and ultimately to the events and people behind them. Audiences can look past or through, for example, an actor representing John F. Kennedy in a docudrama to already existing knowledges and representations of the historical JFK. The continuing attraction of docudrama lies in its merging of modes of understanding that remain fundamental to modern developed societies. It is often evident that docudramas also engage attention beyond their points of first release and transmission, and continue to cause turbulence in the public sphere.

To enter a purely fictional world is a delight difficult to resist – the 'purity' of the fiction virtually guaranteeing suspension of disbelief, and the relaxation involved in encountering fictional worlds during

non-work 'down time' virtually underwriting a willing co-operation. The worlds we encounter in a variety of television and film
dramas offer resolutions to enigmas and temporary closures to sets
of circumstance that both map on to, and offer 'time out' from, the
press of our quotidian lives. This dramatic output goes some way to
suspending the inexorable advance of our own real time and affords
us the opportunity to consider other lives, other patterns of existence, like and not-like our own. The fictional 'inner-scapes' that we
encounter form templates against which it is possible to measure
and take account of the more kaleidoscopic patterns of our own
individual lives. Thus plots and characters can run in parallel to and
even intersect with the 'play' of our own lives, offering *second-order
experience* to compare to or build into our own. Within the world of
the fiction we are insulated from all but empathised pain. We can
also enjoy vicariously the pleasure of others through identification
with them. Robert Hanke summarises:

> when popular fictional plots turn on the empathetic occupation of
> another point of view, 'the borders of the self dissolve, as it occupies
> the position and experiences the problems faced by other creatures'. (in
> Edgerton and Rollins, 2001: 73)[39]

The 'borders of the self' are, indeed, also porous and tend to mix
fact and fantasy. A basis in fact, however thin, offers an experiential
pattern of events, a point of view, more determined (even if more
disputed) than fiction. Any template of facts dramatised in docudrama is governed by a defining paradox: it is both pre-existing and
invented. It is, in a sense, a forgery. But, as Nicolas Spice observes:

> Of all the 'f' words that speak of the relationship between fact and fiction,
> 'forge' is the most expressively two-faced: to forge being both to falsify
> and to create, to fake and to make. (2010: 14)[40]

The pre-existing nature of the dramatised circumstances in docudrama can produce a powerful compulsion in audiences. That
this *did happen*, or that facts say it *could happen*, makes docudrama
a different kind of forgery from the make-believe of fiction. While
this factor has always ratcheted up reaction to the form, it is in this
collision between different sets of determinations that its peren-

nial fascination lies. The worlds of the imagination and the rational mind are yoked together in an active exploration of things that both frighten and fascinate. The scientific term 'immiscibility' sums it up. Used in science to describe the unmixable (as in the proverbial oil and water), in art the claim that fact and fiction, documentary and drama, are 'immiscible' is frequently heard, easily understood, but fundamentally wrong. Art is not science, and the apparently impossible mixing that occurs in docudrama has acquired a new purchase on current times.

There is now a turn towards questions of value, part result of the way politics in particular has evacuated ethical spaces, and this also impacts on the new docudrama. As film critic Robin Wood observes, 'theory and scholarship [have usurped] the place of criticism' in the modern academy's recent history. Theory, scholarship and criticism, he argued, 'should form a triangle of which criticism is the apex ... it is the critic who is primarily concerned with questions of *value*'.[41] There have been many indications that changing trends in contemporary thought are bringing both academy and entertainment industries back to an engagement with questions of value and a concern with ethics. Ethics has always been a concern for the docudrama, because unlike most drama it can and does sail very close to the wind ethically and legally.[42]

I want to re-claim a formerly taboo theoretical notion here, and that is 'the universal'. This word was consigned to the intellectual trashcan with the rest of liberal humanist terminology, not to say ideology, around 1968, when the Paris *évènements* exposed – some thought forever – capitalism's credibility gap. It remains the case that a concept like 'the universal' blanks too much in the way of race, class and gender, among other things. It is a concept also dangerously blind to the specificities of history. But the idea of the 'universal' continues to have a powerful hold on *public* critical discourse (and Humanities disciplines in the academy ignore this at peril of being found irrelevant). A powerful sense of *commonality* is nominated in the word 'universal'. It remains at least potentially useful when trying to convey something that is widely communicable within shared cultures. This 'experiential comparability', to coin a phrase, involves the rough-and-ready measurement it is possible to take when contemplating someone else's experience, especially experience offered through artistic representation. After that measurement of difference, there follows a stage of acknowledgement of degrees of what I think of as 'experiential equivalence'. Here a bearing is taken on how close (or not) one is to an experience depicted in a film, or play, or novel. Second-order experience can never – plainly – be an exact equivalent to first-order experience, but it can hope to supply a deficiency.

Writing on Holocaust films, Joshua Hirsch argues that 'traumatic relay' occurs (2004: 13) for empathising audiences, and that a degree of understanding results. This seems not unlike what I take second-order experience to supply (though clearly ethical and representational stakes are at their very highest in this example). 'Relaying' trauma, like relaying the past itself, is only possible given a compact between maker and audience. The potential is there to make the past as present as we care to make it.[43] Docudramas of the kind I have been discussing in this chapter offer a rich means of effecting states of experiential equivalence. These have something of a consolatory function in a world increasingly sceptical of answers to important questions. As Thomas Elsaesser puts it:

> No longer is storytelling the culture's meaning-making response; an activity closer to therapeutic practice has taken over, with acts of re-telling, re-membering, and repeating all pointing in the direction of obsession, fantasy, trauma. (in Sobchack 1996: 146)

Conclusion

Dramatic means to documentary ends is fashionable in popular factual programming across a wide generic spectrum on television, and also in films that focus on significant people and events. The new citizen being addressed in a new public space dominated by new technology is almost certainly one for whom mediatised performance is a major factor in their ways of making sense of the world in which they live.[44] If this new citizen is one for whom fantasy and reality are so inextricably intertwined as to be elements within the same continuum, it should not necessarily be assumed that this person is the rough beast of Yeats's poem 'The Second Coming', corrupted by an exploitative media and unable to distinguish between fact and fiction.[45] When asked by Macdonald and Cousins to respond to a question about the future of documentary, Direct Cinema pioneers D. A. Pennebaker and Chris Hegedus replied:

> If a new generation of filmmakers is ever going to be interested in a film form called 'documentary' far any reason other than present day career opportunities, it will only be because it can throw off new sparks, not old news. (in Macdonald and Cousins 1996: 390)

It seems to me that the new hybridisation possesses exactly this possibility.

Docudrama is and will remain both an occasional and a difficult form – occasional because of its dependence upon events, difficult because there are always ethical choices to get wrong in its making. In making the claim that docudrama should be approached with 'both/and', rather than 'either/or', arguments, I cannot do other than recognise that the counter-claim that it satisfies neither documentary nor drama expectations is always likely to be heard. To be on guard for the sensationalising 'tabloid tendency', with its perceived preference for the overly emotive treatment of issues, is both important and unimportant in the new ecology. It must remain a critical duty for those interested in mixed forms (in both senses of that word 'critical'). Reviled as it sometimes can be, the docudrama is popular enough with audiences and secure enough in its place in popular culture, and it deserves to be assessed on its own terms. It is best understood first and foremost as itself – a still developing form in its own right rather than an inferior version of something else. That, at any rate, has been the principal thesis of both editions of this book: only by understanding docudrama in and for itself can it be fully known and properly understood.

As well as being watchful for the sensation-for-sensation's sake 'dumbing down' tendency it is still, and equally, necessary to guard against that 'TV priggery' identified by Jib Fowles (1992). No one has been readier that the intellectual to offer holier-than-thou responses, especially to television. But as Fowles remarks, those rubbishing the output of network television by day can themselves sometimes be found watching (even enjoying) a good deal of it by night (1992: ix). As the makers of television programmes and films accede to the demands of a market place driven by ratings and box-office returns, it is as well to be sceptical about cultural production. But measurement of this kind is not, has never been and will never be, the whole story. Docudrama's engagement with public debates about a range of issues has, if anything, grown through hybridisation and I believe it will continue to grow. Leslie Woodhead's classic formula – 'no other way to tell it' – still summarises the justification for docudramatic treatments of real-world issues. But there are reasons to be hopeful about the multiple 'ways' that docudrama now seeks to make a difference in the historical and political world beyond our screens – wherever they are situated.

Notes

1 McFarlane bases his argument on structuralist literary theory. Using Roland Barthes' 'cardinal' and 'catalyser', and Seymour Chatman's similar 'kernel' and 'satellite', narrative functions MacFarlane's theory permits a non-judgemental means of comparison which can 'establish some guidelines for exploring the different natures of the experiences of the two related texts' (1996: 197).

2 John Tulloch for one regards intertextuality as a key feature for *all* television drama, arguing that its 'dynamic succession and synchrony [with] other texts, other *social events*' marks it out in a special way (1990: 130 – my italics). Given television drama's prime place in the general flow of television this seems to me a persuasive notion. Couldry (2003) examines television's connection with events in general through what he terms 'the myth of the mediated centre' (p. 2), through which one myth (that of a society with a centre) is supported by a second myth 'that "the media" has a privileged relationship to that "centre"' (p. 45). This strikes me as a useful corrective to too easy a notion of media centrality in culture, especially in regard to broadcast television.

3 Nelson (1997) argues for 'both/and' critical approaches in a book that sees television drama as, significantly, 'in transition' in the late 1990s.

4 See also Hill (2005) – her Chapter 6 has the title 'Ethics of Care'.

5 The BBC attempted to formalise this idea in the early 1990s by creating a so-called (and short-lived) 'Rapid-Response Unit' in television drama.

6 One of the strongest of Jimmy McGovern's many strong suits is his ability to mine the psychological ramifications of guilt and blame. McGovern

wrote the hugely popular 1990s ITV series *Cracker*, about a clinical psychologist working for the police in Manchester. Some of the Hillsborough families reacted negatively to a 1994 *Cracker* episode ('To Be a Somebody') that depicted a man so traumatised by Hillsborough that he became a serial killer. Following meetings with the families, McGovern agreed to write the docudrama. The Hillsborough Family Support Group was founded shortly after the tragedy in 1989, and continues its campaign for 'Justice for the 96' (see their website: www.hsfg.net).

7 Ultimately the 2000 inquiry did not find in the families' favour, nor have subsequent legal efforts borne the kind of fruit sought by these grieving families, but their struggle continues.

8 *Danielle Cable: Eyewitness* (2003) was an ITV docudrama directed by Adrian Shergold about a 'road rage' murder committed by Kenneth Noye in 1996. The essence of the drama was not just Cable's witnessing of her boyfriend's murder but also her subsequent experience of the so-called 'witness protection scheme'.

9 The BBC's digital channel BBC4 broadcast *Cathy Come Home* as part of the BBC's Autumn 2006 themed programming on homelessness – itself conceived as part-tribute to *Cathy* forty years after its first transmission. *Hillsborough* was repeated on ITV3 in 2008 and 2009 (the latter transmission part of programming marking the twentieth anniversary of the tragedy).

10 It should not be forgotten that docudrama is relatively cheap to make. It continues to cost three or four times as much to fund drama as it does to fund equivalent factual programming . See *inter alia*, *Guardian* (18 February 1997), and also Willis (1997) and Bignell and Orlebar (2005).

11 The former is a professor of politics, the latter of modern history. The official Channel 4 website's special section on Jimmy McGovern's *Sunday* carried these academics' detailed responses to five key questions about the film – precisely the kinds of questions that ordinary viewers ask about docudramas. Question 1, for example, asked: 'How faithful was *Sunday* to the actual events?' See: www.channel4.com/history/microsites/H/history/heads/sunday.html (accessed 16 September 2002). The BBC also ran a website on Paul Greengrass's *Bloody Sunday*, the docudrama it helped to produce. This film (also a cinema release) was based on Don Mullan's book *Eyewitness Bloody Sunday*: www.bbc.co.uk/films/2002/01/18/bloody_sunday_2002.shtml (accessed 18 September 2002). It is worth noting that Greengrass is yet another film director who began his career with *World in Action*.

12 I first heard Mark Lawson make the point about annotated scripts during his talk to the 'Reality Time' conference at the University of Birmingham in 1996. He is one cultural commentator who has been steadfastly suspicious of docudrama. In his 21 February 2005 newspaper column he compared a docudrama – *Cherished* – with a documentary on the same subject

transmitted in the same week – *Angela Cannings: The Real Story*. Preferring the documentary, he concluded that the treatment offered in *Cherished* 'suggests that drama can never improve on fact' (*Guardian 2*, p. 17). There are two volumes of annotated 'Living Newspaper' scripts, both edited by Pierre De Rohan. They were originally published in 1938, and the New York publisher Da Capo produced facsimile editions in 1973.

13 Vidal's claim is somewhat problematical, because 'hits' do not necessarily signify the same level or duration of attention as viewing figures. Be that as it may, the magic figure for large-scale success on British network television is around 10 million. Franny Armstrong's career as a campaigning filmmaker continues. In 2002 she made *Drowned Out*, about the controversial Narmada Dam project in India; in 2008 she made the highly successful *Age of Stupid*, about climate change. For details, see the website: http://spannerfilms.net.

14 The co-pro mini-series has often utilised docudrama methods, one of the earliest examples being NBC/BBC's *Roots* (1977). A sequel to *Band of Brothers, The Pacific*, aired in 2010. HBO's co-production partners for this ten-part series were Seven Network Australia, Sky Movies, Playtone and DreamWorks. For more on *Band of Brothers*, see Paget and Lipkin (2009).

15 If the American television schedules during Autumn 2006 are used as a yardstick, it is remarkable that the made-for-TV-movie seems actually to have been superseded by the film docudrama in the fourth phase. Most docudramas to be found during this period tended to be television transmissions of previously released multiplex films.

16 As I remarked in the Introduction, a great deal of audience research was carried out in the early years of the new century in the UK. See especially Hill (2005). Her research seems to show that the popular audience, far from being dumb, has a pronounced *critical* capacity. Hill concludes (p. 187): 'The way in which television audiences respond to ethical issues in a range of popular factual programmes illustrates their ability to think critically and reflectively about these programmes'.

17 Baudrillard made his claim in 'The Reality Gulf' (*Guardian* 1 January 1991); see also Norris (1992).

18 DeLillo's article first appeared in *Harper's Magazine* in December 2001. It was reprinted in the *Guardian* (22 December 2001). See: www.guardian. co.uk/Archive/Article/0,4273,4324579,00.html.

19 In *One Way Street* (1985 – actually co-written with Asja Lacis in the 1920s) the idea of 'porosity' and its effects is explored in the essay 'Naples' (pp. 167–76).

20 See Whybrow (2005), who draws on Heidegger to make this point (p. 51). It was Whybrow's book that first introduced me to the idea of porosity (p. 18).

21 I think the pejorative tone may come from the idea that something has gone 'out of focus' or has become less sharply focused than it might or should be.

In the first edition of this book I used 'Blurring the Boundaries' for Chapter 5's title. So suspicious have I become of this common – not to say clichéd – phrase that I have dispensed with it for this new edition.

22 In Macdonald's film, climbers Joe Simpson and Simon Yates speak direct to camera about their near-death experience in the Peruvian Andes in 1985, and actors Brendan Mackey and Nicholas Aaron act out their nightmare in reconstructed scenes.

23 I owe the translation of Knopp's phrase (first used in 1998) and the information in much of this section on German docudrama to conversations with Tobias Ebbrecht of the Hochschule für Film und Fernsehen, Potsdam, Germany, and in particular to his 2007 essay 'Docudramatizing History on TV'. Historical-event television in Britain and Germany highlights the differential uses to which docudrama is put in similar-but-different European cultures.

24 CGI effects have proved useful in one other kind of docudramatic representation on offer on early twenty-first-century television. The 1999 BBC series *Walking with Dinosaurs* was not only phenomenally successful, it also spawned many clones. The stock-in-trade of programmes based on computer-generated animation images is effortlessly to leap back millions of years in time. In one case, the 2002 series *The Future is Wild*, the time-leap was forward into a peopleless future. The series presented the evolution of weird animals in a piece of sustained speculative zoology about what might happen post-climate change. Eminent zoologists happily performed as talking heads in order to buttress the speculative factuality of the series. I claim this representation as docudramatic given that the CGI animals 'act out' scenarios that voiceovers explain (and, again, eminent actors are to the fore in these series – Kenneth Branagh, for example). It would take too long to argue this fully in the present book – which also omits the increasingly important new area of animated docudrama, brought to greater prominence by cinema releases such as Ari Folman's 2008 *Waltz with Bashir*. For a good introduction to this area, see Chapter 5 of Ward, 2005.

25 The connection with the religious dimension of bearing witness was suggested to me in an email exchange of 2 and 3 February 2007 by Peter Hughes, editor of the online documentary film journal *Screening the Past* (www.latrobe.edu.au/screeningthepast/).

26 For the full text of the interviews with Range and Finch see: http://news.bbc.co.uk/go/pr/fr/-/1/hi/programmes/the_day_britain_stopped/2992895.stm (accessed 1 November 2006).

27 *Radio Times* (4–10 December 2004, p. 30). Given the legal position outlined in Chapter 2, one can only conclude that Government advisors (assuming they were aware of the film) were prepared to count this use of factual footage as 'fair comment'. Similar things could be said about Simon Cellan Jones's 'speculative' work *The Trial of Tony Blair*, transmitted on More4 in 2007.

28 His piece was reprinted on *Guardian* Unlimited, where I accessed it 13 December 2004 (http://talk.workunlimited.co.uk/business/story.html).

29 The term 'documusical' describes documentaries made mainly for television that use *purpose-composed* verse, music and song within a documentary setting. There is a distinction to be made between a 'documentary musical' (henceforth 'documusical') and a 'musical documentary'. The latter term better describes films that *feature* music centrally in the diegesis, films like D.A. Pennebaker's 1966 Bob Dylan documentary *Don't Look Back*. Like the term 'docudrama', both 'docuopera' and 'documusical' are convenient shorthand. When I interviewed the person I regard as the most significant user of the form, director Brian Hill, on 18 July 2005, he told me he preferred the 'documentary musical' precisely because he wants to emphasis the *documentary* element – see Roscoe and Paget (2006); the article from this online journal can be found in the archive section at www.ejumpcut.org.

30 Prime Minister Blair himself appears in the docuopera, via the very newsreel footage in which he launched this famous soundbite.

31 Goodman was a noted American poet. Another of Adams's frequent collaborators is theatre director Peter Sellars.

32 See Dominic Maxwell's article on Adams, 'A legend out of his own time', in *The Times* (26 January 2007, p. 15).

33 Channel 4 first broadcast *The Death of Klinghoffer* on 25 May 2003. Penny Woolcock herself is the maker of an entirely different series of housing estate-based documentary dramas. These feature the resourceful character Tina (actress Kelli Hollis). In, for example, *Tina Goes Shopping* (2001) Tina's 'shopping' is in fact bespoke shop-lifting carried out by Tina for her neighbours, from whom she collects orders and to whom she later delivers.

34 In the former film, the songs were actually part of a pre-existing Las Vegas show, and not 'purpose-composed'. The latter film, meanwhile, could be described as a documusical but is in my view uneven in documentary quality compared to Hill's work. In an article in *The Providence Journal* (1 June 2007) its director John Kirby (showing unawareness of a body of work by Brian Hill going back to 1998) even claimed to have discovered 'an interesting new genre: the "dramatic-documentary-musical"' (see www.projo.com/opinion/contrributors/content/CT_kirby_06-01-07_935PDFG.1c2eb61.html - accessed 20/08/10).

35 Telephone interviews with Simon Armitage on 9 June 2005 and with Simon Boswell on 13 July 2005.

36 Docuopera can have problems if lyrics are inaudible. Opera itself is not so lyric-dependent. For the film of *The Death of Klinghoffer*, Adams and Woolcock were constrained to use subtitles to back up lyrics potentially at the mercy of the sound on their audience's home television sets. New technological developments may in time make this unnecessary, but it is fair to say that opera is a predominantly musical experience anyway.

37 See Roscoe (2001: 9–20). Brazilian academic Fernando Andacht made perceptive comments on an early draft of Roscoe and Paget (2006), following a presentation I made on the documusical at the 'Visible Evidence XII' conference in Montreal in 2005. He it was who pointed out the essential difference between the 'flickers of authenticity' in Reality TV and the song-moments of documusicals.

38 Lyrics for this song: Simon Armitage, music: Michael Conn.

39 Hanke is quoting here from Bolter and Grusin (1999: 247).

40 Spice was reviewing Peter Carey's 2010 novel *Parrot and Olivier in America*. (Spice, 2010).

41 My emphasis – see Wood (2003).

42 Docusoaps and the various kinds of Reality TV are part of this category too – see, for example, Kilborn (2003), Holmes and Jermyn (2004), Bignell (2005), Biressi and Nunn (2005) and Hill (2005).

43 See also Insdorf (1989) and Shandler (1999). As the latter notes, Holocaust representations are something of 'an ethical touchstone' (p. xl).

44 The idea that performance comes always-already mediatised is elaborated in Auslander (1999).

45 From the 1921 collection *Michael Robartes and the Dancer*, Yeats's poem 'The Second Coming' has, despite its 1921 date, a millennial anxiety about it that is highly suited to the early 2000s. The lines in question are: 'And what rough beast, its hour come round at last, / Slouches towards Bethlehem to be born?'(*Collected Poems*, London: Macmillan, 1963: 210–11).

Bibliography

Ableman, P. (1972), 'Edna and Sheila: Two Kinds of Truth', *Theatre Quarterly*, 2:7, 45–8.

Aitken, I. (1990), *Film and Reform*, London: Routledge.

Aitken, I. (ed.) (2006), *Encyclopedia of the Documentary Film* (3 vols), London and New York: Routledge.

Allen, R., and A. Hill (eds) (2004), *The Television Studies Reader*, London and New York: Routledge.

Ambrose, S. E. (2001), *Band of Brothers: E Company, 506th Regiment, 101st Airborne from Normandy to Hitler's Eagle's Nest*, London: Pocket Books.

Aston, E., and G. Savona (1991), *Theatre as Sign-system*, London and New York: Routledge.

Aubrey, C. (1982), *Nukespeak: The Media and the Bomb*. London: Commedia.

Auslander, P. (1999), *Liveness: Performance in a Mediatized Culture*, London and New York: Routledge.

Auster, A. (1990), 'The Missiles of October: A Case History of Television Docudrama and Modern Memory', *Journal of Popular Film and Television*, 17: 4, 164–72.

Baker, R. (1995), *Media Law: A User's Guide for Film and Programme Makers*, London: Blueprint.

Balio, T. (ed.) (1990), *Hollywood in the Age of Television*, Boston, MA: Unwin Hyman.

Barendt, E., and L. Hitchens (2000), *Media Law: Cases and Materials*, Harlow: Longman.

Barnouw, E. (1966), *A History of Broadcasting in the United States* (3 vols), New York and Oxford: Oxford University Press.

Barnouw, E. (1975), *Tube of Plenty: The Evolution of American Television*, New York and Oxford: Oxford University Press.

Barnouw, E. (1993), *Documentary: a History of the Non-Fiction Film*, New York and Oxford: Oxford University Press.

Barr, C. (ed.) (1986), *All Our Yesterdays: 90 Years of British Cinema*, London: British Film Institute.

Barsam, R. (1974), 'Defining Nonfiction Film', in G. Mast and M. Cohen (eds), *Film Theory and Criticism*, New York: Oxford University Press.

Barthes, R. (1993), *Camera Lucida*, London: Vintage.

Beattie, K. (2004), *Documentary Screens: Nonfiction Film and Television*, Basingstoke and New York: Palgrave Macmillan.

Bell, E. (1986), 'The origins of British Television Documentary: The BBC 1945–55', in J. Corner (ed.), *Documentary and the Mass Media*, 65–80.

Benedetti, J. (2000 – 2nd edn), *Stanislavski: an Introduction*, London: Methuen.

Benjamin, W. (1985), *One-Way Street and Other Writings*, London and New York: Verso.

Bennett, S. (1990 – 2nd edn 2001), *Theatre Audiences: a Theory of Production and Reception*, London and New York: Routledge.

Bennett, T., S. Boyd-Bowman, C. Mercer and J. Woollacott (eds) (1981), *Popular Television and Film*, London and Milton Keynes: British Film Institute/Open University Press.

Bennett, T., L. Grossberg and M. Morris (eds) (2005), *New Keywords: A Revised Vocabulary of Culture and Society*, Malden, MA, and Oxford: Blackwell.

Bentley, E. (1968), *The Theatre of Commitment*, London: Methuen.

Bignell, J. (2002 – 2nd edn), *Media Semiotics: An Introduction*, Manchester and New York: Manchester University Press.

Bignell, J. (2005), *Big Brother: Reality TV in the Twenty-First Century*, Basingstoke and New York: Palgrave Macmillan.

Bignell, J., S. Lacey and M. Macmurragh-Kavanagh (eds) (2000), *British Television Drama: Past, Present and Future*, Basingstoke and New York: Palgrave.

Bignell, J., and J. Orlebar (2005 – 3rd edn), *The Television Handbook*, London and New York: Routledge (1st edn, P. Holland, 1997).

Biressi, A., and H. Nunn (2005), *Reality TV: Realism and Revelation*, London and New York: Wallflower.

Bluem, A. W. (1979), *Documentary in American Television: Form, Function, Method*, New York: Hastings House.

Bolter, J. D., and R. Grusin (1999), *Remediation: Understanding New Media*, Cambridge, MA: MIT Press.

Bourdieu, P. (1984), *Distinction* (trans. R. Nice), London: Routledge.

Brandt, G. (ed.) (1981), *British Television Drama*, Cambridge: Cambridge University Press.

Brandt, G. (ed.) (1993), *British Television Drama in the 1980s*, Cambridge: Cambridge University Press.

Briggs, A. (1995), *The History of Broadcasting in the United Kingdom* (5 vols), Oxford: Oxford University Press.

Brooks, T., and E. Marsh (1999), *The Complete Directory to Prime Time Network and Cable TV Shows: 1946–Present*, New York: Ballantine Books.

Brown, C. (1994), 'Box Office Bonanza', *Screen International* 7–13, 37.

Brown, L. (1992), *Encyclopaedia of Television*, Detroit, MI, and London: Gale Research.

Brown, L. (1995), 'The American Networks', in A. Smith (ed.), *Television: An International History*, 259–84.

Bruzzi, S. (2000 – 2nd edn 2006), *New Documentary: A Critical Introduction*, London: Routledge.

Buscombe, E. (2000), *British Television: A Reader*, Oxford and New York: Oxford University Press.

Carroll, N. (1996), *Theorizing the Moving Image*, Cambridge and New York: Cambridge University Press.

Carveth, R. (1993), 'Amy Fisher and the Ethics of "Headline" Docudramas', *Journal of Popular Film and Television*, 21: 3, 121–7.

Casey, B., N. Casey, B. Calvert, L. French and J. Lewis (eds) (2002), *Television Studies: The Key Concepts*, London and New York: Routledge.

Caughie, J. (1981), 'Progressive Television and Documentary Drama', in Bennett *et al* (eds), *Popular Television and Film*, 327–52.

Caughie, J. (2000), *Television Drama: Realism, Modernism and British Culture*, Oxford and New York: Oxford University Press.

Chambers, C. (ed.) (2002), *The Continuum Companion to Twentieth Century Theatre*, London and New York: Continuum.

Chaney, D. (1993), *Fictions of Collective Life: Public Drama in Late Modern Culture*, New York and London: Routledge.

Chapman, J. (2007), *Documentary Practice: Filmmakers and Production Choices*, Cambridge and Malden, MA: Polity.

Chater, K. (1992), *The Television Researcher's Guide*, Borehamwood: BBC Training.

Chater, K. (2002), *Research for Media Production*, Oxford and Woburn, MA: Focal Press.

Chayefsky, P. (1995), *The Television Plays*, New York: Applause.

Cheeseman, P. (1970), *The Knotty*, London: Methuen.

Clements, P. (1983), *The Improvised Play: The Work of Mike Leigh*, London: Methuen.

Cooke, L. (2003), *British Television Drama: A History*, London: British Film Institute.

Corner, J. (ed.) (1986), *Documentary and the Mass Media*, London: Edward Arnold.

Corner, J. (ed.) (1991), *Popular Television in Britain: Studies in Cultural History*, London: British Film Institute.

Corner, J. (1995), *Television Form and Public Address*, London: Edward Arnold.

Corner, J. (1996 – 2nd edn 1999), *The Art of Record: A Critical Introduction to Documentary*, Manchester and New York: Manchester University Press.

Corner, J., and S. Harvey (eds) (1996), *Television Times: A Reader*, London and New York: Arnold.

Corner, J. (1997), 'Television in Theory', *Media, Culture and Society*, 19: 2, 247–62.

Corner, J. (1999), *Critical Ideas in Television Studies*, Oxford and New York: Oxford University Press.

Corner, J. (2000), 'What Can We Say About Documentary?', in *Media, Culture and Society* 22, 5: 681–8.

Corner, J. (2002), 'Performing the Real: Documentary Diversions', in *Television and New Media* 3, 3: 255–69.

Corner, J. (2007), 'Documentary Expression and the Physicality of the Referent: Observations on Writing, Painting and Photography', in *Studies in Documentary Film*, 1: 1, 5–19.

Corrigan, G. (2003), *Mud, Blood and Poppycock: Britain and the First World War*, London: Cassell.

Couldry, N. (2003), *Media Rituals: A Critical Approach*, London and New York: Routledge.

Cowie, E. (1997), 'The Spectacle of Reality and Documentary Film', *Documentary Box 10*, Yamagata International Documentary Festival, Tokyo, 1–8.

Creeber, G. (ed.) (2001), *The Television Genre Book*, London: British Film Institute.

Creeber, G. (ed.) (2004), *Fifty Key Television Programmes*, London: Arnold.

Crowther, B. (1984), *Hollywood Faction: Reality and Myth in the Movies*, London: Columbus.

Cumings, B. (1992), *War and Television*, London and New York: Verso.

Custen, G. (1992), *Bio/pics: How Hollywood Constructed Public History*, New Brunswick, NJ: Rutgers University Press.

Dayan, D., and E. Katz (1995), 'Political Ceremony and Instant History', in A. Smith (ed.), *Television: An International History*, 169–88.

Domaille, K. (2001), *In the Name of the Father*, London: Longman.

Doncaster, C. (1956), 'The Story Documentary', in P. Rotha (ed.), *Television in the Making*, 44–8.

Dovey, J. (2000), *Freakshow: First Person Media in Factual Television*, London: Pluto Press.

Ebbrecht, T. (2007), 'Docudramatizing History on TV: German and British Docudrama and Historical Event Television in the Memorial Year 2005', *European Journal of Cultural Studies*, 10: 1, 35–53.

Edgar, D. (1988), *The Second Time as Farce*, London: Lawrence and Wishart.

Edgar, D. (1989), 'Faction Plan', *The Listener*, 1 June, 13–14, 32.

Edgar, D. (1993), 'Seeing Isn't Believing', *Sunday Times* 22 August.

Edgerton, G. (1985), 'The American Made-for-TV Movie', in B. Rose (ed.), *TV Genres: A Handbook and Reference Guide*.

Edgerton, G. (1991), 'High Concept, Small Screen: Reperceiving the Industrial and Stylistic Origins of the American Made-for-TV Movie', *Journal of Popular Film and Television*, 19: 3, 114–27.

Edgerton, G., and P. Rollins (eds) (2001), *Television Histories: Shaping Collective Memory in the Media Age*, Lexington, KY: University Press of Kentucky.

Eftimiades, M. (1992), *Letha Lolita: a True Story of Sex, Scandal and Deadly Obsession*, New York: St Martin's Press.

Ellis, J. (1992), *Visible Fictions: Cinema, Television, Video*, London and New York: Routledge.

Ellis, J. (2000), *Seeing Things: Television in the Age of Uncertainty*, London and New York: I. B.Tauris.

Ellis, J. (2007), *TV FAQ*, London and New York: I. B. Taurus.

Ellis, J. C. (1989), *The Documentary Idea: A Critical History of English Language Documentary Film and Video*, Upper Saddle River, NJ, Prentice Hall.

Elsaesser, T. (1996), 'Subject Positions, Speaking Positions: from *Holocaust, Our Hitler*, and *Heimat* to *Shoah* and *Schindler's List*', in V. Sobchack (ed.), *The Persistence of History: Cinema, Television, and the Modern Event*, New York and London: Routledge.

Erven, E. van (1988), *Radical People's Theatre*, Bloomington, IN: Indiana University Press.

Erven, E. van (1992), *The Playful Revolution: Theatre and Liberation in Asia*, Bloomington, IN: Indiana University Press.

Favorini, A. (1995), *Voicings: Ten Plays from the Documentary Theater*, Hopewell, NJ: Ecco.

Feuer, J. (1995), *Seeing Through the Eighties: Television and Reaganism*, London: British Film Institute.

Fielding, R. (1978), *The March of Time 1935–1951*, New York: Oxford University Press.

Finch, J. (ed.) (2003), *Granada Television: The First Generation*, Manchester and New York: Manchester University Press.

Foley, B. (1986), *Telling the Truth: The Theory and Practice of Documentary Fiction*, Ithaca, NY: Cornell University Press.

Forsyth, A., and C. Megson (eds) (2009), *Get Real: Documentary Theatre Past and Present*, Basingstoke and New York: Palgrave Macmillan.

Fowles, J. (1992), *Why Viewers Watch: A Reappraisal of Television's Effects*, London: Sage.

Freed, D. (1970), *Inquest*, New York: Hill and Wang.

Freeman, J. (2002), 'Writing the Self: the Heuristic Documentation of Performance', in *Studies in Theatre and Performance* 22, 2: 95–106.

Freund, E. (1987), *The Return of the Reader: Reader-Response Criticism*, London: Methuen.

Friedman, J. (ed.) (2002), *Reality Squared: Televisual Discourse on the Real*, New Brunswick, NJ: Rutgers University Press.

Fuller, G. (ed.) (1998), *Loach on Loach*, London and Boston, MA: Faber.

Garnham, N. (1972), 'TV Documentary and Ideology', *Screen* 13: 2, 109–15.

Gatfield, L., with A. Millwood Hargrave (2003), *Dramatic Licence: Fact or Fiction?*, London: BSC.

Geraghty, C., and D. Lusted (eds) (1998), *The Television Studies Book*, London: Arnold.

Gilligan, C. (1982), *In a Different Voice: Psychological Theory and Women's Development*, Cambridge, MA: Harvard University Press.

Gitlin, T. (1994), *Inside Prime Time*, London: Routledge.

Goddard, P., J. Corner and K. Richardson (2007), *Public Issue Television: World in Action, 1963–98*, Manchester and New York: Manchester University Press.

Gomery, D. (1983), 'Television, Hollywood, and the Development of Movies Made-for-TV', in E. Kaplan (ed.), *Regarding Television: Critical Approaches – An Anthology*, Los Angeles, CA: University Publications of America/American Film Institute.

Goodenough, O. R. (1989), 'Avoiding Legal Trouble in Preparing Docudramas', *New York Law Journal*, 24 November, 5 and 29.

Goodenough, O. R., and H. J. Blumenthal (2006 – 3rd edn), *This Business of Television*, New York: Billboard.

Goodwin, A. (1986), *Teaching TV Drama-documentary*, London: British Film Institute.

Goodwin, A., P. Kerr and I. Macdonald (eds) (1983), *BFI Dossier 19: Drama-documentary*, London: British Film Institute.

Goodwin, A., and G. Whannel (eds) (1990), *Understanding Television*, London: Routledge.

Grierson, J. (1933), 'The Documentary Producer', *Cinema Quarterly* 2: 1, 7–9.

Gunter, B., and C. McLaughlin (1992), *Television: The Public's View*, London: John Libbey.

Guynn, W. (1990), *A Cinema of Nonfiction*, Rutherford, NJ: Associated Universities Press.

Hallam, J. (2003), 'Introduction', in J. Finch (ed.), *Granada Television: The First Generation*, Manchester and New York: Manchester University Press.

Halliwell, L., and P. Purser (eds) (1986), *Halliwell's Television Companion*, London: Paladin.

Halliwell, L., and J. Walker (eds) (2002 – 17th edn), *Halliwell's Film and Video Guide*, London: HarperCollins.

Hammond, W. and D. Steward (eds) (2008), *Verbatim Verbatim: Contemporary Documentary Theatre*, London: Oberon Books

Hanke, R. (2001), '*Quantum Leap*: The Postmodern Challenge of Television as History', in G. Edgerton and P. Rollins (eds), *Television Histories*, 59–78.

Hardy, F. (ed.) (1979), *Grierson on Documentary*, London and Boston, MA: Faber.

Hare, D. (1984), *The History Plays*, London: Faber.

Hartley, J. (1992), *Tele-ology: Studies in Television*, London and New York: Routledge.

Hayward, A. (2005), *Which Side Are You On? Ken Loach and his Films*, London: Bloomsbury.

Hayward, S. (2006), *Cinema Studies: The Key Concepts*, London and New York: Routledge.

Higson, A. (1986), 'Britain's Outstanding Contribution to Film', in C. Barr (ed.) *All Our Yesterdays*.

Hill, A. (2005), *Reality TV: Audiences and Popular Factual Television*, London and New York: Routledge.

Hirsch, J. (2004), *Afterimage: Film, Trauma and the Holocaust*, Philadelphia, PA, Temple University Press.

Hodge, A. (ed.) (2000), *Twentieth Century Actor Training*, London and New York: Routledge.

Hodgson, T. (1988), *The Batsford Dictionary of Drama*, London: Batsford.

Hoffer, T., R. Musburger and R. Nelson (1980), 'Evolution of Docudrama on American Television Networks: A Content Analysis, 1966–1978', *Southern Speech Communication Journal*, Winter, 149–63.

Hoffer, T., R. Musburger and R. Nelson (1985), 'Docudrama', in B. Rose (ed.), *TV Genres*, 181–211.

Holland, P. (1997 – 1st edn), *The Television Handbook*, London and New York: Routledge.

Holmes, S., and D. Jermyn (eds) (2004), *Understanding Reality Television*, London and New York: Routledge.

Hood, S. (ed.) (1994), *Behind the Screens: The Structure of British Television in the 90s*, London: Lawrence and Wishart.

Horenstein, M. A., B. Rigby, M. Flory and V. Gershwin (1994), *Reel Life Real Life*, Kendall Park, NJ: Fourth Write Press.

Hutcheon, L. (1988), *A Poetics of Postmodernism: History, Theory, Fiction*, London and New York: Routledge.

Independent Television Commission (1992), *Television and the Public's View*. Research monograph.

Insdorf, A. (1989 – 2nd edn), *Indelible Shadows: Film and the Holocaust*, Cambridge and New York: Cambridge University Press.

Izod, J., and R. Kilborn with M. Hibberd (eds) (2000), *From Grierson to the Docusoap: Breaking the Boundaries*, Luton: University of Luton Press.

Jacobs, J. (2000), *The Intimate Screen: Early British Television Drama*, Oxford and New York: Oxford University Press.

Jacobs, L. (1971), *The Documentary Tradition*, New York: Hopkinson and Blake.

Jarvis, P. (1991), *Teletalk: A Dictionary of Broadcasting Terms*, Borehamwood: BBC Training.

Kaplan E. (ed.), (1983) *Regarding Television: Critical Approaches – An Anthology*, Los Angeles, CA: University Publications of America/American Film Institute.

Kearey, A. (n.d. [*ca*1958]), *Emergency – Ward 10*, London: ATV.

Keenan, B. (1992a), *An Evil Cradling*, London: Vintage.

Keenan, B. (1992b), 'Introduction', in McGuinness, *Someone Who'll Watch Over Me*.

Keighron, P., and C. Walker (1994), 'Working in Television: 5 Interviews', in S. Hood (ed.), *Behind the Screens*, 184–212.

Kennedy, D. (ed.) (2003), *The Oxford Encyclopedia of Theatre and Performance* (2 vols.), Oxford and New York: Oxford University Press.

Kepley, V. Jr. (1990), 'From "Frontal Lobes" to the "Bob-and-Bob" Show: NBC Management and Programming Strategies, 1949–65', in T. Balio (ed.), *Hollywood in the Age of Television*, 41–61.

Kerr, P. (1990), 'F for fake? Friction Over Faction', in A. Goodwin and G. Whannel (eds), *Understanding Television*, 74–87.

Kilborn, R. (1994), 'Drama over Lockerbie: A New Look at the Drama-Documentary Debate', *The Historical Journal of Film, Radio and Television*, 14:1, 59–76.

Kilborn, R., and J. Izod (1997), *An Introduction to Television Documentary: Confronting Reality*, Manchester and New York: Manchester University Press.

Kilborn, R., (2003), *Staging the Real: Factual Programming in the Age of Big Brother*, Manchester and New York: Manchester University Press.

Kingsolver, B. (2000), *The Poisonwood Bible*, London: Faber.

Kuehl, J. (1978), 'The Motives for Making Drama Documentaries', *Vision* 3: 1, 3–7.

Kuehl, J. (1981), 'Truth Claims', *Sight and Sound* 50: 4, 272–4.

Lacey, S. (2002), *British Social Realism: From Documentary to Brit Grit*, London: Wallflower.

Laing, S. (1986), *Representations of Working-class Life 1957–1964*, London: Methuen.

Landy, M. (1996), *Cinematic Uses of the Past*, Minneapolis, MN, and London: University of Minnesota Press.

Lazere, D. (ed.) (1987), *American Media and Mass Culture: Left Perspectives*, Berkeley, CA, and Los Angeles, CA: University of California Press.

Leishman, M. (2006), *My Father: Reith of the BBC*, Edinburgh: St Andrews Press.

Lewin, G. R. (1971), *Documentary Explorations*, Garden City, NY: Doubleday.

Lipkin, S. (2002), *Real Emotional Logic: Film and Television Docudrama as Persuasive Practice*, Carbondale, IL: Southern Illinois University Press.

Lipkin, S., D. Paget and J. Roscoe (2006), 'Docudrama and Mock-documentary:

Defining Terms, Proposing Canons', in G. Rhodes and J. Springer (eds) (2006), *Docufictions: Essays on the Intersection of Documentary and Fictional Filmmaking*, 11–26.

Lodge, D. (2005), *Author, Author*, London and New York: Penguin.

Lovell, A., and P. Krämer (eds) (1999), *Screen Acting*, London and New York: Routledge.

Luckhurst, M., and C. Veltman (eds) (2001), *On Acting: Interviews with Actors*, London and New York: Faber.

McArthur, C. (1980), *BFI Television Monograph 8: Television and History*, London: British Film Institute.

McBride, I. (1999), 'Where Are We Going and How and Why?', in A. Rosenthal (ed.) *Why Docudrama?* (111–18).

MacCabe, C. (ed.) (1986), *High Theory/Low Culture: Analysing Popular Television and Film*, Manchester: Manchester University Press.

McCarthy, J., and J. Morrell (1994), *Some Other Rainbow*, London: Corgi Books.

Macdonald, K., and M. Cousins (eds) (1996), *Imagining Reality: The Faber Book of Documentary*, London and Boston, MA: Faber.

McFarlane, B. (1996), *Novel to Film: An Introduction to the Theory of Adaptation*, Oxford: Clarendon Press.

McGrath, J. (1981), *A Good Night Out: Popular Theatre: Audience, Class and Form*, London: Eyre Methuen.

McGuinness, F. (1992), *Someone Who'll Watch Over Me*, London and Boston, MA: Faber.

McKnight, G. (ed.) (1997), *Agent of Challenge and Defiance: The Films of Ken Loach*, Trowbridge: Flicks.

McNeil, A. (1991), *Total Television: A Comprehensive Guide to Programming from 1948 to the Present Day*, New York: Penguin.

Mapplebeck, V. (1997), 'Spoofer's Double Exposure', *The Guardian*, 1 September.

Marill, A. (1987), *Movies Made For Television: The Telefeature and the Mini-Series 1964–1986*, New York: Baseline.

Marris, P. (ed.) (1982), *BFI Dossier 16: Paul Rotha*, London: British Film Institute.

Maxwell, R. (1992), *The Mysteries of Paris and London*, London: University Press of Virginia.

Melvin, M. (ed.) (2006), *The Art of Theatre Workshop*, London: Oberon.

Mendelson, E. (ed.) (1977), *The English Auden*, London: Faber.

Monaco, J. (1977), *How to Read a Film: The Art, Technology, Language, History and Theory of Film and Media*, New York: Oxford University Press.

Mulvey, L. (1989), *Visual and Other Pleasures*, London: Macmillan.

Murray, S., and L. Ouellette (eds) (2004), *Reality TV: Remaking Television Culture*, New York and London: New York University Press.

Musburger, R. (1985), 'Setting the Scene of the Television Docudrama', in *Journal of Popular Film and Television*, 13:2, 92–101.

Nelson, R. (1997), *TV Drama in Transition: Forms, Values and Cultural Change*, London and New York: Macmillan/St Martins.

Newcomb, H. (ed.) (1997), *The Museum of Broadcast Communication Encyclopaedia of Television* (3 volumes), Chicago, IL, and London: Fitzroy Dearborn.

Nichols, B. (1981), *Ideology and the Image*, Bloomington, IN: Indiana University Press.

Nichols, B. (1991), *Representing Reality: Issues and Concepts in Documentary*, Bloomington, IN: Indiana University Press.

Nichols, B. (1994), *Blurred Boundaries: Questions of Meaning in Contemporary Culture*, Bloomington, IN: Indiana University Press.

Nichols, B. (2001), *Introduction to Documentary*, Bloomington, IN: Indiana University Press.

Norris, C. (1992), *Uncritical Theory: Postmodernism, Intellectuals and the Gulf War*, London: Lawrence and Wishart.

O'Connor, J., and L. Brown (1980), *The Federal Theatre Project*, London: Eyre Methuen.

O'Connor, J. E. (ed.) (1983), *American History American Television: Interpreting the Video Past*, New York: Frederick Ungar.

O'Sullivan, T., J. Hartley, D. Saunders, M. Montgomery and J. Fiske (1994), *Key Concepts in Cultural and Communication Studies*, London: Routledge.

Page, A. (ed.) (1992), *The Death of the Playwright: Modern British Drama and Literary Theory*, London: Macmillan.

Paget, D. (1990), *True Stories?: Documentary drama on Radio, Stage and Screen*, Manchester and New York: Manchester University Press.

Paget, D. (1992), 'Oh What a Lovely Post-Modern War: Drama and the Falklands', in G. Holderness (ed.), *The Politics of Theatre and Drama*, London: Macmillan.

Paget, D. (1997), 'Drifting Towards Hollywood: Drama-Documentary Goes West', in *Continuum* 11, 1: 23–42.

Paget, D. (1998 – 1st edn), *No Other Way To Tell It: Dramadoc/docudrama on Television*, Manchester and New York: Manchester University Press.

Paget, D. (1999), '*Cathy Come Home* and 'Accuracy' in British Television Drama', in *New Theatre Quarterly* XV, 1 (no. 57): 75–90.

Paget, D. (2000), 'Disclaimers, Denials and Direct Address: Captioning in Docudrama', in J. Izod and R. Kilborn with M. Hibberd (2000: 197–208).

Paget, D. (2003), 'Preface' to Jeremy Sandford's *Cathy Come Home*, London: Marion Boyars.

Paget, D., and S. N. Lipkin (2009), 'Movie-of-the-Week Docudrama, "Historical-Event Television", and the Steven Spielberg Series *Band of Brothers*', *New*

Review of Film and Television Studies 7, 1, 93–107.

Palmer, G. (2003), *Discipline and Liberty: Television and Governance*, Manchester and New York: Manchester University Press.

Petley, J. (1996), 'Fact Plus Fiction Equals Friction', in *Media, Culture and Society*, 18: 1 11–25.

Pettit, L. (2000), *Screening Ireland: Film and Television Representation*, Manchester and New York: Manchester University Press.

Piroelle, A., and J.-P. Durix (eds) (1994), *Interfaces 6*, Dijon: Université de Bourgogne.

Plantinga, C. (1997), *Rhetoric and Representation in Nonfiction Film*, Cambridge and New York: Cambridge University Press.

Polonsky, A. (edited by J. Schultheiss and M. Schaubert) (1997), *You Are There Teleplays: The Critical Edition*, Northridge, CA: Center for Telecommunication Studies.

Prior, A. (1996), *Script to Screen: The Story of Five Television Plays, From Z Cars to The Charmer*, St Albans: Ver Books.

Rabiger, M. (1987), *Directing the Documentary*, Boston and London: Focal Press.

Rabinowitz, P. (1994), *They Must Be Represented: The Politics of Documentary*, London and New York: Verso.

Rapping, E. (1987), *The Looking Glass World of Nonfiction TV*, Boston, MA: South End Press.

Renov, M. (ed.) (1993), *Theorising Documentary*, London and New York: Routledge.

Renov, M. (2004), *The Subject of Documentary*, Minneapolis and London: University of Minnesota Press.

Rhodes, G., and J. Springer (eds) (2006), *Docufictions: Essays on the Intersection of Documentary and Fictional Filmmaking*, Jefferson, NC, and London: McFarland.

Robertson, G., and A. Nicol (1992), *Media Law*, London: Penguin.

Roscoe, J., and C. Hight (2001), *Faking It: Mock-documentary and the Subversion of Factuality*, Manchester and New York: Manchester University Press.

Roscoe, J. (2001), 'Real Entertainment: New Factual Hybrid Television', in *Media International Australia* 100: 9–20.

Roscoe, J., and D. Paget (2006), 'Giving Voice: Performance and Authenticity in the Documentary Musical', in *Jump Cut: a Review of Contemporary Media* 48, Winter 2006 (online journal: www.ejumpcut.org)

Rose, B. (ed.) (1985), *TV Genres: A Handbook and Reference Guide*, Westport, CT: Greenwood Press.

Rosenstone, R. A. (2006), *History on Film/Film on History*, Harlow: Pearson Longman.

Rosenthal, A. (ed.) (1980), *The Documentary Conscience*, Berkeley, CA, and Los

Angeles, CA: University of California Press.

Rosenthal, A. (ed.) (1988), *New Challenges for Documentary*, Berkeley, CA, and Los Angeles, CA: University of California Press.

Rosenthal, A. (1995), *Writing Docudrama: Dramatizing Reality for Film and TV*, Boston, MA, and Oxford: Focal Press.

Rosenthal, A. (ed.) (1999), *Why Docudrama?: Fact-Fiction on Film and TV*, Carbondale, IL: Southern Illinois University Press.

Rosenthal, A., and J. Corner (eds) (2005 – 2nd edn), *New Challenges for Documentary*, Manchester and New York: Manchester University Press.

Rotha, P. (with S. Road and R. Griffith) (1952 – 3rd edn), *Documentary Film*, London: Faber.

Rotha, P. (ed.) (1956), *Television in the Making*, London: Focal Press.

Sackett, S. (1993), *Prime-Time Hits: Television's Most Popular Network Programs*, New York: Billboard.

Sandford, J. (1973), 'Edna and Cathy: Just Huge Commercials', *Theatre Quarterly*, 3: 10, 79–85, extract also in Goodwin and Kerr (eds), *BFI Dossier 19*, 16–19.

Sandford, J. (2003 – 1st edn 1976), *Cathy Come Home*, London: Marion Boyars.

Scannell, P. (1979), 'The social eye of television, 1946–1955', *Media, Culture and Society*, 1: 1, 97–106.

Scannell, P. (1986), '"The Stuff of Radio": Developments in Radio Features and Documentaries Before the War', in J. Corner (ed.) *Documentary and the Mass Media*, 1–26.

Scheibler, S. (1993), 'Constantly Performing the Documentary: the Seductive Promise of *Lightning Over Water*', in M. Renov (ed.), *Theorising Documentary*, 135–50.

Schulze, L. (1990), 'The Made-for-TV Movie: Industrial Practice, Cultural Form, Popular Reception', in T. Balio (ed.), *Hollywood in the Age of Television*, 351–76.

Self, D. (1984), *TV Drama: An Introduction*, London: Macmillan.

Sendall, B., and J. Potter (1982), *Independent Television in Britain*, London: Macmillan (4 volumes).

Shandler, J. (1999), *While America Watches: Televising the Holocaust*, New York and Oxford: Oxford University Press.

Shubik, I. (2000 – 2nd edn [1st edn 1975]), *Play for Today: The Evolution of Television Drama*, Manchester and New York: Manchester University Press.

Silverstone, R. (1986), 'The Agonistic Narratives of Television Science', in J. Corner (ed.), *Documentary and the Mass Media*, 81–106.

Simon, A. (1996), *Dangerous Knowledge: The JFK Assassination in Art and Film*, Philadelphia PA, Temple University Press.

Sklar, R. (1980), *Prime-Time America: Life On and Behind the Television Screen*,

New York: Oxford University Press.

Smartt, U. (2006), *Media Law for Journalists*, London and Thousand Oaks, CA: Sage.

Smith, A. (ed.) (1995), *Television: An International History*, Oxford: Oxford University Press.

Sobchack, V. (ed.) (1996), *The Persistence of History: Cinema, Television, and the Modern Event*, New York and London: Routledge.

Sparkes, R. (1992), *Television and the Drama of Crime: Moral Tales and the Place of Crime in Public Life*, Milton Keynes: Open University Press.

Spice, N. 'Forged, Forger, Forget', *London Review of Books*, 5 August 2010, pp. 14–16.

Staiger, J. (1997), 'Docudrama', in H. Newcomb (ed.), *The Museum of Broadcast Communication Encyclopaedia of Television*, Chicago, IL, and London: Fitzroy Dearborn, Vol.1: 514–17.

Stott, W. (1973), *Documentary Expression and Thirties America*, Oxford and New York: Oxford University Press.

Styan, J. (1962), 'Television Drama', in J. Russell Brown and B. Harris (eds), *Stratford-upon-Avon Studies 4: Contemporary Theatre*, London: Edward Arnold, 185–204.

Sussex, E. (1975), *The Rise and Fall of British Documentary*, Berkeley, CA, and Los Angeles, CA: University of California Press.

Sussex, E. (1981), 'Getting It Right', *Sight and Sound* 51: 1, 10–15.

Swallow, N. (1956), 'Documentary TV Journalism', in P. Rotha (ed.), *Television in the Making*, 49–55.

Swallow, N. (1966), *Factual Television*, London: Focal Press.

Swallow, N. (1982), 'Rotha and Television', in P. Marris (ed.), *BFI Dossier 16: Paul Rotha*, 86–9.

Swinson, A. (1955 – 2nd edn 1960), *Writing for Television*, London: Adam and Charles Black.

Swinson, A. (1956), 'Writing for Television', in P. Rotha (ed.), *Television in the Making*, 37–43.

Swinson, A. (1963), *Writing for Television Today*, London: Adam and Charles Black.

Tibbetts, J. (2005), 'Elgar's Ear: A Conversation with Ken Russell', in *Quarterly Review of Film and Video*, 22: 1, 37–49.

Toplin, R. (1996), *History by Hollywood: The Use and Abuse of the American Past*, Urbana, IL, and Chicago, IL: University of Illinois Press.

Tulloch, J. (1990), *Television Drama: Agency, Audience and Myth*, London and New York: Routledge.

Tunstall, J. (1993), *Television Producers*, London and New York: Routledge.

Turner, G. (2006 – 4th edn), *Film and Social Practice*, London and New York:

Routledge.

Vahimagi, T. (ed.) (1996 – 2nd edn), *British Television: An Illustrated Guide*, Oxford and New York: Oxford University Press.

Vankin, J., and J. Whalen (2005), *Based on a True Story: Fact and Fantasy in 100 Favorite Movies*, Chicago, IL: Chicago Review Press.

Vaughan, D. (1976), *Television Documentary Usage*, London: British Film Institute.

Vaughan, D. (1986), 'Notes on the Ascent of a Fictitious Mountain', in J. Corner (ed.), *Documentary and the Mass Media*, 161–75).

Ward, P. (2005), *Documentary: The Margins of Reality*, London and New York: Wallflower.

Welsh, T., and W. Greenwood (2003 – 17th edn), *McNae's Essential Law for Journalists*, London: LexisNexis.

Whybrow, N. (2005), *Street Scenes: Brecht, Benjamin and Berlin*, Bristol: Intellect.

Willett, J. (1984), *Brecht on Theatre*, London: Methuen.

Willett, J. (1986), *Brecht in Context*, London: Methuen.

Williams, R. (1988), *Keywords: A Vocabulary of Culture and Society*, London: Fontana.

Williams, R. (1992), *Television: Technology and Cultural Form*, London: Routledge.

Williams, S. (1994), 'Fiction and Reality: The Making of *Hostages*', in A. Piroelle and J.-P. Durix (eds), *Interfaces 6*, Dijon: Université de Bourgogne.

Williamson, J. (1986), *Consuming Passions: The Dynamics of Popular Culture*, London and New York: Marion Boyars.

Willis, E. E. (1951), *Foundations in Broadcasting*, New York: Oxford University Press.

Willis, J. (1997), 'What's Up, Docs?', *Guardian* 6 October.

Winston, B. (1994), 'Public Service in the New Broadcasting Age', in Hood (ed.), *Behind the Screens*, 20–42.

Winston, B. (1995), *Claiming the Real: The Documentary Film Revisited*, London: British Film Institute.

Winston, B. (2000), *Lies, Damn Lies and Documentaries*, London: British Film Institute.

Winston, B. (2008 – 2nd edn), *Claiming the Real: Documentary: Grierson and beyond*, Basingstoke and New York: Palgrave Macmillan.

Wood, R. (2003), 'Editorial', in *Cineaction*, 63: 1.

Woolfe, H. B. (1933–34), 'Commercial Documentary', *Cinema Quarterly*, 2:2, 96–100.

Wyver, J. (1983), 'Invasion', *Time Out*, 15–21 August 1980 (extracted in A. Goodwin, P.Kerr and I. Macdonald [eds], *BFI Dossier 19: Drama-documentary*, 31–3).

Index

Note: 'n' after a page reference indicates the number of a note on that page.